OPEN
to the
PUBLIC

OPEN
to the
PUBLIC

a guide to the museums of Northern California

Charlene Akers

restaurant reviews by

Jobyna Akers Dellar

Heyday Books
Berkeley, California
•
California Historical Society

Co-published by Heyday Books and the California Historical Society. Please address orders, inquiries, or correspondence to Heyday Books, Box 9145, Berkeley, CA, 94709.

Publisher's Cataloging in Publication
(Prepared by Quality Books Inc.)

Akers, Charlene.
    Open to the public : a guide to the museums of Northern California / by Charlene Akers.
    p. cm.
    Includes index.
    ISBN 0-930588-72-X

    1. Museums--Northern California--Guidebooks.   I. Title.
    AM12.C2A34 1994   069'.09794
                                        QBI94-1567

Cover design: Diana Howard
Editing and interior design: Jeannine Gendar
Production: Wendy Low and Jeannine Gendar

Cover photos:
Harbor seal courtesy of Marine Mammal Center, photo by Ken Bach; "Boatmen on the Missouri" by George Caleb Bingham, courtesy of M.H. de Young Museum Rockefeller Collection; photo of frame by Barbara Thompson; wooden Bolivian Carnaval festival mask, ca. 1920, courtesy of San Francisco Craft and Folk Art Museum; hand with bubble courtesy of Exploratorium, photo by Nancy Rodger.

To John, Nate, and Ryan

Acknowledgments

Hundreds of people made this book possible, and my gratitude to all of them is immeasurable.

First of all, to the museum staff and volunteers, too numerous to mention individually, who were so generous with their time and knowledge, my sincerest thanks.

Second, I am grateful to all the people at Heyday Books and most particularly to my editors, Jeannine Gendar and Wendy Low, who painstakingly put it all together—checking facts, selecting photographs, correcting my spelling, designing the layout, and producing the final product. And, of course, thanks also go to Heyday's publisher, the inimitable Malcolm Margolin, who supported this project from the very start and sustained me along the way with his wisdom, humor, and joyous enthusiasm for the beautiful and bizarre world of museums.

There is no way to thank adequately my dear friend, computer genius Paul (Daryl) Raczynski, for his cheerful willingness to guide Jobyna and me through the mysteries of the computer without ever losing patience. And thanks also to my son Ryan, whose sweet-tempered forbearance and delicious teenage wit filled every day with sunshine.

Finally, Jobyna and I offer our eternal thanks to our peerless husbands, John Dellar and Nate Levine. This book would not exist without their understanding, encouragement, and loving support, which enabled us to undertake the exhilaring journey of a lifetime.

Crescent
City

Yreka

Trinity–Shasta–Lassen

Eureka

**North
Coast**

Redding

Susanville

Mendocino

Chico

Quincy

Ukiah

**Sacramento
Valley**

**Wine
Country**

Santa Rosa

Auburn

Sacramento

North Bay

**Sierra
Nevada**

San Francisco

**East
Bay**

Stockton

**Peninsula &
South Bay**

Yosemite
Village

San Jose

Santa Cruz

Monterey

Fresno

**Monterey
Bay Area**

**San Joaquin
Valley**

Porterville

Contents

Introduction

When, as a child, I was given the choice of a Sunday family outing, I invariably begged, "Let's go to the museum." The whole family would pile into the station wagon and head for the only museum we knew, the de Young Museum in San Francisco's Golden Gate Park. As a rather solemn little girl, I could be happy for hours in that hushed, hands-off place. While my sister, Jobyna, would be content to read her book until it was time to go, my rambunctious brothers could be held in check only briefly by the suits of armor and the promise of refreshments to follow in the Japanese Tea Garden. My mother, a transplanted New Yorker, would bemoan California's cultural poverty; compared to the museums and galleries of Manhattan, the Bay Area didn't have much to offer.

My love for museums grew as I did. No visit to another city was ever complete without taking in as many museums as the place had to offer. At home, I indulged my passion with repeated visits to my favorites— the wonderful Oakland Museum, the University Art Museum in Berkeley, the Palace of the Legion of Honor and the ethnic art museums of San Francisco. So when, after finishing our first book together, Jobyna and I were looking for our next project, it didn't take long for me to come up with the suggestion, "Let's go to the museums."

And go to museums we did! For a year we traversed California from the San Joaquin Valley to the Oregon border, visiting almost six hundred museums. On alternate Monday mornings, after throwing our newly washed museum-going outfits in a bag and packing the cooler with brown rice, canned tuna, instant coffee, and cereal, we would load up Jobyna's Volvo and set out on the great museum quest.

Jobyna, the expert on California geography, drove the car and had the challenging task of planning our itineraries and scheduling our visits. My job was to interview museum personnel, take notes, read the literature, and on the off-weeks, write the book. Jobyna selflessly ate her way through the menu of every museum cafe we came across to contribute the restaurant reviews, while I stuck to my diet and lost five pounds.

Our original list included fewer than three hundred institutions. But like Streganona's inexhaustible pot of spaghetti, the list grew and grew. If we were to meet our goal of finishing the research in a year, we found that we would have to visit at least five museums a day. Museum staff and volunteers were invariably gracious in helping us meet this schedule. Busy museum directors interrupted their work to give us personal tours. Many generous people made special efforts, coming early or staying late, and even opening museums on days when they were supposed to be closed.

One would imagine that after the first six months, museum fatigue would have set in. Nothing, however, could be further from the truth. California, with its unparalleled physical beauty, rich history, and ethnic diversity, had us marveling anew each day. Many a time we just looked at each other in wonder at the unimaginable good fortune of having such a variety of experiences laid at our feet. Although we knew before we began that we could expect to see more than pictures on a wall, we were unprepared for the kaleidoscopic abundance of museum experiences that are open to the public.

Children's museums, for example, have been popping up everywhere, like mushrooms after the rain. Having abandoned the old-fashioned, don't-touch-the-precious-objects-in-the-cases format in favor of contemporary interactive exhibitions, these new-style learning institutions are as enticing as playgrounds, and kids are lapping up the lessons they offer like ice cream.

Science museums are proliferating almost as swiftly as the new technologies they interpret, replacing moth-eaten stuffed animals and dusty dioramas with the latest in exhibition design. Making the newest scientific theories, technological innovations, and ecological insights comprehensible and accessible, they do more than educate us—at their best, the new science museums enhance our sense of wonder at the world in which we live.

In every small town, citizens with a new-found historical consciousness are establishing museums, trying to preserve what's left of the old ways before there's no one left who remembers what they were. These museums are often wonderfully personal. Time and again, we were treated to the story behind an object or a juicy bit of gossip about a town's founders. The stories were often based on personal or family memories, but the people who told them were also familiar with the well-known figures from California history. "John Fremont couldn't find his way out of his own back yard," snorted one indignant docent. "It was his guide, Kit Carson, who made all the discoveries!" At first, we were amazed that anyone could have such strong feelings about long-dead personages who were to us no more than names in history books, but as time went on Jobyna and I too began to develop our own favorites.

Ethnic museums are also proliferating. Great cultural wealth, racial antagonism, and ugly stereotyping are all products of California's ethnic diversity. The state's excellent ethnic museums explore the complexity of the Native American, Jewish, Chinese, Mexican, Italian, Japanese, and African-American experiences, generally from an insider's perspective.

Northern California is equally rich in art museums. From Sacramento's Crocker Museum, the first public art museum in the West, to San Francisco's magnificent, spanking new, $60 million Museum of Modern Art, they display treasures from every period in history and every country in the world, in all media and genres. Old World masterpieces share the spotlight with a lavish abundance of California artworks, from exquisite Miwok baskets to the photographs of Ansel Adams or the fanciful folk art of Eureka's Romano Gabriel Sculpture Garden. A trendsetter in food, fashion, and lifestyle, California also produces cutting-edge art that leads the way for the rest of the nation.

Finally, there are museums that defy classification, often the result of an individual's devotion to or even obsession with a subject. Former prizefighter Joe Gavras spent three-quarters of a lifetime putting together the Action Boxing Museum, his personal contribution to the sport. Evelyn Burkhalter, perhaps the world's foremost authority on Barbie dolls, founded a museum to showcase her 16,000-piece collection of Barbiana. A lifelong love affair with the gas engine fueled Charles Parish's desire to build the Agricultural Museum of Merced County, a shrine to the object of his affections. Museums are not put together on a whim, and the passion and creativity that inspired these quirky, idiosyncratic places will astonish you.

Other Museum Activities

On our tour through six hundred of northern California's museums, we were struck by the wide range of services museums provide.

Special events: Museums offer a host of special events, lectures, classes, concerts, performances, workshops, and children's enrichment programs. Full-fledged education departments in the larger museums often schedule programs every weekend, while the smallest museums may host one or two special events each year—Christmas teas, spring wildflower shows, and the like.

Social spaces: As safe and congenial public spaces become harder to find, the local museum often becomes a good place for friends to socialize. Here, one can stroll through the galleries, have lunch in the cafe, browse the gift shop, and after a refreshing hour or two, return to work.

Research: We don't often think of our local museums as resources for research, but many have specialized libraries and extensive archives, and in some cases a well-trained staff to assist you.

Restaurants: Museum cafes have proved to be a financial boon to the institutions and a culinary boon to visitors. More and more museums have traded their nondescript cafeteria-style fare for an upgraded, sophisticated cuisine.

Gift shops: From a few postcards and booklets arranged on the admissions desk to enormous treasure-filled emporia, almost every museum has some wares to peddle. To keep its tax-exempt status, a museum store must stock only items related to the museum's exhibitions. As a result, you'll find a wonderful depth of merchandise, often selected with unusually good taste. Many museum gift shops feature one-of-a-kind items made by local artists and craftspeople.

Facility rental: Although the local museum does not immediately spring to mind when planning a wedding, gala party, or important meeting, many museums rent their facilities for special events. The Victorian parlor of an historic house or a luscious garden may be the perfect romantic setting for a wedding. For painless party-giving, most children's museums and science centers offer birthday party packages: you supply the kids and the museum takes care of the rest.

Getting the most out of a museum visit

After having visited hundreds of museums in the last year, I have developed a few simple rules that may add to your enjoyment of them:

Wear comfortable shoes! Yes, this is prosaic advice, but if your feet hurt, nothing is enjoyable. You're there to see, not to be seen, so forget the four-inch spiked heels. And be sure to bring appropriate cover for outdoor museums.

Limit yourself. The human mind can only absorb so much information and visual stimulation before the dreaded museum fatigue sets in. Many of the smaller museums in this book come in perfect, bite-size chunks, easily taken in on one visit (an hour and a half to two hours is a good time limit). But in a larger institution, don't expect to see everything in one day.

Take a rest. A museum visit is not an endurance test. You can stop, sit on a bench, read your book, have a cup of tea in the cafe, and then continue refreshed.

Take advantage of docent tours or any offer by any staff or volunteer to show you around. People who work in museums are passionate about them, and their passion is contagious. Their love, enthusiasm, and knowledge can never be reproduced on didactic panels. You may find out some wonderful secrets or hear stories you would never find in books. Don't pass up the audio tours either; while they are not as responsive as human guides, they generally enhance your visit.

Getting involved

Anyone who values art, science, and history knows that you can't put a price on the service our museums perform. Yet, in most cases, the cost to us is minimal or free. Ninety percent of the institutions in this book charge no admission fee, and many of those that do have a weekly or monthly free day. In these days of dwindling funding, museums are scrambling for the few dollars available.

It would be wonderful if we could all bestow million-dollar bequests on our favorite institutions, but for those of us who can't, there are ways to help. First, become a member of local museums—you will not only be supporting them, but enjoying the benefits of membership as well, which can include free admission, a monthly publication, invitations to openings and special events, discounts in the gift shops, and perhaps a behind-the-scenes tour. If you visit an institution that is open to the public free of charge—the majority are—slip a dollar or two, or whatever you can afford, in the donation box. Support the museum by shopping in the gift shop or eating in the cafe. Finally, there's hardly a museum in the country that could exist without its cadre of dedicated volunteers. If you don't have money, perhaps you have time—volunteer at your local museum.

How to use this book

The listings in this book include street addresses, phone numbers, hours of operation, and admission costs. Shortly before the book was scheduled to go to press in the spring of 1994, every museum listed was contacted to make sure the information was correct. But changes do occur. Museums move to new locations, change their hours, or raise admission fees. Sometimes a museum closes temporarily to install a new exhibition. So before making a special trip, call to check important facts.

This book is arranged geographically. Travelers can see what an area has to offer and incorporate museum visits into their itineraries. Local residents might be surprised to find their own cities full of delightful places they didn't even know existed.

For those with special interests, we have provided subject information in the index. Classification was difficult—some museums fit equally well into several categories, while others defy classification. We did our best.

We were as conscientious as possible in our selection of museums, striving to include everything and to visit as many as possible. Those few museums I was unable to see with my own eyes are indicated by an asterisk (*). I obtained information about them from telephone interviews and the literature they sent.

The museums we have included range in size from a few display cases in a corner of the public library to major institutions covering entire city blocks. They range in sophistication from down-home folksy to the most advanced state-of-the-art. We saw old-style museums with every object in the collection on display and information hand lettered on yellowing index cards, as well as super-slick exhibitions employing the latest developments in interactive video and computer technology. My object in doing this book was to try to appreciate all, judge each of them on its own terms, and to give you as clear an idea as possible of what to expect.

I plan to revise and reprint this book in the future, so if there is any place that I have missed, or if your experience in visiting any of these museums is far removed from what I described, I would appreciate your comments, care of the publisher.

I hope you enjoy reading this book as much as I enjoyed researching and writing it, and above all that it inspires you to investigate for yourself California's astounding museums. Major public institutions with multi-million dollar budgets; tiny, privately owned collections; small-town museums run by volunteers and operating on a shoe string—every one has its own special delights, and all these magical places are open to the public. Enjoy!

OPEN to the PUBLIC

San Francisco

ALCATRAZ★
Red & White Ferry departs from Pier 41
Phone: (415) 546-2700
Hours: Call for schedule and reservations
Admission: Adults $5.70, seniors $4.75, children 5-11 $3.25; with
audio tour, Adults $9.00, seniors $8.00, children 5-11 $4.50

Some of the most notorious criminals of history—Al Capone, Machine Gun Kelly, and Robert Stroud, the Birdman of Alcatraz, to name a few—did time on The Rock, Alcatraz Island, a mile and a half off San Francisco's shore. From 1934 to 1963 Alcatraz served as a federal prison and before that as a military installation. Not long after the end of a 17-month occupation by Native Americans, the island became part of the Golden Gate National Recreation Area and a popular if chilling (and chilly) tourist attraction in 1972.

Jook Lee, caretaker at the Chinese Historical Society Museum. Photo by Nate Levine.

Visitors can board the Red and White Ferry to the island at Pier 41. Once there, activities include self-guided or ranger-led tours. The excellent Alcatraz audio cassette tour, produced by the Local Antenna Theater, recreates the island's gloomy past through the words of former inmates and guards. Ranger-guided nature tours present a more lighthearted side, with an opportunity to view the many birds and native plants to be found on the island. Wear walking shoes and bring a warm jacket.

CHINATOWN

CHINESE HISTORICAL SOCIETY OF AMERICA
650 Commercial Street, San Francisco
Phone: (415) 391-1188
Hours: Tues.-Sat. noon-4:00 p.m.
Admission: Free

Unless you know what you're looking for, it's easy to miss the modest Chinese Historical Society museum.

Look for the sign over the door that reads "The Promise of Gold Mountain," and descend the stairs to the musty but marvelous museum housing the largest collection of Chinese-American artifacts in the country. Large panels with eloquent and often moving descriptions in English and Chinese trace the major themes of Chinese-American history from the 1850s to the present.

The historic photographs and a remarkable array of artifacts—a Chinese Buddhist altar built in 1880, a 14-foot redwood sampan (fishing boat), a dragon's head from a turn-of-the-century parade, a shrimp winnowing machine, an herb store complete with herbs and scales, opium pipes, and even a long, black queue (the braid traditionally worn by Chinese men)—encased in plexiglass will interest visitors of all ages.

Gift Shop: The tiny shop sells books, cards, and Chinese imports, including porcelain, jewelry, dolls, and delicate wooden bird cages.

CHINESE CULTURE CENTER
750 Kearny Street, San Francisco
Phone: (415) 986-1822
Hours: Tues.-Sat. 10:00 a.m.-4:00 p.m.
Admission: Free

If you park in the Portsmouth Square garage, you can walk across the bridge from the park to the third floor of the Holiday Inn, where you will find the Chinese Cultural Center. Dedicated to fostering understanding and appreciation of Chinese and Chinese-American art, history, and culture in the United States, the center offers a variety of lectures, classes, performances, film productions, art exhibits, and other programs.

The year-round schedule of changing exhibitions has included "Han and T'and Murals from the People's Republic of China," "Huhsien Peasant Paintings," "Modern Chinese Woodcuts," "Laughter in the Palace of the Dragon," paintings from the fishing village of Zhousahan Island, and in 1994, the first U.S. showing of Shiwan Pottery, a Cantonese art form.

For an insider's view of Chinatown, sign up for one of the center's guided tours: Chinese Heritage Walk $15, Chinatown Culinary Walk $30 with lunch, and the special Chinese New Year Walk. Call for reservations.

Gift Shop: In addition to books, cards, porcelain, and jewelry, you will find delightful Chinese papercuts, door gods at $12.50 a pair, and book marks for 30¢ each.

PACIFIC HERITAGE MUSEUM
6008 Commercial Street, San Francisco
Phone: (415) 362-4100
Hours: Mon.-Fri. 10:00 a.m.-4:00 p.m.
Admission: Free

The Bank of Canton of California sponsors the Pacific Heritage Museum, which focuses on the history and cultures of the Pacific Rim. Housed in the original 1874 U.S. Subtreasury building, the three-story museum features a permanent exhibit depicting the building's history. A small exhibition devoted to aviation history is on permanent display. Special exhibits generally run for eighteen months to two years. "Faith, Forms and Harmony of Thailand," which documents Thai culture and Buddhism, Hinduism and Animism, the three main faiths of the Thai people, will be up through 1995. Also on display is "Chinese Antiquities," an exquisite collection of Chinese art bestowed on the Bank of Canton by the National Palace Museum in Taipei.

CIVIC CENTER

BOXING MUSEUM
Civic Center 3rd Floor, San Francisco
Hours: When the auditorium is open
Admission: Free

Once considered the boxing capital of the world, San Francisco is now home to a mini-museum featuring historic photographs of Gentleman Jim Corbett and a host of other prizefighters, and assorted boxing artifacts and memorabilia from the golden age of pugilism. Would-be pugilists can weigh in on an official-looking scale and then find out where they would fall in the range from heavyweight to bantamweight, and with whom they would have fought in the heyday of San Francisco boxing.

SAN FRANCISCO ART COMMISSION GALLERY
155 Grove Street (Civic Center), San Francisco
Phone: (415) 554-9682
Hours: Thurs. noon-8:00 p.m.; Fri. & Sat. noon-5:30 p.m.
Admission: Free

A non-profit exhibition space funded by the city of San Francisco, the gallery presents works in the visual and media arts by emerging and established Bay Area artists. Expect diverse, unusual works on the cutting edge.

SAN FRANCISCO MUSEUM OF MODERN ART
401 Van Ness Avenue, San Francisco
Phone: (415) 252-4000
Hours: Tues., Wed., Fri. 10:00 a.m.–5:00 p.m.; Thurs. 10:00 a.m.–
9:00 p.m.; Sat. & Sun. 11:00 a.m.–5:00 p.m.; closed Monday and
major holidays.
Admission: Adults $4.00, seniors & students $2.00, under age 13
free. Half-price admission Thursday from 5:00–9:00 p.m.
Free first Tuesday of the month.

As this book goes to press, the San Francisco Museum of Modern Art (SFMOMA) is well on its way to completion of one of the most ambitious building projects ever undertaken by an American museum. In January 1995 it will celebrate the grand opening of a new, $60 million home designed by Swiss architect Mario Botta. Located in the Yerba Buena Gardens, an 87-acre redevelopment project, the modernist building will double the museum's exhibit space and features a three-level, stepped-back stone facade distinguished by a soaring cylindrical tower finished in alternating bands of black and white stone.

Through August 1994, SFMOMA is housed on the third and fourth floors of the Beaux Arts-style War Memorial Veterans Building in Civic Center. Despite the limitations of the space it has occupied since 1935, the museum has earned a reputation as the leading modern art museum in the West. Rotating displays feature works from the museum's important permanent collection of 17,000 pieces of modern and contemporary

"Muscle Beach"
by Max Yavno
(photograph, n.d.).
Gift of the Estate
of Max Yavno,
courtesy of
SFMOMA.

art. The museum collects in all media of 20th century art—painting, sculpture, photography—with special strengths in abstract expressionism and photography, and boasts the only department of architecture and design on the West Coast, an impressive department of avant garde media arts, and one of the country's most active departments of photography.

SFMOMA's lively schedule of changing exhibitions keeps visitors coming back again and again. Ambitious, innovative, and beautifully

designed exhibitions international in scope have given Californians a chance to see the best and most adventurous art of the 20th century.

Gift Shop: The Museum Store offers the largest selection of art books in San Francisco, plus a wide variety of children's books, cards, posters, jewelry, and one-of-a-kind gifts.

Restaurant: If you want to take time out from modern art for lunch or a snack, try the museum's pleasant, second-floor cafe. There are individual tables where you can enjoy simple but tasty soups, salads, and sandwiches or the special of the day, all reasonably priced. The sandwiches and salads are made to order. We ordered the soup at $1.50/cup, and a delicious turkey/chili sandwich on foccacia bread at $4.50.

SAN FRANCISCO PERFORMING ARTS LIBRARY & MUSEUM
399 Grove Street, San Francisco
Phone: (415) 255-4800
Hours: Tues.-Fri. 10:00 a.m.-5:00 p.m.; Sat. noon-4:00 p.m.
Admission: Free

San Francisco Performing Arts Library & Museum, PALM, presents four or five exhibits a year related to some aspect of the performing arts. "Jean Cocteau and the Performing Arts" presented numerous original stage and costume designs by this renowned artist. "Martha Graham, a Legend in Her Time" offered a display of photographs by Barbara Morgan and Imogen Cunningham of this legendary dancer. But PALM's crowning glory is its archival collection—the largest of its kind on the West Coast—documenting the history of the performing arts in the Bay Area from the Gold Rush to the present. More than two million historic programs, photographs, playbills, press clippings, scene and costume designs, artifacts, videotapes, periodicals, and books covering the entire spectrum of the performing arts from vaudeville to opera are available to the public for research, education, and enjoyment. San Francisco's lively tradition of support for the arts includes many historic firsts—the first neighborhood arts program and the first full-length production of Swan Lake, for instance—and remains healthy, with the highest per capita arts expenditure and the highest per capita arts attendance in the country. Anyone interested in the performing arts should definitely pay a visit to this low-profile treasure.

CORONA HEIGHTS

RANDALL MUSEUM
199 Museum Way, San Francisco
Phone: (415) 554-9600
**Hours: Tues.-Sat. 10:00 a.m.-5:00 p.m. Animal exhibit closed
    1:00-2:00 p.m.**
Admission: Free

A relatively unknown urban sanctuary operated by the San Francisco Recreation and Park Department, the Randall Museum is part of a 16-acre park that includes playgrounds, tennis and basketball courts, and open spaces.

"You go to some museums to look at things, and some to do something. This is definitely a place you go to do something," our guide explained. Admittedly not much to look at—the museum is currently undergoing renovation—there is still a lot to see. Younger children regularly come to visit the Live Animal Room, by far the most popular of the permanent exhibits, where they might see a raccoon fishing for goldfish in her swimming pool, the opossum eating a grape, and various snakes, spiders, and other creepy crawlies in their cages. Kids can get up close and personal with a long-eared rabbit or a feathery Koshin chicken in the petting corral. All the animals—mostly native to California or endangered species in San Francisco—are either injured or raised by humans, which makes them unfit for survival in the wild.

Founded on the belief that we learn by doing, the museum offers hands-on programs in the arts, sciences, and natural environment for people from age three to adult. Its sprawling hillside facility includes an art room, ceramic studio, darkroom, fully equipped woodshop, lapidary studio, and the museum's crown jewel, a newly renovated, state-of-the-art auditorium. Classes for children, teens, families, and adults span such varied subjects as "Zen and Sawdust" (woodworking), "Family Gardening," "Introduction to Black and White Photography," "Bicycle Workshop," "Polish Paper Cutouts," and "Clowning and Circus Skills." Drop-in programs are offered Saturdays in either art or science, and there is a drop-in ceramics workshop every Saturday at 10:00 a.m.

The San Francisco Amateur Astronomers, Golden Gate Model Railroad Club, San Francisco Hobby Beekeepers Association, Mycological Society of San Francisco, and the Galileo Gem Guild are just a few of the many special interest clubs that meet at the Randall and welcome visitors.

Free buses are available to transport all San Francisco Unified School District elementary and middle school students to the museum for free science field trips, which feature lecture demonstrations and hands-on activities. The schedule includes Creepy Crawlies for Little Kids (K-3), Whales of San Francisco (grades 4 and up), "Skullduggery" (grades 4-7), and "Live Animal Presentations" (all ages).

Rental: For birthday parties, a $30 deposit will reserve space for 30 kids, Saturdays from 10:00 a.m. to 5:00 p.m.

FINANCIAL DISTRICT

FEDERAL RESERVE BANK
101 Market, San Francisco
Phone: (415) 974-3252
Hours: Mon.-Fri. 8:30 a.m.-4:30 p.m.
Admission: Free

Allow an hour to read every word, and you'll find out all you ever wanted to know about money, except maybe how to get your hands on a lot of it. The World of Economics, a gorgeous, block–long permanent exhibit filling the lobby of San Francisco's Federal Reserve Bank, shows what can be done when money is no object. The entertaining format makes it easy to digest a wealth of information about the U.S. economy: press a button to see how money is created; watch a videotape to understand supply and demand; play a computer game that allows you to become a muffin mogul by running your own bakery; design your own fiscal and monetary policy on another computer game; or meet Adam Smith, Karl Marx, and other great economists featured on the Economic Time Line mural. Tours for eighth grade and older students include a film and a tour of the checks department.

Rental: To non-profit organizations only.

THE JEWISH MUSEUM OF SAN FRANCISCO
121 Steuart Street, San Francisco
Phone: (415) 543-8880
Hours: Sun.-Wed. 11:00 a.m.-5:00 p.m.; Thurs. 11:00 a.m.-7:00 p.m.
Admission: Adults $3.00, seniors and students $1.50, children under
    12 free. Free first Wednesday of the month.

Since it was founded only a decade ago, the Jewish Museum of San Francisco has succeeded in creating a cultural bridge between the Jewish community and the rest of the ethnically diverse Bay Area. Changing thematic exhibitions based on Jewish art and culture and their relevance to contemporary America are designed to reach out to people of all ages and ethnic backgrounds. The museum also presents invitational art exhibitions, special performances, lectures, holiday celebrations, and workshops.

Free guided tours available for kindergarten through high school classes include age-appropriate art projects. Artwork by children who participate in the workshops is often displayed in the museum to take the mystery and formality out of the museum setting. Exhibit tours led by college guides are also available.

Gift Shop: The gift shop carries a large selection of books for children and adults on exhibition-related themes, Jewish holidays, and history. Cards, jewelry, and Judaica are also featured.

MUSEUM OF MONEY OF THE AMERICAN WEST
Bank of California (downstairs)
400 California Street (between Montgomery and Sansome)
Phone: (415) 765-0400
Hours: Mon.-Thurs. 10:00 a.m.-4:00 p.m.; Fri. 10:00 a.m.-5:00 p.m.
Admission: Free

Located in the main office of the splendid Bank of California, a financial district landmark since 1867, the Museum of Money of the American

West features hands-off exhibits of money. Gold nuggets, gold coins, ingots, bullion, paper currency, and early bank drafts, all behind glass, recount the history of money in California. Although not worth a special trip on its own, this small, elegant museum certainly deserves a visit if you are in the financial district, especially if you're devoting the day to money and banking-related exhibits in the neighborhood.

Younger kids will probably find the enormous vault, next to but not a part of the museum itself, most interesting; the museum is more appropriate for older children who can read.

TELEPHONE PIONEER COMMUNICATIONS MUSEUM
140 New Montgomery Street, Room 2417, San Francisco
Phone: (415) 542-1570
Hours: Mon.-Fri. 9:00 a.m.-3:00 p.m.
Admission: Free

Pacific Bell has put together the one-room Telephone Pioneer Communications Museum with a collection of artifacts spanning the history of the telephone. On view are historic telephones and antique switchboards, including a recreated Chinatown telephone office. Interactive exhibits invite you to try Beep Baseball for the sightless, test your voice at its best, and compare the speed of dial and touch-tone telephones. Our best results were fifteen seconds dialing versus five seconds pushing buttons, a savings of ten whole seconds.

This 1868 Concord Stagecoach and other artifacts of the Old West recall the history of Wells Fargo, California's oldest bank. Courtesy of Wells Fargo History Museum.

WELLS FARGO HISTORY MUSEUM
420 Montgomery Street (at California), San Francisco
Phone; (415) 396-2619
Hours: Mon.-Fri. 9:00 a.m.-5:00 p.m., except bank holidays
Admission: Free

Neither effort nor money has been spared to make your visit to the Wells Fargo History Museum an exciting adventure. Artifacts from the Old West, photographs, maps, documents, Pony Express stamps, tools,

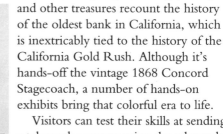

and other treasures recount the history of the oldest bank in California, which is inextricably tied to the history of the California Gold Rush. Although it's hands-off the vintage 1868 Concord Stagecoach, a number of hands-on exhibits bring that colorful era to life.

Visitors can test their skills at sending a telegraph message using the telegraph key and an international telegraph code book in a recreated Wells Fargo office. On the second floor, youngsters will

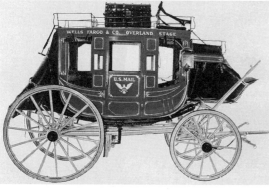

enjoy climbing aboard a replica stagecoach and taking the reins, while their weary elders sit inside. With the help of an audiotape, it's easy to imagine the discomfort of early passengers as they made the journey from Missouri to San Francisco.

Free tours for third grade through high school classes include a packet for in-class use and a follow-up packet. Call early for reservations.

Gift Shop: Wells Fargo souvenirs and memorabilia range in price from 50¢ for postcards to $325 for a stagecoach model.

FISHERMAN'S WHARF

CONTEMPORARY CRAFT MUSEUM
Ghirardelli Square
900 North Point, San Francisco
Phone: (415) 771-1919
Hours: Daily 11:00 a.m.–6:00 p.m.
Admission: Free

A light, bright gallery with a clean, contemporary look, the Contemporary Craft Museum (formerly the California Crafts Museum) presents six to eight shows a year. Imaginative exhibitions of outstanding works in clay, fiber, glass, metal, wood, and paper by established and emerging artists give you a chance to enjoy diverse creative expression in media you might not find in other museums.

Gift Shop: Pricy but gorgeous jewelry, ceramics, and crafts by California artists are available.

GUINNESS MUSEUM OF WORLD RECORDS
235 Jefferson Street, San Francisco
Phone: (415) 771-9890
Hours: Sun.–Thurs. 10:00 a.m.–11:00 p.m.; Fri. & Sat. 10:00 a.m.–midnight
Admission: Adults $6.25, students $5.00, seniors $5.25, children 5-12 $3.25

A favorite with youngsters, the Guinness Museum of World Records translates into three-dimensional forms facts taken from the pages of the world's all-time best seller (next to the Bible), *The Guinness Book of Records.* The world's tallest, shortest, biggest, fastest, costliest, oldest, rarest, tiniest, longest, and fattest, from humans to fingernails, books to bicycles, are all there for you to see, either in three-dimensional wax figure reproductions, large-screen video representations, or the actual artifacts. Interactive exhibits add to the entertainment, if not the educational value.

MARINE MAMMAL STORE AND INTERPRETIVE CENTER
Pier 39, second level, San Francisco
Phone: (415) 289-7339
Hours: Daily 10:30 a.m.–8:00 p.m., winter. Mon.–Fri. 10:30 a.m.–
**   8:00 p.m., weekends 10:30 a.m.–10:30 p.m., summer**
Admission: Free

Learn about sea lions and the marine environment through interactive computer programs, video displays, and other exhibits. Docents answer questions about sea lions at Pier 39. The store has related gifts and books.

MUSEUM OF THE CITY OF SAN FRANCISCO
The Cannery, 3rd Floor
2801 Leavenworth Street, San Francisco
Phone: (415) 928-0289
Hours: Wed.–Sun. 10:00 a.m.–4:00 p.m.
Admission: Free

Step below deck to visit the galley, crew's quarters, and control rooms of the USS Pampanito, a World War II fleet submarine built in 1943. Photo courtesy of National Maritime Museum Association.

The newest and smallest major city museum in the country, the Museum of the City of San Francisco ties the history of the city to the event that most captures the imaginations of residents and visitors alike—the 1906 earthquake. Whether you walk around on your own and examine the collection of artifacts, photographs, and documents of the "big one," or take the free tour, you'll find this little jewel of a museum a real treat. I'd opt for the tour. Our spirited guide had us lying on our backs on the floor to look for the star pattern in the beautiful 13th century mudejar ceiling (a treasure from the estate of William Randolph Hearst), and tapping our feet to the lively music of a 1913 player piano. Running indefinitely, the permanent exhibit "San Francisco, 1906: the Destruction of the Great City" encompasses San Francisco's unique patchwork of humanity and topography.

Gift Shop: A small counter sells San Francisco memorabilia.

Rental: The museum can accommodate up to 300. Call for information

USS *PAMPANITO*
Pier 45, Fisherman's Wharf (near corner of Taylor &
Jefferson), San Francisco
Hours: Sun.–Thurs. 9:00 a.m.–6:00 p.m., Fri. & Sat.
**   9:00 a.m.–8:00 p.m., winter; daily 9:00 a.m.–**
**   9:00 p.m., summer. Open 365 days a year.**
Phone: (415) 929-0202
Admission: Adults $4.00, juniors 12–17 $2.00,
children under 12 and seniors $1.00

Pick up your audio wand at the ticket booth for a

self-guided tour of this World War II submarine narrated by Captain Edward Beach, author of *Run Silent, Run Deep.* You can go below deck to visit the galley, crew's quarters, and control rooms. Imagine what a sailor's life was like in these cramped quarters during long-range cruises in the Pacific. You can also check out the arsenal of ten torpedo tubes and five-inch deck guns. Overnight programs are available for scout groups.

RIPLEY'S BELIEVE IT OR NOT! MUSEUM
175 Jefferson Street, San Francisco
Phone: (415) 771-6188
Hours: Sun.-Thurs. 9:00 a.m.-11:00 p.m.; Fri. & Sat. 9:00 a.m.-midnight
Admission: Adults $7.25, seniors & teens 13-17 $5.50, children 5-12 $4.00

Believe it or not, two floors and ten thousand square feet of exhibits featuring the strange, the unusual, and the unbelievable all started from a simple newspaper cartoon in 1918. One of a worldwide chain, San Francisco's Believe It or Not! Museum recently reopened with eight galleries of animal oddities and natural disasters and a collection of artifacts gathered from all parts of the world, including a two-headed calf, an eight-foot long model of a cable car made from 270,836 match sticks, and an eight-foot tall stegosaurus made entirely from chrome car bumpers. Participatory video displays, a walk-through rotating tunnel, and holographic illusions add a high-tech atmosphere. Kids will love it. A word to the wise: while you earnestly attempt to curl your tongue or touch it to your nose, your facial contortions are on view to other museum visitors via a two-way mirror.

During the 17th century, figureheads and other carved ship's decorations were so elaborate and heavy that captains would sometimes have them cut away and thrown overboard once they got out to sea, to make their ships more seaworthy. Photo of a figurehead at San Francisco's Maritime Museum by Nate Levine.

SAN FRANCISCO MARITIME NATIONAL HISTORICAL PARK
West end of Fisherman's Wharf, Hyde Street to Aquatic Park
Phone: (415) 556-3002

The one-of-a-kind San Francisco Maritime National Historical Park, a unit of the National Park Service, includes the striking Maritime Museum, historic ships, and the J. Porter Shaw Library (see the Fort Mason listings in the Marina District for details on the Shaw Library). The park is a haven for ship lovers, history buffs, and fans of Art Deco architecture.

Rentals: For weddings and receptions at the Maritime Museum or aboard the *Balclutha* or the *Eureka,* call the National Maritime Museum Association at (415) 929-0202.

THE LAST GAM

HYDE STREET PIER HISTORIC SHIPS
Foot of Hyde Street at Jefferson, San Francisco
Hours: Daily 9:30 a.m.–5:00 p.m.
Admission: Adults $3.00; children 12–17 $1.00; seniors & children under 12 free. Free the first Tuesday of the month.

The word "scrimshaw" is said to derive from the French s'escrimer, "to work hard for small results." The traditional art of carefully carving and decorating small pieces of bone, ivory, and shell was refined by sailors on long voyages. This whale tooth by C.R. Hull commemorates a meeting between whaling ships. Courtesy of Danford & Campbell, San Francisco Maritime National Historic Park.

A fleet of floating national landmarks spanning a century of working history is docked at the Hyde Street Pier. Your entrance fee will get you aboard and let you explore three of them—the *Eureka, C.A. Thayer,* and *Balclutha.*

Older visitors may remember crossing the bay on the sidewheel ferry *Eureka,* in her day the world's largest passenger ferry. Today you can examine the massive, four-story steam engine that once powered the ship, and a large collection of vintage vehicles, a reminder of the many autos (up to 120 at a time) she hauled. Visitors can see much of the ongoing restoration work.

The square-rigged *Balclutha,* an 1886 sailing vessel that made the perilous voyage from Europe to San Francisco, recalls the danger and romance of rounding Cape Horn. Movie buffs may recognize the *Balclutha* from the 1930 version of "Mutiny on the Bounty."

Fishing fans can fantasize hauling in salmon off the coast of Alaska or cod in the Bering Sea while exploring the graceful, three-masted schooner *C.A. Thayer,* the last commercial sailing vessel to operate from a West Coast port.

Less elegant than her sister ships, the boxy, flat-bottomed scow schooner *Alma,* the last of her kind, has recently been restored and opened to the public for tours once a day. *Alma* serves as the park's ambassador, sailing to Bay Area ports for special events.

The tug *Eppleton Hall* is presently undergoing reconstruction and is not accessible to the public, but you may catch a glimpse of a volunteer crew at work.

For nothing more than the price of admission you can also choose from a rich menu of shipboard programs, including chantey sings, figurehead modeling workshops, and maritime culinary demonstrations. Check the chalkboard at the ticket booth for schedules, or call the ranger desk at (415) 556-3002. Boat-building classes and workshops are offered for a fee in the Small Boat Shop on the pier. Admission also includes other activities, such as puppet shows and living history programs, on the pier.

THE MARITIME MUSEUM
Foot of Polk Street at Beach Street, San Francisco
Hours: Daily 10:00 a.m.–5:00 p.m.
Admission: Free

Touted as one of the most sophisticated WPA projects of all, the 1932 ferroconcrete, glass, and stainless steel structure that now houses the

Maritime Museum is classic Art Deco, right down to the chrome chandeliers. Hilaire Hiler's enormous interior mural depicting the underwater world of the lost continent of Atlantis and the gorgeous marble floors based on a shoal chart of the bay will take your breath away.

Permanent exhibits of ship models, historic photographs, and maritime artifacts, including a painted figurehead and a shipboard medicine chest, display the rich history of West Coast seafaring, the California Gold Rush, and the whaling industry. "Days of the Tule Sailor" is about scow schooners like the *Alma* that plied the bay hauling bricks and hay—the semi trucks of the pre-bridge era. In the Steamship Room you can learn how steam technology revolutionized shipping, or just admire the model steamers. Interactive and hands-on exhibits keep even young children entertained.

THE MARITIME STORE
Hyde Street Pier, San Francisco
Phone: (415) 775-2665
Hours: Daily 9:30 a.m.-5:30 p.m., winter; 9:30 a.m.-6:00 p.m., summer.

The best place in town to find books about virtually all maritime subjects, as well as games, models, ship plans, nautical art, and other gifts of the sea. Shop proceeds support educational and conservation projects.

WAX MUSEUM AT FISHERMAN'S WHARF
145 Jefferson Street (between Taylor & Mason), San Francisco
Phone: (800) 439-4305
Hours: Daily 9:00 a.m.-11:00 p.m., summer; 9:00 a.m.-10:00 p.m., winter.
Admission: Adults $8.95, seniors & teens 12-17 $6.95, children 6-12 $4.95, under 6 free.

Even the most reluctant museum-goer among the younger set will jump at a chance to visit the Wax Museum. Despite the high admission price and questionable educational value, this bizarre and eclectic hodgepodge of life-size wax figures is strangely compelling. On the four floors of the hundred-year-old former grain warehouse you will find assembled the oddest assortment of historical, fictional, and contemporary figures imaginable, roughly categorized under the broad headings of Palace of Living Art, Gallery of Stars, Hall of Religions, King Tutankhamen's Tomb, and Chamber of Horrors. We couldn't decide if the intent was high camp tongue-in-cheek or deadly serious. In any case, you don't often get an opportunity to see Albert Einstein, Jim and Tammy Bakker, and Jesus all under one roof. Young

Joe Montana is just one of the famous people you can see at the Wax Museum, not to mention King Tutankhamen and Albert Einstein. Courtesy of Wax Museum at Fisherman's Wharf.

children and nightmare-prone adults should skip the Chamber of Horrors—it is truly gruesome.

Rental: Available Monday through Thursday, except holidays, $895 for the first hour, $275 for each additional half hour.
Wheelchair access first floor only.

GOLDEN GATE PARK

San Francisco's pride and joy, Golden Gate Park, covers over one thousand acres of gardens, lakes, meadows, bridle paths, and recreation areas. Several of San Francisco's major museums are here, all within walking distance of each other. For $10 you can buy a Golden Gate Park Culture Pass good for admission to five attractions. Although you save 30% this way, it's hard to imagine taking in all these splendid sights in a limited time.

ASIAN ART MUSEUM
Golden Gate Park, San Francisco
Phone: (415) 668–8921
Hours: Wed.–Sun. 10:00 a.m.–4:45 p.m.
Admission: Adults $5.00, youths 12–17 $2.00, seniors $3.00
(good for admission to the de Young Museum as well).
Free first Wednesday of the month, 10:00 a.m.–8:45 p.m.,
and first Saturday, 10:00 a.m.–noon.

As America's gateway to Asia, San Francisco is a most fitting home for the Avery Brundage Collection, considered the largest and best collection of Asian art in the world outside Asia.

Most of the first floor is devoted to Chinese art, which makes up more than half the collection, and includes ceramics, jade objects, bronzes, and paintings on scrolls, fans, and albums. Examples of Chinese art date back seven thousand years. To put this in perspective, consider the contemporary charm of some of these objects, and then think about what was happening in Europe seventy centuries ago when they were being made. The Korea gallery is also on the first floor.

The second floor galleries are divided among the arts of India, Tibet and the Himalayas, Japan, Southeast Asia, and the Middle East—forty different countries in all. Objects from the huge collection are periodically rotated, which gives repeat visitors a chance to see new works, but always has me rushing to familiar spots to make sure my favorites (a wonderful Chinese camel, an intricately carved stone sculpture of the elephant-headed god Ganesha, and a particularly graceful, seated Buddha) are still on display.

With most of the objects behind glass and the rest strictly "do not touch," this is not a museum geared to young children. However, it's not unusual to find children quite taken with the works of art. I watched a pair of ten-year-olds stare in utter fascination at the collection of ancient Indian sculpture, the multi-headed, multi-armed gods and goddesses holding various weapons and ritual objects. A perennial favorite with all ages is the enormous jade collection presented with the Chinese collection. A promise of tea and cookies in the serenely beautiful Japanese Tea Garden, visible through several gallery windows, may encourage patience in young visitors.

In 1998 the museum will begin to build a new home in Civic Center Plaza, in the Beaux Arts building currently housing the public library.

Library: A resource library of 12,000 books, periodicals, photographs, microfilms, and slides is available for curators and scholars of Asian art.

Gift Shop: The gift shop carries postcards, notecards, books, and other tastefully selected merchandise.

Rental: The museum is available for private and corporate use and receptions. Call (415) 668-6313.

CALIFORNIA ACADEMY OF SCIENCES
Golden Gate Park, San Francisco
Phone: (415) 221-5100
Hours: Daily 10:00 a.m.–5:00 p.m.; 10:00 a.m.–7:00 p.m. summer.
Admission: Adults $7.00, students, seniors, youths 12–17 $4.00,
children 6–11 $1.50. Free first Wednesday of the month.

I must confess that the Academy of Sciences was not on my list of favorite places when I was a child—a bunch of musty stuffed animals in dusty dioramas, I thought. Well, let me tell you, things have changed in

From dinosaur skeletons to crocodiles to cartoons by Gary Larson, the California Academy of Sciences has something for everyone. Photo by Susan Middletown, courtesy of California Academy of Sciences.

the last forty years! New exhibits have been added, including the Laserium, the Living Coral Reef, Wild California, Life Through Time, and the Fish Roundabout, and old ones have been renovated. Even the least scientifically inclined will find plenty to enjoy in this magnificent institution.

With over 14,000 specimens, including fresh and saltwater fishes, reptiles, amphibians, and marine mammals, Steinhart Aquarium is the oldest and most diverse aquarium in North America. If speed and motion

excite you, you'll enjoy the Fish Roundabout, where you, the visitor, stand in the middle while fast-swimming salt-water fishes (including sharks from the San Francisco Bay) swim madly around you. The effect is mesmerizing, though not recommended for anyone susceptible to sea sickness. The Swamp, ornamented with lush tropical plants and a waterfall, is home to the more sedate frogs, snakes, lizards, crocodiles, and alligators. If you want something really cute, you can watch eighteen formally dressed penguins waddle and swim in their own breeding colony. For adorability, nothing beats the three harbor seals and two dolphins at feeding time which, fortunately, happens every two hours. If you simply must get a closer view, the aquarium's newest exhibit, the California Tidepool, lets you put your hands in the water and pick up a starfish or sea urchin.

As a child on school field trips to the Morrison Planetarium, I never quite understood how there could be so many stars out in the daytime. Now I know that the famous Sky Shows are realistic simulations of the night sky. You might see a blue moon or meteor showers, or follow Galileo's thoughts as he discovered the secrets of our moon, the planets, and the galaxy. Shows cost $2.50 for adults, $1.25 for seniors and kids, and they change every few months. For evening entertainment, a live laserist performs a dazzling, multi-colored light show to musical accompaniment Thursday through Sunday at the Laserium (not recommended for children under six).

Other state-of-the-art exhibits in the Natural History Museum offer a million possibilities for fun and learning: the magnificent African Safari Hall, where visitors pick up a telephone receiver to hear "a meal for all," the dramatic story of the African lion family at dinner; toddlers to senior citizens can be seen standing transfixed before the African waterhole exhibit, complete with recordings made on location; I found myself laughing aloud at the hilarious cartoons of Gary Larson in the Far Side of Science Gallery; and when I stood under the giant microscope and looked up, I could swear the giant eye looking down winked at me. All this and much, much more make the Academy of Sciences a sure-fire winner. After all, a million and a half visitors a year can't be wrong.

The Discovery Room, for children K-6 and limited to twenty visitors at a time, is a mini-museum without glass or ropes to restrain eager hands or dampen curiosity. Youngsters can try on clothes from other countries, hold a dinosaur bone, or watch a tree frog eat a cricket. School groups may visit the academy between 10:00 a.m. and 5:00 p.m. any day of the year. Admission is $1.00 per person, San Francisco school groups free. Call for reservations early in the school year, (415) 750-7159.

Library: The non-circulating, scientific library is open by reservation. The Bio-Diversity Resource Center, a lending library about the environment with magazines, videos, and a computer network, is open to the public.

Gift Shop: Three separate shops include the small Swamp Shop, which sells aquarium-related objects, the main Academy Store, filled with a

Penguins can't fly, but they can swim at speeds up to 25 miles per hour, using their wings as paddles. Photo by Charlotte Fiorito, courtesy of California Academy of Sciences.

marvelous selection of beautifully displayed gifts ranging from Safari Socks to Pueblo pottery, and The Book Shop.

Rental: The entire Museum may be rented for $10,000 for one night. It sounds like a lot but you can throw a pretty spectacular party there.

THE CONSERVATORY
Golden Gate Park, San Francisco
Phone: (415) 666-7017
Hours: Mon.-Sun. 9:30 a.m.-5:00 p.m.
Admission: General $1.50, seniors and students 75¢. Free Mon.-
  Fri. 9:00-9:30 a.m.

The graceful, ornate, glass Conservatory, touted as the outstanding example of Victorian architecture in the Bay Area, is the oldest building in Golden Gate Park, and the oldest continuously operating conservatory in the country. It boasts the only public collection of cold-growing orchids in the world (they come from the Andes). The philodendron, planted in 1884, is considered one of the most magnificent specimens in the world—the leaves are three feet across and the flowers are twenty inches long and weigh five pounds each. There are also the Victoria Pond and the Cloverleaf Pond, filled with tropical water lilies and Egyptian lotus, and the children's garden. Since kids are mostly interested in plants they can eat or plants that eat something else, this special garden is planted with edibles like mango, guava, papaya, vanilla, coconut, and banana, and a host of carnivorous plants.

Rental: The Conservatory accommodates up to two hundred and is available evenings from 6:30 to midnight. You won't find a more romantic place to celebrate a wedding in the entire Bay Area. The perfect garden setting—no need to worry about the weather and no need to buy flowers. Call (800) 707-1879 for information.

Gift Shop: A kiosk sells San Francisco souvenirs, postcards, publications, and small plants.

Fond of the chill of its Colombian homeland, Masdevallia caudiovulvula *has very specific temperature require-ments, making it very hard to grow even in San Francisco's cool, foggy climate. The Conservatory's conservation program for endangered, high-altitude orchids struggles to keep such plants in cultivation, as many are extinct now in the Andes.* Courtesy of The Conservatory.

M.H. DE YOUNG MEMORIAL MUSEUM
Golden Gate Park, San Francisco
Phone: (415) 863-3330
Hours: Wed. 10:00 a.m.-8:45 p.m.; Thurs.-Sun. 10:00 a.m.-5:00 p.m.
Admission: Adults $5.00, seniors $3.00, youth 12-17 $2.00 (Good for
  admission to the Asian Art Museum as well). Free first Wednes-
  day of the month, 10:00 a.m.-8:45 p.m., and first Saturday
  10:00 a.m.-noon.

Along the lines of your traditional, all-purpose, history-of-art museum, the de Young has a little bit of this and a little bit of that in its quite

"Mrs. Robert S. Cassatt, the Artist's Mother" (Katherine Johnston Cassatt), by Mary Cassatt (ca. 1889, oil on canvas, 38" x 27"), part of the de Young's extensive collection of American painting. Courtesy of the M.H. de Young Memorial Museum.

respectable collection, which ranges from Greek vases to Tiffany glass.

Thanks to gifts in 1979 and 1992 from John D. Rockefeller III, the de Young is the best in the West when it comes to American paintings. Pick up a map at the entrance, walk through the stately Hearst Court, and follow the alphabetical course for a chronological tour of the American Galleries. They include paintings and sculpture from the colonial period through work by contemporary Bay Area artists. Along the way you'll find furniture and examples of the decorative arts (a silver tankard by Paul Revere II, Amish quilts, and the like) and even a federal period room.

Art from other times and other places is also represented, including the requisite Egyptian mummy, works from Africa, Central, South and Mesoamerica, and English paintings, furniture, and silver.

For kids: Saturday Morning at the de Young, a free drop-in program; Big Kids/Little Kids, where kids from ages 3-1/2 to 6 and their parents see and do art together; Doing and Viewing Art, docent tours and studio workshops for 7- to 12-year-olds.

Library: The African Art Study Center is open by appointment only.

Gift Shop: The shop at the museum features art books, prints, posters, cards, and gift items. The Museum Store at Macy's, in Union Square, sells merchandise to make giving an art form, including Escher ties, Frank Lloyd Wright scarves, Picasso notecards, reproductions, jewelry, sculptures and toys by contemporary artisans, and art books.

Rental: Corporate evening rentals are available. Call (415) 750-3683.

Restaurant: If you didn't mind paying the $5.00 entrance fee to the museum, the cafe at the de Young could be a destination in itself. You can dine in an attractive room with art-covered walls, or outdoors in the garden (bring a sweater, San Francisco gets chilly). The food, served cafeteria-style, is made to order. Lunch is served from 11:00 to 3:30. Coffeecakes and fabulous desserts, coffee and tea are always available. Sandwich prices range from about $4.00 to $5.50, and homemade soups are about $2.50. Specials are about $6.50—on our visit, a savory Mexican quiche with zucchini, lima beans, mild chilis, carrots, and broccoli was served with salad for this price, and an anchovy-dressed Caesar salad was $5.50.

JAPANESE TEA GARDEN
Golden Gate Park, San Francisco
Phone: (415) 666-7200
Hours: Daily 9:00 a.m.-6:30 p.m., summer; 8:30 a.m.-6:00 p.m.
Oct.-March
Admission: $2.00 adults, $1.00 seniors and children, free first
Wednesday of the month

Tea and cookies and a stroll through the exquisite Japanese Tea Garden
will cap your visit to the de Young and the Asian Art Museum perfectly.
Designed in 1893, the meticulously manicured tea garden offers the
perfect balance between human creations—bridges, pagodas, footpaths,
a large bronze Buddha, and an ornate Temple Gate—and nature's
wonders. Cherry trees in bloom, maples, and bonsais are tempered by
the gardener's artistry. As a child I delighted in the terror of climbing the
steep moon bridge. As a grown-up I prefer a leisurely stroll, with a stop
to watch the koi swimming lazily in the ponds.

Gift Shop: A large assortment of souvenirs and tourist items with a
Japanese bent is available in the gift shop.

Restaurant: Kimono-clad waitresses serve tea and cookies ($2.00 per
person) in the charming tea house.

STRYBING ARBORETUM & BOTANICAL GARDENS
9th Avenue and Lincoln Way, San Francisco
Phone: (415) 661-1316
Hours: Mon.-Fri. 8:30 a.m.-4:30 p.m.; Sat. & Sun., holidays
10:00 a.m.-4:00 p.m.
Admission: Free

I know a bank where the wild thyme blows,
Where cowslip and the nodding violet grows:
Quite overcanopied with luscious woodbine,
With sweet musk roses, and with eglantine.

William Shakespeare could have been describing the luscious Strybing
Arboretum and Gardens, a beautifully landscaped, 70-acre section of
Golden Gate Park filled with 7,500 plants. Thanks to San Francisco's
temperate climate, hundreds of plants are in bloom year round. Take a
free, docent-led Garden Walk (1:30 p.m. weekdays, 10:30 a.m. and
1:30 p.m. weekends) or explore on your own. Don't miss the Garden
of Fragrance, the Biblical Garden, New World Cloud Forest, the Moon-
Viewing Garden, or the Redwood Trail.

For schools, docent-led walks with a Teacher's Resource Guide
containing pre- and post-curriculum classroom materials are free. Call
(415) 661-0822. Children's programs and family programs include story-
telling, gardening, and crafts.

Library: The Helen Crocker Russell Library of Horticulture, open daily from 10:00 a.m. to 4:00 p.m. except Tuesdays, is a lovely place to read about garden design, landscaping, and horticulture. This non-circulating library contains more than 14,000 volumes, including a rare book collection, and receives over 300 periodicals.

Gift Shop: Miraculously squeezed into the tiny bookstore is a selection of gifts and an extensive collection of horticulture, botany, and gardening books—more than 2,000 titles. The store is open daily from 10:00 a.m. to 4:00 p.m., telephone (415) 661-5191.

Rental: The garden itself is not available but the adjacent San Francisco County Fair Building, a large, nondescript edifice, can be rented in its entirety (14,000 square feet, 2,000 person occupancy) or smaller rooms. Call (415) 753-7090. The San Francisco Recreation and Park Department also rents hedges, trees, bushes, plants, and cut-flower arrangements at astonishingly low rates. Check them out for your next event, (415) 666-7200.

HUNTERS POINT

GOLDEN GATE RAILROAD MUSEUM
Phone: (415) 363-2472
Hours: By appointment only
Admission: Free

We might never have learned about the Golden Gate Railroad Museum if vandals had not cut a hole in a chain link fence and sprayed paint on the vintage cars. The media coverage of the event let this well-kept secret out of the bag.

Restoration and preservation of historic locomotives and railcars is the primary activity at the facilities, although museum members are currently refurbishing and modifying the existing buildings to create a first-class car and locomotive shop, railroad yard, and visitor/docent areas.

"Doubleheader at Benicia, SP 2472 and SP 4449." At the Golden Gate Railroad Museum, you can see #2472, a fully restored steam locomotive built for Southern Pacific in 1921. Courtesy of Golden Gate Railroad Museum.

The museum's prize exhibit is the fully restored steam locomotive #2472. This high-speed mainline passenger steam locomotive was delivered to the Southern Pacific in 1921 and was originally used to pull the famous Overland Limited. Later it saw service in the commuter fleet in the San Francisco Bay Area and was retired in 1957. Today the locomotive, the only one of its class that has been fully rebuilt and restored to active service, can best be seen when it travels to various railroad displays around the state. Call for information.

To visit the museum, you must contact them in advance to arrange for a pass onto the Hunters Point Naval Shipyard. A valid driver's license, current vehicle registration, and proof of insurance must be presented at time of arrival.

THE MARINA

THE EXPLORATORIUM
Palace of Fine Arts
3601 Lyon Street, San Francisco
Phone: (415) 563-7337. Tactile Dome reservations:
(415) 561-0362.
Hours: Daily 10:00 a.m.–5:00 p.m. (10:00 a.m.–
9:30 p.m. Wednesdays), Memorial Day–Labor Day;
closed Mondays after Labor Day.
Admission: Adults $8.00, seniors $6.00, youth $4.00,
family $20.00. Free first Wednesday of the month.

"The whole point of the Exploratorium is to make it possible for people to believe they can understand the world around them. I think a lot of people have given up trying to comprehend things. And when they give up with the physical world, they give up with the social and political world as well. If we stop trying to understand things, I think we'll all be sunk." So said physicist Frank Oppenheimer, explaining why he came up with the concept of the Exploratorium. Considered by many to be the best and most original science museum ever, the Exploratorium has inspired similar institutions all over the world since it opened in 1969.

All 650 exhibits at San Francisco's Exploratorium offer hands-on experiences to enhance our understanding of how things work. Courtesy of the Exploratorium.

The Exploratorium is housed in the restored Palace of Fine Arts, designed by Bernard Maybeck for the Panama-Pacific Exposition of 1915. The fanciful, pink, pseudo-classical exterior, with its pillared rotunda overlooking a serene, swan-filled lake, offers a striking contrast to the noisy and cavernous interior, roughly divided into thirteen subject areas: life sciences, color, electricity, heat and temperature, language, light, motion, patterns, sound and hearing, touch, vision, waves and resonance, and weather. All 650 exhibits—and more are being added all the time—are meant to be manipulated by visitors, enhancing our understanding of what we see, hear, smell, feel, and otherwise experience of the world around us.

In the no-frills atmosphere, where something is always blinking, clanking, or splashing and children are rushing from one exhibit to another, the pace can get almost frenzied at times. But the exhibits are built to withstand the most arduous physical examinations, and Explainers, high school students wearing bright orange jackets, are on hand to explain an exhibit if you ask. Separated from the museum floor by a low fence is the workshop where all the museum's exhibits are created; the Exploratorium's dedication to showing how things work includes exhibiting the exhibit builders at work sawing, painting, and welding.

Although the hands-on exhibits were created with children in mind, the Exploratorium is not just for children. After all, over 60% of its half a million annual visitors are adults. Some exhibits are too complicated for a child to understand without an adult's explanation, and even the most straightforward kid-pleasing exhibits have a secondary level of scientific sophistication to appeal to adults.

The Tactile Dome, a series of rooms, tunnels, and slides of different textures through which visitors make their way in complete darkness using only their sense of touch, can be visited by reservation only—call (415) 561-0362.

Library: A non-circulating library is open to the public by appointment.

Gift Shop: Shopping at the Exploratorium store is almost as much fun as visiting the museum itself. You'll find a unique collection of gadgets, gizmos, games, and books related to the exhibits, and glorious t-shirts.

Rental: The Exploratorium, all 100,000 square feet of it with exhibitions fully operational, can be rented for evening events.

Restaurant: Since you'll probably be spending the day at the Exploratorium, at some point you *will* need to eat. Angel's Cafe offers you a large choice of flavorful foods without gouging you in the pocketbook. This cafeteria-style eatery sits right in the heart of the Exploratorium, so expect a lot of noise while you dine. The full lunch menu includes sandwiches and a large variety of salads, soups, and hot dishes. We were well satisfied with meals costing about $5.00 each. Children's sandwiches are about $3.00. For a quick fix, down a breakfast muffin, ice cream, or cookies.

FORT MASON CENTER

Used by the military for over two hundred years, Fort Mason's piers and warehouses stood barren and deserted twenty-two years ago. Since 1972, when it was entrusted to the National Park Service, Fort Mason has been converted into a thriving cultural center, home to over fifty nonprofit groups—from theaters and ethnic museums to galleries and environmental groups. Located between the Golden Gate and the Bay Bridge in a setting of incomparable beauty on San Francisco's northern waterfront, Fort Mason Center forms the hub of the Golden Gate National Recreation Area, the world's largest, most successful urban national park.

FORT MASON ART CENTER GALLERY
Fort Mason Center, Building B, San Francisco
Phone: (415) 561-1840
Hours: Mon.-Fri. 9:00 a.m.-8:00 p.m., Sat. 9:00 a.m.-5:00 p.m.
Admission: Free

Known as the Coffee Gallery, this comfortable, informal dining area showcases work by students and faculty from the City College of San Francisco Art Center at Fort Mason.

SS *JEREMIAH O'BRIEN*
Fort Mason Center, San Francisco
Phone: (415) 441-3101
Hours: Weekdays 9:00 a.m.–3:00 p.m., weekends
9:00 a.m.–4:00 p.m.
Admission: Adults $2.00, children & seniors $1.00,
family $5.00

On D-Day, June 6, 1944, the greatest armada in history stormed the beaches of Normandy to liberate Europe. Of those 5,000 ships, only one survives intact— the liberty ship SS *Jeremiah O'Brien*.

During World War II, liberty ships carried troops, arms, machinery, and food through the submarine-infested waters of the Pacific and Atlantic oceans. Run by merchant marines, the ships were subject to the same hazards as their armed service counterparts. Of the 2,700 liberty ships built between 1941 and 1944, only the *Jeremiah O'Brien* survives in its original condition, fully operational; every piece of machinery on board, from the dual-acting, triple-expansion, reciprocating steam engine to the whistle, functions exactly as it did in 1943.

Robert Davidson, an engineer aboard the Jeremiah *O'Brien. Photo by Nate Levine.*

Although you are welcome to explore the ship on your own, I strongly recommend the free tours led by dedicated and knowledgeable volunteers. This way you will be sure to see everything and you will hear some fascinating tidbits. For example, the radio room aboard ship is always called the Radio Shack and the operator—no matter what his or her name—is always called Sparks. Your guides may show you how to steer the ship and tap out your name in Morse Code.

You might want to time your visit for Steaming Weekend, the third weekend of the month, when the engine is fired up (at slow speed) and the original coal-burning range in the galley turns out hot dogs and "Chocolate Ship Cookies." The truly smitten may sign up for the annual May cruise, when the ship sails out the Golden Gate with one thousand guests aboard and returns five hours later. Lunch and live music of the 1940s are included in the $75 per person tab.

Gift Shop: A small, on-board gift shop open on Steaming Weekends carries nifty nautical items priced from $1.00 up.

Rental: Children can celebrate their birthdays with a tour of the ship, followed by cake in the Gunners' or Crew's Mess for $25, plus regular admittance. Number Two Hold and the Officers' Mess are available for standing receptions, dinner, and dancing, for a small cleaning fee and $3.00 per person.

THE MEXICAN MUSEUM
Fort Mason Center, Building D, San Francisco
Phone: (415) 441-0445
**Hours: Wed.-Sun. noon-5:00 p.m.; first Wednesday of the month
noon-8:00 p.m.**
**Admission: Adults $3.00, students & seniors $2.00, children under
10 free. Free on first Wednesday of the month.**

A former garage for military equipment now houses the first museum in
the country dedicated to the work of Mexicano (Mexican, Mexican-
American, and Chicano) and Latino artists. Museum-generated shows
range from Mexican surrealism to graffiti art, with a few blockbuster
shows, like Frida Kahlo in 1986, originating elsewhere.

Children's educational art programs invite children to the museum for
story-telling, tours, and hands-on workshops tailored to the exhibit on
view. Traveling Trunks are the museum's traveling mini-exhibitions,
designed to encourage children in elementary and high school to explore
Mexicano culture through art in the classroom.

The museum plans to relocate to a newly constructed building on
Mission Street in 1998.

Library: The extensive library is available to scholars on a limited basis.

Gift Shop: La Tienda, the museum's gift shop, overflows with folk art
from Mexico and Latin America. A unique selection of handcrafted
masks, ceramics, jewelry, and lacquerware is available, as well as books
on contemporary and traditional Latino art and culture.

MUSEO ITALO AMERICANO
Fort Mason Center, Building C, San Francisco
Phone: (415) 673-2200
Hours: Wed.-Sun. noon-5:00 p.m.
**Admission: Adults $2.00, seniors & students $1.00. Free on the first
Wednesday of the month.**

The pleasant Museo Italo Americano shows works of Italian and Italian-
American artists and occasional historical exhibits in the gallery, and offers
Italian language classes in the library. C.I.A.O. (Children's Italian Art
Outreach), the in-school program offered free to all schools, covers
Italian history and art, and generates completed art projects, like building
a Renaissance palace. Call to reserve free tickets for the popular Christmas
play "La Befana," presented at the museum in December.

Gift Shop: For things Italian—ceramics, jewelry, books—try the museum
gift shop.

SAN FRANCISCO AFRICAN AMERICAN HISTORICAL & CULTURAL SOCIETY

Fort Mason Center, Building C, San Francisco
Phone: Fort Mason: (415) 441-0640; Fulton Street: (415) 292-6172
Hours: Wed.-Sun. noon-5:00 p.m.
Admission: Adults $1.00, youth 50¢, seniors 75¢. Free on the first
   Wednesday of the month.

Founded in 1955, the San Francisco African American Historical & Cultural Society has facilities at Fort Mason and on Fulton Street. The Fort Mason facility includes a museum, art gallery, and gift shop, with the museum's permanent exhibition featuring artifacts and archival materials on African-American life and culture from the 19th century to the present. The gallery showcases works by new and master artists of African descent. Exhibits have included photogravures of Carl Van Vechten's photos of heroes of the Harlem Renaissance, and a photographic retrospective on the last five years of the life of Martin Luther King, Jr.

The Howard Thurman Listening Room, located at the Society's 762 Fulton Street location, is a quiet room for listening to the taped lectures of Howard Thurman, speeches by African-American leaders, and musical compositions by local, national, and international African-American artists.

Library: Also located 762 at Fulton Street, the library includes a collection of books, periodicals, and files available for research. It is open Wednesday through Saturday from noon to 5:00 p.m.

Gift Shop: The gift shop at Fort Mason carries gorgeous African and African-American arts and crafts.

SAN FRANCISCO CRAFT & FOLK ART MUSEUM

Fort Mason Center, Landmark Building A, San Francisco
Phone: (415) 775-0990
Hours: Tues.-Sun. 11:00 a.m.-5:00 p.m.
Admission: $1.00. Free Sat. 10:00 a.m.-noon and first Wednesday
   of the month.

This small, exciting museum offers six to ten always beautiful and often ground-breaking exhibitions a year of contemporary fine crafts, American folk art, and traditional ethnic art

The museum's Folk Art in the Schools Program brings hands-on experiences with traditional ethnic arts to Bay Area schoolchildren in third to eighth grade.

Gift Shop: A delightful gift shop carries work by local craftspeople and imports from Mexico, Haiti, India, and Indonesia.

"Ugly Jar" (left) by Mathew Hewell, 1983, alkaline glaze on stoneware, kaolin, and "Face Jug" (right) by Clayton Bailey, 1990, pink glaze on stoneware, kaolin. "Face vessels" were made by African-American potters in South Carolina in the 1800s. Later, "ugly jars" were produced by white potters throughout the South, and the tradition continues today. Photo by Clayton Bailey, courtesy of San Francisco Craft & Folk Art Museum.

SAN FRANCISCO MUSEUM OF MODERN ART RENTAL GALLERY
Fort Mason Center, Building A, San Francisco
Phone: (415) 441-4777
Hours: Tues.-Sat. 11:30 a.m.-5:30 p.m.; closed August
Admission: Free

If viewing art in museums has given you a yen to hang some on your own walls, this might be just the place for you. An adjunct of the SFMOMA, the Rental Gallery rents and sells works by over 900 northern California artists. Purchase prices range from $100 to $15,000. Art lovers daunted by the high price of collecting will find renting simple and affordable. For as little as $15 a month, you may take home a painting, sculpture, photograph, or print. After two months (corporate clients get three), you either return the work or buy it, with half the rental fee being credited toward the purchase price. You rummage through racks and racks of paintings on the gallery's second floor until you find the perfect piece. Corporate clients get a little more assistance in selecting art, plus delivery and installation.

The gallery also mounts eleven exhibitions a year, each showcasing the talents of three contemporary Bay Area artists. The light-flooded, split-level space accommodates larger paintings, sculpture, and installations on the first floor and smaller works on the second floor.

J. PORTER SHAW LIBRARY
Fort Mason Center, Building E, San Francisco
Phone: (415) 556-9870
Hours: Tues. 5:00-8:00 p.m.; Wed.-Fri. 1:00-5:00 p.m.;
    Sat. 10:00 a.m.-5:00 p.m.
Admission: Free

A "fou-fou band" (an ensemble formed on the spur of the moment to make music with whatever is on hand) poses on the deck of a turn-of-the-century squarerigger in this historic photograph from the J. Porter Shaw Library. Courtesy of Danford & Campbell, San Francisco Maritime National Historic Park.

Part of the San Francisco Maritime National Historical Park, the Maritime Museum Library makes available to the public its extensive collection of books, log books, manuscripts, ship plans, oral histories, periodicals, and nautical ephemera. Maritime artifacts and fine arts from the Collections Management Department (telephone 415-556-3797) may be examined by appointment only.

THE MISSION

San Francisco's Mission district boasts at least fifty organizations offering performances or visual arts exhibitions on a regular basis.

ATA (ARTISTS' TELEVISION ACCESS) GALLERY
992 Valencia Street, San Francisco
Phone: (415) 824-3890
Hours: Call for evening hours & reviewing reservations

A non-profit media arts center, ATA exhibits videos and films, as well as interdisciplinary works that emphasize the media arts. Evening screenings include such avant-garde works as "The Ad and the Id: Sex, Death and Subliminals," an exploration of the psychological aspects of advertising, and "Zygosis," an update of the Dada satirists' photomontage techniques into the expanded electronic vocabulary of scratch video.

"If this is Death, I like it," by Ester Hernandez, serigraph. Photo by Rubén Guzman, courtesy of Galería de la Raza.

Daytime passers-by can get a taste of what goes on inside from the weird and wonderful window installations, which incorporate video and mixed media. Lovers of the bizarre may find these gutsy creations worth a trip.

GALERÍA DE LA RAZA/STUDIO 24
2857 - 24th Street, San Francisco
Phone: (415) 826-8009
Hours: Tues.-Sat. noon-6:00 p.m.
Admission: Free

Located in the heart of the Mission district, Galería de la Raza (Gallery of the People) has been presenting innovative, relevant, Chicano/Latino art exhibitions since 1970. Six to eight shows a year cover the artistic spectrum, including paintings, performance art, videos, traditional weaving, altars, sugar skulls, and graffiti that reflect current, regional social and political issues. You never know if the current exhibition will be showcasing an emerging talent or an established artist working in new forms or traditional Chicano styles, but you can be sure it will be great. The annual Day of the Dead exhibition and celebration (October 15–November 2) have become one of San Francisco's most colorful cultural events. Galería offers scheduled docent tours for children and teens—call for current schedules.

Library: There is a research and resource library of photographs and slides of works by Chicano artists.

Gift Shop: Adjacent to the Galería, Studio 24 is a collector's dream store. It is packed to the rafters with fanciful folk art by Mexican, South and Central American, and local artists. Beautifully decorated windows and outstanding displays highlight a diverse selection of whimsical toys,

"El Caliente" by Armando Cid, serigraph. Photo by Rubén Guzman, courtesy of Galería de la Raza.

textiles, jewelry, posters, cards, clothing, pottery, paper cutouts, and Spanish and English literature. You'll find something for everybody and every pocketbook, including limited edition fine prints in the $800 range.

LA RAZA GRAPHIC CENTER
2868 Mission Street, San Francisco
Phone: (415) 648–0930
Hours: Mon.-Fri. 9:00 a.m.-5:00 p.m.
Admission: Free

Currently housed in the Mission Cultural Center, La Raza Graphic Center shows art by emerging artists from the community who haven't been able to show downtown. The gallery tries to incorporate the whole Chicano movement and Latino culture in six to eight exhibitions a year, including a children's exhibition and a traditional approach to Day of the Dead. Free art classes for children 8–14 are taught in Spanish.

MISSION CULTURAL CENTER
2868 Mission Street, San Francisco
Phone: (415) 821–1155
Hours: Tues.-Fri. noon-6:00 p.m.; Sat. 10:00 a.m.-4:00 p.m.
Admission: Donations accepted

Unless you are on the look-out you can walk right by the unpretentious, three-story building that houses the Mission Cultural Center. If you did, you would miss out on one of the richest cultural experiences in town.

Established in 1977 for the purpose of promoting Latino visual arts, the Galería Museo presents a year-round program of local, national, and international exhibitions. Ten shows a year include an annual exhibition of children's art, a women's show and, in November, the popular Day of the Dead show which displays thirty rooms for the dead built by local artists. On view during our visit were the moving and beautiful "Listen to Our Elders/Listen To Our Children," a multimedia exhibition inspired by elders in the Mission district and produced by middle school students of the Mission community, and "A Life in Color," a 50-year retrospective of the works of Peter Rodriquez, one of the country's most prominent Chicano artists.

The Cultural Center also offers a full schedule of classes in visual arts, music, and dance, as well as theater performances for children and adults.

Misión Gráfica, an internationally-known graphic arts facility directed by Chilean master silkscreen artist René Castro, offers classes in silkscreen and design and has produced some remarkable posters for the community. Misión Gráfica Textiles offers classes as well as full-service production of silkscreened t-shirts at competitive rates.

Gift Shop: Alas, there is no gift shop. But people in the know ask to see the gorgeous, colorful, posters produced by Misión Gráfica, which can be purchased at bargain prices. T-shirts from Misión Gráfica Textiles are also available.

MISSION SAN FRANCISCO DE ASIS (MISSION DOLORES)
3321 - 16th Street, San Francisco
Phone: (415) 621-8203
**Hours: Daily 9:00 a.m.-4:30 p.m. Tours Tues., Thurs., Fri. 9:30 or
    10:30 a.m.**
Admission: $1.00

Founded in 1776, Mission San Francisco de Asis (known as Mission Dolores) boasts the oldest building in the city—it survived both the 1906 and Loma Prieta earthquakes. California's first book, Palou's *Life of Junipero Serra*, was written here. Manuscripts and Mission artifacts are displayed in the small museum.

LEVI STRAUSS MUSEUM
250 Valencia Street, San Francisco
Phone: (415) 565-9159
Hours: Wed. by appointment
Admission: Free

In 1853, a 24-year-old German immigrant dry goods merchant named Levi Strauss used heavyweight brown canvas intended for gold miners' tents to make a sturdy pair of pants instead. "Those pants of Levi's" soon grew popular with the miners. When the brown canvas was gone Levi switched to a sturdy, blue fabric from Nîmes, France called "serge de Nîmes," since conveniently shortened to "denim." Levi's denims soon became the work uniform of farmers, mechanics, cowboys, and miners. By the 1940s a mystique had developed around the pants worn by movie cowboys like Gary Cooper and Roy Rogers in popular western films. Their popularity was assured when movie idols James Dean and Marlon Brando wore jeans in "Rebel Without a Cause" and "The Wild Ones," and "levis" became the uniform of the baby boom generation.

The complete history of these most recognizable of American icons is revealed in the Levi Strauss Museum. A visit to the yellow, wood-framed factory, a 1906 commercial Victorian structure, begins with a 10-minute video of classic Levi's television commercials and a look at the exhibits in the small museum, which feature historic photos, early jeans, and some fancifully-decorated entries in the 1973 Levi's Denim Art Contest. The tour includes a walk through the oldest and smallest operating Levi's facility in the world, where you will see workers engaged in producing the ever-popular pants.

NOB HILL

SAN FRANCISCO CABLE CAR MUSEUM
1201 Mason Street (at Washington), San Francisco
Phone: (415) 474-1887
Hours: Daily 10:00 a.m.-6:00 p.m.
Admission: Free

This photo from an air exhibition at San Francisco's Crissy Field ca. 1914 is from the North Beach Museum's collection of photographs documenting the city's lively history. Courtesy of North Beach Museum.

The Scotsman Andrew Hallidie introduced the cable car to San Francisco 120 years ago, after witnessing a horrible accident when a horse-drawn streetcar broke down trying to negotiate one of the city's steep hills. Hallidie's invention, perhaps influenced by his family's ownership of a cable manufacturing company, consisted of streetcars latched to underground steel cables powered by giant flywheels driven by steam engines enclosed in large barns.

All the cable cars in San Francisco are run by the enormous cables, engines, and wheels right out of this very Cable Car Barn. You can watch the whole operation at work either from the underground excavation that gives you a view of the Sheave Room or from observation decks looking down on the great spinning wheels. Antique cable cars and artifacts—many over 100 years old—are also on view, along with a 17-minute film on the cable car system. (This place is noisy! Bring ear plugs.)

NORTH BEACH

NORTH BEACH MUSEUM
EurekaBank Mezzanine
1435 Stockton Street, San Francisco
Phone: (415) 391-6210
Hours: Mon.-Thurs. 9:00 a.m.-4:00 p.m., Fri. 9:00 a.m.-6:00 p.m.
Admission: Free

Changing displays of photographs and artifacts celebrate the history of North Beach, one of San Francisco's most colorful neighborhoods, as well as Fisherman's Wharf and Chinatown.

TATTOO MUSEUM
841 Columbus Avenue (near Lombard), San Francisco
Phone: (415) 775-4991
Hours: Mon.-Sat. noon-10:00 p.m.; Sun. noon-8:00 p.m.
Admission: Free

The world's largest collection of tattoo artifacts and memorabilia awaits the curious at Lyle Tuttle's studio-cum-tattoo museum. You can browse through hundreds of tattoo designs, examine photographs of ritual tattoos from around the world, and see archaic tattooing instruments in the single, wooden-floored room reminiscent of a Victorian parlor. You may even see a tattoo artist at work behind the brass rail that separates the museum from the studio. "Yes it hurts," reads a sign on the wall. This is a bloody spectacle, definitely not for children or the faint of heart.

PACIFIC HEIGHTS

HAAS-LILIENTHAL HOUSE
2007 Franklin, San Francisco
Phone: (415) 441-3004
Hours: Wed. noon-3:15 p.m.; Sun. 11:00 a.m.-4:15 p.m.
Admission: Adults $5.00, seniors & children $3.00

Built in 1886 by Peter Schmidt for William Haas, a Bavarian-born wholesale grocer, the Haas-Lilienthal House survived the disastrous 1906 earthquake and the fire that raged only a block away. The Queen Anne Victorian, occupied by the Haas and Lilienthal families until 1972, is the only fully-furnished Victorian open to the public in San Francisco.

OCTAGON HOUSE
2645 Gough Street, San Francisco
Phone: (415) 441-7512
Hours: Noon-3:00 p.m., second Sunday of the month and second and fourth Thursdays except January; closed holidays.
Admission: Donations accepted

In 1848, successful publisher and phrenologist Orson Fowler published *A Home For All,* a popular book promoting the eight-sided house as the ideal design, ensuring the most efficient use of space, maximum natural light, and a healthful environment. A rash of octagonal houses across the nation resulted, including eight in San Francisco. One of only two surviving in San Francisco, the 1861 William McElroy house now serves as the headquarters of The National Society of Colonial Dames of America in California, and the only museum west of Texas devoted to artifacts of the colonial and federal periods. There is a colonial-style garden, and collections representing the decorative arts contain examples of American furniture, portraits, housewares, Chinese export porcelain, and documents pertaining to colonial and early American history.

A stunning example of the Queen Anne style, the Haas-Lilienthal House is the only fully-furnished Victorian in San Francisco that is open to the public. Courtesy of the Haas-Lilienthal House.

SAN FRANCISCO FIRE DEPARTMENT
   PIONEER MEMORIAL MUSEUM
655 Presidio Avenue (at Pine), San Francisco
Phone: (415) 861-8000, ext. 3065
Hours: Thurs.-Sun. 1:00-4:00 p.m. Hours may vary—call ahead.
Admission: Free

Over half the visitors to the San Francisco Fire Department museum
are firefighters from all over the world, but you don't have to be one
to enjoy this charming, one-room museum located next to a working
firehouse. You can hear the dispatchers as you tour, and you may even
see the fire engines go out on a call.

With every corner filled with equipment, artifacts, astounding historic
photographs, and memorabilia, you can get a fairly thorough lesson in
San Francisco firefighting history from 1849 to the present. Antique
equipment—hand-pulled pumps that required forty men to move them,
horse-drawn vehicles capable of pumping 1,000 gallons of water per
minute, and the first motorized fire engine—shares space with model
engines, leather buckets, life guns with spear harpoons, a gallery with
photographs and the helmets of San Francisco fire chiefs, and a collection
of uniform patches from all over the world.

Even though most of the exhibits are not for touching, kids will still
find this a thrilling place. Where else can you open a real fire box and
find out what happens when you pull the alarm? Signage is minimal but
our volunteer guide, docent Al Sassus, was so knowledgeable and full of
humorous anecdotes that we could hardly tear ourselves away.

Gift Shop: Although there is no gift shop per se, stashed behind the
admission desk is a supply of unique firehouse memorabilia including
postcards, badges for $5.00, t-shirts for $12.50, posters for $1.00, an
admirable photograph of the 1906 fire, and a self-guided tour book to
all the vintage San Francisco firehouses.

THE PRESIDIO

Established in 1776 by the Spanish, the Presidio of San Francisco is one of
the oldest military establishments in the country. Currently the headquarters of the U.S. Sixth Army, the Presidio will be turned over to the
National Park Service in October 1994. By the turn of the century,
this choice piece of San Francisco real estate is expected to be a thriving
cultural center, home to dozens of new and relocated San Francisco arts
and cultural organizations.

FORT POINT NATIONAL HISTORIC SITE
Marine Drive, San Francisco
Phone: (415) 556-1874
Hours: Wed.-Sun. 10:00 a.m.-5:00 p.m.
Admission: Free

Early plans for the Golden Gate Bridge called for the demolition of Fort Point, built before the Civil War. Fortunately, the bridge engineers figured out a way to preserve the fort by spanning it with a graceful, steel arch. Nestled under the bridge's southern foot, Fort Point offers a breathtaking view of the Golden Gate and the bay. Built between 1853 and 1861 as a part of the National System of Coastal Defense, the masonry building boasts walls of brick and granite 7-1/2 feet thick to shield ninety arched gun rooms known as casemates. Before the building was finished, the technology to breach it had already been found. Nevertheless, the fort was armed with cannons and mortars and occupied by Union soldiers during the Civil War. During World War II, soldiers manned rapid-fire guns while a submarine net was stretched across the entrance to the bay as a coastal defense.

Fort Point, built before the Civil War and used for coastal defense during World War II. Photo by Nate Levine.

Even on the warmest day, a visit to Fort Point can be a bone-chilling experience, so be sure to bring an extra coat. You can watch a 17-minute movie covering the history of Fort Point from 1776 to World War II, and rent an audio tour to experience a typical day in the life of a Civil War soldier stationed there. Rangers also give tours of the fort and cannon-loading demonstrations, using volunteers from the audience as cannoneers.

PRESIDIO MUSEUM
Golden Gate National Recreation Area
Lincoln Boulevard & Funston Avenue, Building 2
Phone: (415) 556-0856
Hours: Wed.-Sun. 10:00 a.m.-4:00 p.m.
Admission: Free

In the look-but-don't-touch tradition, the Presidio Museum relates two hundred years of Presidio history through glass-cased exhibits of Army uniforms, weapons, artifacts, models, and dioramas. Although the technique may be old-fashioned, the results are not in the least dry or dull. A case of Civil War medical instruments, for example, can be eloquently expressive. Of special interest are a pair of refugee cottages built by the Army to house survivors of the 1906 earthquake.

RICHMOND AND SUNSET DISTRICTS

CALIFORNIA PALACE OF THE LEGION OF HONOR
Lincoln Park
34th Avenue and Clement, San Francisco
Phone: (415) 750-3614
Hours: Presently closed for seismic improvements and renovation

In 1990, the jointly-governed M.H. de Young Memorial Museum and the California Palace of the Legion of Honor underwent a major reorganization that had collections jumping across town from one museum to another. The Legion of Honor, which formerly contained only French art, will show European paintings, sculpture, and decorative art works from the 14th to the 20th centuries, many previously housed at the de Young. The collection features outstanding paintings by El Greco, Georges deLaTour, Rubens, Rembrandt, Boucher, Fragonard, and Seurat, and the extensive Achenbach collection of 100,000 prints and 3,000 drawings, as well as the Legion's collection of Rodin sculptures, one of the finest in the world.

Plans call for the renovated building, which sits high on a hill overlooking the Golden Gate, to reopen in 1994. The $25 million remodeling project will add six new galleries. The museum's signature sculpture, Rodin's "The Thinker," will remain in the magnificent, columned courtyard to greet visitors.

Scheduled for 1995, "Ballets Suédois: A Modernist Vision in France" will document the Parisian avant-garde dance company through drawings, costume and set designs, posters, and photographs. In 1996 "Color Woodcuts," an exhibition of 85 woodcuts, linocuts, and wood engravings from the museum's collection, will chronicle the rise in popularity of the color block print during the period from 1895 to 1950.

"Wizard Predictions" one of a multitude of machines "whose only purpose," according to the owner of the Musée Mécanique, "is to amaze and delight." Photo by Nate Levine.

MUSÉE MÉCANIQUE
Cliff House
1090 Point Lobos Avenue, San Francisco
Phone: (415) 386-1170
Hours: Mon.-Fri. 11:00 a.m.-7:00 p.m.; weekends & holidays 10:00 a.m.-8:00 p.m.
Admission: Free

Edward G. Zelinsky began collecting antique automata in 1933 when he won a one-cent penny arcade machine in a raffle. The collection now includes more than 300 coin-operated machines, ranging from Barbary Coast orchestrians to today's video games. A permanent rotating exhibit of these fascinating machines, some dating back as far as the 1880s, can be seen in the marvelous Musée Mécanique. Pop in a coin to see early San Francisco's idea of a bawdy peep show or test your strength against a masked, mechanical wrestler. Old-time San Franciscans are likely to feel twinges of nostalgia when they see Laughing Sal, who delighted (or terrified) visitors to Playland at the Beach from 1940 to 1972.

THE SAN FRANCISCO ZOOLOGICAL GARDENS
1 Zoo Road, San Francisco
Phone: (415) 753-7172
Hours: Daily 10:00 a.m.-5:00 p.m.
Admission: Adults $6.50, seniors & youths $3.00,
   children 6-11 $1.00

The San Francisco Zoo, the major zoological park in northern California, welcomes one million visitors a year. Developed in the 1930s with WPA funds, the Zoo is situated on 125 acres of land, including a five-acre Children's Zoo, and houses over 350 different animal species. In operation at its present site since 1929, the zoo has undertaken a major remodeling project, "Zoo 2000," with plans to usher in the 21st century as a premier zoological institution and a world leader in wildlife conservation and education.

The formidable-looking Gorilla gorilla, *largest of the great apes, is actually a vegetarian and attacks only when provoked.* Photo taken at the San Francisco Zoo by Nate Levine.

TREGANZA MUSEUM OF ANTHROPOLOGY
San Francisco State University
1600 Holloway, San Francisco
Phone: (415) 338-1642
Hours: Weekdays by appointment, 9:00 a.m.-5:00 p.m.
Admission: Free

The Treganza Museum of Anthropology, located in a small room on the third floor of San Francisco State's science building, mounts two exhibits a year. Tentatively planned for 1994, contingent on funding, is a student Master of Arts show, "Run Away Kids," combining anthropology, archaeology, and art. Clothing and artifacts belonging to runaways will be on display as well as photographs taken by the children themselves. An exhibit on mural painting and one on Marin County archaeology are planned for 1995.

SOUTH OF MARKET

ANSEL ADAMS CENTER FOR PHOTOGRAPHY
250 - 4th Street, San Francisco
Phone: (415) 495-7000
Hours: Tues.-Sun. 11:00 a.m.-5:00 p.m., first Thursday of the
month 11:00 a.m.-8:00 p.m.
Admission: Adults $4.00, students $3.00, seniors and youth $2.00,
children under 12 and members free.

In 1967, Ansel Adams and other prominent photographers founded
The Friends of Photography in Carmel, California, to further photography as an art and as a reflection of human experience. Twenty-two years
later, the Friends established headquarters in a former health department
clinic in the Yerba Buena Gardens cultural district and opened the Ansel
Adams Center for Photography, a museum dedicated to creative photography. One of the center's five galleries is devoted exclusively to exploring the photographic legacy of Ansel Adams. In the four remaining
galleries, The Friends mount fifteen exhibits a year showcasing the best
of contemporary and historical photography in all styles and genres, from
fragile 19th century works to avant-garde photographic installations
utilizing mixed media and video.

Gift Shop: The Friends of Photography bookstore carries the best selection of photography books in the Bay Area and calendars, notecards,
posters, jewelry, and photo-related gift items.

CARTOON ART MUSEUM
665 Third Street, 4th Floor (Brannan and Townsend), San Francisco
Phone: (415) 456-3922
Hours: Mon.-Fri. 9:00 a.m.-5:00 p.m.
Admission: Adults $3.00, students & seniors $2.00, children $1.00

Comics were born in America almost a hundred years ago, but only
recently have they gained recognition as a legitimate art form. The
Cartoon Art Museum was founded in 1984 to increase public awareness
of this uniquely accessible art form by exhibiting original cartoon art and
animation cels. Four major exhibits a year present American and international cartoon art from the museum's collection or on loan. The Bay
Area Spotlight Gallery exhibits the work of local cartoon artists. Comics
are treated as serious art here, but children will probably like it anyway.
Class tours, available for $1.00 per student, include an excellent curricu-
lum packet.

Library: A small library is available.

Gift Shop: The tiny store sells comic books, reference works, limited
edition posters, t-shirts, and original cartoon art.

CENTER FOR THE ARTS AT YERBA BUENA GARDENS
701 Mission Street (at Third), San Francisco
Phone: (415) 978-2787 or 978-ARTS
Hours: Tues.–Sun. 11:00 a.m.–6:00 p.m.
Admission: Adults $3.00, seniors and youth under 16 $1.00.
   Free first Thursday of the month, 6:00–9:00 p.m.

In 1993, after thirty years of planning, controversy, designing and revising, San Francisco celebrated the opening of Center for the Arts, located in the Yerba Buena Gardens. One of the major urban architectural projects in the world, Yerba Buena Gardens includes a five-acre esplanade park, a state-of-the-art performing arts theater, galleries, the San Francisco Museum of Modern Art (scheduled to relocate there in 1995), and the Moscone Convention Center. By the turn of the century, the Jewish Museum and Mexican Museum will have relocated to the site.

The heart of this vital arts complex is Center for the Arts, an architectural masterpiece housing three exhibition galleries, a 96-seat theater for video and film, the Forum (a huge space for innovative performances), a cafe, and a gift shop. Designed by Japan's leading architect, Fumihiko Maki, the futuristic building, wrapped in a skin of corrugated sheet aluminum and glass, resembles a cross between a high-tech factory and a ship. The airy, light-filled building, a blend of Western and Eastern aesthetics, is graced with distinctive Japanese details like a black bamboo garden and a wall of white glass blocks resembling shoji screens.

The center, which does not have a permanent collection, provides a showcase for a wide range of artistic expression from fine art to popular culture, from traditional to cutting edge, in an ongoing series of temporary exhibitions. Painting, sculpture, photography, computer arts, film, video, and installations created by local artists reflect the Bay Area's cultural diversity.

Rental: Call (415) 978-2700 for information.

Restaurant: You've spent the whole morning shopping in downtown San Francisco, you're starving and don't want to spend a lot for a really nice

Panorama of Yerba Buena Gardens (l-r): Center for the Arts Galleries and Forum, San Francisco Museum of Modern Art (in background), Center for the Arts Theater. Photo by Ken Friedman, courtesy of Center for the Arts at Yerba Buena Gardens.

lunch, so take a break and walk the two or three blocks to the OPTS Cafe at Center for the Arts. The cafe adjoins the upstairs gallery and gives you a complete view of the Yerba Buena Gardens. Now you can enjoy a really nice lunch for a little. The guest chef program, with a new chef each month from a top local restaurant, keeps the menu perpetually new and exciting. When we were there, for instance, choices included a Tunisian salad with lentils, tomatoes, dried apricots, and sweet peppers; a Mongolian sesame pocket sandwich stuffed with teriyaki tofu; and a roast turkey breast sandwich with garlic jack cheese on a polenta roll. Prices for salads, sandwiches, and specials are in the $5.00 to $6.50 range. Dessert choices included giant chocolate chip cookies for $1.25 and an elegant gingerbread trifle layered with pears and served with caramel sauce for $4.25. Beer, wine, and assorted other beverages are available.

THE OLD MINT

88 Fifth Street (at Mission), San Francisco
Phone: (415) 744-6830
Hours: Mon.-Fri. 10:00 a.m.-4:00 p.m.
Admission: Free

San Francisco seems to have more than its fair share of money museums, but for my money the best of the lot is the Old Mint. Touted as one of the finest examples of federal classic revival architecture in the West, this monumental national historic landmark has 22 rooms on two levels open to the public. In operation from 1874 until 1937, the Old Mint has witnessed a lot of California history, some knowledge of which you can acquire painlessly if you take the free, guided tour, offered hourly.

With a little something for everyone, hands-off exhibits include a furnished Victorian bedchamber, an authentic recreation of a miner's cabin, an 1860s stagecoach, and more. You can step right into the steel vault where, until 1936, one-third of all the nation's gold was stored. For showmanship you can't do better than the original coining room: with an appropriately dramatic flourish, the guide dons white gloves and ear plugs to strike a medal on the original press. For a dollar, you can buy a brass blank and strike your own medal.

The Old Mint, a national historic landmark where money was made from 1874 until 1937. Courtesy of the Old Mint.

Library: Numismatic library, by reservation only.

Gift Shop: The gift shop, known officially as the Numismatic Sales Room, carries coins, jewelry made from coins, medals and postcards. Because it is located on federal property this "factory outlet" charges no sales tax—thus, the more you buy the more you save.

SAN FRANCISCO CAMERAWORK
70 Twelfth Street, 3rd floor, San Francisco
Phone: (415) 621-1001
Hours: Tues.-Sat. noon-5:00 p.m.
Admission: Free

As one might expect from an organization on the cutting edge, Camerawork is not a slick, downtown gallery. Don't be put off by the frankly funky building nor by the fact that you must climb three flights of dubious-looking stairs or hitch a ride in the even more suspect freight elevator to get there. You will be rewarded, and brought up-to-date on the latest happenings in the world of photography. Camerawork presents six to eight exhibitions a year of national and international photographers, the majority emerging artists not shown in commercial galleries. Lectures and performances are offered in conjunction with the exhibitions.

Library: The non-circulating collection of 2,500 books, magazines, monographs, and other reference materials is open to the public.

Gift Shop: You can find a good selection of monographs, theoretical and critical works, paperbacks, a few upper-end coffee-table books, and a small collection of fine prints offered at the bargain price of $250 (expect to pay $500 elsewhere) in the bookstore.

Rental: For a change of pace, you can rent the space. Rates are negotiable.

SOUTH OF MARKET CULTURAL CENTER
934 Brannan Street (at 8th), San Francisco
Phone: (415) 552-2131
Hours: Mon.-Sat. 9:00 a.m.-5:00 p.m.
Admission: Free

A stroll through the colorful community garden will bring you to the SOMAR Gallery, a cavernous exhibition space with 40-foot ceilings. Part of the South of Market Cultural Center, a 30,000-square-foot warehouse arts facility which includes the SOMAR Theater, the gallery presents about 15 exhibitions a year featuring the work of professional, multi-cultural artists and gifted students, and exchange shows with other cultures and countries.

The center also offers community arts classes, graphic services, a mural resource center for artists whose main focus is on public art, and technical services in the form of light, sound, and stage equipment for performing and visual arts.

Rental: A dance studio, theater, and classrooms are available for rent at low cost to community artists and art groups.

TREASURE ISLAND

TREASURE ISLAND MUSEUM
Treasure Island Naval Base, Building 1
Phone: (415) 395-5067
Hours: Mon.-Sun. 10:00 a.m.-3:30 p.m.
Admission: Free

Tour buses routinely stop just outside the gates of Treasure Island Naval
Base, half-way across the Bay Bridge, to take in one of the most spectacular views of San Francisco in the Bay Area, but most tours do not include
a visit to the Treasure Island Museum. This is an unfortunate oversight.
Located in the sole remnant of the enormous Art Deco complex built to
house the 1939 Golden Gate International Exposition, this charming
museum celebrates two former residents of Treasure Island, the 1939
Exposition itself and Pan American's China Clipper Flying Boats, as well
as the history of the Navy, Marines, and Coast Guard in the Pacific.

Our volunteer docent, a former Navy man, made history come alive
for us. We were especially enchanted by the Exposition—historic
photographs of Pontiac's lucite car and clips from the first color home
movies made us wish we could have been there. If you have time, take in
the free films about the Blue Angels or one about the Exposition narrated
by Art Linkletter. To help youngsters enjoy the museum, pick up the
children's activities sheet, which includes fun suggestions like, "Fog Bell.
Ring it hard: *one* ring per person, please."

Library: Limited, non-circulating, research library.

Gift Shop: World's Fair and Navy memorabilia.

East Bay

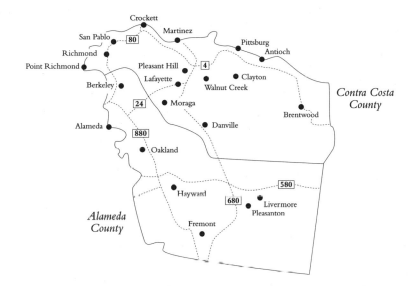

Crockett
San Pablo
Martinez
Pittsburg
Antioch
Richmond
80
Point Richmond
Pleasant Hill
4
Berkeley
Lafayette
Clayton
Walnut Creek

Contra Costa County

24
Moraga
Alameda
Brentwood
880
Danville
Oakland

580
Hayward
Alameda County
Livermore
680
Pleasanton
Fremont

East Bay

ALAMEDA COUNTY

ALAMEDA

ALAMEDA HISTORICAL MUSEUM
2324 Alameda Avenue, Alameda
Phone: (510) 521-1233
Hours: Wed.-Fri., Sun. 1:30-4:00 p.m.; Sat. 11:00 a.m.-4:00 p.m.
Admission: Free

Located on the ground floor of the old Masonic Temple in Alameda's historic Park Street district, the cavernous Alameda Historical Museum is filled with a collection of artifacts ranging from relics of the native Chochenyo Ohlone to a 1931 bicycle built for six. Toys, dolls, vintage garments, two period kitchens, and a 1904 Mission-style living room represent the museum's historic component. Works by local artists are featured in a changing exhibition gallery. A very up-to-date, hands-on exhibit combining history and modern technology in the form of a computer program invites you to paint electronic images of Alameda's Victorian houses.

Library: The Homeowners Library contains how-to books on home repair.

CRAB COVE VISITOR CENTER★
1252 McKay Avenue, Alameda
Phone: (510) 521-6887
Hours: Wed.-Sun. 10:00 a.m.-4:30 p.m.
Admission: Free

Located at Robert Crown Memorial State Beach, a two-and-a-half-mile stretch of sandy beach, mudflat and rocky shore better known as Alameda Beach, Crab Cove Visitor Center houses a large saltwater aquarium filled with seldom-seen San Francisco Bay fish and provides information on sharks, whales, shells, and other marine subjects. Photographs tell the story of the Neptune Beach area, known in its heyday as the Coney Island of the West.

BERKELEY

BERKELEY ART CENTER
1275 Walnut Street, Berkeley
Phone: (510) 644-6893
Hours: Thurs.-Sun. noon-5:00 p.m.
Admission: Free

Hidden behind Live Oak Park is the Berkeley Art Center, Berkeley's only non-profit community art gallery, known for its innovative presentation of multi-cultural, contemporary art, including an annual national juried exhibition, a performance series, and a membership exhibition. Informal artists' salons on the third Thursday evening of the month often inspire discussions of important arts issues.

Rental: A $2500 membership donation will earn you free use for one day or evening of this charming creekside gallery surrounded by stately oak trees.

"That Which Has Been Appropriated," a screenprint by Enrique Chagoya (1992, 24" x 32"), an example of the innovative, multi-cultural works presented by the Berkeley Art Center. Courtesy of BACA and Alliance Graphics.

BERKELEY HISTORICAL SOCIETY MUSEUM
1931 Center Street, Berkeley
Phone: (510) 524-9880
Hours: Thurs., Fri., Sat. noon-5:00 p.m. (4:00 p.m. winter & fall)
Admission: Free

After years without a home, the Berkeley Historical Society recently opened this small museum in the Veterans Memorial Building. Exhibits of historical photographs and artifacts document Berkeley history. "Berkeley in the Sixties" will be on view in 1994.

Library: The Historical Society Archives contain over 8,000 photos, oral histories, Berkeley newspapers from 1905 to 1944, Berkeley High School yearbooks, and Berkeley history books for research.

HALL OF HEALTH
2230 Shattuck Avenue (lower level), Berkeley
Phone: (510) 549-1564
Hours: Tues.-Sat. 10:00 a.m.-4:00 p.m.
Admission: Free

"You own a magical machine. Learn to treasure it. It's yours for life. It's your body." The Hall of Health, a hands-on health museum cosponsored by Oakland's Children's Hospital and Berkeley's Alta Bates Medical Center, has been delivering this message to everyone from pre-schoolers to senior citizens since 1974. Displays, games, electronic quizzes, multi-media exhibits, and even a few antique medical artifacts are all used to help visitors understand the wonders of their bodies and teach them how to live healthier lives. You can ride an exercycle to find out how many calories you can burn in a minute (discouragingly few), take your blood pressure, study the nervous system under a microscope, or deliver a baby (doll) by Cesarean or natural methods. The two newest hands-on exhibits, "Ashtown" and "Drugs and Your Nervous System," make irrefutable arguments for clean living.

JUDAH L. MAGNES MUSEUM
2911 Russell Street, Berkeley
Phone: (510) 549-6950
Hours: Sun.-Thurs. 10:00 a.m.-4:00 p.m.
Admission: Free

Named for the first American rabbi ordained west of the Mississippi, the third largest Jewish museum in the United States started out in 1962 in two rooms above an Oakland movie theater. Four years later it moved to its present home, a 1908 mansion on a half-acre setting in a quiet Berkeley neighborhood. In the sculpture-filled gardens designed by John McLaren, landscape architect for Golden Gate Park, California symbolically meets the Middle East in the form of redwood and palm trees.

Inside the beautifully renovated mansion, the museum offers exhibits and two excellent libraries. The permanent collection of over 10,000 objects reflects the amazing variety of Jewish life over the centuries. Family ritual objects, communal treasures created for synagogues, and objects rescued from vanishing Jewish communities comprise the large ceremonial art collection. The museum recently acquired an interesting piece of Judaica, the 1936 Art Deco-style Torah Ark from the *Queen Mary*, which housed the first synagogue built as a permanent part of an ocean liner.

The fine art collection includes paintings, sculpture, prints, and drawings, focusing primarily on genre painting and works by European, Israeli, and American Jewish artists of the 19th and 20th centuries. Two changing exhibition galleries feature group and individual shows by contemporary Jewish artists such as Ben Shahn, Chana Orloff, and Raphael Soyer, and thematic exhibits documenting Jewish history and culture around the world. Themes range from the experience of Kurdish Jews in Israel to art as a form of spiritual resistance in the Nazi camps.

Library: The Blumenthal Library, open by appointment for research, houses 12,000 rare books and manuscripts, Jewish recorded and sheet music, a Holocaust collection, and thousands of photographs. The Western Jewish History Center, a research repository focusing on Jews of the American West, contains over 300 archival collections

Part of the permanent collection of ceremonial art at the Judah L. Magnes Museum, this Moroccan Hanukah lamp was cut from a heavy brass sheet. The engraved "Hamsa" (hand), designed in arabesques, and the Star of David were appliqued. 20.5" x 11". Courtesy of Judah L. Magnes Museum.

including correspondence, synagogue records, diaries, photos, scrapbooks, genealogical charts, oral histories, newspapers and periodicals, and fine press books.

Gift Shop: The museum shop carries ceremonial objects and crafts by Bay Area and Israeli artists, books, and catalogs.

PACIFIC SCHOOL OF RELIGION MUSEUM
17798 Scenic Avenue (at Le Conte), Berkeley
Phone: (510) 848-0529
Hours: Mon.-Thurs. 9:00 a.m.-noon & 1:00-4:30 p.m.,
    Fri. 9:00 a.m.-noon & 1:00-4:00 p.m.
Admission: Free

An oasis of calm amidst the hustle and bustle of the University of California's Northside, the Pacific School of Religion campus shelters a relatively unknown museum. Housed in the elegant English Gothic reading room of the former library, the museum—actually three museums in one—includes the Bade Institute of Biblical Archaeology, the Howell Bible Collection, and the Ellen Carey Sherwood Changing Exhibit Area, plus an outstanding library of books, journals, and slides related to Syro-Palestinian archaeology, historical geography, and biblical texts.

The Bade's permanent exhibit displays artifacts from one of the earliest scientific excavations in Palestine. Lamps, pitchers, bowls, jars, jewelry, and cosmetic items (eye make-up was the most popular) from Mizpah, an ancient city inhabited by Old Testament Israelites, give you an idea of what life was like in a provincial town three thousand years ago. Excavation tools depict the methods of Near Eastern archaeology in the 1920s.

The Howell Collection of approximately 300 volumes, the largest collection of rare Bibles west of the Mississippi, boasts four incunabula (books printed before 1501) and two 1611 editions of the King James Version among its treasures.

Changing exhibitions in the Ellen Carey Sherwood Gallery feature contemporary works of art inspired by the Bible or spirituality, or that reflect ethical, moral, or socio-political issues of importance to the Pacific School of Religion community.

For kids: Free tours for children fourth grade and above include a slide show and a museum treasure hunt. Traveling Suitcase exhibits containing authentic artifacts from the Mizpah excavation can be shipped anywhere in the country for a minimal fee ($24 to $45). Easily assembled displays can turn the classroom into a mini-museum and allow students to examine actual antiquities from 3,000 years ago.

Library: The library contains one of the largest theological collections in the United States. It is at 2400 Ridge Road, telephone (510) 649-2400, and is open to the public Monday through Friday, 8:30 a.m. to 5:00 p.m.

Gift Shop: GTU Bookstore has the largest selection of theological books in the Bay Area. Located at 2465 LeConte Avenue, telephone (510) 649-2470, it is open Monday through Friday, 9:30 a.m.–5:00 p.m. and Saturday, 11:00 a.m.–5:00 p.m.

TATTOO ARCHIVES RESEARCH CENTER
2804 San Pablo Avenue, Berkeley
Phone: (510) 548-5895
Hours: Mon.–Sat. noon–8:00 p.m.
Admission: Free

The Tattoo Archives are currently located at the very site where tattoo artist C.W. Eldridge plies his trade. Because some clients prefer privacy while Eldridge enhances their appearance, it's best to call before your visit. Dedicated to the documentation and preservation of tattoo history around the world, the Archives present four exhibits a year of tattoo-related art and artifacts. One exhibit featured the work of underground artist Greg Irons, who produced rock posters for the Avalon, Fillmore, and Winterland ballrooms and underground comix before moving into tattoo art. Another exhibit displayed bookplates from the 1700s and a third, historical tattoo postcards.

Because most tattoo collections are not accessible to the public, Eldridge and friends and colleagues from the tattoo community have established the Paul Rogers Tattoo Research Center, which hopes to open a tattoo museum by the turn of the century.

TILDEN REGIONAL PARK BOTANIC GARDEN
Wildcat Canyon Road & South Park Drive, Berkeley
Phone: (510) 841-8732
Hours: Daily 8:30 a.m.–5:00 p.m.
Admission: Free

Imagine 160,000 square miles of California set in a ten-acre garden and you have the Botanic Garden in Tilden Park. Divided into ten sections from the desert to the Pacific rain forest, the garden provides an opportunity to see the rich diversity of California's native plants in a few hours. Specimens brought from all corners of the state include 300 rare and endangered plants and large collections of manzanita, ceanothus, conifers, ornamental grasses, bulbs, and perennials. On Saturdays from November through January, slide shows and lectures are presented in the visitor center, where there is usually also an exhibit on native plants. Free tours are offered Saturdays and guided group tours can be arranged by appointment.

For visitors with children in tow, Tilden offers several special attractions: the antique Hershell Spillman merry-go-round, the Tilden Nature Area, which includes the Little Farm, and the park's famous miniature steam train.

UNIVERSITY OF CALIFORNIA AT BERKELEY

BOTANICAL GARDENS
Centennial Drive, Berkeley
Phone: (510) 642-3343
Hours: Every day except Christmas 9:00 a.m.–4:45 p.m.
Admission: Free

Some 95,000 people come every year to stroll in the 34-acre University of California Botanical Gardens, admiring and studying the plants, or just sitting and enjoying the peaceful surroundings. With more than 12,000 different types of plants, this is the largest as well as the oldest university botanical garden in the United States.

Flower lovers will find colorful plants from all over the planet arranged by region of origin, with the largest area devoted to California native plants. For people with a practical bent, the Western Herb Garden has plants for cooking, fragrances, and medicinal use, and the Chinese Medicinal Herb Garden displays herbs according to their functions in traditional Chinese medicine. Indoor gardeners will enjoy the green-houses. The humid Desert and Rain Forest House, displaying a collection of cacti, succulents, and orchids, is as good as a trip to the tropics. The Fern and Insectivorous Plant House, complete with fly traps, is a sure kid-pleaser.

There is something to see at every time of year. The rhododendrons are absolutely spectacular in March. The Garden of Old Roses, with its old-fashioned roses laid out like an eighteenth century garden, is at its peak in May. And food gardeners will want to schedule a visit to the Garden of Economic Plants in the late summer, when many of the crop plants from around the globe are ready for harvest. The serene Japanese Pool is a balm to the spirit any time. Free, docent-led tours are available for the public year-round, on Saturdays and Sundays at 1:30 p.m.

Gift Shop: A garden lover's delight, with books (over 700 titles), plants, gardening things, and a kids' section. The Annual Spring Plant Sale on Mother's Day weekend draws crowds of gardeners looking for good buys on bromeliads, bulbs, cacti, succulents, orchids, roses, trees, rhododen-drons, and many more.

ESSIG MUSEUM OF ENTOMOLOGY
311 Wellman Hall, UC Berkeley
Phone: (510) 642-4779
Hours: By appointment only
Admission: Free

Ranked number one among university entomology museums in the country, the Essig Museum contains more than four million specimens, and is the richest source of geographical and biological data on the insects of California. Essentially a research museum without facilities for dealing with casual visitors, the museum welcomes school children on pre-arranged tours. If you're on campus, however, you might want to check out the cases outside the museum exhibiting a gorgeous array of butter-flies, bees, wasps, and other creatures originally assembled for the 1939 World's Fair.

PHOEBE APPERSON HEARST MUSEUM OF ANTHROPOLOGY
103 Kroeber Hall, UC Berkeley
Phone: (510) 642-3681
Hours: Tues.-Fri. 10:00 a.m.-4:30 p.m. (Thurs. until 9:00 p.m.);
   Sat. & Sun. noon-4:30 p.m.
Admission: Adults $2.00, seniors $1.00, children 50¢

Formerly known as the Lowie Museum, the University of California at Berkeley's anthropology museum was recently renamed to honor the woman who provided the money to get the whole thing started. It seems that Phoebe Apperson Hearst fell in love with anthropology, and since the University of California had neither a museum nor an anthropology department, she agreed to fund the department and subsidize expeditions to Egypt in 1895, and later Peru. From its inception in 1901, the museum has amassed the largest anthropological collection west of Chicago, with more than four million items. Important holdings include objects from Peru, Ancient Egypt, and the Mediterranean, and artifacts from native peoples of North and South America, the Arctic, Oceania, Africa, Malaysia, the Philippines, Europe, and Asia. The museum's collections from the native people of California are unparalleled anywhere in the world.

Since 1960, the museum has been housed in Kroeber Hall, with the smallest exhibition space (5,000 feet) allotted to any museum of compa-rable inventory in the country. Such cramped quarters allow only a fraction of the collection to be shown—if the entire collection were to be exhibited, each artifact would be on view once every 300 years. Museum exhibits feature selections drawn from the collections or current developments in archaeology and ethnology, presenting programs designed to appeal to the public. Popular favorites include the museum's ancient Egyptian collection, and the exhibition (recently updated) dedicated to Ishi, the last surviving member of California's Yahi tribe.

Gift Shop: The Museum Store features a wonderful selection of books, ethnic arts, jewelry, and cards.

Inuit bear, contemporary, from the Eastern Arctic. Collection of Nelson and Catherine Graburn. Courtesy of Phoebe Hearst Museum of Anthropology, University of California at Berkeley.

LAWRENCE HALL OF SCIENCE
Centennial Drive, Berkeley
Phone: (510) 642-5132
Hours: Daily 10:00 a.m.–5:00 p.m.
Admission: Adults $5.00, students & seniors $4.00,
  children 3-6 $2.00

Children climb on a model of a DNA molecule, 5.5' tall and 60' long, at UC Berkeley's Lawrence Hall of Science. The scientifically accurate climbing and learning structure is over eight million times larger than the real thing. A real person with DNA this large would be standing with one foot in Berkeley and the other in Honolulu! Courtesy of Lawrence Hall of Science.

An imposing, gray concrete structure resembling the fictional SMERSH headquarters stands out among the eucalyptus trees and brown-shingled houses of the Berkeley hills. It's the Lawrence Hall of Science, the world-famous public science museum of the University of California. The octagonal shape represents the eight branches of physical science, the olive trees in the plaza are a symbol of peace, and the colorful sculpture with kids crawling all over it is a model of a DNA strand.

Opened in May 1968, the Lawrence Hall of Science pioneered the hands-on approach to learning about science and math. Kids of all ages love this amusement park for the mind. Permanent exhibits include "Within the Human Brain," using puzzles and games to show how the brain works; "Math Rules," which allows children to explore math tactually; a mini-planetarium; and a two-story periodic table. The Hall also hosts large visiting exhibits that change about twice a year.

Come on weekends for planetarium shows, visits with gentle animals, interactive experiments with electricity, the Science Discovery Theatre, and more. LHS publishes a catalog filled with workshops, assemblies, festivals, and teacher education classes for preschool through high school.

Gift Shop: As good as any commercial enterprise, the large, exciting Discovery Store stocks an extensive inventory of scientific and educational toys, instruments, books, games, puzzles, music, and gifts.

Rental: Kids ages 4 through adult can celebrate their birthdays with a Party Workshop, $65 for 15 kids. The list of workshops includes Bubbleology, Mystery Party, Slime and Slippery Stuff, and more. To reserve a party call (510) 642-5134. For evening rentals—receptions, parties, buffet dinners—call (510) 642-2275.

Restaurant: The magnificent view of the entire Bay Area would compensate for any imperfections in the food at the Galaxy Cafeteria, but the made-to-order food is actually quite good and reasonably priced. Sandwiches made with fresh ingredients, including hot dogs and hamburgers, range from about $2 to $3, and salads are available as side orders. Give the children change and they can buy a complete lunch at the vending machines, which offer sandwiches ($1.00), chips, candy, fruit, drinks, and other lunchables. After bussing your dishes and putting trash into the recycling bins, you can play the computer game "What's in Your Lunch" to find out the nutritional value of the food you just consumed.

MUSEUM OF PALEONTOLOGY
Valley Life Science Building, UC Berkeley
Phone: (510) 642-1821
Hours: Mon.-Fri. 8:00 a.m.-5:00 p.m.
Admission: Free

UC's renowned paleontology research museum houses the largest fossil collection (an estimated five million) west of the Mississippi. It is not a public museum, but significant fossils, including a complete Tyrannosaurus rex, marine mammals, and spectacular invertebrates, will be exhibited in the three-floor atrium of the Valley Life Science Building when it opens in 1994.

UNIVERSITY ART MUSEUM AND PACIFIC FILM ARCHIVE
2625 Durant Avenue, Berkeley
Phone: (510) 642-1207
Hours: Wed.-Sun. 11:00 a.m.-5:00 p.m.,Thurs. 11:00 a.m.-9:00 p.m.
Admission: Adults $6.00, youth 12-17 $4.00, children under 12 free.
Free Thurs. & Sat. 11:00 a.m.-noon.

UC Berkeley students once voted to convert this 95,000-square-foot structure of tiered, concrete blocks into a skating rink, but the plan never went into effect and the building continues to function as the University Art Museum and Pacific Film Archive, one of the largest university museums in the world. The architect selected to design the UAM/PFA from 366 entries in an international competition was the San Francisco firm of Mario J. Ciampi, who claimed that never having designed a museum before gave them the advantage of a fresh approach. The exposed-concrete-walled galleries connected by terraced ramps and cantilevered landings jutting out into space are a breathtaking sight, ideal for the exhibition of contemporary work.

Since it is a teaching museum obliged to collect and exhibit a broad range of art, the UAM/PFA collections cover most periods and media of visual art. Two highlights of the collection are an 800-piece Asian collection, considered one of the finest in the U.S., and the world's largest collection of works by abstract expressionist Hans Hofmann. In fact, it was Hofmann's bequest in 1963 of 48 paintings and $250,000 that initiated plans for the museum's present building. The most extensive holdings are in 20th century Western art, including paintings by Francis Bacon, Joan Miro, Fernand Leger, Robert Delaunay, Georges Rouault, and Rene Magritte, and sculptures by Alexander Calder, David Smith, Peter Voulkos, Joseph Cornell, and Donald Judd.

The museum's impressive collection of pop, assemblage, kinetic, California figurative, funk, and realist art shows to advantage in the space and seems to delight children who are often bored by art museums.

The UAM/PFA has originated its share of major traveling exhibitions, including a Juan Gris retrospective and a Richard Avedon photography retrospective, and hosted blockbuster shows of works by Claes Oldenburg, Diane Arbus, Johnathan Borofsky, and Robert Mapplethorpe. An outdoor sculpture garden provides a dramatic space for large-scale sculpture and a quiet spot for contemplation.

"Rotante del Foro Centrale" (1971), bronze, by Arnaldo Pomodoro (Italian, b. 1926), is a striking example of works in the sculpture garden at the University Art Museum and Pacific Film Archive. Courtesy of the UAM/PFA.

MATRIX, one of the boldest and most creative temporary exhibition programs in the Bay Area, presents ten to twelve small-scale shows a year, giving Bay Area audiences exposure to the breadth of contemporary art on the cutting edge, from video to conceptual and performance art.

The Pacific Film Archive, housing a collection of over 6,000 films, screens 750 films a year in a daily program encompassing works from every film-producing nation in the world: documentaries, animation, shorts, rare silent movies, avant-garde works, and children's films.

Library: The Pacific Film Archive library and film collection is available for research.

Gift Shop: The store sells art and film books, cards, posters, and jewelry.

Rental: For an unusual setting for receptions, meetings, performances, and lectures, you can rent the UAM/PFA galleries, lobby, terraces, sculpture garden, or 234-seat theater. Call (510) 642-5188.

Restaurant: A good reason to visit the University Art Museum and Pacific Film Archive is Cafe Grace. Treat yourself to a tasty, moderately priced, healthy lunch, and see some contemporary art while you're at it. On a fine day you can enjoy your meal or just coffee outdoors, or you may decide to sit inside and look out on the sculpture garden. The menu offers lots of choices: soups, salads with or without meat, sandwiches, and special dishes like sausage with potato salad and garlic bread, or chicken quesadilla with jack cheese and sun-dried tomatoes. I loved the cream of butternut squash soup with chickpeas and ate every bit of the pizza du jour (primavera) with garden salad ($5.95). A salad and half-sandwich combination on foccacia bread went for $4.50. Kids will go for the children's pizza, only $2.50.

UNIVERSITY OF CALIFORNIA AND JEPSON HERBARIA
Valley Life Science Building, UC Berkeley
Phone: (510) 642-2465
Hours: 8:00 a.m.-noon, 1:00-5:00 p.m.
Admission: Free

When you first come face-to-face with the aisles of metal filing cabinets that comprise the UC and Jepson Herbaria, they look pretty dull. Anything but dull, the herbarium, the largest this side of New York, contains a beautiful collection of 1.7 million plant specimens, many long-disappeared from the face of the earth. Large folio pages covered with delicate, spidery, 19th century script contain fragile dried plants collected as early as 1830. Prized among the many specimens is the 1875 John Muir collection. In 1993 the herbarium staff created a big stir in the botanical world with the release of the updated *Jepson Manual: Higher Plants of California*, a definitive work ten years in the making which revised classification of California flora.

Unfortunately the herbarium and its library of botanical literature, specimens, archival materials, photographs, and field books are available only to serious researchers and artists. Appointments can be made for first-time orientations and college-level class tours may be arranged. Temporarily housed off campus, the herbarium will move to the Valley Life Science Building in 1994, and plans to make parts of the collection more accessible to the general public at that time.

FREMONT

ARDENWOOD HISTORIC FARM
34600 Ardenwood Blvd., Fremont
Phone: (510) 796-0663
Hours: Thurs.-Sun. 10:00 a.m.-4:00 p.m., April through
  mid-November
Admission: Adults $6.00, seniors $4.00, children $3.50

One of the nicest things you can do for and with your family is spend a day at Ardenwood Historic Farm. Leave your car in the parking lot and travel via horse-drawn vehicles back to the late 19th century.

Over a hundred years ago, a disappointed gold seeker from the Midwest gave up mining and found even greater riches farming the fertile land of the East Bay. By the 1880s, George Patterson had acquired 6,000 acres and established himself as one of the wealthiest men in the area. Today's Ardenwood is a 205-acre recreation of Patterson's self-contained family farm, complete with orchards, fields, farm animals, and antique farming equipment. Volunteers and staff dressed in Victorian garb grow the same kinds of crops Patterson tended. The blacksmith fires up the forge to shoe the draft horses that pull wagons, plows, and railcars. Visitors are invited to help out with the chores—hand-planting potatoes, threshing wheat, harvesting pumpkins, pressing cider. On one visit our young guests scraped corn from the cob, ground it into meal, and shaped corn cakes, which a naturalist cooked for us on an outdoor grill—a bit grimy, but good.

Tours of the Patterson Home—an elaborate, three-story, Queen Anne addition to the Pattersons' original modest farmhouse—are available (children over six only). Luxuries like the clay tennis court, the first concrete swimming pool in the county (now covered) and a Victorian garden were added as the family grew more and more prosperous.

I have paid several visits to Ardenwood and never fail to fall under its spell. My companions, all city dwellers ranging in age from small children to grandparents, have been enchanted by the bucolic atmosphere of a gentleman-farmer's farm—perhaps a tiny bit sanitized to meet contemporary tastes.

Gift Shop: The General Store, located in the Arden Train Station, carries a large inventory of old-fashioned toys, penny candy, cookbooks, spices, and Victorian-style gifts.

Rental: Ardenwood offers idyllic sites for weddings, family picnics, and other special events. Call (510) 462-1400 for reservations.

Restaurant: You must eat at least something at the Farmyard Cafe, because the food is first-rate. Almost all items are made from scratch and the menu is geared to children's likes. Delicious cornbread is available for 95¢ to accompany chili or beef stew (about $3.00). We tried the hot apple pie à la mode (about $2.50) and licked the plate. Have a root beer float to wash everything down.

Volunteers and staff in Victorian garb use antique farming equipment and traditional techniques at Ardenwood Historic Farm, where visitors can also see a blacksmith in action, tour the elaborate, three-story Patterson home, and help plant potatoes, thresh wheat, or pick pumpkins. Courtesy of East Bay Regional Parks.

COYOTE HILLS VISITOR CENTER
8000 Patterson Ranch Road, Fremont
Phone: (510) 795-9385
Hours: Tues.-Sun. 9:30 a.m.-5:00 p.m.
Admission: $3.00/car parking fee on weekends and holidays

A visit to Ardenwood transports you to the 19th century, but a visit to nearby Coyote Hills Regional Park can take you back two thousand years. Before the area was a part of the Spanish land grant known as Potrero de los Cerritos, or of George Patterson's 6,000-acre ranch, it was home to the native Ohlone people. Park naturalists have reconstructed parts of a traditional Ohlone village—a dome-shaped tule house, an underground sweat house, and other structures—near one of the park's four shell mounds. You must make reservations to visit this area with a guide.

You can learn more about the Ohlone way of life in the modern, two-room visitor center. Exhibits demonstrate techniques for starting fires, making acorn soup, and weaving baskets. "Please open" discovery drawers let you see Ohlone tools, games, trade items, and foods. An Ohlone-style tule boat is on display.

Weekend classes are offered on many aspects of native technology and the natural history of the park. You can also pick up a brochure for a self-guided tour of the one-mile Muskrat Trail, which traverses the marsh, at the visitor center.

MISSION SAN JOSE CHAPEL AND MUSEUM*
43300 Mission Boulevard, Fremont
Phone: (510) 657-1797
Hours: Daily 10:00 a.m.-5:00 p.m.
Admission: Donation $1.00/adult, 50¢/child

Established in 1797, the original Mission San Jose adobe buildings had all but disappeared by 1831. The present church was reconstructed in 1985 and lavishly decorated as in the 1830s. The small museum features exhibits on the Ohlone and the restoration of the mission.

NILES DEPOT HISTORICAL FOUNDATION MUSEUM
36997 Mission Boulevard, Fremont
Phone: (510) 797-4449
Hours: First and third Sunday of the month, 10:00 a.m.-4:00 p.m.
Admission: Donations accepted

The 1904 Niles Station was moved to its present location in 1982 to house the Niles Depot Museum. The Model Engineers have set up a model HO gauge railroad in the basement, "to watch and enjoy but not touch." The upstairs houses an extensive collection of railroadiana—uniforms, tools, maps, photos, tickets, schedules, et cetera. A caboose is being restored outside.

SAN FRANCISCO BAY NATIONAL WILDLIFE REFUGE VISITOR CENTER
1 Marshlands Road, Fremont
Phone: (510) 792-0222
Hours: Tues.-Sun. 10:00 a.m.-5:00 p.m.
Admission: Free

Operated by the U.S. Fish and Wildlife Service, the visitor center offers displays on the creatures that inhabit the nation's largest urban wildlife refuge—over 20,000 acres set aside to protect the flora and fauna of the San Francisco Bay and migratory birds that use the Pacific Flyway. Follow the 1-1/3 mile nature trail through wildflower-laced uplands, over Newark Slough, and down to the salt marsh, or sign up for one of the many weekend activities.

Gift Shop: Books, field guides, jewelry, and t-shirts are for sale.

JAMES SHINN HOUSE
1251 Peralta Avenue, Fremont
Phone: (510) 656-9076
Hours: First Wednesday of the month, third Sunday,
    noon–4:00 p.m.
Admission: Adults $3.00, seniors & children $1.50

Built in 1856 by James Shinn, a pioneer in the nursery business, the redwood, Victorian-style farmhouse is authentically furnished to represent a prosperous ranching operation. The barracks in back that once housed Chinese serf-labor recall another aspect of the house's history. The 4-1/2 acres of park surrounding the house are home to many of the exotic trees Shinn imported from around the world, and a charming, walled Japanese garden.

Rental: For outdoor weddings and events contact the Department of Recreation, (510) 791-4340.

Exhibits at the Hayward Area Historical Society Museum range from antique fire engines to contemporary themes. Courtesy of Hayward Area Historical Society Museum.

HAYWARD

HAYWARD AREA HISTORICAL SOCIETY MUSEUM
22701 Main Street, Hayward
Phone: (510) 581-0223
Hours: Mon.-Fri 11:00 a.m.–4:00 p.m.; Sat. noon–4:00 p.m.
Admission: $1.00

Located in a 1926 masonry building that once served as Hayward's post office, the Hayward Area Historical Society Museum is folksy, friendly, and cheerful. A restored 1923 fire engine, an 1830 hand-pumper, and a portion of the original Castro Valley post office are featured in the permanent exhibits devoted to early police, fire, and post office memorabilia and local history.

Changing exhibits put a fresh face on things and keep the local residents coming back. Each year an ethnic group in the area is invited to design an exhibit about their culture. The museum staff stages two additional temporary exhibitions each year, one with a local history theme (in 1993, "Play Ball" celebrated local baseball teams), and the annual holiday display of vintage toys. Shows are invariably bright, attractive, and jolly, with something to interest visitors of all ages.

Library: The non-circulating library, open Mondays, offers extensive research materials relating to local history, including 13,000 photographs from the mid-1800s to the present.

Gift Shop: The Corner Store has the feel of a small-town antique shop with a little of everything—miniatures, toys, dolls, and reproductions of museum-related collectibles.

HAYWARD SHORELINE INTERPRETIVE CENTER
4901 Breakwater Avenue, Hayward
Phone: (510) 881-6751
Hours: Daily 10:00 a.m.-5:00 p.m., closed Mondays seasonally
Admission: Free

Bring your bike or your hiking boots to explore the eight miles of trails at the Hayward Shoreline, a large, flat marshland teeming with wild creatures. From microscopic organisms to the endangered salt marsh harvest mouse, you can find more life in one square inch of mudflats and salt marsh than in a mile of hills—you just need to know where and how to look and what to look for. A good place to learn is the Hayward Shoreline Interpretive Center, a contemporary wooden structure perched on stilts overlooking the salt marsh and the bay. Changing exhibits are featured, and the Habitat Room, a laboratory/classroom, is filled with hands-on displays, murals, and three aquaria. "Lunch with the Lepidoptera" and "Snakes Alive" are just two of the programs presented by enthusiastic, friendly, and knowledgeable staff naturalists.

Library: The non-circulating library focuses on shoreline natural history and wetland restoration. *Tidal Tales,* the center's newsletter, provides information on events and news of the shoreline for $2.00/year.

Gift Shop: Tides & Currents gift shop sells books, t-shirts, and an interesting assortment of nature-related items from bug boxes to shark tooth fossils.

Rental: The facility is available for groups related to the San Francisco Bay or wetlands. Call for information.

JAPANESE GARDEN
22373 North Third Street, Hayward
Phone: (510) 881-6715
Hours: Daily 10:00 a.m.–4:00 p.m.
Admission: Free

Designed by landscape architect Kimio Kimura, Hayward's lovely
Japanese Garden occupies three and a half acres that housed the Hayward
High School agricultural studies program from 1913 to 1962. Where
Future Farmers and 4-H members once studied botany and horticulture,
visitors now stroll through the garden, enjoying its simplicity, balance,
and harmony. The first of its kind to combine the principles of traditional
Japanese garden art with native California trees, plants, and stones,
the garden is actually made up of many smaller gardens and areas.
The Hayward Area Recreation and Park District provides information
on plants and their sources, encouraging visitors to duplicate portions of
the garden on their own property.

McCONAGHY ESTATE
18701 Hesperian Blvd., Hayward
Phone: (510) 276-3010
Hours: Thurs.–Sun. 1:00–4:00 p.m.
Admission: Adults $2.00, seniors $1.50, children 50¢. Special
   Christmas rates: adults $3.00, seniors $2.00, children 50¢.

This 12-room farmhouse, with carriage house and tank house, has been
restored to its Victorian splendor and authentically furnished in the style
of 1886, the year it was built. The house is decorated to the nines for
Christmas and other holidays, and features a show and sale of antiques
and collectibles the third weekend in July. The laundry equipment on the
porch seems to be especially fascinating to youngsters. Neighboring
Kennedy Park, complete with playground, petting zoo, merry-go-round,
and train, offers an ideal site for a picnic.

Gift Shop: An upstairs bedroom has been turned into the McConaghy
House Boutique, featuring Victorian and country-style gifts, books,
and toys.

CLARENCE E. SMITH MUSEUM OF ANTHROPOLOGY
Meiklejohn Hall, California State University, Hayward
Phone: (510) 881-3104 (office); (510) 881-7414 (museum gallery)
Hours: Mon.–Fri 10:00 a.m.–4:00 p.m.
Admission: Free

Working with a small, two-room space on a tiny budget, this teaching
museum manages to produce a first-rate, well-designed exhibit every
year. The museum has an impressive collection of Hopi kachinas.

Collectors of Native American art look forward to the annual Holiday Trading Post, a two-week sale of contemporary Navaho and Hopi artifacts held late in November.

SULPHUR CREEK NATURE CENTER
1801 D Street, Hayward
Phone: (510) 881-6747
Hours: Tues.-Sun. 10:00 a.m.-5:00 p.m.
Admission: Free

Sulphur Creek Nature Center is an idyllic spot nestled in a heavily wooded canyon in a ten-acre park. It's hard to believe the lovely wildlife garden, picnic grounds, nature trail, and trickling creek smelling ever so faintly of sulphur exist only one mile from the heart of downtown Hayward. The center's wildlife rehabilitation program receives over 1,300 injured and orphaned creatures a year to care for with the goal of releasing them back to the wild. Over 100 non-releasable wild animals— coyotes, opposums, foxes, owls, hawks, songbirds, lizards, snakes, frogs, toads, salamanders, scorpions, spiders—reside in naturalistic habitats at the center. Changing exhibits in the rustic Discovery Center teach youngsters about local wildlife. The center also offers nature study classes, Wildlife Camp, and other special programs.

Library: The Animal Library offers a choice of guinea pigs, rats, mice, and hamsters, each with cage and food, for a one-week rental.

Rental: Kids can celebrate their birthdays at the center—$65 for up to 20 guests.

SUN GALLERY
1015 E Street, Hayward
Phone: (510) 581-4050
Hours: Wed.-Sat. 11:00 a.m.-5:00 p.m.
Admission: Free

The only non-profit, community-based art gallery in Hayward, Sun Gallery mounts seven exhibits a year showcasing northern California artists.

For Kids: School field trips include a tour and discussion about the exhibit and a hands-on art project in the art studio, at $65 per class.

Library: A small non-circulating collection of art books.

Gift Shop: A wonderful place to find unusual, unique gifts, each one a work of art, created by northern California artists and craftspeople. Gorgeous earrings, handmade cards, and fine ceramics are available at bargain prices.

Other than humans, coyotes (Canis latrans) are the most common large mammals in California's scrub communities— so prevalent that some seeds (holly-leafed cherry and possibly others) need the acid chemicals of a coyote's digestive tract to germinate. Like many other injured or orphaned animals, these two coyotes were brought to Hayward's Sulphur Creek Nature Center to be cared for. Courtesy of the Hayward Area Recreation and Park District.

LIVERMORE

COMPUTER MUSEUM
Livermore
Phone: (510) 423-6095
Hours: By appointment
Admission: Free

To some of us, 1953 seems like yesterday, but in the world of computers it's ancient history. 1953 marks the date the Livermore Computer Center bought its first computer, a UNIVAC I. This huge machine with buttons, switches, bells, and lights filled an entire room but had less power than today's little personal computers. The UNIVAC I and the generations of computers that replaced it are on view at the Lawrence Livermore Laboratory's Computer Museum. A hand-operated adding machine from 1887, a programmer's office of forty years ago, and an assortment of obsolete computers trace the evolution of the machine that changed the world. Computer buffs will love this place. Visitors do not need to be computer experts to enjoy the exhibits, but it helps.

As this book goes to press, the Computer Museum is in storage. You can call the Associate Director of Computation's Office at the Lawrence Livermore Laboratory (see number above) to find out if the museum has relocated yet.

LAWRENCE LIVERMORE NATIONAL LABORATORY
VISITOR CENTER
7000 East Avenue, Livermore
Phone: (510) 422-9797
Hours: Mon., Tues., Thurs., Fri. 10:00 a.m.-4:30 p.m.;
    Wed. 12:30-4:30 p.m.
Admission: Free

Whether for better or worse, there's no denying that since Lawrence Livermore National Laboratory was established in 1952 it has shaped the 20th century. Managed by the University of California for the U.S. Department of Energy with a billion dollar annual budget, LLNL is one of the leading applied science research laboratories in the world. Ten thousand employees work on the lab's major programs—defense, lasers, fusion, biotechnology, energy, and the environment. Visitors 18 and over can take a tour of NOVA, the largest, most powerful laser in the world, and NERSC, the National Energy Research Super Computer Center.

Visitors of all ages are welcomed at the visitor center, a handsome, modern structure with inviting landscaping outside and scientific displays and videos within. Exhibits give an overview of the lab's current research programs and their applications. You can watch a video on space exploration and see a sample of Aerogel. Developed for NASA to use in the space shuttle, Aerogel feels as light as air—it is 99% air—but is the strongest material in existence for its density, with the greatest insulating powers. Exhibits make highly technical information comprehensible and interesting to ordinary folk.

LIVERMORE HERITAGE GUILD HISTORY CENTER
2155 - 3rd Street, Livermore
Phone: (510) 449-9927
Hours: Wed.-Sun. 10:30 a.m.-3:00 p.m. summer; 11:30 a.m.-
   4:00 p.m., Sept.-May.
Admission: Free

The Livermore History Center shares space with the Art Association Gallery in a 1911 Carnegie Library building. Changing exhibits depict various aspects of life in Livermore, from the days of the Spanish land grants to the present. A 1993 exhibit tracing the history of a local drugstore and soda works featured a popular exhibit of suburban archaeology—artifacts from a refuse pit from the 1906 earthquake.

Library: Open by request, the library has photographs and a complete index of Livermore newspapers from 1874 to the 1940s.

Gift Shop: Cards and pamphlets on Livermore are available here.

OAKLAND

CAMRON-STANFORD HOUSE
1418 Lakeside Drive, Oakland
Phone: (510) 836-1976
Hours: Wed. 11:00 a.m.-4:00 p.m.; Sun. 1:00-5:00 p.m.
Admission: Adults $2.00, seniors $1.00, children under 12 free

The Italianate Camron–Stanford house is the only remaining Victorian mansion on Oakland's Lake Merritt. Designed and built in 1876 by Samuel Merritt, the house was first owned by Will and Alice Camron, and sold in 1882 to Josiah Stanford, brother of Leland Stanford, one of the Big Four railroad barons. The story goes that C.P. Huntington, another of the Big Four, planned to fill in Lake Merritt and build a railroad station on the site but was disuaded by Stanford. For more than sixty years, the mansion housed the Oakland Public Museum until 1967, when it was replaced by the new museum building a few blocks away. Saved from the wrecking ball, the refurbished house opened to the public in 1978 with five rooms furnished in the style of 1880 by the Camron–Stanford House Preservation Association.

Rental: The Camron–Stanford House is a popular site for weddings, receptions, and other special events.

CHABOT OBSERVATORY & SCIENCE CENTER
4917 Mountain Boulevard, Oakland
Phone: (510) 530-3480
Hours: Fri. & Sat. 7:30 p.m.
Admission: Observatory free. Planetarium shows: adults $4.00,
　　children $2.50.

The public is invited to gaze at the evening sky through two large telescopes in the Chabot Observatory and watch changing star shows in the 100-seat planetarium.

Astronomy, according to the staff of the Science Center, is the beautiful wrapping paper that makes you want to open the present of science. The Science Center focuses on astronomy and offers programs in the natural and physical sciences. A new, 65,000-square-foot Chabot Observatory and Science Center facility is scheduled to open to the public in 1996 on a 10-acre site near the present location.

DUNSMUIR HOUSE & GARDENS
2960 Peralta Oaks Court, Oakland
Phone: (510) 562-3232
Hours: Tues.-Fri. 10:00 a.m.-4:00 p.m., Feb.–Oct.; Thurs. & Sun. ,
　　11:00 a.m.-3:00 p.m., April–Sept. Also open for special events.
Mansion tours Wednesday, noon & 1:00 p.m.; Thurs. & Sun. noon,
　　1:00 & 2:00 p.m., April–September.
Admission, estate grounds: adults $2.00, seniors & juniors $1.00.
　　Mansion tour: adults $4.00, seniors & juniors $3.00.

Bagpipes are part of the Christmas festivities at Dunsmuir House. Courtesy of Dunsmuir House & Gardens.

A wedding gift from lumber and mining heir Alexander Dunsmuir to his wife Josephine, with whom he had cohabited for twenty years before the marriage ceremony, the elegant, 37-room mansion became Josephine's alone when Dunsmuir died in New York on their honeymoon. The colonial revival home designed by San Francisco architect J. Eugene Freeman, with its Tiffany-style dome, mahogany paneling, inlaid parquet floors, lavish furnishings, and stark servants' quarters, testifies to the social stratification of the era.

In 1906, I.W. Hellman, Jr. of Wells Fargo fame purchased the 40-acre estate and engaged Golden Gate Park's landscape architect, John McLaren, to design lavish gardens. At one time the estate contained a golf course, croquet court, tennis court, swimming pool with Roman bathhouse, glass conservatory, aviary, formal garden maze, Japanese garden, carriage house, stables, and farm buildings, some of which remain, in various states of disrepair.

The mansion is decorated for a turn-of-the-century Christmas celebration every year, offering carriage rides, a Victorian tea, and special entertainment.

THE EBONY MUSEUM OF ARTS
30 Jack London Village, Suite 209, Oakland
Phone: (510) 763-0745
Hours: Tues.-Sat. 11:00 a.m.-6:00 p.m.; Sun. noon-6:00 p.m.
Admission: Free

Founded in 1980 "because I saw a need for a place that would showcase the art and history of the black people," the unique Ebony Museum of Art is a testimony to the personal vision and determination of its founder, Aissatoui Ayola Vernita.

When I first encountered the museum, it was housed in Vernita's large Victorian home in East Oakland. A disastrous fire prompted the move to the present interim site in the Jack London Village shopping center. Antiquities from all parts of Africa—masks, drums, baskets, textiles, ancestor figures, lavish cowry shell headdresses, bronze busts— fill one room. Another room displays the museum's collection of African-American memorabilia and stereotypical images in art and advertising. A collage of greeting cards and postcards, and cases displaying products like Uncle Ben's Rice, Negro Head Oysters, Darkee Toothpaste, Black Joe's juice grapes, and Aunt Jemima cookie jars offer an ironic, thought-provoking commentary on American culture.

"Soul Foods out of the Closet into Art," an arresting collection of jewelry created by Vernita from chicken, beef, and ham bones, dried greens, chitterlings, rice, beans, and peanuts, is on permanent display in another room. According to Vernita, the collection represents an effort to "tackle the soul food issue. To name it: slave food; to state the issue of it: survival food; and thus to purge the shameful memories it still evokes in the descendants of the slaves."

Library: Back issues of *Ebony* magazine from 1956 to the present are available for research.

Gift Shop: African imports, including baskets, clothing, dolls, and jewelry, are available.

THE JUNIOR CENTER OF ART AND SCIENCE
558 Bellevue Avenue, Oakland
Phone: (510) 839-5777
Hours: Tues.-Fri. 10:00 a.m.-6:00 p.m.; Sat. 10:00 a.m.-2:00 p.m.
**   Summer hours: Mon.-Thurs. 9:00 a.m.-5:00 p.m.**
Admission: Free

Housed in an airy, light-filled building on the banks of Lake Merritt, the Junior Center of Art and Science welcomes drop-in guests, who can participate in free activities or visit the Children's Gallery. The gallery features three first-rate exhibits every year based on themes from the Oakland Public School social studies and science curricula. Exhibits have featured African-American inventors, California Native Americans, the birds of Lake Merritt, and indigenous architecture from around the world. East Bay artists are featured in three additional exhibits.

For a nominal fee children 5 to 16 can sign up for after-school classes held in the center's four well-equipped studios. The center also holds free art and science workshops in public school classrooms, and offers a school tours program.

Rental: Art parties on Saturdays from 1:00-3:00 p.m. for a maximum of 15 kids include an art project or science activity, decorations, and t-shirt ($120 and up).

THE JACK LONDON MUSEUM OF OAKLAND
30 Jack London Square, Suite 104, Oakland
Phone: (510) 457-8218
Hours: Tues.-Sun. 10:30 a.m.-6:00 p.m.
Admission: Free

Housed in a storefront in the Jack London Village shopping center, the Jack London museum is as sleek and spare as they come. When I visited just after it opened, the museum's premiere exhibition, featuring books by or about Jack London, artifacts, and London ephemera, was displayed in glass cases. In their recently expanded location, "Jack London in the Movies" features films made from London's books and actual footage of Jack London and friends.

While Jack London devotees and aficionados of other Bay Area authors of the period will find the museum of interest, it will not hold the attention of younger children for any great length of time. Fortunately, the spectacular waterfront location offers a fascinating parade of boats, ships, and barges passing through the Oakland Estuary.

Just a hop, skip, and a jump away, in neighboring Jack London Square, sits the sod-covered log cabin Jack London lived in while he was prospecting for gold in the Klondike in 1897. Purchased by the Port of Oakland and plopped down on the pavement without further ado, the cabin loses some of its romance in its new urban environment, but is still the stuff kids' fantasies are made of.

Only big kids (21 and over) are allowed to enter the neighboring Heinold's First and Last Chance Saloon, an 1883 historic landmark constructed from the timbers of an old whaling ship. You can soak up the historic atmosphere in this dimly-lit bar as you sip your drink at the very same table frequented by schoolboy Jack London, President William Howard Taft, Robert Louis Stevenson, Joaquin Miller, Ambrose Bierce, and other notables.

Gift Shop: The shop features new and used books, including first and second editions by Jack London and other Bay Area authors, limited edition prints, tapes, gift cards, and White Fang non-alcoholic zinfandel from Jack London's ranch.

MILLS COLLEGE ART GALLERY
ANTONIO PRIETO GALLERY
5000 MacArthur Boulevard, Oakland
Phone: (510) 430-2004
Hours: Tues.-Sat. 11:00 a.m.-4:00 p.m.; Sun. noon-4:00 p.m.
Admission: Free

The lovely Mills College campus houses two art galleries. The Mills College Art Gallery, located in a recently restored, Spanish-style building, offers ten or more shows a year featuring works from the college's extensive private collection, Master of Fine Arts and faculty exhibitions, and traveling shows from major American museums. The smaller Antonio Prieto Gallery presents works by local artists.

MUSEUM OF CHILDREN'S ART (MOCHA)
560 Second Street, Oakland
Phone: (510) 465-8770
Hours: Mon.-Sat. 10:00 a.m.-5:00 p.m.; Sun. noon-5:00 p.m.
Admission: Free

A visit to MOCHA (located right across the street from Cost Plus) is the perfect activity for children who are more interested in creating art than looking at it; although the large, open gallery space (4,800 square feet) showcases art by children, most kids will be more interested in the bustling studio in the back, where drop-in visitors are welcome to work on projects using the museum's materials. Classes in mixed media, sculpture, paper-making, fiber art, and papier mache are offered at a nominal fee.

Exhibition art is created off site by kids participating in the museum's visiting artist program, which sends artists into schools and community groups and provides a unique opportunity for kids to see their work in a formal setting. MOCHA also hosts visiting shows, recently including a medley of Eastern and Central European children's art, and a commemorative exhibition created by children in response to the fire in the East Bay hills.

Gift Shop: T-shirts and bumper stickers are available.

Rental: Birthday parties, $100 for 15 kids, include an artist and materials.

NORTHERN CALIFORNIA CENTER FOR AFRO-AMERICAN HISTORY AND LIFE

5606 San Pablo Avenue, Oakland

Phone: (510) 658-3158

**Hours: Tues. noon-7:00 p.m.; Wed. & Thurs. 10:00 a.m.-
5:30 p.m.; Fri. noon-5:30 p.m.; Sat. 10:00 a.m.-5:30 p.m.;
closed Sunday & Monday**

Admission: Free

Brought to California as a slave in 1849, Alvin Aaron Coffey earned enough money in the gold fields to buy freedom for himself and his family, but his owner cheated him. Coffey returned to California in 1854 with a different owner, saved $7,000, and finally succeeded in freeing himself, his wife, and his children. He went on to become a home-steader in Red Bluff, and his great-grandson was one of the first African-American policemen in Oakland. Courtesy of Northern California Center for Afro-American History and Life.

The Northern California Center for Afro-American History and Life is currently housed in the Golden Gate branch of the Oakland Public Library, a neoclassic red brick 1918 Carnegie building. Plans are to move the Center to much larger headquarters in another Carnegie building on 14th Street in Oakland. Although primarily a research center for African-American History in California, the reading room also mounts informative and elegantly designed exhibits which tell the rich and diverse story of African-Americans in northern California with historic photographs, documents, and artifacts. A permanent time line painted on the wall gives an overview of the contributions made by the Bay Area's remarkable African-American community. Free, guided tours are offered for classes 4th grade and older, and free education packets are available for 3rd, 4th, and 5th grades.

Library: Students, researchers, and educators may use the archives— a treasure trove of original manuscripts, letters, diaries, personal papers, oral histories, periodicals, and 10,000 photographs—by appointment.

THE OAKLAND MUSEUM OF CALIFORNIA

1000 Oak Street, Oakland

Phone: (510) 238-3401

Hours: Wed.-Sat. 10:00 a.m.-5:00 p.m., Sunday noon-7:00 p.m.

Admission: Suggested donation $4.00 general, $2.00 seniors and students. Free to children 6 and under, free on Sundays from 4:00 to 7:00 p.m.

I fell in love with The Oakland Museum the day it opened, and 25 years and some 600 museums later it is still my all-time favorite.

Collections from three earlier Oakland museums (the Oakland Public Museum, the Oakland Art Museum, and the Snow Museum of Natural History) were culled, combined, and reorganized around a single theme—California—to create the new museum in 1969. A young architect, Kevin Roche, was hired to design the building on a four-square-block site on the south shore of Lake Merritt. The three-tiered complex of sandblasted concrete is constructed so that the roof of each level becomes a garden and terrace for the one above. The maze of galleries, terraces, ponds, hidden patios, green lawns, and lush gardens is considered one of the area's most beautiful structures. The museum has something to offer visitors of all ages, interests, and ethnic backgrounds.

Exhibits focus on California ecology, history, and art. On the first level, the Hall of California Ecology recreates California's eight biotic zones. Case exhibits, lifelike dioramas, and detailed topographical models are arranged to allow visitors to take a simulated walk across California from the coast to the Sierra Nevada. The new Aquatic California Gallery shows what life is like for creatures in aquatic habitats as diverse as rivers, estuaries, snowbanks, hot springs, and the ocean.

In a case just outside the Hall of Ecology, the Chang Wen Ti Sacred Jade Pagoda, carved by more than 150 master carvers over a ten-year period and assembled from 1,046 interlocking pieces of translucent, apple-green jade, continues to delight and astonish visitors.

An arresting and colorful exhibit of California history from the earliest native peoples to the complex, multi-ethnic, technological society of today is on view in the second-level Cowell Hall of California History. More than 5,000 objects—tools, costumes, furniture, machines, games, toys, graphics, and other printed materials—are displayed in thought-provoking settings that attest to the genius of The Oakland Museum's exhibition-design team. The Great Hall, which spans the second and third levels, is the site for the museum's excellent changing exhibitions of art, history, and ecology.

The third-level Gallery of California Art shows art by California artists or dealing with California themes and subjects. Circling the gallery counterclockwise, the viewer can trace the chronological evolution of California art from Thomas Hill to Christopher Brown in an unusual display that integrates painting, crafts, and photography. The outstanding, 20,000-object permanent collection ranges from works by artist-explorers who were recording information about the exotic West, to the landscape artists and photographers whose work influenced Congress to establish the National Park System, to cutting-edge contemporary artists: Richard Diebenkorn, Mel Ramos, Wayne Thiebaud, Robert Arneson, Manuel Neri, William Wiley, Roy De Forest, Sam Francis, Viola Frey, and more—all California's best are represented.

Library: The California Library of Natural Sounds, a unique regional sound library, features live recordings from natural habitats. It is open by appointment. The Archives of California Art, also open by appointment, document the life and work of thousands of contemporary and historic painters, sculptors, printmakers, craftspeople, and photographers identified with art in California. The Index of Contemporary Artists consists of individual files and slides representing more than 5,000 artists currently working in California. The entire collections of fine arts and history photographs, on videodisk, are available to researchers.

The Oakland Museum's Aquatic California gallery features a greatly-magnified model of this jaunty, moss-dwelling microscopic creature— Echiniscus laterculus— a tardigrade (water bear). During dry spells, tardigrades shrivel up and cease all activity, including metabolism, but do not die—at least not irrevocably. They can exist for years or even centuries in suspended animation, to come alive again with the return of water. Electron scanning microscope image by Carrie Adams, courtesy of the Oakland Museum.

Gift Shop: The large museum store carries a good selection of books, toys, handcrafted jewelry, and gifts. The Collector's Gallery offers original paintings, graphics, photographs, prints, fiber arts, ceramics, and glass by California artists and artisans for rental and for sale.

Rental: The restaurant is available for rental.

Restaurant: If you're going to the Oakland Museum, plan to have lunch in the large cafe overlooking the garden and koi pond. The changing menu features California cuisine served cafeteria-style—soups, salads, sandwiches, and specials, all under $7.00. Tasty and colorful ingredients abound: on our visit, there was a salad made with white beans, smoked chicken sausage, spinach, roasted peppers, and croutons, and an open-faced polenta sandwich with goat cheese, sun-dried tomatoes, and basil. The desserts will tempt you, so give in—the cakes and cheesecakes are delicious.

Gibbons, the lesser apes, live in the rainforests of Southeast Asia, keeping in touch with their relatives through loud, musical calls that carry for long distances and echo among the trees. Here, a white-handed gibbon swings through its tropical island home at The Oakland Zoo. Photo by Rick Mannshardt, courtesy of The Oakland Zoo.

OAKLAND MUSEUM SCULPTURE COURT AT CITY CENTER
1111 Broadway, Oakland
Phone: (510) 238-3402 (office hours Monday-Friday)
Hours: Mon.-Fri. 7:00 a.m.-7:00 p.m.; Sat. 8:00 a.m.-4:00 p.m.;
**   Sun. 10:00 a.m.-4:00 p.m.**
Admission: Free

A ten-minute walk from the Oakland Museum, the Sculpture Court in Oakland's City Center is a satellite gallery presenting three shows a year of California sculpture.

THE OAKLAND ZOO
Knowland Park, Oakland
Phone: (510) 632-9525
Hours: Daily 10:00 a.m.-4:00 p.m.
Admission: Adults $4.50, seniors and children 2-14, $3.00. Parking
**   is $3.00 per car, $7.50 per bus. Group rates available.**

Nestled in the rolling hills of Knowland Park, the Oakland Zoo has garnered national acclaim for its spacious, naturalistic habitats. A pride of six African lions enjoys a one-and-a-half acre home on a grassy hillside. African elephants have a 7-foot-deep swimming hole in addition to their yard and barn. The white-handed gibbons and siamangs swing in 30-foot trees on their tropical island homes.

Underway in the Oakland Zoo's 15-year renovation and expansion program are rain forest and savanna areas, as well as an educational exhibit featuring five species that are now extinct in California and thirty others that are in dramatic decline.

Other attractions are the Children's Zoo, a miniature train ride and rides for the kids, a skyride, gift shop, cafe, and picnic areas.

Docents offer free tours, and the education department conducts classes for school groups, a summer Zoo Camp, and Zoomobile outreach programs for local schools and organizations.

THE PARDEE HOME MUSEUM
672 - 11th Street, Oakland
Phone: (510) 444-2187
Hours: Tours by reservation only
Admission: $4.00 per person, $3.00 seniors

Collectors of Victoriana and early 20th century artifacts, and anyone else who just likes things, are going to love this grand, three-story Italianate villa built in 1868. Home of the illustrious Pardee family, the mansion has been left exactly as it was in 1981 at the death of the last family member. Unlike the approach used in many historic houses, no attempt has been made to resore it strictly to its original period; a splendid music box once used for dancing, a gramophone, an electric phonograph, and a color television can be found side by side.

The contents of the house—a staggering number of artifacts representing three generations of avid collectors—set the Pardee mansion apart from other historic house museums. The first Mrs. Pardee carried the Victorian mania for collecting objects from around the world to an extreme. With valuable objects of art sitting next to pieces of tourist trash, the very eclectic collection of her collections—teapots, miniatures, candlesticks, china, brassware—gives a good picture of what was available at the turn of the century. More than sixty thousand items have been catalogued to date, and the curator hasn't seen the end of it yet.

Library: Archives are available for use by appointment.

ROTARY NATURE CENTER
Lakeside Park
552 Bellevue, Oakland
Phone: (510) 238-3739
Hours: Mon. noon-5:00 p.m.; Tues.-Sun. 10:00 a.m.-5:00 p.m.
Admission: Free

A medical doctor who became governor of California (1903–1907), George Pardee became nationally known as the "earthquake governor" as he personally directed relief operations for six weeks after the 1906 disaster. He is shown here with his family, whose collection of collections numbers sixty thousand pieces and counting. Courtesy of the Pardee Home Foundation.

Located on the shores of Oakland's Lake Merritt, the Rotary Nature Center has a low-tech charm sure to appeal to even the most Nintendo-saturated kid or jaded adult.

The main attraction is Lake Merritt itself, 150 acres of water in the heart of Oakland, where the first wildlife refuge in the country was established in 1870. The lake's five small islands are home or hotel to over fifty species of resident and migratory waterfowl. What with migration, breeding, nesting, and rearing of the young, there is something to see all year round. You can feed the birds, sit in the park, play in the playground, go on a staff-led nature walk, or watch films and visual presentations in the Nature Center.

Established in 1953, the Nature Center served as a model for the newer, more elegant interpretive centers around the state. Although the homey exhibits are old and funky, visitors still love to watch the bees in the glass hive going about their business, or lift the little wooden trap doors to smell native plants. Extensive remodeling is in the planning stages, so try to visit soon before they spruce it up.

Library: A selection of nature specimens, books, magazines, and photographs is available in the library.

WESTERN AEROSPACE MUSEUM
8260 Boeing Street, Building 621, Oakland
Phone: (510) 638-7100
Hours: Wed.-Sun. 10:00 a.m.-4:00 p.m.
Admission: Adults $3.00, children $2.00, Flying Boat $2.00 extra

In 1937, Amelia Earhart took off from Oakland Airport's North Field on a journey that would have made her the first woman to fly around the world. Earhart and her Lockheed 10-A Electra disappeared without a trace somewhere over the Pacific, but you can see the sister ship to her downed craft, as well as photographs and Earhart memorabilia, in Oakland's Western Aerospace Museum.

Located in a vintage hangar built in 1939 at North Field by the Boeing School of Aeronautics, the museum's 25,000 sqare feet of indoor space and 33,000-square-foot outdoor exhibition area showcase working planes (actual and model size), historical documents and photos, signatures, uniforms, medals, memorabilia, artifacts, and mystical murals by aviation artist Robert Hope. Themed rooms highlight women in aviation, early aviation, African-American pilots, and General James Doolittle of Doolittle's Raiders.

The most spectacular exhibit, the Short Solent 4-Engine Flying Boat once owned by Howard Hughes, is the last of its kind. Built in 1946 as an upgraded version of the World War II British Sunderland and converted into a luxury passenger airliner in 1949, the airship played a starring role in "Raiders of the Lost Ark." You can watch clips of her performance and a video chronicling her history in the video screening room, which is furnished with airline seats. Kids will enjoy trying out the fully-functioning Link Instrument Trainer and seeing the wonderful models on display in the room sponsored by the Western Association of Modelers.

PLEASANTON

AMADOR–LIVERMORE VALLEY HISTORICAL SOCIETY MUSEUM
603 Main Street, Pleasanton
Phone: (510) 462-2766
Hours: Wed.-Sun. 11:00 a.m.-4:00 p.m.; Sat. & Sun. 1:00-4:00 p.m.
Admission: Free

Pleasanton's Old Town Hall, built in 1914, has been refurbished to house a pleasant, spacious museum that combines professional museology with a homey, small-town flavor. Three changing exhibits a year cover a range of topics spanning prehistory to the present. In 1993 "Collectibles," an eclectic display of antiques and collectibles on loan from several valley collectors, included well-researched collections of knife rests, lead crystal cut glass, Lalique glass, and pigs! Permanent exhibits portray yesteryears' lifestyles with reconstructions of a 19th century parlor, 1930s kitchen, blacksmith's and cooper's shops, and a dentist's office.

Library: The archives/reference library has books, manuscripts, maps, photographs and videos, and transcripts and tapes of oral history interviews.

Gift Shop: The museum store offers local history materials, including a copy of a 1910 *Pleasanton Times* for $1.00.

CONTRA COSTA COUNTY

ANTIOCH

ANTIOCH HISTORICAL MUSEUM
519 F Street, Antioch
Phone: (510) 757-7351
Hours: Wed., Fri., Sat. 1:00-4:00 p.m.
Admission: Free

This tiny museum is bursting at the seams with the history of business and life in Antioch, from the late 1800s to 1940. Once the town library, the museum is now a resource for information about coal mines, farming, and the area's fishing industry.

BLACK DIAMOND MINES MUSEUM
5175 Somersville Road, Antioch
Phone: (510) 757-2620
Hours: Daily 8:00 a.m.-dusk (park hours)
Admission: $3.00 per vehicle

The 4,000-acre Black Diamond Mines Regional Preserve is located at the site of California's largest coal-mining operation, the Mount Diablo

Coalfield. From the 1860s through the turn of the century, nearly four million tons of coal (black diamonds) were removed from the earth by men and boys working under the most arduous and dangerous conditions.

The park's visitor information center offers historic photos, videos, and information about the history and natural history of the park. Five short tunnels are available for visitors to explore, including the 200-foot Prospect Tunnel, created in the 1860s by miners in search of commercial-quality coal.

BRENTWOOD

EAST CONTRA COSTA HISTORICAL SOCIETY MUSEUM*
Sellers Avenue & Zelma Sunset Road, Brentwood
Phone: (510) 634-3216
Hours: First Saturday & third Sunday of the month, 2:00–4:00 p.m.
   May–October and by appointment.
Admission: Free

The historic Beyer/Nail House, a two-story wooden house dating back to the 1840s, is furnished to the period except for its 1950s kitchen. The Brentwood, Byron, and Oakley Rooms have been furnished with artifacts from each of these small, east Contra Costa communities.

CLAYTON

CLAYTON HISTORICAL SOCIETY MUSEUM
6101 Main Street, Clayton
Phone: (510) 672-0240
Hours: Sun. & Wed. 2:00–4:00 p.m. and by appointment
Admission: Free

At the head of the Diablo Valley, nestled at the base of Mount Diablo, sits Clayton, once a rip-roaring copper and coal mining town with the highest murder rate in California, now a serene suburban town with a sense of history. The Clayton Historical Society relocated the home of town founder Joel Clayton, another early Clayton residence, the old jail, and even an outhouse (for the sake of authenticity) to a site on Main Street to form the Clayton Museum. The two little Victorian houses joined together display furnishings and memorabilia typical of the 1860s, Miwok artifacts, and the ubiquitous barbed wire collection. The outside boasts a period flower garden, a disassembled almond huller and other vintage ranch machinery, and a flagpole rescued from the 1906 San Francisco earthquake. Photos, tapes, books, and clippings are on file. Special events include a February Camellia Silver Tea, a May Garden Tour, and a 4th of July Front Porch Auction.

Clayton's Old Timers' Group meets in the museum boardroom to swap stories. Constance Rehr, the museum's curator, also has quite a few stories to tell, making a visit entertaining for kids and adults.

Gift Shop: The gift shop sells books, cards, and historical replicas.

CROCKETT

CROCKETT HISTORICAL MUSEUM
900 Loring Avenue, Crockett
Phone: (510) 787-2178
Hours: Wed. & Sat. 10:00 a.m.-3:00 p.m.
Admission: Free

In 1865, Judge Joseph Crockett settled a land grant dispute and received as his fee a strip of land on the Carquinez Straits one mile wide and three miles long. The strip of land, now the town of Crockett, is known principally for the C&H Refinery, the largest sugar cane refinery in the world. Directly across the street from the enormous brick refinery building, in the former railroad depot, is the Crockett Historical Museum. The 4,000-square-foot museum boasts the most eclectic, least-organized collection of memorabilia we've come across.

The three remarkable curators, Jo Smaker, Dick Boyer, and Tony Machado, all former C&H employees, know the provenance of every artifact (nothing is written down) and regale visitors with endless streams of fascinating anecdotes. By their own admission, the museum looks like a flea market. "This is a people's museum," Jo informed us. "Everything in here has come out of somebody's attic or basement. If a kid brings an old airplane down, we put it in here someplace. And next time he comes in, that's the first thing he looks for."

Among the thousands of items, you'll find a world's record, nine-and-a-half-foot stuffed sturgeon; an eight-by-three-foot model of St. Peter and Paul Cathedral, complete with stained glass windows and interior furnishings; the town's original switchboard, retired in 1969 when Crockett moved to the dial telephone; and Leo Ghilarducci's bowling ball.

Crockett's model railroad club, headquartered in the museum's back room, operates N-scale trains on 125 feet of track divided into sections, each one decorated according to the desires of a club member.

Library: Crockett archives, stored in vintage wooden filing cabinets, contain the best collection in the world of photos of Crockett, local newspapers dating back to 1906, oral histories, and 16 mm sound movies.

Rental: The Old Homestead, original home of Crockett's first settlers, can be rented for weddings and other events.

DANVILLE

THE MUSEUMS AT BLACKHAWK
Blackhawk Plaza, an upscale shopping center, features a two-acre waterway with fountains and reflecting gardens, the Behring Auto Museum, and the UC Berkeley Museum of Art, Science & Culture.

THE BEHRING AUTO MUSEUM
3700 Blackhawk Plaza Circle, Danville
Phone: (510) 736-2277
Hours: Tues.–Sun. 10:00 a.m.–5:00 p.m. (Wed. to 9:00 p.m.)
Admission: Adults $7.00, seniors & students $4.00

A spectacular exhibition space, the 63,000-square-foot Behring Museum presents cars dating from 1897 to the 1980s as works of art, encouraging visitors to view the "rolling sculptures" as masterpieces of design, engineering, and craftsmanship. Turn-of-the-century horseless carriages, jazz age speedsters, and dream cars of the fifties and sixties gleam as if they just rolled off the assembly line. The opulent building of polished granite and vaulted, copper-hued glass could easily eclipse less dazzling exhibits, but the 120 classic, vintage, and rare automobiles on display here are as magnificent as their setting.

Temporary exhibits, including vehicles on loan from local, national, and international collectors, and video documentaries on auto designers, enhance the permanent collection. Automobile fans of any age will be mesmerized for hours and even those with only a passing interest in cars will want to spend at least half an hour.

For kids: Free school tours are available. The museum pays transportation costs for classes from public schools in Contra Costa County.

Library: The W.E. Miller Automotive Research Library, open Tuesday through Sunday from 10:00 a.m. to 4:45 p.m. (closed from 1:00 to 2:00 p.m.) is the most extensive automotive library outside of Detroit. The non-circulating collection includes general automotive books, periodicals, sales brochures, vehicle catalogs, owner's manuals, and original art and photographs.

Rental: The Blackhawk museums' extensive dining, reception, and gallery facilities are available for corporate and private use for parties, evening receptions, luncheons, and banquets.

Blackhawk's Behring Auto Museum prides itself on presenting automobiles as "rolling sculptures" in a dramatically elegant setting. This 1954 De Soto Adventurer II— body by Ghia—was a one-of-a-kind show car built for De Soto. Courtesy of The Behring Auto Museum.

UC BERKELEY MUSEUM OF ART, SCIENCE & CULTURE
3700 Blackhawk Plaza Circle, Danville
Phone: (510) 736-2277
Hours: Tues.-Sun. 10:00 a.m.-5:00 p.m.
Admission: Adults $7.00, students and seniors $4.00

Opened in 1991, the 28,000-square-foot Museum of Art, Science and Culture is an inspiring example of the use of state-of-the-art exhibit techniques to engage the senses.

The "Artistic Spirit" exhibit features over three hundred ancient and traditional artifacts from the University of California at Berkeley's Phoebe Apperson Hearst Museum of Anthropology. The significance of objects representing 5,000 years of culture and creativity—life-size New Guinean ancestor figures, Egyptian glass jewelry and a sarcophagus, Persian armor inlaid with gold—becomes clear when they are presented in universal themes, like "The Domain of Woman," "Images of Childhood," and "Death and Afterlife."

A display dedicated to discoveries from nine million years ago found at the Blackhawk Ranch Fossil Quarry recreates prehistoric life in the Bay Area, with reconstructions and fossils of one-toed horses, ancient camels, pigs, and the complete skeleton of Gomphotherium, a four-tusked mastodon. In an ongoing exhibit developed in conjunction with the University of California at Berkeley's Museum of Paleontology, prominent paleontologists share their enthusiasm for the science in video interviews, while hands-on games like "Match the Mammals" and "Who Traveled, Who Didn't" illustrate animal evolution.

For a change of pace, visitors can sit in the quiet game room and play Ayo, a Yoruba game from Nigeria, or Tingmiujang, an Eskimo game. This is a very child-friendly museum, also interesting to adults.

For kids: Free school tours are available. The museum pays transportation costs for classes from public schools in Contra Costa County.

Rental: The Blackhawk museums' extensive dining, reception, and gallery facilities are available for corporate and private use for parties, evening receptions, luncheons, and banquets.

EUGENE O'NEILL NATIONAL HISTORIC SITE
P.O. Box 280, Danville
Phone: (510) 838-0249
Hours: Wed.-Sun. 10:00 a.m. and 12:30 p.m., by reservation only.
Admission: Free

Using his 1936 Nobel prize money, Eugene O'Neill and his wife Carlotta built Tao House in the secluded hills of the San Ramon Valley. Its name inspired by O'Neill's interest in Eastern thought and Carlotta's passion for Asian art and furniture, the Spanish colonial house has been completely restored, from the deep blue ceilings, red doors, black mirrors, and black-stained floors within to the Mediterranean garden and crooked path outside. The National Park Service is slowly and painstakingly refurnishing the house with authentic pieces—with the exception of O'Neill's study, furniture is presently sparse.

Visitors are picked up in a parking lot in Danville and transported by Park Service mini-van up the steep, narrow road that leads to the property. The hour-and-a-half tour provides an excellent and informative lecture on the long day's journey of America's great playwright, with time left over for a self-guided tour of the grounds. O'Neill fans will be enthralled, children under high school age will find this a deadly bore.

Gift Shop: A small visitor center sells postcards and books.

LAFAYETTE

MUSEUM OF VINTAGE FASHION
1712 Chaparral Lane, Lafayette
Phone: (510) 944-1896
Hours: By appointment
Admission: $15 pre-paid includes tour and tea

Patti Parks McClain has been collecting vintage clothing since she was 18. The collection, which now numbers over 19,000 pieces dated from 1736 to 1990, fills the closets and numerous armoires, trunks, and chests in Patti's suburban home. For students and people who seriously love fashion, Patti will literally open the doors to her closets and show you their contents, including her favorite designer pieces, handbags, compacts, hats, shoes, wedding gowns, lingerie, children's garments, and items worn by such famous women as Eleanor Roosevelt and Jacqueline Kennedy.

Thirteen acres in nearby Alamo have been donated to Patti for the Museum of Vintage Fashion's next home. The new 20,000-square-foot facility will make the collection accessible to the public. Until that time, *please do not attempt to visit the Museum of Vintage Fashion without an appointment!*

Groups of eight or more are invited to book a Closet Tour, which includes tea and light refreshment. Patti's idea of a light refreshment was our idea of a full meal. She served us delicious ham and egg salad sandwiches, spinach quiche, homemade brownies, raspberry cream cake, and grapes.

Library: A large collection of books on fashion design, costume, and fashion-related subjects is available for research.

MARTINEZ

MARTINEZ HISTORICAL SOCIETY MUSEUM★
1005 Escobar Street, Martinez
Phone: (510) 228-8160
Hours: Tues. & Thurs. 11:30 a.m.–3:00 p.m.; first & third Sunday
of the month, 1:00–4:00 p.m.
Admission: Free

Built in 1890 by Dr. J.S. Moore as a residence and dental office, this little Victorian cottage houses a vast collection of Martinez memorabilia, photographs, and oral histories. The County Room, Barber Shop, School Room, Olden Days Room, and Waterfront Room display tools, housewares, costumes, and office machines.

Library: The library makes videos, slides, scrapbooks, and a variety of books and records chronicling the history of the city available for research.

JOHN MUIR NATIONAL HISTORIC SITE
4202 Alhambra Avenue, Martinez
Phone: (510) 228-8860
Hours: Wed.–Sun. 10:00 a.m.–4:30 p.m.
Admission: $2.00, children 16 and under free

In my eagerness to get to the main attraction, I am sometimes tempted to overlook the visitor centers at historic sites. Don't miss the film at the John Muir Historic Site. This superb, half-hour film accompanies stunning scenery with selections from Muir's writings, a perfect vehicle for conveying his passion for wilderness.

Throughout his life, John Muir championed the cause of preserving American wilderness. He convinced President Teddy Roosevelt to protect forest lands from commercial exploitation and was one of the founders of the Sierra Club. It was largely through his efforts that the Yosemite and Sequoia/Kings Canyon national parks were established. Although the footloose Muir loved nothing more than tramping through the wilderness, he curtailed his global wanderings for a time to provide for his wife and two daughters, securing a modest fortune from growing fruit.

At this historic site, you can explore the house Muir lived in from 1890 until his death in 1914, as well as a small part of his orchards. The seventeen-room Victorian home, built in 1882 by Muir's father-in-law, John Strentzel, cost $20,000—a considerable sum in those days. Furnished to the period of 1890–1914,

John Muir had such passion for nature that it was said he could identify a tree by listening to the wind in its leaves. After marrying Louie Strentzel in 1880 at the age of 42, he lived in the house built for them by her father, supporting his family by growing fruit. It was during this period that he successfully advocated establishing Yosemite as a national park, and became the first president of the Sierra Club. Photo by Fred Mang, Jr., courtesy of National Park Service.

the house gives an idea of upper middle-class Victorian life and of the Muirs' family life. One of the more interesting rooms is Muir's study, or "scribble den" as he called it. Children will enjoy exploring the attic filled with family discards and climbing the stairs to ring the bell in the bell tower.

A path leads from Muir House to the Martinez Adobe built in 1849 by Vincente Martinez, son of the commandant of the Presidio of San Francisco. Muir's daughter Wanda lived here with her husband, Thomas Hanna. Presently closed for seismic retrofit (it was damaged in the 1989 Loma Prieta earthquake), the adobe will reopen in 1995.

"Mount Lyell, California Sierra" (1874) by William Keith. An eminent Bay Area bohemian and a mystic, Keith was a prolific painter, selling landscapes (which he could complete in a few hours) and occasional portraits to railroad and mining magnates of the day at very respectable prices. The Hearst Gallery at Saint Mary's College in Moraga features an extensive collection of works by Keith, as well as works by other artists. Courtesy of Hearst Art Gallery.

MORAGA

HEARST ART GALLERY
Saint Mary's College, Moraga
Phone: (510) 631-4379
Hours: Wed.-Sun. 11:00 a.m.-4:30 p.m.
Admission: Free

If you've never seen Saint Mary's College, a visit to the Hearst Gallery might be just the reason you need to visit this beautiful, Spanish-style campus tucked away in a quiet Contra Costa valley.

One of the college's gleaming white, red-tile-roofed buildings houses the 2,000-square-foot Hearst Gallery, most of which is devoted to high-quality changing exhibitions in a wide variety of media, periods, and cultures. A small gallery showcases paintings from the museum's extensive William Keith collection. In addition to the works of Keith, a prolific and highly regarded interpreter of the California landscape, the gallery collects and exhibits 19th and 20th century California landscapes by other artists. Christian imagery in art, another focus of the collection, is represented in occasional exhibitions, along with ethnographic art and a Master Artist Tribute series.

Gift Shop: In the entry area is an interesting selection of jewelry, catalogs, children's art books, and notecards.

PITTSBURG

PITTSBURG HISTORICAL SOCIETY
40 Civic Avenue, Pittsburg
Phone: (510) 439-7501 and 439-8730
Hours: By appointment. Closed November–April.

"Were it not for the preservation of memorabilia, the history of this area would fade and pass without record," reads the sign over the door of the former Standard Oil pump station that now houses the Pittsburg Historical Society. Not a terribly catchy slogan, but it speaks to the heart and soul of the handful of volunteers who have organized this remarkable, small-town museum. Making use of every inch of the 1,600-square-foot site and a fine collection of historic artifacts, the museum presents a lively history of Pittsburg from the earliest Ompin Miwok occupants through successive industrial heydays as a coal mining, ranching, fishing, and cannery town. Recreations of a laundry room, dressmaker's shop, meat market, barber shop, schoolroom, and the Bayview Saloon convey the feeling of everyday life in a bygone era. Members of the Historical Society have also set up historical vignettes in shop windows of the old downtown area along Railroad Avenue.

Gift Shop: Publications and cards about Pittsburg are available.

PLEASANT HILL

DIABLO VALLEY COLLEGE MUSEUM
Golf Club Road, Pleasant Hill
Phone: (510) 685-1230, ext. 303
Hours: Call ahead—hours change every semester
Admission: Free

Budget cuts to public education have taken their toll at Diablo Valley College Museum and it's a shame. Once fully-functioning, this fine little museum has been forced to reduce hours and limp along with scant funds for staffing, developing exhibits, or repairing and maintaining the collection.

Changing exhibits feature items from the museum's eclectic collection of freeze-dried and taxidermied Bay Area wildlife specimens—mammals, reptiles, amphibians, local and exotic insects—and artifacts from California's native peoples. On permanent display, a Foucault pendulum demonstrates the rotation of the earth, a 1960 seismograph registers earth tremors, and a vintage printing press can be inked up to print greeting cards. For something a little out of the ordinary, there is the quirky collection of "quack machines"—Hair Restorer, Abunda-Beauty machine, Micro Dynamiter—all testaments to human gullibility.

There's enough here to interest most children if an accompanying adult can provide explanations. Outdoors, you can stroll through a botanical garden of native plants or sit by the pond. Planetarium shows take place Tuesday and Thursday mornings, by appointment only.

PLEASANT HILL HISTORICAL SOCIETY MUSEUM*
2050 Oak Park Boulevard, Pleasant Hill
Phone: (510) 932-6267
Hours: Third Sunday of the month, 1:00-4:00 p.m. Closed July
    & August.
Admission: Free

The 1920 Pleasant Hill Grammar School houses early 20th century household artifacts and the American Indian Collection of the Pleasant Hill Historical Society.

POINT RICHMOND

POINT RICHMOND HISTORY ASSOCIATION MUSEUM
139-1/2 Washington Avenue, Point Richmond
Phone: (510) 234-5334 or (510) 235-1336
Hours: Thurs. & Sat. 11:30 a.m.-2:00 p.m.
Admission: Free

The large, industrial city of Richmond traces its origins to a charming but little-known community known as Point Richmond. On the hillside overlooking San Francisco Bay are some lovely old houses and churches, the historic Hotel Mac and Masquers Theater, and the tiniest of museums imaginable. The oldest commercial building on the Point, the 125-square-foot structure has been restored to its original 1903 appearance and moved to its present location, next to the modern firehouse. Photographs on the wall and in albums recreate the history of the area.

RICHMOND

GOLDEN STATE MODEL RAILROAD MUSEUM
Miller/Knox Regional Shoreline
900 Dornan Drive, Richmond
Phone: (510) 234-4884
Hours: Sun. 1:00-5:00 p.m. May–October
Admission: Adult $2.00, children & seniors $1.00, families $5.00

Located in Oakland since 1933, the East Bay Model Engineers Society recently relocated their Golden State Model Railroad Museum to a former paint factory across from the picnic area on Richmond's Miller/Knox shoreline. With 10,000 square feet of floor space, the layout, one of the largest model railroad exhibits west of the Mississippi, is a model railroader's dream. Model train aficionados can enjoy the largest O scale models, representing one quarter inch to a foot, the HO layout which reproduces the rail line from Oakland to Martinez, and the tiny N scale train running from a miniature Sacramento through Bakersfield.

"Juggler" by Lisa Clague (clay and metal, 22" x 25" x 8", 1993). Photo by Scott McCue Photography, courtesy of Richmond Art Center.

RICHMOND ART CENTER
Civic Center Plaza
25th & Barrett, Richmond
Phone: (510) 620-6772
Hours: Tues.-Fri. 10:00 a.m.-4:30 p.m.;
  Sat. & Sun. noon-4:30 p.m.
Admission: Free

Founded in 1936, the Richmond Art Center moved in 1951 to what was called by *Architectural Forum* magazine "the first modern civic center built in any American city." The 25,000-square-foot facility has some of the best-equipped studios in the Bay Area, and 5,000 square feet of exhibition space presenting six shows a year that feature emerging and well-known Bay Area artists. Outstanding exhibitions have established the center's reputation as a "discovery gallery" and one of the most influential contemporary art spaces in the country; Richard Diebenkorn, Jasper Johns, and Nathan Olivera are among the many famous artists shown at the center early in their careers.

RICHMOND MUSEUM OF HISTORY
400 Nevin Avenue, Richmond
Phone: (510) 235-7387
Hours: Thurs. noon-4:00 p.m.; Sat. & Sun. 1:00-4:00 p.m. and
  group tours by appointment
Admission: Free

We picked up a postcard in the Richmond Museum of History that read, "What, a museum in Richmond?" In fact, there are three museums in Richmond, including the first-rate Richmond Museum of History. Started in the 1950s in the basement of the 1910 Carnegie Library, the museum now occupies the entire renovated and expanded building.

   The ducks were flying too high to hit on the day in 1895 when A.S. Macdonald went duckhunting in what is now Richmond, so he went for a walk instead, and conceived the idea of a transcontinental rail terminal and port. Five years later, two hundred passengers boarded a ferry in San Francisco, landed in Richmond, and climbed aboard Santa Fe's first through train to Chicago. Mementos of the city's origins and community history from the Ohlone people through the 1940s are exhibited in the museum's permanent history gallery. Artifacts and memorabilia that chronicle Richmond's growth include the first Model A off the Richmond Ford Plant assembly line in 1931 and the dress worn to christen one of the 563 military vessels produced at the Richmond shipyards. The museum's main floor houses the Seaver Gallery, where changing exhibits highlight community history. On view during our visit was an extraordinarily moving and well-documented exhibit on child care centers during World War II, with paintings created by children in Richmond's centers.

Gift Shop: There is no shop, but you can purchase handsome mugs, t-shirts, and totes.

SAN PABLO

ALVARADO ADOBE & BLUME HOUSE MUSEUM
1 Alvarado Square, San Pablo
Phone: (510) 236-7373 or (510) 234-7518
Hours: Fourth Sunday of the month, noon–4:00 p.m.
Admission: Free

Dwarfed by Richmond, its bigger and better-known neighbor, the tiny town of San Pablo is often overlooked by Bay Area residents and tourists alike. The handsome Alvarado Square, with its beautifully landscaped courtyards and two well-kept museums, is a worthy destination for a Sunday afternoon outing. (Be sure to make it the fourth Sunday of the month.)

The original Alvarado Adobe, built in 1845 by Jesus Maria Castro for his young bride, Josefa Alviso, was occupied over the years by generations of Castros and Alvarados, including Juan Alvarado, the first native-born governor of California. Reconstructed in 1978 on the original site, the adobe is now a part of Alvarado Square, the modern, Spanish-style complex that houses the city offices. The San Pablo Historical Society has furnished the living room and bedroom as befits a prosperous California rancho at the end of the Mexican period, with locally-manufactured goods, Chinese imports, and items shipped around the Horn from New England.

A typical, turn-of-the-century farmhouse built in 1905 by Henry and Frederika Blume, the Blume House was moved to Alvarado Square when the newly-formed San Pablo Historical Society convinced the developers of Hilltop Mall, Chevron Land and Development Corporation, to donate the house and outbuildings to the city of San Pablo. Immigrants from Germany, the Blumes acquired over a thousand acres of land in the northern section of Rancho San Pablo, which they farmed for over half a century. Visitors can tour the bottom floor of the two-story farmhouse and the barn.

WALNUT CREEK

THE LINDSAY MUSEUM
1931 First Avenue, Walnut Creek
Phone: (510) 935-1978
Hours: Wed.-Sun. 1:00-5:00 p.m., Sept.-June; Wed.-Sun. 11:00 a.m.-
5:00 p.m., July & August.
Admission: Adults $3.00, seniors and children $2.00, members free.

The Lindsay Museum, America's oldest wildlife rehabilitation center and one of the largest, has saved the lives of thousands of injured, orphaned, and displaced creatures since it opened in 1970.

Thirty-five species of non-releasable native birds and mammals live at the museum, including foxes, eagles, falcons, hawks, snakes, and a bobcat that looked like an overgrown house cat as he paced restlessly in his cage during our visit. Museum exhibits are designed to showcase the work that goes into the care and stewardship of these animals. Two large areas provide the public with a view of their daily feeding, bathing, and exercising.

The Exhibit Hall's focal point is a 35-foot Balancing Rock, cast from a real rock formation on Mount Diablo, and supporting over 100 plant and animal specimens local to the mountain. A wall full of natural history objects—furs, bones, skins, and more—is set up for hands-on learning. A small theater shows continual nature films, a rotating drum displays local insects, and aquaria highlight the fish and amphibians of the region's waterways. Information extends beyond the Exhibit Hall to encompass threats to wildlife from loss of habitat, accidents, pesticides, and pets.

In a separate room called "Especially for Children" and designed to look like a house and back yard, families who prowl through the exhibit can find snakes in the woodpile, raccoons under the deck, fawns under a tree, and many more examples of wildlife in an urban setting. There is a Petting Circle just outside this room.

The nation's oldest wildlife rehabilitation center, Walnut Creek's Lindsay Museum features natural history exhibits that do not fail to entertain while they educate visitors of all ages. Courtesy of The Lindsay Museum.

The Lindsay Museum emphasizes one-on-one learning and community action. Over 250 classes and trips for children are offered each year.

Library: Museum members can check out hamsters, rabbits, guinea pigs, and rats from the Pet Library, and more than 10,000 nature objects are available on loan from the Natural History To Go program.

Gift Shop: The museum store sells books and nature items for children and adults.

MOUNT DIABLO SUMMIT VISITOR CENTER*
Mt. Diablo State Park, Walnut Creek
Phone: (510) 837-6119
Hours: Tues.-Sun. 11:00 a.m.-5:00 p.m.
Admission: $5.00/vehicle

From the observation deck of the stone tower built at the summit of
Mount Diablo in the thirties, more than 40,000 square miles of California
are visible; on a clear day you can see Mount Lassen, Mount Whitney,
and the Sierra Nevada. Inside the tower, the brand-new Mount Diablo
Summit Museum chronicles the history of the mountain; a rock wall
with instructional videos examines the geological forces that created it,
panels describe the Native American history of the area, and a diorama
complete with recorded natural sounds offers an overview of the park's
ecosystems. The Summit Gallery presents changing exhibitions by artists
and photographers whose works depict Mount Diablo and other places
in California.

SHADELANDS RANCH HISTORICAL MUSEUM
2660 Ygnacio Valley Road, Walnut Creek
Phone: (510) 935-7871
Hours: Wed., Thurs. 11:30 a.m.-4:00 p.m.; Sun. 1:00-4:00 p.m.
Admission: Adults $2.00, seniors $1.00, children under 12 free

Shadelands Ranch Historical Museum exists today in its original state on
a corner of Shadelands Office Park, once a successful, 500-acre fruit and
nut ranch. Built in 1903 by Hiram P. Penniman, one of the founders of
the town of Walnut Creek, the colonial revival house is furnished with
actual family furnishings and memorabilia, a turn-of-the-century kitchen,
and a closetful of Victorian ladies' wear and lace-trimmed baby clothes.

Library: The Sherwood D. Burgess History Room holds some 500 books
and vintage newspapers, historical photos, maps, and oral histories.

Rental: The grounds are available for weddings and other events for $95
per hour.

North Bay

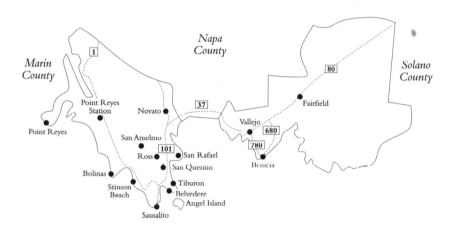

Marin County · Napa County · Solano County

1 · 80 · 37 · 101 · 680 · 780

Point Reyes Station
Novato
Point Reyes
San Anselmo
Ross
San Rafael
San Quentin
Bolinas
Tiburon
Stinson Beach
Belvedere
Angel Island
Sausalito
Vallejo
Benicia
Fairfield

North Bay

MARIN COUNTY

ANGEL ISLAND

ANGEL ISLAND STATE PARK★
Angel Island
Phone: (415) 435-3522 or (415) 435-1915
Hours: Daily 8:00 a.m.-sunset. Ferries depart from Tiburon,
** San Francisco, and Vallejo.**
Admission: Included in ferry fee

The largest island in San Francisco Bay, covered with grass and forest, Angel Island was for thousands of years a hunting and fishing site for Coast Miwok people. From 1859, when the island became the property of the U.S. government, it served as a Civil War fort, a quarantine station, an immigration facility, an embarkation center during both world wars, a prisoner-of-war processing facility, and a nike missile base. In 1963 it was turned over to the state of California for use as a park.

Visitors can enjoy biking and hiking and the spectacular views all year round. The museums are open when volunteer docents are available. The Immigration Museum is a reminder of the days when Angel Island, "the Ellis Island of the Pacific," served as a detention center for Asian immigrants. The Camp Reynolds Museum traces history back even further to the Civil War, when Angel Island was used to defend the Union against a possible Confederate attack. A few of the fort's old wooden buildings, including the old bake house and the former bachelor officers' quarters, have been restored.

Angel Island can be reached by commercial ferry service from Tiburon, San Francisco, and Vallejo. Contact the Angel Island State Park Ferry Company at (415) 435-2131, or the Red and White Fleet at (415) 546-2896.

BELVEDERE

CHINA CABIN MUSEUM
52 Beach Road, Belvedere
Phone: (415) 435-2251
Hours: Wed. & Sun. 1:00–4:00 p.m., April–October.
Admission: Free—donations accepted

When the *SS China,* a wooden sidewheel steamer, was brought to the marine crematory in Tiburon Cove to be burned for scrap metal, the social saloon and two attached staterooms deemed too beautiful to burn were saved. After serving for ninety years as part of a private residence, the Victorian reception room, with its highlighted goldleaf decor, walnut woodwork, cut-glass floral windows, and brass and crystal chandeliers, has been restored and opened to the public as a maritime museum with a panoramic vista of the San Francisco skyline.

Rental: The China Cabin is once again available for use as a setting for private parties, as well as weddings and concerts.

BOLINAS

BOLINAS MUSEUM
48 Wharf Road, Bolinas
Phone: (415) 868-0330
Hours: Thurs. 5:00–7:00. p.m., Fri.-Sun. 1:00–5:00 p.m.
Admission: Free

The tiny Bolinas Museum, housed in an historic white clapboard building that has done duty as a hotel, library, and general store, combines sophisticated museum technology with a folksy community spirit, focusing on the art and history of coastal Marin County. A floating wall divides the permanent historical exhibit from the larger space devoted to changing art and historical exhibits. Artifacts from the original Bolinas post office, blacksmith shop, and general store share space with an exhibit dedicated to the *Owl,* a schooner that carried cargo and sometimes passengers to and from San Francisco.

Each year the museum presents seven to nine highly professional rotating exhibitions, including an historical show, a juried exhibition, a Focus exhibition examining the life work of an individual artist, and the popular miniature show featuring two hundred tiny works, none larger than 6 by 6 inches.

Gift Shop: The Bolinas Museum store showcases work by local artists and craftspeople, and one-of-a-kind donated antiques and collectibles.

NOVATO

MARIN MUSEUM OF THE AMERICAN INDIAN
2200 Novato Boulevard, Novato
Phone: (415) 897-4064
Hours: Wed.-Fri. 10:00 a.m.-3:00 p.m.; Sat. & Sun. noon-
4:00 p.m.
Admission: Free

This small but beautifully put together museum, located in Miwok Park on a Coast Miwok archaeological site, does a fine job of telling visitors about California's rich Native American heritage. The museum's primary focus is on children, whose tour includes the permanent exhibit, "Coast Miwok Indians, the First People of Marin," the native plant garden surrounding the museum, and the downstairs education room, where they can pound acorns on an authentic stone mortar, feel a rabbitskin blanket, try on clothing, and drill holes with a pump drill. A mobile "Hands On, Will Travel" classroom takes artifacts and replicas of Native American ethnographic items into classrooms.

Baby baskets are still used by some California families. A treasured link to tradition, they also provide a safe and comfortable spot from which to learn about the world. © Catherine Karnow, courtesy of Marin Museum of the American Indian.

A "Trade Feast," celebrated the first or second Saturday in June, features Native American dancers, games, story-telling, demonstrations of traditional skills and crafts, and delicious fry bread.

Library: The non-circulating research library of works on archaeology, anthropology, California history, and Native Americans, including exclusive holdings on the Coast Miwok, is open by appointment.

Gift Shop: The tiny store sells books, maps, posters, games, jewelry, and novelties on Native American themes.

Rental: Birthday parties for up to 30 kids can be arranged for $60.

NOVATO HISTORY MUSEUM
815 DeLong Avenue, Novato
Phone: (415) 897-4320
Hours: Thurs. & Sat. 10:00 a.m.-4:00 p.m.
Admission: Free

The volunteers who run the folksy Novato History Museum have filled every nook and cranny of the historic 1850 postmaster's home with displays of Novato's yesteryears, and are running out of space. Two rooms are chockablock with historic photographs, household goods, tools, toys, costumes, and furniture, and a third chronicles military aviation at Hamilton Field Air Force Base. Schoolchildren can ring the old schoolhouse bell on free class tours.

Library: Reference materials available to the public include history books, school yearbooks, newspapers, and oral history interviews.

OLOMPALI STATE HISTORIC PARK
8901 Redwood Highway, Novato
Phone: (415) 892-3383
Hours: Daily 10:00 a.m.–sunset; summer, 10:00 a.m.–7:00 p.m.
Admission: $2.00/auto, $1.00/dog (dogs & bikes are not permitted on hiking trails)

Very few traces remain of the large Coast Miwok trading village that once existed on the land now occupied by Olompali State Historic Park, but visitors will see the remains of other historic periods as they explore the 700-acre park. Be sure to pick up a copy of the self-guided tour book, which relates the history behind the park's confusing jumble of structures.

A shingled, plywood shed protects an old adobe dating from the time of Camilo Ynitia, a Coast Miwok leader whose Rancho Olompali was one of the few Mexican land grants to a Native American to be confirmed by the U.S. government. Ynitia's adobe was later enclosed by a modest wood frame house, which subsequently became the heart of James Burdell's grand, 26-room mansion. The mansion and gardens, once the showplace of Marin, passed through a string of owners until their final incarnation as a hippie commune known as "The Chosen Family." A fire gutted the mansion in 1969, but the walls of the adobe still remain, as well as the cookhouse, barn, generator house, blacksmith shop, two saltbox houses, and the remnants of Marin County's first formal garden.

POINT REYES NATIONAL SEASHORE

A day may not be enough time to enjoy the natural wonders and cultural facilities of the 65,000-acre Point Reyes National Seashore, so get an early start. Within the Point Reyes Peninsula—a one-hundred-square-mile living museum—the National Park Service operates six interpretive facilities that focus on the cultural and natural heritage of the area.

BEAR VALLEY VISITOR CENTER
Bear Valley Road, Point Reyes National Seashore
Phone: (415) 663-1092
Hours: Daily 9:00 a.m.–5:00 p.m.
Admission: Free

A good place to begin your visit is the Bear Valley Visitor Center, a large and handsome, barn-like structure at the Bear Valley entrance to the park. The rangers are happy to screen "Something Special," a 20-minute orientation film, or the dramatic slide show "The Enchanted Shore" in the center's auditorium, to give you an overview of the area.

The 2,500-square-foot exhibition hall examines the physical aspects of Point Reyes, the history of the Coast Miwok, early English and

Spanish explorers, ranching, shipwrecks, and plant and animal life. From the center's weather station you can monitor the weather, which varies drastically from hour to hour, noting the velocity and direction of the wind, temperature, and rainfall. Kids can climb the observation tower to view (stuffed) birds through the scope. Walk-through nature dioramas display taxidermied specimens (mostly roadkills) of the animals you may encounter when you explore the outdoors.

EARTHQUAKE TRAIL
Hours: Daily, sunrise to sunset

Setting out from the Visitor Center, follow the half-mile Earthquake Trail tracing the fracture zone of the San Andreas Fault. Here, in 1906, the earth's crust separated and moved 16 feet. Signs include pictures of the 1906 San Francisco earthquake and information on present-day earthquake theories.

KULE LOKLO
Hours: Daily, sunrise to sunset

From the Visitor Center, a quarter-mile trail will lead you to Kule Loklo, a replicated Coast Miwok village constructed by volunteers in 1978 usingtraditional methods and tools. On Saturdays you may find volunteers demonstrating such traditional skills as making clamshell disk beads or flintknapping obsidian. During the week the village may be overrun with schoolchildren on field trips, but if you are fortunate enough to arrive, as we did, on a rainy winter Tuesday and find yourselves the only visitors, you may experience a primordial peacefulness capable of calming the most city-weary soul.

A sweat house at the Coast Miwok village of Kule Loklo. Photo by Selena Filippis.

MORGAN HORSE RANCH
Bear Valley Road, Point Reyes National Seashore
Phone: (415) 663-1092
Hours: Daily 8:00 a.m.-4:30 p.m.
Admission: Free

It's a short walk from the Visitor Center to the Morgan Horse Ranch, a working ranch where the National Park Service raises and trains Morgan Horses. Rangers use these sturdy creatures—Morgan Horses were the first American-bred horses—to patrol park trails. Visitors can see what it takes to raise a colt from birth and train it.

KENNETH C. PATRICK VISITOR CENTER
Drakes Beach, Point Reyes National Seashore
Phone: (415) 669-1250
**Hours: Weekends & holidays 10:00 a.m.-5:00 p.m., closed for lunch
   from noon to 12:30.**
Admission: Free

It is here, on beautiful Drakes Beach, that Sir Francis Drake is believed
to have stopped to repair his ship, the *Golden Hinde,* in 1579. Exhibits in
the Visitor Center focus on the 16th century explorer and the ocean's
ecology. A salt-water aquarium filled with plant and animal life from the
bay has recently been installed for a fish-eye view of life beyond the surf.
A Minke whale skeleton can be viewed up close.

PIERCE POINT RANCH
Pierce Point Road, Point Reyes National Seashore
Phone: (415) 669-1534
Hours: Daily, sunrise to sunset
Admission: Free

When California was under Mexican rule, the entire Point Reyes
peninsula was divided into three land grants. When the United States
took over, Point Reyes was entrusted to a San Francisco law firm, which
broke the land up into dozens of dairy ranches controlled by the senior
partners of the firm. Cattle have roamed the fields of Point Reyes ever
since. Pierce Point Ranch, established in 1858, is one of the oldest dairy
ranches on the peninsula. It has been renovated, and a short, self-guided
trail tour is open to the public. Although you may not enter the structures, you may wander through the ranch complex.

POINT REYES NATIONAL SEASHORE LIGHTHOUSE
VISITOR CENTER
Sir Francis Drake Highway, Point Reyes National Seashore
Phone: (415) 669-1534
**Hours: Thurs.-Mon. 10:00 a.m.-5:00 p.m.; lighthouse stairs
   10:00 a.m.-4:30 p.m., weather permitting**

Perched on the rocky Point Reyes headlands, the Lighthouse Visitor
Center features exhibits on whales, wildflowers, geology and lighthouses.
Hearty souls who wish to descend the 300 steps down to the lighthouse
will be treated to an impressive view. The lighthouse observation
platform is an excellent place to see the gray whale migration, which
takes place during January through April, and watch for marine wildlife.
The historic, 118-year-old lighthouse is open for tours on weekend
mornings, January through March 20. A limited number of spaces are
available for the evening lighthouse tour, which features the dusk lighting
of the giant crystal lens. Call for reservations.

POINT REYES STATION

THE BOLINAS MUSEUM'S LIVING ARTISTS PROJECT RESOURCE CENTER
1101 Highway 1, Pt. Reyes Station
Phone: (415) 868-0330
Hours: Fri.-Mon. 11:00 a.m.-5:00 p.m., and by appointment.
Admission: Free

The Living Artists Project Resource Center, the Bolinas Museum's
satellite gallery in Point Reyes Station, maintains a library of 1,000 slides
representing the work of 200 coastal Marin artists, and a state-of-the-art
slide registry viewing system. One-person art exhibits change monthly.

ROSS

MARIN ART & GARDEN CENTER
Sir Francis Drake Boulevard, Ross
Phone: (415) 454-5597
Hours: Mon.-Fri. 11:00 a.m.-4:00 p.m.; Sat. & Sun. noon-4:00 p.m.
Admission: Free

In 1857 James Ross (for whom the town of Ross is named) acquired
the Mexican land grant called Rancho Punto de Quentin. His wedding
present to his daughter, a 21-acre parcel of the rancho, later became
the Marin Art & Garden Center. This venerable Marin institution, maintained by a coalition of community arts and garden groups, encompasses
beautiful gardens and an arboretum, the José Moya del Pino Library, and
an art gallery showing works by local residents and presenting monthly
juried exhibitions. The barn is now used by the Ross Valley Players,
the oldest continuously operating little theater group in the United States.

Library: The José Moya del Pino Library is housed in the first building
constructed on the Garden Center site, a charming octagonal structure
designed as a tank house and used as a temporary dwelling. An excellent
selection of books on art and gardening is available for reference use.

Gift Shop: Laurel House Antiques, open Tuesday through Friday,
11:00 a.m. to 4:00 p.m., offers an outstanding selection of Asian and
Western antiques and collectibles.

Restaurant: We thought we were in for a disastrous meal at the Ross
Garden Restaurant & Patio when our waitress asked if we wanted ice
in our red wine. Much to our relief, our lunch was as pleasant as the
cheerful surroundings and amiable volunteers who staff this quaint cottage
restaurant. We had a choice of three meals—a hot entree of raspberry
chicken breasts with a green salad, a meatloaf sandwich with potato-
mushroom soup, or a green salad with shrimp and the soup. Lunches,

priced under $8, included homemade cake for dessert. The restaurant is open from 11:30 a.m. to 2:00 p.m., Tuesday through Friday.

SAN ANSELMO

SAN ANSELMO HISTORICAL MUSEUM
10 Library Place, San Anselmo
Phone: (415) 258-4666
Hours: Tues. 10:30 a.m.-12:30 p.m.; Sat 2:00-4:00 p.m., and by appointment.
Admission: Free

The tiny San Anselmo Historical Museum, located in two basement rooms of the San Anselmo library, may close temporarily while the library is retrofitted for earthquake safety, so call before you visit. Specializing in historic photographs of San Anselmo, the museum features a time line ranging from the original Coast Miwok inhabitants to the present, illustrated with photographs, documents, and artifacts. Museum displays highlight the railroads, the town's original raison d'être in the days when San Anselmo was simply called "the junction."

Library: The large photo archive is available for research.

SAN QUENTIN

SAN QUENTIN PRISON MUSEUM
Bldg. #106 Dolores Way, San Quentin
Phone: (415) 454-8808
Hours: Mon.-Fri. 10:00 a.m.-4:00 p.m.
Admission: Adults $2.00, children $1.00, family $6.00

Built in 1853, San Quentin was California's first prison, with inmates ranging from the Californio bandit Tiburcio Vasquez to labor leader Tom Mooney, San Francisco political boss Abraham Ruef, and Soledad Brother George Jackson. This photo of men in the stereotypical striped prison uniform is from the prison museum's extensive photo archives. Courtesy of the San Quentin Prison Museum.

For some reason, prisons hold an irresistible fascination for youngsters. Even the most reluctant museum-goer will jump at a chance to visit the San Quentin Prison Museum. Approaching the museum, parking in the visitors' lot with its unique view of San Francisco Bay, and entering through the actual prison gates is quite a thrill in itself, and the museum is not a letdown. Opened in 1992 after seven years of preparation, San Quentin's beautifully designed museum tells a moving and arresting story through historic photographs and artifacts which span its 140-year history as California's first prison.

Although most displays serve as grim reminders of the wages of crime— a 1913 cell measuring 4'8" by 10'6", a case of prisoners' restraints featuring straitjackets and leg irons, and a sobering exhibit on the history of the death penalty—our guide discussed prison industry jobs, educational opportunities, and other less gloomy aspects of prison life as well. In testimony to human ingenuity, a case of contraband items confiscated from prisoners features an escape rope braided from tire cords, a hollowed-out toilet paper roll used to secret drugs, a tattoo gun, and a small still fashioned out of a tobacco can.

Call for reservations for free, docent-led class and youth group tours.

Gift Shop: The museum gift shop sells San Quentin souvenir items: belt buckles, t-shirts, earrings, pencils, "Pen" pens, books, cards, convict dolls, and a cassette of the San Quentin Choir. The San Quentin Handicraft Shop, located outside the prison gates, sells t-shirts, crafts, and original art by inmates.

SAN RAFAEL

CALIFORNIA CENTER FOR WILDLIFE (WILDCARE)
76 Albert Park Lane, San Rafael
Phone: (415) 456-SAVE
Hours: Daily 9:00 a.m.-5:00 p.m.
Admission: Free

Founded forty years ago as the Junior Museum of Marin, the California Center for Wildlife, as it is currently known, concentrates its energy on the Wildlife Rehabilitation Hospital, which treats over 4,000 animals a year. Although emphasis has shifted from educating people to rehabilitating injured, orphaned, and sick birds and mammals, there is still plenty for visitors to see.

Inside the large, one-room exhibit hall, hands-on puzzles and games as well as stuffed wildlife, birds' nests, and a lovely mural are all designed to teach environmental responsibility. The best, however, is outside in the courtyard, where creatures too badly injured to be able to survive in the wild make their homes. Two blind squirrels, Acorn and Walnut, scamper seemingly unhampered by their disability, the ravens Edgar and Leanore have not yet been heard to utter "Nevermore," and Azor, a frisky sparrow hawk whose wing was shot off with an air gun, preventing him from every flying again, peers out at visitors. You can view familiar and unfamiliar species through one-way glass as they convalesce.

Docent tours are offered at the center for school and after-school groups at $1 per child. Docent presentations in the classroom for $75 include live and taxidermied animals, slides, and a discussion of animal care and rehabilitation.

Library: There is a lending library of ecology books.

CHINA CAMP STATE PARK & MUSEUM*
North San Pedro Road, San Rafael
Phone: (415) 456-0766
Hours: Daily 10:00 a.m.–5:00 p.m.
Admission: $3.00 auto fee

The 1,640-acre China Camp State Park is located on the site of the last of the Chinese shrimp-fishing villages that thrived on San Francisco Bay in the 1880s. The pier and several of the village buildings have been restored. The small museum tells the story of the Chinese immigrants who made their livings here—nearly five hundred people lived in China Camp at one time. Today Frank Quan, a descendant of one of the original settlers, is the only resident. Quan still operates a fishing business, selling most of his catch for bait. Occasionally you can purchase delicious, fresh grass shrimp at the snack bar.

FALKIRK CULTURAL CENTER
1408 Mission Ave. at E Street, San Rafael
Phone: (415) 485-3328
Hours: Tues., Wed., Fri. 10:00 a.m.–4:30 p.m.; Thurs. 10:00 a.m.–
9:00 p.m.; Sat. 10:00 a.m.–1:00 p.m.
Admission: Free

The splendid Victorian mansion now known as Falkirk Cultural Center presents a thoroughly contemporary range of cultural exhibits and events. Photo by Thea Schrack, courtesy of Falkirk Cultural Center.

A splendid, 17-room, Queen Anne Victorian mansion set on an 11-acre garden estate, Falkirk was designed by Clinton Day, better known for the glorious and now-defunct City of Paris department store in San Francisco. If you like your historic houses with period furnishings, you may be disappointed. Excellent exhibits and programs presenting visual, performance, and literary works by regional and national artists should offer adequate compensation, not to mention the floor-to-ceiling stained glass windows, beautifully handcrafted fireplaces, rolling lawns studded with magnolias and towering oak trees, a reflecting pool, exotic Bunya-Bunya trees, the occasional herd of deer, and a historic, Gothic-arched greenhouse.

Library: The Falkirk Reading Room features Bay Area poetry and historic preservation literature.

Rental: The first floor of the mansion, the veranda, and gardens are available year-round for private parties, receptions, photography shoots, filming, and memorable weddings. Maximum capacity 125.

MARIN COUNTY HISTORICAL SOCIETY
1125 B Street at Mission, San Rafael
Phone: (415) 454-8538
Hours: Thurs.-Sat. 1:00-4:00 p.m.
Admission: Free

We were fortunate to have as our guide Bill Vanderbilt, whose grand-father built the 1879, two-story, Victorian Gothic house where the Marin County Historical Society now resides. Filled with artifacts, memorabilia, clothing, and the personal effects of Arctic explorer Louise Boyd, Warden Clinton Duffy of San Quentin, and other historic figures, this folksy museum gives you a lot of information about Marin County from its earliest settlers to recent days.

Library: Many Marin County documents, including old newspapers, deeds, journals, books, maps, and photographs, are available for research by appointment.

Gift Shop: This is the place to find Marin-related videos, photos, cards, books, and t-shirts.

MISSION SAN RAFAEL ARCANGEL*
1104 - 5th Avenue, San Rafael
Phone: (415) 454-8141
Hours: Daily 11:00 a.m.-4:00 p.m.
Admission: Free

Established in 1817, this was the only mission founded as a hospital, named for the angel of bodily healing. The current building, built in 1949, is a replica.

SAUSALITO

BAY AREA DISCOVERY MUSEUM
557 East Fort Baker, Sausalito
Phone: (415) 289-7268
Hours: Wed.-Sun. 10:00 a.m.-5:00 p.m., winter; Tues. Sun. 10:00 a.m.-5:00 p.m., summer.
Admission: $4.00, free first Thursday of the month.

Occupying a turn-of-the-century army fort and a new, two-story facility on seven acres of what is quite possibly the most spectacular piece of real estate in northern California, the Bay Area Discovery Museum offers hands-on exhibits guaranteed to delight children of all ages, but designed with one- to twelve-year-olds in mind.

Each exhibit contains a wealth of information about the world around us, but the educational aspect is as subtle and palatable as the vitamin D in an ice cream cone. Making discoveries is part of the action, as young

Kelvin Amos at the helm, at Sausalito's Bay Area Discovery Museum. Photo by David Allen, courtesy of Bay Area Discovery Museum.

visitors don hard hats and build a high-rise, crawl through an underwater tunnel, fish for salmon from a rocking boat, dissect a squid, pump gas into a Model T, dress up in fabulous costumes and perform on stage, make multi-track sound recordings, or create their own videos. The media center, with a broadcast studio and computer stations, and the Maze of Illusions, a funhouse of mirrors and holograms, were created to appeal to the more sophisticated, pre-teen set.

The modest scale of the old army buildings, which once housed a blacksmith shop, an ordnance storehouse, a bakery, a horse stable, and wagon shed, is ideal for pint-sized visitors. The location, a quiet cove directly under the Golden Gate Bridge, provides the perfect setting for picnics and nature walks. Take a ride on the foot-powered handmade carousel created especially for the museum by master carousel-maker Bill Dentzel.

Gift Shop: Children can find items for a dime and grown-ups will be delighted with the imaginative selection of books, games, and toys in the big, beautiful Discovery Store.

Rental: Kids can celebrate their birthdays in the colorful birthday party room. Hands-on theme parties tailored to each child's age and interests include art, science, or theater. The entire museum can be rented for parties after museum hours.

Restaurant: The Discovery Cafe offers a lunch menu for adults as well as children, and the food tastes great, too! Food is prepared to order, so don't wait until the kids are starving because there will probably be a line. Grown-ups can choose from savory homemade soup, vegetarian chili, sandwiches, and salads, all for about $5 or less. For the kids there's grilled cheese, hot dogs, and The Kid's Sandwich (peanut butter & jelly), all under $2.50. Muffins, cookies, and drinks are available for quick snacks.

HEADLANDS CENTER FOR THE ARTS
944 Fort Barry, Sausalito
Phone: (415) 331-2787
Hours: Tues.-Sun. noon-5:00 p.m.
Admission: Free

The primary focus of the Headlands Center for the Arts is an artist-in-residence program that provides studios and housing for local, national, and international artists and thinkers of all disciplines. The public has a chance to meet the artists and see their work at open studios held three times a year. The rest of the year, visitors can see the eleven historic army buildings and enjoy the spectacular natural beauty of the coastal setting.

Four major American artists, David Ireland, Anne Hamilton, Bruce Tomb, and John Randolph, participated in renovating the 1907 army barracks building that serves as the center's headquarters. It's worth a drive to the Headlands just to see these avant-garde renovations. My particular favorite is the unisex latrine—flying in the face of convention, the renovators used a chilly palate of gray steel and concrete, and amplified sound wherever possible.

Rental: Building 944 is available for film shoots, meetings, retreats, weddings, and events for up to 200 people.

THE MARINE MAMMAL CENTER★
Marin Headlands, Sausalito
Phone: (415) 289-SEAL
Hours: Daily 10:00 a.m.-4:00 p.m.
Admission: Free

The Marine Mammal Center rescues hundreds of sick and injured animals each year, and gives them round-the-clock care so they can be returned to their ocean homes. Although caring for and studying the animals is their primary focus, the Center welcomes visitors, who can view the recuperating patients and study the illustrated panels or participate in education programs.

SAN FRANCISCO BAY HYDRAULIC MODEL
2100 Bridgeway, Sausalito
Phone: (415) 332-3871
Hours: Tues.-Fri. 9:00 a.m.-4:00 p.m., Sat. & Sun. 10:00 a.m.-
6:00 p.m., summer; Tues.-Sat. 9:00 a.m.-4:00 p.m., winter.
Admission: Free

A great deal of effort has been put into making the Bay Model an interesting and educational attraction, but don't expect a replica of the San Francisco Bay with miniature bridges, tiny cars, and little people. Built in 1954 by the Army Corps of Engineers, this one-and-a-half-acre model reproduces the rise and fall of the bay's tides and the flow of the currents so that engineers, scientists, and planners can study problems that can't be solved by hypothetical thinking alone.

You can pick up a free, self-guided audio tour at the desk to learn everything you ever wanted to know about the ecology, biology, history, and water resources of the bay and the San Joaquin River delta. Depending on scheduled experiments, the model may not be operating.

In the beautiful and up-to-date Bay Model visitor center you will find an added bonus, "Marinship 1942-1945," a nostalgic exhibit developed by the Sausalito Historical Society and the Army Corps of Engineers to commemorate the remarkable shipyard located on this very site during World War II.

At up to 16 feet long and 5,000 pounds, the northern elephant seal (Mirounga angustirostris) is the largest seal in the northern hemisphere. Adult males have remarkable, foot-long snouts to amplify the threatening noises they make in battles for their "harems"— 85% of the pups come from only 4% of the males. Photo of elephant seal pup by Jane Oka, courtesy of The Marine Mammal Center.

The *Wapama*, a rugged steam schooner, and the *Hercules*, an ocean-going tug, are docked outside the Bay Model. Tours of the ships are available Saturdays at 11:00 a.m. and 12:30 p.m. Wear flat shoes. No children under 12 allowed.

Gift Shop: The Bay Model gift shop carries books, postcards, and maps.

SAUSALITO HISTORICAL SOCIETY MUSEUM*
420 Litho Street, Sausalito
Phone: (415) 289-4117
Hours: Wed. & Sat. 10:00 a.m.-2:00 p.m.
Admission: Free

Photographs and historical artifacts—some brought up from the bottom of the bay by scuba divers—filling two rooms and a hallway on the third floor of Sausalito's city hall make up the Sausalito Historical Society Museum. The Historical Society has also mounted an exhibit downtown in the Village Fair building at 777 Bridgeway.

STINSON BEACH

AUDUBON CANYON RANCH
4900 Highway One, Stinson Beach
Phone: (415) 868-9244
Hours: Sat., Sun., & holidays 10:00 a.m.-4:00 p.m., March-July.
Admission: Free

Every spring, great blue herons and great egrets return to the thousand-acre Bolinas Lagoon Preserve to nest atop the redwood trees. Visitors can watch the show through spotting scopes situated on lookout points, and what a show it is. The huge birds swoop in and settle in the tree tops. The male herons perform their showy mating dance, displaying the nuptial plumes on their necks and breasts and uttering eerie calls. Later, there will be eggs and chicks and the sight of the parent birds feeding their young. Although the egrets and herons are the main feature, the ranch offers a host of other natural wonders, including over ninety species of land birds, mammals, plants, and insects, and exhibits in the display hall, which is located in the converted milking barn— the sanctuary is a former dairy ranch. Displays include the heronry, the lagoon, plant communities, animal life, Native American culture, local 19th century history, and the San Andreas fault.

The ranch is open to the public on weekends and holidays, and to schools and other groups Tuesdays through Fridays by appointment. Some busing scholarships are available.

Travelling as they do in such huge numbers, water birds have developed special traits to stake out their individual places on the food chain. The snowy egret (Egretta thusa) attracts curious fish with its yellow toes. Photo by Clerin Zumwalt, courtesy of Audubon Canyon Ranch.

Gift Shop: The well-stocked bookstore carries field guides, binoculars, natural history books, and small gift items.

TIBURON

BELVEDERE–TIBURON LANDMARKS SOCIETY
1600 Juanita Lane, Tiburon
Phone: (415) 435-1853
**Hours: Mon.-Fri. 9:00 a.m.-4:00 p.m.; Sat. 9:00 a.m.-
   3:00 p.m.**
Admission: Free

The Belvedere–Tiburon Landmarks Society mounts four exhibitions a year in their large, light-filled, one-room gallery, featuring historic and local artists. The Society also oversees projects involving the preservation of local landmarks.

Gift Shop: This high class thrift shop/gift shop sells antiques and collectibles.

Old St. Hilary's, now a local history museum with a remarkable wildflower preserve. Courtesy of the Belvedere-Tiburon Landmarks Society.

OLD ST. HILARY'S CHURCH MUSEUM & ST. HILARY'S PRESERVE
via Beach Road at Tiburon Blvd., Tiburon
Phone: (415) 435-2251
Hours: Wed. & Sun. 1:00-4:00 p.m., April–October.
Admission: Free—donations accepted

Constructed of redwood in 1886, the deconsecrated Old St. Hilary's is one of the few 19th-century Carpenter Gothic churches to survive in its original condition and setting. Botanist John Howell described St. Hilary's Preserve as "one of the most interesting and remarkable and beautiful wildflower gardens in California (and therefore in all the world!)." The tiny wildflower garden, adjacent to the church, features 217 species of plants, including four rare and endangered species.

Rental: Old St. Hilary's is available for weddings and concerts.

UNKNOWN

THE UNKNOWN MUSEUM
Address unknown
Phone: (415) 383-2726

The Unknown Museum, "a treasure trove of everything your mother ever made you throw away," was once a cultural highlight of Marin County, but has been closed and the collection in storage since 1989. We were lucky enough to catch "This Is Your Life," an exhibition comprised of excerpts from the Unknown Museum at Falkirk Cultural Center in 1993. Words cannot convey the evocative power and nostalgic

What can you say about a mannequin bathing in hair rollers? For glimpses of everyday objects displayed in wacky and anthropologically revealing juxtaposition, seek out The Unknown Museum. Courtesy of Mickey McGowan.

thrill of Mickey McGowan's funky, frenetic, fantastic, funny-yet-serious recreation of everyone's childhood through massive accumulations of everyday objects displayed in wacky and witty juxtaposition. A mannequin in a bridal dress supine on a bed of rice, surrounded by bride and groom cake-toppers; a wall papered with board games; a reproduction of the Last Supper embellished with miniature beers and hot dogs; an aquarium of Mr. Potatoheads; and millions of other quotidian objects that surround us present, according to McGowan, the real answers to life's mysteries. If you are searching for the meaning of life, or just an afternoon of unparalleled entertainment, it is worth the effort to track down The Unknown Museum. Call or write Mickey McGowan at P.O. Box 1551, Mill Valley, CA 94942, telephone (415) 383-2726.

SOLANO COUNTY

BENICIA

BENICIA CAMEL BARN MUSEUM
2060 Camel Road, Benicia
Phone: (707) 745-5435
Hours: Wed.-Sun. 1:00-4:00 p.m.
Admission: Donation

Benicia's Camel Barn Museum derives its name from a little-known bit of American military history. In the 1850s, Secretary of War Jefferson Davis decided that camels would be ideal pack animals in the deserts of the Southwest. The U.S. Camel Corps, established with 78 camels imported from the Near East, used the animals to transport materiel and mail for ten years. At the outbreak of the Civil War the project was abandoned, and 35 camels were shipped up the coast of California to be auctioned off at the Benicia arsenal building. Although the camels were only in Benicia for forty days and were never housed in the arsenal, the name stuck.

Exhibits at the Camel Barn Museum focus on Benicia's local history and role in U.S. Army history. A large camel collection dramatizes the story of the failed Camel Corps. Permanent exhibits include a diorama of von Pfister's store, where, as the story goes, Sam Brannan first announced the discovery of gold. Housed in a graceful sandstone building with arched doors and window openings, the museum building is part of a complex consisting of two (misnamed) camel barns, the engine house, and a powder magazine.

Gift Shop: Camels of all descriptions, t-shirts, caps, books, paper dolls, and Civil War memorabilia are for sale in the gift shop.

BENICIA FIRE MUSEUM
160 Military West, Benicia
Phone: (707) 745-1688
Hours: First & third Sunday of the month, noon-5:00 p.m.
Admission: Free

The Benicia Fire Department, California's first, dates back to 1847, when the first fire engine arrived in the state. The Benicia Fire Museum may be small (1,500 square feet) but it's a fine resource for firefighting history, especially if Ron Rice shows you around. We learned from him why firemen traditionally wore red (the King of Holland decreed that red shirts should replace white as a reminder of the blood-soaked shirt of a courageous Dutch fireman), the iniquitous history of fire marks, and the fact that the first fire department in the United States was started in 1608. On display in the museum are an 1820 Phoenix with buffalo-hide hoses, an 1855 Solano Engine, and an 1860 Griffin, along with 7,000 hats from all the fire departments in California and a collection of antique water grenades and fire extinguishers.

BENICIA STATE CAPITOL HISTORIC PARK
First and G Streets, Benicia
Phone: (707) 745-3385
Hours: Daily 10:00 a.m.-5:00 p.m.
Admission: Adults $2.00, children $1.00 (also good for admission to the Fischer-Hanlon house)

The capital of California moved around a bit before finally settling in Sacramento. For a period of 13 months in 1853 and 1854, the seat of government was located in Benicia, a city founded in 1847 by Robert Semple, Thomas Larkin, and General Mariano Vallejo on Vallejo's land and named for his wife. In fierce competition with other cities to become the capital of California, Benicia set up a kiln to bake bricks, took masts from abandoned ships for columns, and paid laborers $16 a day (quite a princely sum in those days), and in three months' time had constructed a stately city hall intended to serve as the State Capitol. Although their tenure here was brief, the Legislature passed significant legislation—the first laws giving women property rights, the first fish and game laws in the country, and authorization for the construction of San Quentin Prison. The building has been completely restored, exactly as it was when the first session met, right down to the hats, quill pens, newspapers, and canes of the early legislators.

FISCHER-HANLON HOUSE & GARDENS
137 West G Street, Benicia
Phone: (707) 745-3385
Hours: House, Sat. & Sun. noon–3:30 p.m. Garden, daily 10:00 a.m.–
**   5:00 p.m.**
Admission: Adults $2.00, children $1.00 (also good for admission to
**   Benicia State Capitol)**

In 1856, Benicia merchant Joseph Fischer purchased the White House
Hotel, moved it to its present location next door to the Capitol building,
and converted it into his family residence. Three generations of Fischers
occupied the building until the last surviving Hanlon (nee Fischer)
donated the house and all its contents to the State in 1969. Family
treasures—a sea shell collection and a statue of Little Egypt from the 1898
Exposition—and household features like the linoleum carpet provide a
glimpse at Victorian life. Knowledgeable tour guides explain architectural
history and construction details.

Rental: The lovely, restored gardens may be rented for weddings and
special events.

FAIRFIELD

TRAVIS AIR FORCE MUSEUM
661 E Street, Bldg. 80, Fairfield
Phone: (707) 424-5605
Hours: Mon.-Fri. 9:00 a.m.-4:00 p.m.; Sat. 9:00 a.m.-5:00 p.m.;
**   Sun. noon-5:00 p.m. Closed federal holidays.**
Admission: Free

To receive an entry pass to enter Travis Air Force Base, the location of
the museum, you must present your driver's license and vehicle registration at the base's visitor center, but for aircraft enthusiasts it is well worth
the effort. Built in 1942 as a jumping-off point for the war in the Pacific,
Travis became a major aerial port, a role it continues to play today.
The museum, founded in 1986, focuses on Travis' role in military
aviation history. In the three and a half acres of outdoor exhibit space
you can examine thirty historic aircraft—bombers, fighters, transports,
helicopters, trainers, and observation craft.

The cavernous indoor museum is filled with photographs, uniforms,
aviation memorabilia, and historic exhibits. Kids will enjoy trying out the
T-37 navigator trainer and the Link flight simulator, as well as the large
model collection. Our favorite exhibit features the Gonzales No. 1
biplane, one of the first successful airplanes flown in the Bay Area.
Twins Willy and Arthur Gonzales built the plane of pine, spruce, and
bicycle spokes in their backyard, using photos and drawings as models.

Because San Francisco prohibited flying machines within the city limits, the Gonzales boys would dismantle the plane, pack it up in crates, and move it by train to the town of Woodland, where they would do their flying, experimenting, or whatever they had to do until they ran out of gas or food. The Gonzales brothers later operated a flying school and aircraft manufacturing business from their home, although it is not known if they ever had a student or ever sold a plane.

Gift Shop: The large gift shop has every kind of aircraft-related item you could imagine—books, models, mugs, shirts, even astronaut munchies.

WRIGHT MUSEUM OF SPACE ACTION
732 Ohio Street, Fairfield
Hours: By appointment
Admission: Free

While sitting in an orchard one day, Isaac Newton saw an apple fall to the ground and discovered gravity—a force that comes from the earth and *pulls* things down. This is what we all learned in school, right? According to Walter Wright, Newton was wrong. Gravity is a *push,* not a pull. For the past twenty-five years, Wright, a retired electrical engineer, has been trying to convince the world that his push-gravity theory is the correct one. In his Museum of Space Action, the funkiest of home-grown museums, housed in two rooms in the back of his modest, suburban home, Mr. Wright has constructed more than fifty colorful models to prove his theory. Despite his patient explanations, most of Mr. Wright's demonstrations were over my head. However Mr. Wright has received rave reviews for his television and classroom appearances. "If Wright is correct, his ideas would put him in a class with Copernicus, Darwin, and Einstein," wrote one UPI reporter. I suggest you make an appointment to visit the Wright Museum of Space Action and decide for yourself.

VALLEJO

MARINE WORLD AFRICA USA
Marine World Parkway, Vallejo
Phone: (707) 644-4000 or 643-ORCA
Hours: Wed.-Sun. 9:30 a.m.-5:00 p.m.; Memorial Day–Labor Day,
**   daily 9:30 a.m.-6:30 p.m.**
Admission: Adults $23.95, seniors (60+) $19.95, children 4-12
** $16.95, children 3 and under free.**

Situated about 30 miles northeast of San Francisco, Marine World Africa USA bears little resemblance to the original marine theme park that opened in Redwood City in 1968. Although it maintains that glossy, commercial feel (and the high ticket price), the park has developed into

A trainer at Marine World Africa USA feeds a very large, hand-raised Bengal tiger milk out of a carton. Photo by Darryl W. Bush, courtesy of Marine World Africa USA.

a unique wildlife park and oceanarium whose goal is to educate the public about wildlife and environmental issues, and whose educational philosophy maintains that learning should be fun. There's no denying, this place is great fun. Although extremely skeptical at first about the educational value, I was soon converted.

It's impossible to take in all the sights in one day. The best bet is to arrive early and decide which of the eight animal shows to attend, select from more than a dozen exhibit areas, and leave time to chat with the trainers and meet and touch the animals (two-day passes are also available). We selected for our first stop the exquisite Butterfly World, home to over 500 free-flying butterflies from all over the world. On Tiger Island, we were so fascinated by the sight of hand-raised Bengal tigers and one young lioness playing, wrestling, and relaxing with their trainers and even drinking milk out of a carton that we stayed and stayed. We couldn't miss the $5.5 million Shark Experience, so we got on the moving walkway that carried us into a clear acrylic tunnel through a 300,000-gallon tropical reef habitat, with sharks and fish swimming over and alongside of us. The Aquarium, with its hands-on tide pool and tropical and California coast displays of more than 2,000 fish, was another must-see. Families with small children will want to save time for "Dinosaurs! A Prehistoric Adventure," open through October 1994 and featuring over 20 moving, roaring, "living," robotic dinosaurs, with a supporting cast of all the big name fellows and starring the 24-foot tall, 47-foot long Tyrannosaurus rex.

Gift Shop: There are many opportunities to purchase souvenirs, including the main gift shop just inside the entrance gate, and specialty shops adjacent to Butterfly World, Shark Experience, Elephant Encounter, and inside Dinosaurs. Most sell film, fine gifts, clothing, and souvenirs. Numerous merchandise kiosks and other specialty shops are located throughout the park.

Restaurants:
Lakeside Market: An array of restaurants featuring fried chicken, deli sandwiches, Asian food, nachos, french fries, corn dogs, soft drinks, beer, and wine.
The Broiler: Hamburgers, hot dogs, grilled chicken sandwiches, fries, sodas, desserts.
Mobe's: Fish & chips, chicken strips, salads.
Tacos: South of the border cuisine.
Pizza Safari: Pizza, Caesar salad.
Clock Tower Cafe: Oudoor restaurant (open spring/summer).
Kiosks, snack carts, and drink stands can be found throughout the park.

VALLEJO NAVAL & HISTORICAL MUSEUM
734 Marin Street, Vallejo
Phone: (707) 643-0077
Hours: Tues.-Fri. 10:00 a.m.-4:30 p.m.; Sat. 11:00 a.m.-4:30 p.m.
Admission: Adults $1.50, seniors & students 75¢

Misled by the name, many people think of the Vallejo Naval & Historical
Museum as a maritime museum. While it does a splendid job of interpreting the history of the Navy at Mare Island, this fine museum has much
more to offer. Located in downtown Vallejo in the former city hall, an
imposing 1927 Italian Renaissance Revival building designed by Charles
Perry, the museum occupies over 25,000 square feet, with five galleries
on three levels. Works from the permanent collection, sixty percent of
which document Vallejo's community history, are displayed in two
imaginatively conceived and well-designed thematic exhibits a year;
exhibits are not "just a bunch of neat stuff that people can look at,"
but an interpretation of local history through the visual arts and historic
artifacts. A newly-opened Community Gallery invites community groups
to display their collections.

In 1853 Mare Island became the first naval base in the western United
States and David Farragut, famous for his Civil War battle cry, "Damn
the torpedoes—full speed ahead!" its first commandant. The Staircase of
Sea Power, dominated by a 1/4-scale model of the bow of USS *Saginaw,*
the first ship built at Mare Island (in 1859), features the Museum's
showpiece, a working submarine periscope installed through the roof.
Visitors can rotate the periscope for a 360-degree view of the city and
Mare Island.

Library: Open for research by appointment, the library contains the city
archives and an extensive naval history collection.

Gift Shop: The unusual museum bookstore offers not only educational
materials in support of the museum's mission, but also a complete
selection of the latest popular fiction and non-fiction.

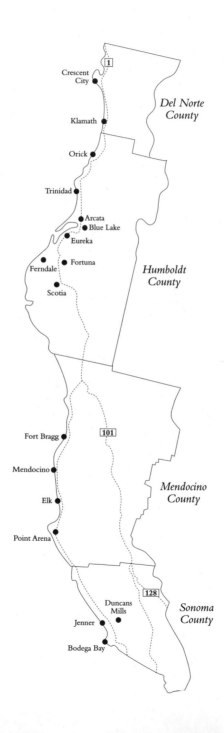

North Coast

DEL NORTE COUNTY

CRESCENT CITY

BATTERY POINT LIGHTHOUSE
Battery Point Island, Crescent City
Phone: (707) 464-3089
Hours: Wed.–Sun. 10:00 a.m.–4:00 p.m., summers only.
Admission: Adults $2.00, children 50¢

Battery Point Lighthouse sits on the highest point of Battery Point Island, a solid hunk of rock measuring about three quarters of an acre, three hundred yards from the mainland. The only way to get to this 1856 historical landmark is to walk across the rocky ocean floor when the tide is out and climb another two hundred yards to the little Cape Cod-style lighthouse. Sturdy shoes are a must.

Jerry and Nadine Tugel, the lighthouse keepers, will give you a guided tour that includes a history of the lighthouse, a visit to the lantern room upstairs, and a stop in the small museum. The lighthouse beacon, a 375-mm Drumm lens reactivated in 1982, can be seen fourteen miles out at sea. An earlier light, a fourth order Fresnal lens, is on view in the museum. The tour even includes a walk through the Tugels' own living quarters, furnished with a few prize artifacts. Among them are a working banjo clock issued to the lighthouse in 1857 and, for the kids, a pirate's treasure chest filled with candy.

Library: A small corner of the museum holds the lighthouse archives, with keepers' logs and lighthouse history books.

Gift Shop: You can purchase cards, lighthouse memorabilia, and monographs by Nadine Tugel, current keeper.

DEL NORTE COUNTY HISTORICAL SOCIETY MUSEUM
577 H Street, Crescent City
Phone: (707) 464-3922
Hours: Mon.-Sat. 10:00 a.m.-4:00 p.m., May through September.
Admission: Adults $1.50, children (under 12) 50¢

An exhibit of Victorian women's fashions on display behind cell bars reminds visitors that the Del Norte County Historical Society Museum building was originally the county jail. Today it chronicles the history of California's northernmost county with a staggering number of artifacts, photographs, and personal memorabilia. Every aspect of county life is represented; farming, logging, mining, and railroad equipment document Del Norte industries, while beautiful period rooms, an extensive quilt collection, vintage fashions, musical instruments, and a country kitchen recall the past. A 19th century lens, eighteen feet high, from the St. George Reef lighthouse serves as a reminder of the treachery of the sea along the rugged Del Norte coast. Photographs and clippings document the 1964 tsunami (tidal wave) that devastated Crescent City.

The museum has a splendid collection of Native American baskets, recently cleaned and restored. Two rooms dedicated to Native Americans feature the core collection of beautiful baskets of local origin (Yurok, Tolowa, Hupa, Karuk) and photo carousels filled with images of local Native American residents.

Library: Archives include photographs, clippings, articles, books, newspapers, the Book of Memories, and more.

Gift Shop: A small counter display of books, mugs, and items pertaining to the county.

NORTHCOAST MARINE MAMMAL CENTER
424 Howe Drive, Crescent City
Phone: (707) 465-6265
Hours: Summer daily 10:00 a.m.-5:00 p.m.; winter hours vary.
Admission: Free

Injured seals, sea lions, and other marine mammals recuperate in specially-designed tanks at the Northcoast Marine Mammal Center. Visitors can watch feedings three times a day and see the animals returned to the ocean when their recovery is complete.

Gift Shop: Stocks items with a marine mammal theme.

RELLIM DEMONSTRATION FOREST
Hamilton Road, Crescent City
Phone: (707) 464 3144
Hours: Daily 9:00 a.m.–5:00 p.m.
Admission: Free

Sixty-five million years ago, when dinosaurs roamed the earth, groves of towering redwood trees extended over much of the northern hemisphere. These giants with massive trunks and skyscraping tops outlived the dinosaurs and survived the Ice Age. What they almost didn't survive was human beings. During the California Gold Rush, the search for new routes to the gold mines led men to the redwood forests. The first mills appeared in the 1850s, and trees that had taken centuries to grow were cut down. By the turn of the century, the old forests that once seemed inexhaustible were decimated. In 1918, the Save the Redwoods League began its efforts. State and national parks were established, and rules and restrictions began to be imposed upon the timber industry.

The Rellim Demonstration Forest is one of many in the region, through which timber companies tell their side of the story and acquaint the public with the aims and methods of industrial forest management. At the entrance to the forest, a modern redwood building exhibits tools and photographs of early logging and of the modern lumber industry. Pick up a printed tour guide and follow the trail: signs will help you identify dozens of plants, shrubs, and trees, as well as skid roads down which logs were dragged, abandoned rigging cable, and a fallen tree with baby trees sprouting from its trunk.

UNDERSEA WORLD
304 Highway 101 South, Crescent City
Phone: (707) 464-3522
Hours: Daily 8:00 a.m.–8:00 p.m., until September 15; 9:00 a.m.–
**   5:00 p.m., winter.**
Admission: Adults $5.95, seniors & teens $4.95, children $2.95

This may look like just another roadside attraction, but a visit to Crescent City's Undersea World can be both educational and fun. Your guide on the required 45-minute tour will tell you all about the varieties of marine life—perch, ling cod, flounder, crab, eels, leopard shark—that inhabit several large aquaria in the bottom of a landed ship. (It used to be a floating aquarium, but it kept drifting off.) The hands-on component of the tour includes a tide pool, feeling a shark skin, and patting a large octopus. The tour ends with an opportunity to toss a fish to Ralph and Elliot, two playful, 1,000-pound sea lions. (Crescent City's little Undersea World is currently being sued by Anheuser-Busch Corporation, owners of Sea World, to change their name. Whatever the new name, the location will stay the same.)

Gift Shop: Billed as the complete sea shop, this large gift shop stocks shells, star charts, shark bags, books, t-shirts, and a host of ocean-related gift items.

KLAMATH

TREES OF MYSTERY
END OF THE TRAIL INDIAN MUSEUM
Highway 101, Klamath
Phone: (707) 482-2251
Hours: Daily 8:00 a.m.–8:00 p.m. (dawn to dusk)
Admission: Museum free; Trees of Mystery: adults $6.00, seniors $4.00, children 6-12 $3.00.

The 49-foot-tall Paul Bunyan at the Trees of Mystery does justice to, or perhaps even exceeds the myth of the giant logger and his blue ox, Babe. Enticed by the statues, children may learn something along the Trail of Mysterious Trees or in the End of the Trail Museum. Courtesy of Trees of Mystery.

Enthralled by the talking, winking, waving, 49-foot-tall Paul Bunyan, kids will insist on stopping at the Trees of Mystery. Adults will be delighted to discover that despite its resemblance to a tacky roadside attraction (although a spotlessly clean and beautifully landscaped one) there is more to see here than figures carved out of redwood with chain saws; here is the perfect opportunity to put into practice the trade-off theory of family museum-going.

First, something for the kids. Enter through the hollow log and follow the Trail of Mysterious Trees (actually illustrating arboreal methods of survival) and the Trail of Tall Tales—recorded music and stories illustrated by figures carved out of redwood.

Then, a visit to the enormous gift shop will lead past miles of merchandise to the End of the Trail Museum, where adults (and children, too) can enjoy one of the finest private collections of Native American arts in the country. Marylee Thompson Smith began collecting in 1946,

when her interest in Native American arts was sparked by local women wearing beautiful basket hats. Today her collection is on display in floor-to-ceiling glass cases, in a large, well-lit museum with five rooms, each representing a geographic area of the United States.

The focal point of the museum is the collection of baskets and ceremonial garments of the local people, mainly Yurok, Tolowa, Hupa, and Karuk. Using the materials at hand: hazel and willow sticks, spruce and willow roots, grasses, ferns, bark, and porcupine quills, the women of the area wove, and continue to weave, baskets for every use, from kitchen utensils to huge storage baskets. Smith has gathered some fine examples. Also displayed are beautiful buckskin dresses, adorned with shells, seeds, and braided beargrass, which occasionally leave the museum to be worn by local women in ceremonial dances. The collection also includes a unique gathering of cradleboards from 25 different North American tribes, and several Edward Curtis "Gold Tones" photographs depicting Native Americans in the first half of this century.

Gift Shop: The enormous gift shop sells handcrafted items, redwood furniture, rain sticks, and tourist-type gifts—over 12,000 items.

HUMBOLDT COUNTY

ARCATA

HUMBOLDT STATE UNIVERSITY NATURAL HISTORY MUSEUM
1315 G Street, Arcata
Phone: (707) 826-4479
Hours: Tues.-Sat. 10:00 a.m.-4:00 p.m.
Admission: Free

Visitors are often surprised to find a world-class natural history museum in a town the size of Arcata—the Maloney Fossil Collection consists of about 2,000 mint-condition specimens that represent life from 570 million years ago to modern times across the spectrum of plant and animal forms, from every continent on Earth except Antarctica. Tom and Hilda Maloney, professional fossil collectors and brokers for 25 years, supplied museums around the world with specimens, always keeping the very best for themselves. When the Maloneys' personal collection became available, major museums vied to acquire it, but because the Maloneys wanted the entire collection to be on view to the public and not hidden away in storage, Humboldt State University walked away with the prize.

Paleontologists agree that the museum owns some pretty rare stuff, including the full skeleton of a mesosaur, a two-foot-long, freshwater reptile that died out about 250 million years ago. Found both in Africa and South America, mesosaur fossils substantiate the theory of continental drift. Most of the exhibits are under glass, but the wall-mounted dinosaur tail that can be touched and discovery boxes that can be checked out for examination are favorites with kids.

Natural history exhibits include a butterfly collection containing examples of 75% of northern California's butterfly species and a display of shells of northern California. Rotating art exhibits display botanical drawings and other works with a natural history theme.

Gift Shop: The gift shop offers a fine selection of natural history books, field guides, posters, and kid-pleasing gift items.

PHILLIPS HOUSE MUSEUM
7th and Union Streets, Arcata
Phone: (707) 822-4722
Hours: Sun. noon-4:00 p.m. and by appointment.
Admission: Donation

Dating from the 1850s, the recently-restored Phillips House is the probably the oldest house in Arcata. Humboldt County's newest museum, an unpretentious farmhouse, has been furnished as it might have been in the 1880s, with the exception of the 1930s kitchen, a jewel of a room. Occupied

"A jewel of a room," this 1930s kitchen is the most modern room in the unpretentious Arcata farmhouse recently restored as the Phillips House Museum. Courtesy of Phillips House Museum.

continuously until the 1970s, the house was the site of some rip-roaring goings on—you can still see where a musket ball was fired into a wall. The best view of Arcata in town is from the back porch.

BLUE LAKE

BLUE LAKE MUSEUM
330 Railroad Avenue, Blue Lake
Phone: (707) 668-5752
Hours: Tues., Wed. 1:00-4:00 p.m., Sun. noon-4:00 p.m., April–Sept.
Admission: Free

If I were ever to give up the excitement of big city life it would be for Blue Lake. Among the many charms of this beautifully preserved Victorian town is the Blue Lake Museum. The volunteers who put the museum together attended classes in museum science, which resulted in a happy combination of big city professionalism and small-town folksiness.

The museum is housed in the meticulously restored 1893 train depot. The Railroad Room pays homage to the Arcata and Mad River Railroad, a 12-mile-long common carrier that operated between 1854 and 1983, earning more money per mile of track than any other railroad in the country during the lumber boom after World War II. Also featured is the now defunct resort town of Korbel, founded by the Korbels of champagne fame. A hallway housing temporary exhibits leads to the main exhibition room, where the history of the town is told. Yurok and Hupa baskets and utensils represent the first inhabitants of the area. Displays of household articles and equipment used in logging recreate the work and home life of a past century. Be sure to ask the docent to tell you the story of the wooden wheelbarrow that served as Blue Lake's first garbage truck.

Library: The Documents Room is a good place to research local history with local genealogy charts, photographs, school yearbooks, scrapbooks, and back issues of the *Blue Lake Advocate.*

Gift Shop: The Blue Lake Museum Cookbook, hats, cups, plates, and other logo items are available.

EUREKA

BLUE OX MILLWORKS
Foot of X Street, Eureka
Phone: (707) 444-3437
Hours: Mon.-Sat. 9:00 a.m.-5:00 p.m., Sun. 11:00 a.m.-4:00 p.m.
Admission: Adults $5.00, seniors $4.00, children $2.50

When the federal government hosted a conference on the timber industry, President Clinton and Vice President Gore invited Eric Hollenbeck. "I went and told them whose hog ate the cabbage," said Hollenbeck, a logger, millwright, blacksmith, plasterer, poet, modern-day Renaissance man, and co-owner, with his wife Viviana, of the Blue Ox Millworks. Not exactly your run-of-the-mill mill, Blue Ox is the last historically-accurate "job shop" in the country; they turn out made-to-order Victorian millwork, going from the log to the finished product using fully operational machinery dating from 1852 to 1940. This is a working museum (complete with sawdust, wood chips, and noise) preserving the old way of doing things and educating visitors about the history of the timber business.

The largest of the museum buildings is the mill proper, an 8,000-square-foot, 1904 industrial building that formerly housed the North Mountain Power Plant, which burned redwood trees for power. Visitors can watch men and machinery in action from a series of paths and landings. If things aren't too busy, Viviana Hollenbeck may demonstrate the oldest tool in the mill, an 1852 picket pointer, which can turn a piece of wood into a Victorian picket in seconds. A working blacksmith shop forges parts for antique machinery, and the plaster shop turns out ceiling medallions, composition moldings, and picture rails using a lost technique Hollenbeck rediscovered. Four buildings from a 1919 "skid town" were relocated to the site and will be restored to house the museum gift shop, a bunk house, and a theater offering classes and lectures as well as videos on the history of logging.

The Hollenbecks are planning hands-on programs that will allow visitors to work with craftspeople, creating objects to take home. Longer-term classes, workshops, and full apprenticeship programs will also be offered in woodworking, pottery, glassblowing, blacksmithing, etc.—call for current schedules and prices.

At the Blue Ox Millworks, you can watch made-to-order Victorian millwork in progress in the last historically accurate "job shop" in the country. You may also want to look into the hands-on workshops, classes, and apprenticeships they offer. Photo by J. Patrick Cudahy, courtesy of Blue Ox Millworks.

CLARKE MEMORIAL MUSEUM
3rd and E Streets, Eureka
Phone: (707) 443-1947
Hours: Tues.-Sat. noon-4:00 p.m.
Admission: Free—donations accepted

Everyone is a collector at heart. When a personal collection outgrows
its home, the owner may lend or donate it to the local historical society,
and another small town museum is born. Eureka High School teacher
and eclectic collector Cecile Clarke went one step further: she purchased
the palatial Bank of Eureka building and founded the Clarke Memorial
Museum. The 1912 marble and granite, Italian Renaissance-style
building is considered the largest historical artifact in the museum's
collection. The collections inside range from charming curiosities to
works of major import. The museum staff has the wisdom to display
them accordingly.

Clarke's collections of gems and minerals, cut crystal, and stuffed birds
are exhibited in cases reminiscent of early cabinets of curiosities. Nineteenth century paintings are hung salon-style, and furniture is arranged
in period rooms. The museum's collection of Native American artifacts,
including one of the most complete and extensive collections of Hupa,
Yurok, and Karuk dance regalia, stonework, and baskets in the world,
is displayed in state-of-the-art exhibits in a special wing added in 1979.
In the rest of the museum, exhibits of shipbuilding, logging, milling,
and maritime trade represent the history of Humboldt County industry.
A 1901 drugstore interior, a fine collection of antique duck-hunting guns,
vintage fashions, quilts, and "Eureka at the Movies" recall 19th and early
20th century life.

FORT HUMBOLDT STATE HISTORIC PARK
LOGGING MUSEUM
3431 Fort Avenue, Eureka
Phone: (707) 445-6567
Hours: Daily 9:00 a.m.-5:00 p.m.
Admission: Free

Established in 1853 to protect settlers, Fort Humboldt was abandoned by
the United States government as a military post after thirteen years. Its
major claim to fame is the fact that a Captain Sam Grant, better known
as U.S. Grant, was stationed there. The one remaining original building,
an 1863 hospital, has been restored to serve as a museum. Future plans
call for the complete restoration of the fort.

Currently located at the north end of the park is the Logging Museum,
consisting of informational panels recounting logging history in the
Redwood Empire, an outdoor logging display, and two restored and
working steam locomotives. Active children will love this outdoor

museum, where they can enjoy a furnished logger's cabin and large-scale
logging machinery, and plenty of space to run around. The State hopes
to move the museum to a more appropriate site and establish an interna-
tional-scale California State Logging Museum.

ROMANO GABRIEL SCULPTURE GARDEN
315 Second Street, Eureka
Hours: Always on view
Admission: Free

Tucked away in a brick-walled
triangle between a restaurant and
a bank, the Romano Gabriel
Sculpture Garden delights
children and adults alike. Over
a period of thirty years, Italian-
born Eureka resident Romano
Gabriel filled his front yard with
hundreds of amazing, brilliantly
colored sculptures. This imaginative jumble includes fanciful
objects, like the Ferris wheel

with flower-filled Mason jars for riders, animated with motors;
satirical sculptures, like the Italian Salami Tree; and a host of people,
angels, and imaginary creatures. The work of the reclusive carpenter/
gardener has been designated an important piece of folk art by the
California Arts Council.

Romano Gabriel built this startling and lively sculpture garden in his thirty-by-sixty-foot front yard in downtown Eureka over a period of some thirty years. An introvert, he used this medium to express his opinions about contemporary people, events, religion, and politics. Courtesy of Eureka Redevelopment Agency.

HUMBOLDT ARTS COUNCIL GALLERY
214 E Street, Eureka
Phone: (707) 442-2611
Hours: Tues.-Sat. noon-5:00 p.m.
Admission: Free

The Humboldt Arts Coucil Gallery exhibits painting, sculpture, and other
visual arts that reflect the cultural diversity of California's northwest.

HUMBOLDT BAY MARITIME MUSEUM
1410 Second Street, Eureka
Phone: (707) 444-9440
Hours: Daily 11:00 a.m.-4:00 p.m.
Admission: Free

Housed in a replica of the McFarlan House, a sea captain's home that was
the oldest house in Eureka, the Humboldt Bay Maritime Museum is
packed with maritime relics. The walls are plastered from floor to ceiling

with curled photographs and yellowed newspaper clippings documenting the hundreds of marine disasters that occurred in treacherous Humboldt Bay from 1850 to 1975. A porthole from the cruiser USS. *Milwaukee*, the anchor from the tug *Ranger*, and a five-ton buoy manufactured in 1907 are some of the shipwreck remains salvaged by museum members for display. You will also see a fourth order Fresnal lens, old navigational instruments, a radio direction finder, an early radar unit, cork and glass floats, ship-building tools, and a beautiful private rowing skiff that once belonged to lumber baron William Carson.

The museum operates the tour boat *Madaket*, the oldest continuously operating ferry boat in California.

SAMOA COOKHOUSE MUSEUM
Off US 101, across the Samoa Bridge, Eureka
Phone: (707) 442-1659
Hours: Daily 6:00 a.m.-3:30 p.m., 5:00-9:00 p.m.
Admission: Free

In the heyday of the logging industry, every logging camp had a cookhouse which provided hard-working loggers with three hot meals a day, except for a cold Sunday supper. Food was served family-style on long, oilcloth-covered tables with mismatched chairs. Today, visitors can relive the past at the Samoa Cookhouse, the last logging camp cookhouse in the West, which looks much as it did in 1885. A small museum features logging relics, cookhouse artifacts, and an assortment of historical aparati from old hair dryers and curling irons to a PBX machine, a washing machine, and ancient office equipment.

Gift Shop: The Christmas Wreath Gift Shop sells ornaments and Christmas items.

Restaurant: The food is the thing at the Samoa Cookhouse; the museum takes a back seat to the family-style restaurant. Breakfast, lunch, and dinner are served at long tables in a huge room with an open kitchen. Eat all you can. The price is fixed according to your age (3-6 years, 7-11 years, adult) from about $3.50 to $6.00 for breakfast or lunch, and $4.45, $6.95, or $10.95 for dinner. Milk is 95¢ extra. Lunch and dinner include soup, salad with choice of dressing, a meat entree, lots of home-made white bread, and of course, dessert. We ate a lunch of hearty vegetable beef soup, fresh iceberg lettuce salad, roasted turkey with all the trimmings (dressing, string beans, and mashed potatoes), and vanilla custard topped with lots of whipped cream for dessert. Coffee and iced tea are included.

FERNDALE

FERNDALE MUSEUM
Third & Shaw Streets, Ferndale
Phone: (707) 786-4466
Hours: Tues.-Sat. 11:00 a.m.-4:00 p.m., Sun. 1:00-4:00 p.m.;
closed January.
Admission: Adults $1.00, children 6-16 50¢, under 6 free

Founded in 1852 by two brothers looking for good farmland, Ferndale
soon became a thriving dairy community, known as the Cream City
and populated with lavish Victorian homes known as Butterfat Palaces.
Largely unchanged since the 1800s, the entire town of Ferndale has been
designated a State Historical Landmark.

In the early 1970s the Arts Council of Ferndale decided to build
a museum, although none of the members had any museum experience.
With a little bit of luck and a lot of persistence they managed to enlist
the services of a Canadian museum consultant, finagle their way into
a conference sponsored by the Smithsonian Institution for professionals,
and convince the County to donate a building. As a result, Ferndale has
a first-rate museum created and staffed by volunteers.

Housed in the old County maintenance barns, the Ferndale Museum
displays artifacts that were used by early residents. Exhibits include
Victorian rooms and shops, a player piano, and working crank telephones. An annex houses a blacksmith shop, farm and dairy equipment,
and a variety of tools. A working, vintage 1900 Bosch-Omori seismograph donated by the University of California at Berkeley is read daily.
The original reading of the 1906 earthquake printed on smoked paper
hangs on the wall nearby.

Library: The research library, open by appointment, has a complete
collection of the *Ferndale Enterprise* from 1878 to present on microfilm,
and oral histories of long-time residents on tape.

Gift Shop: The small lobby shop sells books and pamphlets on local
history, cards, prints, homemade jams and jellies, and handcrafted items.

KINETIC SCULPTURE MUSEUM
580 Main Street, Ferndale
Phone: (707) 725-3851
Hours; Daily 9:30 a.m.-5:00 p.m.
Admission: Free

The annual Arcata to Ferndale Cross-Country Kinetic Sculpture Race
has been featured in national television shows, numerous magazines,
and even in the film "If It's Fun." Started in 1969 by Ferndale artist
Hobart Brown, the three-day race must be among the world's zaniest

competitions: it features bizarre, handmade, people-powered machines that must traverse sand dunes, highways, Humboldt Bay, and the Eel River. The machines that survive the grueling ordeal are on view in the Kinetic Sculpture Museum, a 7,500-square-foot, warehouse-like space.

The exhibits change every year with each race, but the high level of art and insanity coupled with engineering sophistication and careful fabrication remain constant. The incredible moving sculptures, composed for the most part of bicycle, motorcycle, and power lawnmower parts, take such unlikely forms as iguanas, dinosaurs, flying saucers, giant slippers, and insects. Machines in progress are visible behind a wall made of bicycle parts.

FORTUNA

CHAPMAN'S GEM AND MINERAL SHOP AND MUSEUM
Highway 101, 4 miles south of Fortuna
**Hours: Mon.-Sat. 10:00 a.m.-5:00 p.m., Sun. 1:00-5:00 p.m., May-
    September. Closed Tuesdays and major holidays in winter.**
Phone: (707) 725-4732
Admission: Free

The quintessential roadside attraction, Chapman's Gem and Mineral Shop and Museum allots 3,000 square feet for each component. The shop sells jewelry, agates, rough rocks, lapidary supplies, fossils, and minerals. The museum features Warren Chapman's private collection of agates, petrified stones, petrified palms, animal and plant fossils, crystals, and Native American and pre-Columbian artifacts. A safe builder by trade, Chapman has created a kid-pleasing vault to house the valuable cut stone collection. A velvet-curtained fluorescent display room contains a shining assortment of glow-in-the-dark minerals. Chapman has been assembling this collection since 1936.

FORTUNA DEPOT MUSEUM
4 Park Street, Fortuna
Phone: (707) 725-2495
**Hours: Daily noon-4:30 p.m., June-September; Wed.-Sun. noon-
    4:30 p.m., September-June.**
Admission: Free

Housed in the restored 1893 Northwestern Pacific Train Depot in Rohner Park, the Fortuna Depot Museum displays a conglomeration of articles too numerous to mention. Mannequins so startlingly lifelike that I mistook them for real people inhabit the train room, which is filled with train memorabilia, including a toy train from the thirties. The major collections, most accumulated by local residents, include fishing gear, locks, spark plugs, tools, typewriters and business machines, dolls, hats, police patches, and a large barbed wire collection. Exhibits change to coincide with the Fortuna Rodeo and Autorama, and to allow the curator to display the museum's large collection of vintage fashions.

Library: A researcher's dream for local area newspapers, maps, city records, photos, and high school yearbooks from 1906 to present.

Gift Shop: The tiny gift shop sells train memorabilia and country items.

ORICK

STONE LAGOON SCHOOLHOUSE MUSEUM
Redwood Trails Campground, Highway 101, Orick
Phone: (707) 488-2061
Hours: Daily 10:00 a.m.-6:00 p.m., April–October
Admission: Free

A hundred years ago, one-room schoolhouses like the little redwood Stone Lagoon Schoolhouse were a common sight across the country. Today, they are a rare sight indeed. Built in 1897, the Stone Lagoon Schoolhouse was an active center of learning and community activity until 1956, when the last class was held and the building was abandoned. Relocated and restored, the schoolhouse had been furnished "the way it was" by Orick residents.

SCOTIA

SCOTIA MUSEUM
Main Street, Scotia
Phone: (707) 764-2222
Hours: Daily 8:00 a.m.-4:00 p.m., summer
Admission: Free

The Scotia Museum is housed in a 1920s Parthenon look-alike constructed entirely of redwood, including the columns. Owned and operated by the Pacific Lumber Company, the logging museum offers sedate displays of photographs, products from redwood, and logging equipment, including a steam locomotive outside. This is also the place to pick up your pass and directions printed on a piece of redwood to tour Mill B, the largest redwood sawmill in the country, where the real action is. Yellow signs and arrows direct you on this self-guided tour up stairways to overhead walkways from which you can see and hear the giant pieces of machinery in operation. Begin with the mill pond, proceed to the hydraulic barker, where high-powered water jets blast the bark off the logs, then see the sawmill, and end your tour in the lumber products factory.

The town of Scotia is a fascinating relic itself—one of the few company towns left, with housing for families of 270 company employees. Many original buildings, constructed more than a hundred years ago, are intact and a new shopping center is being built.

TRINIDAD

HUMBOLDT STATE UNIVERSITY MARINE LAB
Edwards & Ewing, Trinidad
Phone: (707) 826-3671
Hours: Mon.-Fri. 9:00 a.m.-5:00 p.m.
Admission: Free

Although the primary mission of the marine lab is teaching and research, Humboldt State University does allow the public access to two hallways featuring exhibits on coastal marine life, and aquaria with fresh and salt-water creatures. A sign at the entrance advises visitors to take notes so they can answer the computer quiz at the end. Outside, kids can visit starfish, anemones, and other sea creatures in the touch tank, while grown-ups examine the Schatz Solar Hydrogen Project, which aims to demonstrate that solar hydrogen is a reliable and abundant energy source.

PATRICK'S POINT STATE PARK—SUMEG INDIAN VILLAGE
4150 Patrick Point Drive, Trinidad
Phone: (707) 677-3570
Hours: Daily 8:00 a.m.-6:00 p.m.
Admission: $5.00 parking fee

Sumeg Village, a historically accurate Yurok village, was created in 1990 to revive and carry on Yurok cultural traditions and spirituality, and for public education. Located amidst the 640 acres of forest and meadow-covered headlands of Patrick's Point State Park, the village includes a redwood house like the ones in which Yurok women and children traditionally slept; a sweat house, used for purification rituals and slept in by men and older boys; and a Brush Dance pit, which is now used for demonstrations of traditional skills and ceremonial dances. Plants used by the Yurok people for basketry, food, and medicines are growing in the neighboring native plant garden.

TRINIDAD MUSEUM
529B Trinity Street, Trinidad
Phone: (707) 677-3883
Hours: Fri.-Sun. 1:00-4:00 p.m., May–October; or by appointment.
Admission: Free

The small Trinidad Museum concentrates on the natural history and first inhabitants of the area. A mural depicts the native Yurok people making a dugout canoe. Displays include Native American artifacts and a large collection of freeze-dried mushrooms. A native plant garden encircles the building.

MENDOCINO COUNTY

ELK

GREENWOOD CREEK STATE BEACH VISITOR CENTER
Highway 1, Elk
Phone: (707) 877-3458 or (707) 937-5804
Hours: Call for hours.
Admission: Free

Once a roaring mill town called Greenwood, the tiny hamlet of Elk is the site of Greenwood Creek State Beach, 47 acres of headlands offering spectacular views and fishing, diving, and picnic facilities. A new visitor center will open in 1994 in the 1917 Goodyear Redwood Company mill office building on the headland, with exhibits on local history. When we visited, an artist was at work at the mill office, painting a mural of the town as it was when sailing ships came in to collect lumber. On the north side of the building is the old Elk Post Office, which was founded in 1887 and operated in this location until 1994. Thanks to a donation from the U.S. Postal Service, the old post office will become a museum, preserved as it was on the day it closed.

FORT BRAGG

THE GUEST HOUSE MUSEUM
343 North Main Street, Fort Bragg
Phone: (707) 961-2840
Hours: Wed.-Sun. 10:00 a.m.-2:00 p.m., April-October;
Sat. 10:00 a.m.-2:00 p.m., November-March.
Admission: Free

The three-story redwood Victorian built in 1892 has always held a certain mystique for citizens of Fort Bragg. In the days when this was strictly a company town, the house was a symbol of the rich, namely the owners and executives of Union Lumber Company. Designed by local architect A.T. Carmichael for Union Lumber founder C.R. Johnson, the building served as the family residence until 1912. It was used as a guest house for friends and business associates until 1969, when the company was sold to Boise Cascade. Today, the gracious old matriarch of downtown belongs to the city of Fort Bragg, and is used as a museum and repository for historical pictures, artifacts, and records. Although she could use a coat of paint, her good bones show through in the twelve-foot ceilings, decorative moldings, fireplaces, marble basins, and stunning stained glass window. Each room documents an aspect of Fort Bragg's history: transportation, logging, milling, and everyday life.

The museum's larger artifacts are displayed in Fort Bragg Depot, which is across the street (401 N. Main Street), adjacent to the Skunk Train Depot. Sitting amidst the retail shops and restaurants you will find logging equipment and historic trains, including "Daisy," the restored Forny engine in use from 1885 to 1945.

MENDOCINO COAST BOTANICAL GARDENS
18220 North Highway 1, Fort Bragg
Phone: (707) 964-4352
Hours: Daily 9:00 a.m.-5:00 p.m., summer; 9:00 a.m.-4:00 p.m., winter.
Admission: General $5.00, seniors $4.00, students and juniors $3.00, under 12 free

The 47-acre Mendocino Coast Botanical Gardens include formal gardens, a wild-flower meadow, a heather collection, a coastal pine forest, bluffs overlooking the Pacific Ocean, and this lush, green, fern-filled canyon.
Courtesy of Mendocino Coast Botanical Gardens.

A garden for all seasons, the 47-acre Mendocino Coast Botanical Gardens offers something for every kind of gardener—manicured formal gardens, a wildflower meadow, a dense coastal pine forest, a lush, fern-covered canyon, coastal bluffs overlooking the pounding Pacific Ocean. Whale fanciers can take shelter in the Cliff House to watch for gray whales during their winter and spring migrations; bird watchers can identify the eighty species of birds that live in or visit the gardens. Serious botanists can visit the American Ivy Society Standard Reference Collection and the premier heather collection. Rosarians will enjoy a collection of old-fashioned roses in the fenced Heritage Rose Garden.

Founded in 1961 by retired nurseryman Ernest Schoefer, the gardens were purchased by the Mendocino Coast Recreation and Park District in 1992. A small staff and hundreds of dedicated volunteers are constantly at work—salvaging an old apple orchard, moving the iris garden to a sunnier spot, adding twenty new species to the spectacular heather garden, or deadheading the dahlias—but they are always willing to answer questions. Picnickers and small wedding parties are welcome. Two electric carts are available at no charge for those with special needs. Plan to spend at least a couple of hours. If it rains, you can borrow an umbrella.

Gift Shop: In addition to the retail nursery, the garden shop carries a good selection of gardening books, supplies, and seeds, and beautiful t-shirts, aprons, and pillows.

MENDOCINO

FORD HOUSE VISITOR CENTER AND MUSEUM
Main Street, Mendocino
Phone: (707) 937-5397
Hours: Mon.-Fri. 10:40 a.m.-4:30 p.m.; Sat. 11:00 a.m.-4:00 p.m.;
   Sun. noon-4:00 p.m.
Admission: Free

When the clipper ship *Frolic* sank off the coast of Mendocino, mill owner
Henry Meiggs sent Jerome Bursley Ford to find the ship and salvage the
cargo. Ford returned with something even more
lucrative, the report of a vast forest of huge redwood
trees. Meiggs sent him back to Mendocino to find a
site for a sawmill. By 1854, Ford was part owner of
the new mill on the Mendocino headlands, and the
proud possessor of the second house built in
Mendocino. The Fords and their six children lived
in this house until 1872. One hundred years later,
the house and surrounding property became part of
the Mendocino Headlands State Park.

Ford House, which now serves as the visitor
center for the park, interprets the beautiful natural
environment and the history of the area. A local craftsman is responsible
for the wonderfully detailed models of Mendocino in the year 1890,
including a logging industry skid road and the ingenious apron chute used
to get logs from the shore to the ships. Changing exhibits feature seasonal
displays of natural history (seaweed, bats) and works by local artists with
an environmental theme.

THE KELLEY HOUSE MUSEUM
45007 Albion Street, Mendocino
Phone: (707) 937-5791
Hours: Daily 1:00-4:00 p.m., May–September; Mon.-Fri. 1:00-
   4:00 p.m., October–April.
Admission: $1.00

William Henry Kelley, a native of Prince Edward Island, Canada, arrived
in Mendocino as a ship's carpenter in 1850 on the brig that brought the
first mill. By 1861 he had purchased almost all of the Mendocino peninsula for the sum of $2,650, entered into various business ventures,
journeyed back to Prince Edward Island to fetch a bride, and built
a home for his family.

The two-story Kelley House, its gardens and spring-fed duck pond
located on three-quarters of an acre between Main and Albion Streets,

*In 1850, after a
career in the opium
trade, the clipper
ship* Frolic *ran
aground off Point
Cabrillo. The ship
was mostly ignored
from the 1880s
until the 1960s,
when divers began
to salvage what
remained of the
cargo. The Kelley
House, Mendocino
County Museum,
and the Grace
Hudson Museum
are collaborating on
exhibits featuring
the* Frolic. *Cour-
tesy of The Kelley
House Museum.*

houses the museum. Two exhibits a year explore aspects of Mendocino County history; the theme coordinates with a book published each year by Mendocino Historical Research. In 1994 the Kelley House will host an exhibit on the 1850 *Frolic* shipwreck in conjunction with the Grace Hudson Museum in Ukiah and the Mendocino County Museum in Willits.

Library: The reference library and archives, run by Mendocino Historical Research, Inc., have the most extensive collection of documents, records, genealogical data, historic photographs, books, and other artifacts pertaining to the ethnic, economic, and social history of Mendocino County in existence. Research, by appointment, is encouraged.

Gift Shop: Sells publications of Mendocino Historical Research.

POINT ARENA

POINT ARENA LIGHTHOUSE AND MUSEUM
Lighthouse Road, Point Arena
Phone: (707) 882-2777
Hours: Daily 11:00 a.m.–2:30 p.m.; weekends only Thanksgiving
through Christmas.
Admission: Adults $2.00, children 50¢

The 115-foot-tall Point Arena Lighthouse was built in 1908 to replace the original 1870 structure, which was irreparably damaged in the 1906 earthquake. The company hired to build the new, earthquake-proof lighthouse had experience building factory smokestacks, which accounts for the unusual design. Today, energetic visitors who climb the 145 stairs to the top will be greeted with a spectacular view of the coastline and the two-ton, first order Fresnel lens. Over six feet in diameter, with 666 hand-ground glass parts, the lens literally floats on a bath of mercury contained in a large tub. The lens, which once relied on oil lamps for light, was retired in 1977 and replaced with an automated aircraft-type beacon.

In the museum housed in the 1869 Fog Signal Building you will see, along with other historical artifacts and photographs, the compressed air foghorn which was retired in 1976. The many-windowed Whale Watching Room offers a perfect site for gazing out at gray whales when they are migrating.

Rental: Three furnished, three-bedroom, two-bath houses, built on the property for lighthouse keepers, are rented out.

SONOMA COUNTY

BODEGA BAY

BODEGA MARINE LABORATORY
Bay Flat Road, Bodega Bay
Phone: (707) 875-2211
**Hours: Fri. 2:00–4:00 p.m. Group tours by appointment on Tues. &
   Thurs. (maximum 40 visitors/tour).**
Admission: $1.00

As a unit of the University of California with the primary function of
conducting research in population biology and ecology, cell and develop-
mental biology, and aquaculture and fisheries, the Bodega Marine
Laboratory is not generally open to the public. However, if you drop by
on a Friday afternoon between 2:00 and 4:00, a docent will take you on
a tour of the facility, which includes numerous aquaria, greenhouses, and
an algae/shellfish culture lab. The setting, the spectacular rocky coast of
Bodega harbor, is one of the most scenic locations on the northern
California coast.

Library: The library collection consists of journals, monographs, photographs, maps, charts, atlases, technical reports, and more than 2,300
student reports.

DUNCANS MILLS

DUNCANS MILLS MUSEUM
Moscow Road, Route 116, Duncans Mills
Phone: (707) 865-1424
Hours: Sat. 10:00 a.m., by appointment.
Admission: Free

Duncans Mills, population 20 or 85, depending upon which side of town
you enter from, is more a restored Victorian shopping center than a real
town. Once a thriving mill town, it was established in the 1860s by the
Duncan brothers, Alexander and Samuel, who had built a mill at what is
now Bridgehaven in 1862. The Duncan brothers brought the mill into
town in 1877, and the North Pacific Coast Railroad followed. From the
1890s through the 1920s Duncans Mills was a mecca for tourists from all
over California. The last train left town in 1935, and by 1970 Duncans
Mills consisted of not much more than a few ramshackle buildings. In
1971 Duncans Mills Trading Company bought and slowly restored the
original buildings that were still standing and built new ones in the same
early California style. The Trading Company has also restored several
local railroad cars and is presently working on a new acquisition, the
North Pacific Coast Caboose #2.

The restored 1909 Northwestern Pacific Railroad Depot won the Best Restoration of the Year award from the Conference of California Historical Societies in 1972. It now houses the Duncans Mills Museum, which is filled with a rather haphazard assortment of local relics. It's difficult to know exactly what the artifacts represent, as there are no signs or brochures, but visitors are welcome to touch them and soak up the old-time atmosphere. David Ferreira, whose office is in the depot, described a busload of students on a museum tour who fell in love with the place at once: "Wow! This is great. This place is dusty!" they exclaimed. "How does it feel—how does it smell—rub against the old stove and get a bit dirty," is Ferreira's advice.

JENNER

FORT ROSS STATE HISTORIC PARK
19005 Coast Highway 1, Jenner
Phone: (707) 847-3285
Hours: Daily 10:00 a.m.–4:30 p.m.
Admission: $5.00 per private vehicle

The first Russian Orthodox structure in North America, the chapel at Fort Ross served the colony of hunters and traders who settled here to grow food for their Alaskan holdings and hunt sea otters. Courtesy of California State Parks.

In 1812, a commercial hunting and trading company chartered by the tsar of Russia arrived on the Sonoma coast; the Russian-American Company was to establish a colony to grow food for their Alaskan holdings, and to hunt profitable sea otters. The settlement, named Ross from Rossiia (the word for Russia) was constructed along the lines of the traditional stockades found in Siberia and Alaska. For the next thirty years, Fort Ross represented the southernmost point of Russia's adventure into North America. By 1841, the sea otters had been virtually wiped out and the colony's agricultural efforts proved insufficient to supply the company's Alaskan holdings. Fort Ross was sold to John Sutter for $30,000.

Although most of the fort was destroyed in the 1906 earthquake, the State has done an excellent job of recreating ten of the original buildings. The chapel, the first Russian Orthodox structure in North America, reconstructed as it was in 1825, is still used for Orthodox religious services every Memorial Day and Fourth of July.

The museum, located in the stunning new visitor center at the entrance to the park, presents an excellent graphic interpretation of the area's first inhabitants, the Kashaya Pomo, as well as the Russian occupation and the early American ranching period. Plan to spend at least half an hour at the museum to acquaint yourself with the history of the area before exploring the buildings of the fort.

Park staff and volunteers dressed in Russian costumes enact a typical day as it may have been in the early 19th century on the last Saturday of July, when Fort Ross celebrates Living History Day.

Gift Shop: In addition to the usual selection of books, the gift shop has a unique stock of Russian gift items, including Matreska (stacking dolls), lacquerware, and folk scarves.

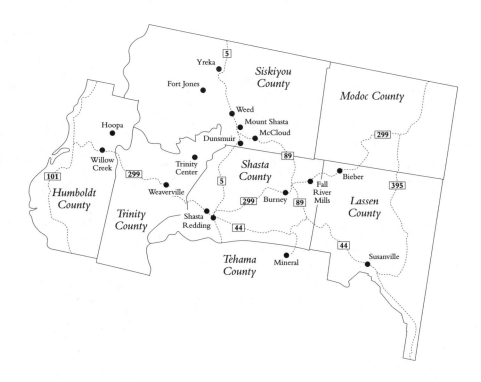

Trinity-Shasta-Lassen

HUMBOLDT COUNTY

HOOPA

HOOPA TRIBAL MUSEUM
Hoopa Shopping Mall, Hoopa
Phone: (916) 625-4410
Hours: Mon.-Fri. 8:00 a.m.-5:00 p.m., all year; Sat. 9:00 a.m.-
   4:00 p.m., May-September.
Admission: Free

For generations receding into prehistory, the Hupa people have lived along the Trinity River, gathering willow roots, hazel shoots, bear grass, and wild iris to make the baskets they used for cooking, storage, carrying babies, and ceremonial dances. Today many Hupa baskets, along with ceremonial regalia, redwood dugout canoes, and tools used by the Hupa and other local tribes are on display in glass cases in the Hoopa Tribal Museum. Most of the collections—some containing rare baskets dating back seven hundred years—are on loan from members of the local community. Exhibits are changed periodically to allow the baskets' spirits to move around, and many artifacts are taken out to participate in the traditional tribal ceremonies. As the curator explained to us, "It took time and love to make these baskets, which were meant to be used every day. If they sit unused, the colors start to fade because the spirit begins to die. But when they are dancing, the spirit still lives." The Hupa religion, language, songs, and dances are part of a living culture passed down from generation to generation, and the tribally owned and operated museum is a "living museum."

Acorns were once a staple food almost everywhere in California. Here, a Hupa woman, Mrs. Freddie, demonstrates how to leech the bitter taste out of acorn flour by pouring water through it. Traditional tools and baskets are displayed at the tribal museum on the Hoopa Reservation. Courtesy of Hearst Museum of Anthropology.

Ask to see the video "Where the Trail Returns," developed by the tribe to document their traditions and tribal government.

Library: Limited access to the archives.

Gift Shop: Changing selection of one-of-a-kind pieces by local artists and craftspeople.

WILLOW CREEK

WILLOW CREEK–CHINA FLAT MUSEUM
Hwy 299 behind the Flame Restaurant, Willow Creek
Phone: (916) 629-2653
Hours: Fri.-Sun. 10:00 a.m.-4:00 p.m., May through September.
Admission: Free

"Seven years ago we started losing old people in the valley, and some of us older folks who are history buffs started getting scared, because the new generation looked upon a lot of this as junk. People were too young; they weren't into their cultural history. So we hunted all these old things down and opened the museum." Thus was created the Willow Creek–China Flat Museum, a two-room history museum displaying artifacts related to the Trinity Valley.

Exhibits include Native American baskets on loan from local families, a display of native medicinal plants, mining memorabilia from old gold mine claims, and artifacts from the now-vanished Chinese community. A gravity-fed gas pump and cash register recall bygone days of the Gambi resort. Wallace Beebe's violin serves as a reminder of Saturday night hoedowns. Displays in the living history case change annually to feature mementos contributed by local families. Large farming and mining implements are on view in the back room.

Gift Shop: Don't pass up the jams and jellies made by museum members. Also available are local history books, t-shirts, and hats.

TRINITY COUNTY

TRINITY CENTER

SCOTT MUSEUM
Trinity Center
Phone: (916) 266-3378
Hours: Tues.-Sun. 1:00-5:00 p.m., May 15 to September 15.
Admission: Free

Set in a grove of cedar trees overlooking Trinity Lake, its broad front porch supported by natural oak pillars and furnished with rustic chairs, a handsome brick building houses Trinity Center's Scott Museum. Edwin Scott, a Trinity County pioneer, founded the museum in 1967, donating

the land, the building, and its contents in order to show future generations how the pioneers lived. Inside the massive handmade front door
are carefully labeled and displayed artifacts of Scott's past (he died at the
age of 96 in 1989): his slate and slate pencil from the one-room school
he attended, household items he grew up with, and the largest collection
of barbed wire in the country, with 500 of the 700 known patents
represented. Outdoor exhibits include old buggies and wagons and
a blacksmith shop.

WEAVERVILLE

J.J. JACKSON MEMORIAL MUSEUM
Trinity County Historical Park
508 Main Street, Weaverville
Phone: (916) 623-5211
Hours: Daily 10:00 a.m.–5:00 p.m., May through October; noon–
**   4:00 p.m., April and November.**
Admission: Free

The handsome brick building looks right at home on Weaverville's
historic Main Street, even though it was constructed fairly recently
(1968). Starting with fossils and rocks from Trinity County's prehistory,
the 5,000-square-foot J.J. Jackson Memorial Museum displays artifacts
and photos to dramatize the lives and events of the people who inhabited
the county—Wiyot Indians, pioneers, miners, Chinese residents—right
up to the pair of shoes local teacher Gail Jones wore when she ran the
Boston Marathon in 1988. Kay Jackson provided the core of the museum's
large collection when he left his collection of antique firearms in the care
of his brother Jake while he went off to fight in World War I. In addition
to the usual bottles, tools, household items, garments and such, there are
reminders of the area's less worthy moments: weapons from the 1854
tong war, during which white residents stood on the sidelines and egged
on the participants in the hopes of seeing more blood; photographs of
two young Native American girls, sole survivors of the massacre at
Natural Bridge; and relocated jail cells with prisoners' graffiti intact.

An old ditch tender's cabin has been relocated to the museum grounds.
The museum has also relocated and restored an original Weaverville
blacksmith shop, Max Lang's tin shop, and a two-stamp mill built in 1904
to crush gold-bearing ore at the Paymaster gold mine. The stamp mill and
the blacksmith and tin shops are fully operational and are fired up for
special demonstrations.

Library: The reference library has old schoolbooks, photo albums, and
books on the history of Trinity County.

Gift Shop: Homemade jams and jellies and gold-panning equipment are
among the items you will find on the shelves here.

WEAVERVILLE JOSS HOUSE STATE HISTORIC PARK
Oregon & Main Streets, Weaverville
Phone: (916) 623-5284 & 938-5050
Hours: Daily 10:00 a.m.-5:00 p.m.
Admission: $2.00

"The Temple of the Forest Beneath the Clouds" read the Chinese characters over the door of the Weaverville Joss House. The oldest continuously used Taoist worship site in the western hemisphere was built in 1874 to replace another that had burned. Visitors cross a wooden bridge in the quiet park to reach the temple, whose facade is painted bright blue with white lines to resemble the tile on the temple's Chinese prototype. Two large doors open to disclose two more doors, "spirit screens" to keep out evil spirits, which can only go in straight lines. On the small wooden table before the altar, visitors may see incense, candles, and offerings of food and paper money left by Chinese worshippers, who come to the temple from all over California. Attached to the temple building are a Chinese courtroom and temple attendants' quarters. A small museum in the modern visitor center displays Chinese art objects, pictures, mining tools, and wrought iron weapons used in the 1854 tong war.

SISKIYOU COUNTY

DUNSMUIR

DUNSMUIR MUSEUM★
4101 Pine Street, Dunsmuir
Phone: (916) 235-0733
Hours: Wed.-Sun. 10:00 a.m.-3:00 p.m., summer. Closed after
  Labor Day for the winter.
Admission: Free

Located in the Old Weed Hotel (1904), Dunsmuir Museum tells the story of the town's railroad past. Other exhibits feature a 1919 Western Electric telephone switchboard, Native American artifacts, clothing, furniture, office equipment, cameras, and skis.

FORT JONES

FORT JONES MUSEUM
11913 Main Street, Fort Jones
Phone: (916) 465-5125
Hours: Mon.-Fri. 10:00 a.m.-4:00 p.m., summer
Admission: Free

The Fort Jones Museum was built in 1947 to display an excellent collection of Native American baskets and artifacts. Other items, added to depict the lives and activities of trappers, miners, explorers, soldiers, and settlers, include a period kitchen and the bedroom belonging to Mr. and Mrs. Ernest Reichman when they started housekeeping in 1890. Photographs and calling cards of Scott Valley beaux of 1877 to 1880 are one of the more unusual photo carousel displays. But the most unusual artifact of all is the museum building itself. The stone structure was built on an old brewery framework with native material from Siskiyou County. Imbedded in the walls are, among other items, a whole truck-load of mortars, pestles, and grinding plates plowed up a hundred years ago on the old Campbell Ranch, petrified wood, chunks of meteorites, sparkling slabs of iron pyrite, quartz, black obsidian, jade, and marble. There are grist mill stones made in France and shipped around Cape Horn, "shell rock" patterned with fossilized fish, snails, and mollusks, and a Pelton wheel. Embedded in the north wall is the famous two-ton soapstone Rain Rock used by the Shasta tribe to produce rain and snow. Legend says it will rain and snow all summer unless the rock is covered.

FORT JONES CARRIAGE HOUSE
Sterling & E Street, Fort Jones
Hours: Mon.-Fri. 10:00 a.m.-4:00 p.m., summer
Admission: Free

The carriage house contains seven horse-drawn vehicles, including a harvester, and other relics.

MOUNT SHASTA

SISSON MUSEUM
3 Old Shasta State Road, Mount Shasta
Phone: (916) 926-5508
Hours: Daily 10:00 a.m.-5:00 p.m., summer; noon-4:00 p.m., winter.
Admission: Free

The Sisson Museum owes much of its appeal to its unique location on the grounds of the Mount Shasta Hatchery. The oldest remaining hatchery building, built in 1909, houses the museum's exhibits exploring the history of Mount Shasta City and surrounding areas. Science and natural history displays include a seismograph, exhibits on the weather conditions on the 14,162 foot Mount Shasta, a volcanic rock collection, and a mural depicting native wildlife. There are also a turn-of-the-century parlor, a pharmacy, a post office, a 1915 Ford fire engine, photographs, and paintings.

The museum is, naturally, a repository for information about Mount Shasta Hatchery, the oldest operating fish hatchery in the West, in production since 1888. Pick up a brochure for a self-guided tour of the hatchery. Hundreds of thousands of trout in all stages of growth fill the ponds. In summer you can feed them with food provided on site. Check the fall and winter schedule for the fascinating spawning days.

McCLOUD

HERITAGE JUNCTION OF McCLOUD HISTORIC CENTER*
320 Main Street, McCloud
Phone: (916) 964-2604 or 964-2626
Hours: Tues.-Sat. 11:00 a.m.-3:00 p.m., Sun. 1:00-3:00 p.m.,
**   summer; by appointment in winter.**
Admission: Free

A turn-of-the-century building houses a large collection of logging industry memorabilia, including the 1903 Corliss engine that once powered the McCloud Steam Log Mill and created steam to heat the business buildings and executives' homes. Early firefighting equipment and office equipment, and clothing and accessories from the 1850s to the early 1900s are also on view.

Photo of Corliss engine by John and Naomi Brazier, courtesy of Heritage Museum.

WEED

WEED HISTORIC LUMBER TOWN MUSEUM
303 Gilman Avenue, Weed
Phone: (916) 938-2352
Hours; Thurs.-Mon. 10:00 a.m.-4:00 p.m., summer; by appointment
**   in winter.**
Admission: Free

Abner Weed, an early lumber baron, gave his name to the town and linked its future to the lumber industry. Until 1960, Weed was a company town—housing, store, theater, restaurant, the works were owned by Long Bell Lumber Company, who paid their workers in company scrip. The Roseburg Mill, which employs 150 workers, is the only mill still in operation today, but you can learn all about the local lumber industry from the turn of the century to the present in the folksy Weed Historic Lumber Town Museum. The museum is housed in the unimposing 1930s municipal building, which once served as courthouse and jail. A few jail cells have been turned into period rooms, and the chief of police's office is now an old-fashioned bedroom. One cell and the booking room remain as they were. A more recent annex displays a stagecoach from the Overland Express, a 1923 fire engine, a wine-making exhibit contributed by Weed's Italian community, and the de rigueur blacksmith shop, which functions as a lesson to youngsters that "…in them days you didn't go to a hardware shop to buy your tools—you made them or somebody made them for you."

YREKA

KLAMATH NATIONAL FOREST INTERPRETIVE MUSEUM
1312 Fairlane Road, Yreka
Phone: (916) 842-6131
Hours: Mon.-Fri. 8:00 a.m.-4:00 p.m.
Admission: Free

The handsome headquarters of the Klamath National Forest also contains
the Klamath National Forest Interpretive Museum. Visitors are invited
to tour the museum and the building—a helpful brochure will guide you
through the hallway exhibits. The centerpiece of the one-room museum
is a model lookout tower, complete with a hands-on Bosworth fire
finder. Surrounding exhibits and photo displays present information on
timber and fire management, wildlife, recreation, watershed, and the like.
Exhibits along the first-floor hallways feature works of local artists and
collectors. The second-floor hallways showcase historic posters and maps,
timber-cutting equipment, and telephones, radios, and communication
equipment of yesteryear. Forest Service employees occasionally look up
from their desks to bestow a welcoming smile.

Library: The non-circulating reference library has materials on
archaeology, timber, fire, logging, and a complete set of the Code
of Federal Regulations.

Gift Shop: You can purchase books, t-shirts, hats, belt buckles, etc.
in the lobby.

SISKIYOU COUNTY MUSEUM
910 South Main Street, Yreka
Phone: (916) 842-3836
Hours: Mon.-Sat. 9:00 a.m.-5:00 p.m., summer; Tues.-Sat.
**   9:00 a.m.-5:00 p.m., winter.**
Admission: Adults $1.00, children 7-12 75¢

The Siskiyou County Museum was built in 1950 to display the county's
vast collection of historical artifacts. For more than forty years, nothing
changed in the folksy institution, until the present director came on
board. Today you will find the museum undergoing extensive remodeling, in transition from the old cabinet-of-curiosities style to a modern
interpretive museum. The two styles of museumship are represented in
the 8,200 square feet of exhibition space. The downstairs galleries offer
viewers state-of-the-art exhibits interpreting the cultures of the area's
Shasta and Karuk tribes, and fur trapping. Agriculture, lumbering, gold
mining, and 20th century history are presented in the upstairs galleries
in the best of the old style, with old-fashioned cases full of artifacts,
and charming period rooms.

Open only in summer, the 2-1/2 acre Outdoor Museum features half a dozen restored or replicated buildings, an herb garden, and large mining and agricultural equipment. Visitors can tour the original one-room Spring School, a blacksmith shop, a smokehouse, an early rancher's cabin, a hard rock miner's cabin, and the first Catholic church in the area.

The Christmas Candlelight Tour, held weekends after Thanksgiving with costumed historical interpretation, period food, and the museum orchestra, is an event you won't want to miss.

Library: Photographs, manuscripts, books, newspapers, printed ephemera, maps, and an extensive clipping file are available for research.

Gift Shop: Denny Bar Mercantile Company sells old-fashioned candy, handmade quilts, jewelry, and other 19th-century-style merchandise in summer. Books, jewelry, and small mementos are for sale in the museum year-round.

SHASTA COUNTY

BURNEY

McARTHUR–BURNEY FALLS MEMORIAL PARK
VISITOR CENTER
24898 Hwy 89, Burney
Phone: (916) 335-2777
Hours: Daily 8:00 a.m.-dusk, June-October.
Admission: $5.00 auto

The tiny log cabin (12 by 20 feet) built in 1934 by the Civilian Conservation Corps features an exhibit of the plant and animal life to be found in the park, with hands-on exhibits for kids. The park's stellar attraction is the 129-foot-high waterfall, over which 100 million gallons of water flow every day.

FALL RIVER MILLS

FORT CROOK MUSEUM*
Fort Crook Avenue, Fall River Mills
Phone: (916) 336-5110
Hours: Tues.-Sun. noon-4:00 p.m., May through October.
Admission: Free

The Fort Crook Historical Society built the Fort Crook Museum to "preserve the past for the future." Six small buildings, including a one-room schoolhouse, homesteader's cabin, old jail house and old equipment building, display items of interest such as Fall River Valley's first motor coach, a dugout canoe, firearms, Native American baskets, and a host of books, Bibles, scrapbooks and photographs that tell the area's history.

SHASTA

SHASTA STATE HISTORIC PARK
SR 299, Shasta
Phone: (916) 243-8194
Hours: Thurs.-Mon. 10:00 a.m.-5:00 p.m., summer; Fri.-Sun.
10:00 a.m.-5:00 p.m., winter.

In 1855, you could walk the streets of Shasta, referred to as "Queen City of the North," and witness a Gold Rush town at the peak of prosperity, with five hotels, five stagecoach companies, three bookstores, seven general stores, and so on. By the turn of the century, Shasta, like many California mining towns, had become an abandoned, crumbling ghost town. Thanks to the efforts of the preservation-minded Shasta Historical Society, the remarkable Mae Helene Bacon Boggs, and the California State Parks, you can now visit renovated or reconstructed historic buildings and, with guidebook in hand, learn the histories of other, abandoned brick buildings.

The State, as usual, has done an outstanding job of meticulous restoration and scholarly interpretation, bringing the past to life for today's visitors. But, the unusual—the truly extraordinary—item that makes Shasta stand out from the rest of the historic parks is the Boggs Collection. This premier collection of three hundred paintings by California artists spans a hundred-year period, from the old masters to more contemporary times. In her hundred-year life span, Mrs. Boggs, an intelligent, original woman, was involved in women's suffrage, spearheaded the San Francisco Panama Pacific Exposition of 1914, was responsible for the State's acquisition of Shasta Historic Park, and assembled one of the finest collections of California art in the state. On permanent display at the Courthouse Museum are one hundred paintings, including works by Thaddeus Welch, Gideon Jacques Denny, Enoch Pery, Edwin Deakin, William Keith, Maynard Dixon, and Grace Hudson, and a striking portrait of John Sutter by Emmanuel Leutze.

Buildings from Shasta, once the "Queen City of the North," have been restored by the California State Parks system, and paintings from the collection of Mae Helene Bacon Boggs are on display at the Courthouse Museum. Photo of Shasta ca. 1860 courtesy of Shasta State Historic Park.

Gift Shop: The Litsch Store, in a late 1800s general store museum setting, displays the original Litsch inventory of goods. Staffed by park volunteers, it is presently open weekends from noon to 4:00 p.m., May through October.

TEHAMA COUNTY

MINERAL

LOOMIS MUSEUM★
Lassen Volcanic National Park
Park Road (Highway 89), 39 miles outside Mineral
Phone: (916) 595-4444
Hours: Daily 9:00 a.m.–5:00 p.m., summer.
Admission: Park entrance $5.00 per auto

The Loomis Museum recently reopened after a twenty-year hiatus. The historic structure, built of native volcanic rock in the 1920s, was believed to be located in a rock avalanche hazard zone. Up-to-date information from the United States Geological Survey indicates that the museum is out of the rock fall zone and safe for day use.

In addition to a park information station and audio visual programs screened in the auditorium, the highlights of the museum are the B.F. Loomis exhibit of photographs of the Lassen Peak eruption taken by Loomis between 1915 and 1917, and an interactive volcano exhibit. This first-class exhibit, developed by Redding's Carter House Natural History Museum, is a real kid-pleaser.

Gift Shop: A bookstore sells printed matter on the natural and cultural history of the park.

Lassen Peak (10,457') is at the southern end of the Cascade Range, of which Mount Saint Helens is presently the most notable member. Lassen last erupted in 1917, but there is still plenty of geothermal activity in the area. B.F. Loomis photo courtesy of National Park Service.

LASSEN COUNTY

BIEBER

BIG VALLEY HISTORICAL MUSEUM★
Pumpkin Center Road, Bieber
Phone: (916) 294-5368
Hours: Tues.–Thurs. 1:00–4:00 p.m., May 1–October 1.
Admission: Free

Big Valley Historical Museum serves the three small towns of Bieber, Adin, and Lookout. Although we didn't get a chance to visit the museum, we were assured by Erma Conley, the curator-cleaning lady, that it really is pretty nice. The museum, she informed us, has a little bit of everything—old dishes, guns, Pit River baskets, quilts, arrowheads, and ladies' hats and garments, all well-arranged in glass cases or hanging on the walls.

SUSANVILLE

LASSEN HISTORICAL MUSEUM*
75 North Weatherlow Street, Susanville
Phone: (916) 257-3292
Hours: Mon.-Fri. 10:00 a.m.-4:00 p.m., May 1–November 1.
Admission: Free

In the 1940s, local Explorer Scouts gathered artifacts on the trails and constructed a log building (with a little help from the community) to house them. The two-room Lassen Historical Museum displays artifacts from early Lassen County, including farm and logging equipment, household goods, Native American artifacts, and early photographs. Next door to the museum is the town's original trading post, Roop's Fort, which was owned by Isaac Roop, governor of the Provisional Territory of Nevada and Nataqua. Susanville is named for his daughter.

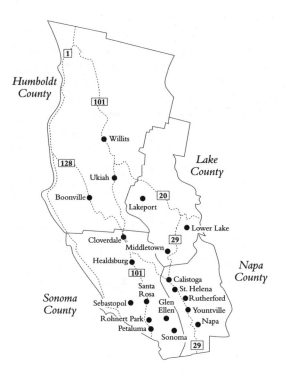

Humboldt County

Lake County

Napa County

Sonoma County

1

101

Willits

128

Ukiah

Boonville

20

Lakeport

Lower Lake

Cloverdale

29

Middletown

Healdsburg

101

Calistoga

Santa Rosa

St. Helena

Sebastopol

Glen Ellen

Rutherford

Rohnert Park

Yountville

Petaluma

Napa

Sonoma

29

Wine Country

MENDOCINO COUNTY

BOONVILLE

ANDERSON VALLEY HISTORICAL MUSEUM★
Highway 128, Boonville
Phone: (707) 895-3207
Hours: Fri.-Sun. 1:00-4:00 p.m., closed Dec. 10-Jan. 10.
Admission: Free

Housed in the one-room Con Creek Schoolhouse (1891) and three new structures, the museum exhibits represent aspects of Anderson Valley home life, schools, agriculture, lumbering, and "Boontling," the valley's unique folk language.

UKIAH

THE GRACE HUDSON MUSEUM AND THE SUN HOUSE
431 South Main Street, Ukiah
Phone: (707) 462-3370
Hours: Wed.-Sat. 10:00 a.m.-4:30 p.m.; Sun. noon-4:30 p.m.
Admission: Free

One of the first artists to depict native people respectfully, Grace Hudson enjoyed commercial success and a national reputation as an important regional portrait artist. Aided in her work by her husband, John Hudson, a prominent collector, ethnographer, and linguist, Hudson aimed to preserve for posterity a record of the local Pomo people, whom she (mistakenly) perceived as a dying race.

Although trained as a medical doctor, John Hudson gave up medicine a few years after his marriage to Grace to devote his life to collecting,

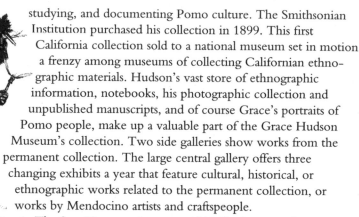

studying, and documenting Pomo culture. The Smithsonian Institution purchased his collection in 1899. This first California collection sold to a national museum set in motion a frenzy among museums of collecting Californian ethnographic materials. Hudson's vast store of ethnographic information, notebooks, his photographic collection and unpublished manuscripts, and of course Grace's portraits of Pomo people, make up a valuable part of the Grace Hudson Museum's collection. Two side galleries show works from the permanent collection. The large central gallery offers three changing exhibits a year that feature cultural, historical, or ethnographic works related to the permanent collection, or works by Mendocino artists and craftspeople.

Pen and ink study of a Pomo dancer wearing an eagle feather cape, by Grace Hudson. Courtesy of the Grace Hudson Museum.

The Sun House, a six-room, 1911 Craftsman-style bungalow designed by San Francisco photographer and architect George Wilcox for Grace and John Hudson, was named for the Hopi symbol of fertility and growth which stands over its front door. The striking, redwood structure is a paragon of simplicity, reflecting the hallmark of the Craftsman style, a reaction against the excesses of Victorian architecture. In keeping with the back-to-nature approach of the Arts and Crafts Movement, the house features redwood wainscoting, coarse cloth to cover the walls, exposed beams, and sleeping porches and doors opening out to the garden. Furnished entirely with items from the Hudsons' collection, the house reflects the unconventional lifestyle of its original owners.

Library: The Hudson Archives contain the voluminous writings, including notebooks, unpublished manuscripts, and correspondence, and the photographs of John Hudson, and correspondence and writings of Helen McCowen Carpenter, Grace's mother.

Gift Shop: The fine selection of books is divided into Native Americans, women's history, California history, and the children's corner. Grace Hudson prints, jewelry, and other gift items are for sale in this lovely shop.

POMO VISITOR CENTER★
Marina Drive at Lake Mendocino, Ukiah
Phone: (707) 485-8685
**Hours: Wed.-Sun. 9:00 a.m.-5:00 p.m., summer; Sat. & Sun. 1:00-
    5:00 p.m., fall.**
Admission: Free

The round visitor center, modeled on a Pomo ceremonial dance house, was built by the Army Corps of Engineers and is operated by local Native Americans. Exhibits, demonstrations, and special programs seek to pass down knowledge of the Pomo culture.

WILLITS

MENDOCINO COUNTY MUSEUM
400 East Commercial Street, Willits
Phone: (707) 459-2736
Hours: Wed.-Sat. 10:00 a.m.-4:30 p.m.
Admission: Free

When it opened in 1972, the Mendocino County Museum resembled a community attic filled with donated artifacts. Today, the museum focuses on the lives of the people of Mendocino County. Using oral history as a unifying theme, exhibits reveal the stories that the many objects have to tell; descriptive labels feature words of the people who made or used the artifacts.

Elsie Allen, a renowned Pomo basketweaver, promised her mother that she would preserve her baskets and those of other weavers, although this meant breaking with the Pomo tradition of destroying a weaver's baskets when she dies. The exhibit of the Elsie Allen Family collection, called "A Promise Kept," is one of the best collections of Pomo baskets in the world.

A large portion of the 7,500 square feet of exhibition space is devoted to the history of small businesses in Mendocino County. A favorite of local residents is the Willits Creamery and Soda Fountain, a beloved local institution which was moved intact, right down to the dishrag on the ice cream freezer, from its downtown location when it closed up shop in 1985.

The museum's award-winning staff offers a fresh approach to typical county museum exhibits. A hearse displaying a wicker body basket set amidst rubbings from local tombstones is the centerpiece of an exhibit entitled "Farewell." A restored "hippie van," labeled a "contemporary homesteader's cabin," provides a more recent slant on Mendocino County settlers. A window looking back into museum storage gives visitors a first-hand view of what goes on behind the scenes. Outdoor exhibits of early day machinery from the North Coast timber industry feature regular steam power exhibitions by the Roots of Motive Power volunteers.

In 1994, in conjunction with the Grace Hudson Museum in Ukiah and the Kelley House Museum in Mendocino, the Mendocino County Museum will open a new permanent exhibit telling the almost forgotten story of the 1850 shipwreck of the *Frolic*. When steamships began to put commercial sailing vessels out of business, the owners of the clipper *Frolic,* which had been employed in the opium trade between India, China, Great Britain, and the United States, outfitted her with a cargo of Chinese trade goods for one final voyage. The ship was wrecked on the coast of Mendocino. The men sent to salvage the cargo took one

A Pomo ceremonial basket, ca. 1906. The finely trimmed grasses and shoots from which it is made, the even stitches, carefully worked pattern, and tasteful decoration with quail feathers and clamshell beads attest to the artistry of Pomo weavers. A fine collection of baskets can be seen at the Mendocino County Museum. Courtesy of The Brooklyn Museum.

look at the giant redwood trees in the area and returned to inform their employer, Henry Meiggs, that they had found a treasure much more valuable than the cargo of the *Frolic*.

In 1851 the first large-scale lumber mill was established in Meiggsville—now the town of Mendocino—and the sunken *Frolic* was forgotten by all but a few Pomo people, who salvaged green bottle glass, silks, and blue and white Chinese porcelain from the wreck. In the 1980s archaeologist Tom Layton discovered arrowheads and beads made of these salvaged items, and rediscovered the story of the *Frolic*.

Gift Shop: The well-stocked shop has information on how to preserve your own family collections and record your family history, as well as lots of local history, including books about Native Americans, and great things for children.

LAKE COUNTY

LAKEPORT

LAKE COUNTY MUSEUM
255 North Forbes Street, Lakeport
Phone: (707) 263-4555
Hours: Wed.-Sun. 11:00 a.m.-4:00 p.m.
Admission: Suggested donation adults $2.00, children $1.00

Formerly the Lake County Courthouse, the spacious Lake County Museum is packed with historic artifacts. Courtesy of Lake County Museum.

The lovely, two-story brick building that was Lake County's courthouse from 1871 until 1978 is now the Lake County Museum. The main gallery features the museum's renowned collection of Pomo baskets, enhanced by a detailed exhibit that includes photographs of weavers.

Some of the exquisite baskets are elaborately decorated with the red and yellow feathers of the red-headed woodpecker, green feathers from the heads of mallards, plumes from the male valley quail, shells, and beads.

Exhibits about early pioneers include period rooms, costumes, and a display of firearms featuring pistols and rifles dating from the early 1800s through the early 1900s. Such Lake County celebrities as Lillie Langtry, George Piner, and Corabelle Knight are recalled in paintings, clothing, and ephemera collections. Pink and lavender "Lake County Diamonds" are the highlight of the gem and mineral collection.

Library: The research library contains historical photographs dating to the mid-1800s and more than 1,000 volumes of Lake County Genealogical Society materials.

Gift Shop: The small bookstore features books about Lake County history and Native Americans, and books by local authors. The store also sells jewelry made by local Native Americans.

LOWER LAKE

ANDERSON MARSH STATE HISTORIC PARK★
Highway 53, Lower Lake
Phone: (707) 994-0688
Hours: Fri., Sat., Sun. 10:00 a.m.–4:00 p.m.
Admission: $2.00 per auto

The 1,000–acre Anderson Marsh State Historic Park was saved from development through the efforts of archaeologist John Parker, who spearheaded efforts to preserve the site because of its archaeological and natural wealth. The 540–acre Natural Preserve, representing more than half of the remaining wetland habitat at Clear Lake (84% of the original marsh area has been destroyed), provides a home to a wonderful diversity of fish, birds, and other wildlife, including the American bald eagle, peregrine falcons, and great blue herons. Following the four nature trails of a little over one mile each leads you through riparian, grassland, and oak woodland environments, and along the marsh. The park contains 36 Native American archaeological sites, some inhabited by Pomo people ten thousand years ago.

The park is named for the historic Anderson Ranch, owned and operated by the Anderson family from 1885 and until the late 1960s. The two-story ranch house, built in 1855, is furnished with some of the original family belongings and period antiques. Costumed docents offer historic tours through the home and ranch buildings. You may want to schedule your visit to take in one of the park's special events: a tea and musicale in April, the Blackberry Pie Social in August, Heritage Days in October, and Christmas at the Anderson Ranch House in December.

MIDDLETOWN

THE OLD STONE HOUSE★
Highway 29, Hidden Valley Lake, Middletown
Phone: (707) 987-3138
Hours: Tues. & Thurs. 1:00–3:00 p.m., or by appointment.
Admission: Donations

In 1854, Captain R. Steele and Robert Sterling, managers of the 21,200–acre Rancho Guenoc, built the Stone House. The oldest house in Lake

County, it was rebuilt in 1894 by Charles M. Young, and has been designated a historical landmark. The house's furnishings include some local antique pieces.

NAPA COUNTY

CALISTOGA

PETRIFIED FOREST
4100 Petrified Forest Road, Calistoga
Phone: (707) 942-6667
Hours: Daily 10:00 a.m.-6:00 p.m.; 10:00 a.m.-5:00 p.m., winter
Admission: Adults $3.00, seniors $2.00, children $1.00

Three million years ago, Mount St. Helena erupted with an awesome volcanic blast that felled trees like matchsticks, covering the entire area with a thick layer of volcanic ash. Over the millennia, rainwater laden with silicates soaked the fallen trees until the wood fibers were replaced by crystallized silica and the trees turned to stone. In 1870, Charles Evans found a stump of petrified tree while tending his cows. A man who knew a tourist attraction when he saw one, "Petrified Forest Charlie" began charging admission to see the natural phenomenon. One of the visitors, Robert Louis Stevenson, immortalized Charlie and the trees in *The Silverado Squatters*. In 1910, Ollie Bockee, a woman who was also savvy about public attractions and the value of publicity, settled in the area and soon had people coming from around the world to visit the Petrified Forest. Today Ollie's descendents still own the property.

You can follow the circular trail through the forest to examine the fallen giants—most of the redwoods were over 2,000 years old when they were buried. The small museum located in Ollie Bockee's house behind the gift shop offers a brief and understandable history of the petrified forest and Sonoma County geology.

Library: Visitors to the forest can peruse geology books in the small library.

Gift Shop: You can purchase polished petrified wood, fossils, and a host of other related items at the Nature Store.

SHARPSTEEN MUSEUM
1311 Washington Street, Calistoga
Phone: (707) 942-5911
Hours: Daily 10:00 a.m.-4:00 p.m., April-October; noon-4:00 p.m.
**   November-March**
Admission: Free

A resort town from the get-go, Calistoga loves visitors and entertains them with this first-rate historical museum. A tour begins with Ben's

Room, dedicated to museum founders Ben and Bernice Sharpsteen, whose personal memorabilia commemorate Ben's thirty-year association with Walt Disney Studios. Following a small exhibit of Pomo Indian artifacts, three-dimensional dioramas recreate scenes from Napa County's colorful past: the arrival of the railroad, Calistoga's Chinese shanty town, and Robert Louis Stevenson's honeymoon in the abandoned Silverado Mines bunkhouse.

The focal point of the museum is an extraordinary replica of the elegant Hot Springs Resort as it looked in the 1860s when Sam Brannan first turned Calistoga into the "Hot Springs of the West." Brannan looms large in California history as the man who introduced Abraham Lincoln at the Republican Convention, published the first newspaper in San Francisco, started the California Gold Rush, became California's first millionaire, and subsequently lost all in a scandalous divorce. He is also credited with naming the town, when his toast to the "Saratoga of California" came out "To the Calistoga of Sarafornia."

Life-size mannequins riding a restored stagecoach may be familiar to local residents, as their faces were created from life masks of museum volunteers. Reproductions of a 19th century general store, kitchen, and blacksmith shop showcase historic artifacts. A simulated barn interior serves as a visible storage area for more museum artifacts. One of the original resort cottages, elaborately furnished with period antiques, has been relocated to the museum site. An 84-year-old volunteer working at a quilting frame informed us that she was the museum's only living antique.

Gift Shop: Gift shop shelves are generously stocked with historical books, collectibles, pretty china teacups and teapots, porcelain boxes, and other Victorian reproductions.

NAPA

ACTION BOXING MUSEUM AND ATHLETIC CLUB
1729B Action Avenue, Napa
Phone: (707) 224-4977 or (707) 938-0120
Hours: Daily 7:30 a.m.-noon; call for afternoon hours.
Admission: Free. No donations accepted.

Joe Gavras, a lightweight prizefighter known in his heyday (1933 to 1941) as Newsboy Joe Gavras, spent three-quarters of a lifetime putting the Action Boxing Museum together. "This museum is a contribution to boxing from me," Joe told us. "Bank of America has a lot of money but they ain't got no pictures like this," he continued, pointing to the floor-to-ceiling display of more than two thousand photographs, posters, and programs featuring past, present, and future boxing champions. Nor does Bank of America have the original boxing ring from San Francisco's

"This is one of the most important signs in the Boxing Museum," says Joe Gavras. "Boxing is one sport where you better save your money." Photo by Joe Gavras, courtesy of Action Boxing Museum.

Kezar Stadium, where Rocky Marciano defended his heavyweight championship of the world in 1957. Joe does. Lining the perimeter of the museum are at least a hundred wooden chairs from the Navy hospital that Joe painted with the names of champion prizefighters. Beside the ring are punching bags and workout equipment where Joe and his friends work out and aspiring boxers train. To add authenticity to the atmosphere, a bell sounds out every three minutes. Joe gave us a personal tour of the locker room, which was neat as a pin, and pointed out the right-hand boxing glove Joe Louis wore when he knocked out Jack Roper in 1939. He handed us a printed sheet to share with our readers. "The Boxing Museum is the finest of its kind anywhere in the country," it reads. "If you are planning on having out-of-town guests and they are boxing or sporting fans this will be a treat for them. They will find both the museum and athletic club gym *clean, exciting* and *presentable*." We couldn't agree more. One suggestion: telephone before your visit to make an appointment to have Joe show you around. This is one tour you definitely don't want to miss.

THE HESS COLLECTION WINERY
4411 Redwood Road, Napa
Phone: (707) 255-1144
Hours: Daily 10:00 a.m.-4:00 p.m.
Admission: Free (wine-tasting $2.50)

Swiss architect Beat Jordi restored this 1903 winery, now the home of the extensive Donald Hess art collection, as well as a winery with a tasting and retail room. The 13,000-square-foot gallery—a light-filled space integrating the stone walls of the original structure with the clean lines of a contemporary art museum—features a permanent exhibition of 130 post–World War II paintings and sculptures by 29 contemporary American and European artists including Francis Bacon, Georg Baselitz, Robert Motherwell, Morris Louis, Frank Stella, and Magdalena Abakanowicz.

RUTHERFORD

ST. SUPÉRY WINE DISCOVERY CENTER
8440 St. Helena Highway, Rutherford
Phone: (707) 963-4507
Hours: Daily 9:30 a.m.-4:30 p.m.
Admission: $2.50, good forever

Ninety percent of the wine produced in the United States comes from California, and ninety percent of California's premium wine comes from the Napa Valley: commercial wineries and winery tours abound here. Although connected to a commercial enterprise, the St. Supéry Wine Discovery Center offers a comprehensive, noncommercial overview of wine history and production, as well as a tour of a historic Queen Anne farmhouse and a lovely drought-tolerant garden, and an art gallery featuring changing exhibits of work by local contemporary artists.

The tour begins in the Education Vineyard, where eight varieties of grapes grow on various forms of trellising. From growing and picking we follow the grape through the processes of crushing, fermenting, aging, and bottling. A topographical map of the Napa Valley illustrates how the climate is ideal for wine production. A "smellovision" exhibit uses plexiglass sniffer tubes to demonstrate that taste is largely in the nose. The mouth can only distinguish between hot, cold, bitter, sweet, sour, and salty, but the nose can detect pepper, black cherry, olive, and an array of other scents that give a wine its characteristic flavor. The tour ends with wine tasting.

Gift Shop: In addition to wine, the gift shop sells t-shirts, glasses, mugs, and wine-related items.

Rental: For special occasions, the lovely Joseph Atkinson House and the Wine Discovery Center are available to groups interested in the wine experience.

ST. HELENA

BALE GRIST MILL STATE HISTORIC PARK
3 miles northwest of St. Helena on SR 29
Phone: (707) 942-4575
Hours: Daily 10:00 a.m.-5:00 p.m.
Admission: Adults $2.00, children $1.00

Meticulously restored by California State Parks and open to the public since 1988, the Bale Grist Mill and its lush park setting offer something for everyone.

In 1847, Dr. Edward Bale built this impressive grist mill, whose towering redwood waterwheel measures 36 feet in diameter, generates 40 horsepower, and uses 450 gallons of water a minute to turn the millstone. Nowadays, rangers and volunteers explain the history and mechanical workings of the mill, a film covers further aspects of milling, and on weekends and holidays at 1:00 and 3:00 p.m. you can actually see the millstone grind corn, wheat, and rye into flour, from which the rangers and volunteers bake cornbread in the woodburning oven. For only $1.00 you can walk away with your own bag of freshly ground flour.

Nineteenth-century mills didn't just provide flour—they were community gathering places, and enriched our language with a wealth of folk expressions: "hung on tenterhooks," "grist for the mill," "rule of thumb," "manhandle," "run of the mill," and "keep your nose to the grindstone" among them. Of the original $5,000 spent on the Bale Grist Mill, $2,700 covered the cost of the millstone, an indication of the significance of having "a millstone around your neck." Our park ranger/ tour guide enlivened our visit with the etymological origins of these and other phrases.

Gift Shop: You can buy freshly ground cornmeal and flour, as well as cookbooks and other books, cards, and maps.

NAPA VALLEY MUSEUM
473 Main Street, St. Helena
Phone: (707) 963-7411
Hours: Mon.-Fri. 9:00 a.m.-4:00 p.m.; Sat. & Sun. 11:00 a.m.-
**   3:00 p.m.**
Admission: $2.00, children free

From Wappo baskets to historic agricultural implements, this small museum shines like a whole jewelry box full of artifacts. Currently occupying 1800 square feet on the second floor of the stately Vintage Hall, (formerly St. Helena's high school), the Napa Valley Museum concentrates on the history, natural history, and art of the Napa Valley.

Robert Louis Stevenson. Courtesy of California State Parks, R.L. Stevenson Collection.

A new permanent exhibit, "The Land, The People, The Industry," traces the history of the area from the beginning of time to the present by means of beautifully executed vignettes. Changing exhibits feature works by local artists or dramatize Napa Valley themes, like phylloxera, the American root louse that nearly destroyed the vineyards in 1873 and is again devastating the local wine industry. The small permanent collection includes 19th century watercolors by Sophie Alstrom, wildflower prints by Henry Evans, and Charles O'Rear photographs.

The museum plans to begin construction on a permanent home on four and a half acres in Yountville soon.

Gift Shop: In addition to prints, cards, and such, the gift shop recently acquired a large collection of Henry Evans California native wildflower prints.

THE SILVERADO MUSEUM
1490 Library Lane, St. Helena
Phone: (707) 963-3757
Hours: Tues.-Sun. noon-4:00 p.m.
Admission: Free

As the story goes, the young Robert Louis Stevenson fell in love with Fanny Osborne, a married woman ten years his senior, and followed her to California. While waiting for her divorce, Stevenson lived briefly in the French

Hotel (now the Stevenson House) in Monterey. Married on May 19, 1880 and unable to afford the $1.00-a-day rental on a Calistoga cottage, the nearly penniless Stevensons spent their honeymoon rent-free in an abandoned bunkhouse in the old Silverado Mine—after Fanny had chased away the rattlesnakes.

Located since 1979 in its own wing of the St. Helena Public Library Center, the cheerful, red-carpeted Silverado Museum is a repository of manuscripts, letters, first editions, paintings, sculptures, photographs, and Stevenson memorabilia, including Fanny and Robert's wedding rings, the lead soldiers immortalized in *A Child's Garden of Verses*, and Henry James' gloves. The privately endowed museum houses over eight thousand items from the personal collection of ardent Stevenson fan Norman Strouse.

Library: The reference library, for use by scholars by appointment only, contains rare books, letters, Fanny's cookbooks, etc.

Gift Shop: Sells Robert Louis Stevenson's books, of course.

YOUNTVILLE

CALIFORNIA VETERANS MUSEUM
Veterans Home of California, Yountville
Phone: (707) 944-4600
Hours: Fri., Sat., Sun. noon–2:00 p.m.
Admission: Free

In 1882, the newly incorporated Veterans Home Association purchased 910 acres of Napa Valley farmland at a cost of $17,750 to provide shelter and care for their wounded com-

rades. Although the original three-story building no longer exists, the sprawling Mediterranean-style complex with lush, green lawns and tidy gardens welcomes visitors. Guests may tour the grounds and visit the California Veterans Museum, which chronicles 110 years of military history. Located in the restored Armistice Chapel, a delicately proportioned English Country Gothic church featuring two lovely stained glass windows, Gothic trusses, and a plank ceiling, the museum collection includes a portrait of Abraham Lincoln donated by the Daughters of the American Revolution, the 36-star flag carried on Lincoln's first inaugural trip, a Norden bombsight, a 1943–44 World War II display, and a corner dedicated to women at war.

Civil War veterans on the steps of Yountville's original Veterans Home, built in the late 19th century. Courtesy of Veterans Home of California.

SONOMA COUNTY

CLOVERDALE

CLOVERDALE HISTORICAL SOCIETY MUSEUM
215 North Cloverdale Boulevard, Cloverdale
Phone: (707) 894-2067
Hours: By appointment
Admission: Free

The red brick, gingerbread-trimmed Gould-Shaw home houses the
Cloverdale Historical Society Museum, where photographs and abundant
memorabilia take visitors back to the time when this northernmost
community in Sonoma County was first settled. Cloverdale is proud of
its history, beginning with the Makahmo Pomo, whose chief village was
located on Sulphur Creek and the Russian River. From 1870 to 1910,
the town enjoyed a prosperous period as a resort known for its geysers
and mineral springs and the world-famous Pop McCray's. Members of
the Historical Society are currently restoring the old stagecoach that used
to carry tourists to the geysers. Word has it that after that precarious
seventeen-mile ride, most preferred to walk back.

In 1869 oranges were brought from Panama and a citrus belt was
created. A carousel features photos of the fabulous scenes and themes
created with citrus fruit by local citizens for the annual Citrus Fair.
The fair is still around, but much to the regret of old timers, the elaborate, fanciful displays have been toned down. In the 1880s, Cloverdale
was the site of a utopian commune founded by a French group known
as the Icarians, and the home of a religious cult led by Madame Preston,
a spiritual healer. Bits and pieces of all this history are on view in the
rather jumbled museum. The front rooms feature a furnished Victorian
bedroom and the photo carousel, the middle room offers an excellent
slide show of Cloverdale history, and the back room, described by our
guide as "a hodgepodge of everything," is known as the general store.

The museum garden is actually several gardens in one, with rose,
herb, and wildflower gardens and an English garden accentuated by a
brick walkway and a gazebo. When we asked if the garden could be
rented for special events, we were told, "I suppose someone could just
get married there, and if they were kind enough they would make a
donation to the museum."

Library: Historical photographs and county records on microfilm are
available.

GLEN ELLEN

JACK LONDON STATE HISTORIC PARK MUSEUM
2400 London Ranch Road, Glen Ellen
Phone: (707) 938-5216
Hours: Daily 10:00 a.m.-5:00 p.m.
Admission: $5.00 per car

Movie-star handsome, exuberant, and adventuresome, Jack London was not only a traveller, lecturer, war correspondent, socialist, and rugged individualist, but also the highest paid, most popular fiction writer of his day. Internationally famous by the age of 29, London purchased farmland in Sonoma County for a quiet getaway from Oakland and the "man-trap" of city life. Filled with enthusiasm for living off the land, London planned to operate Beauty Ranch employing the latest scientific agriculture techniques, and began construction on Wolf House, his 26-room dream mansion, which mysteriously burned down the night before the Londons were to move in. London died three years later at 40, still planning to rebuild Wolf House.

After his death London's widow, Charmian, built a smaller, more formal house similar to Wolf House in its tiled roof and volcanic stone. The House of Happy Walls, now a museum dedicated to London, chronicles his life and adventures through photographs and memorabilia. You will see furniture designed by the Londons for Wolf House, items from London's study, and a great collection of curiosities and treasures amassed by the Londons on their world travels. Charmian's dressing room and closets filled with elaborate frocks, furs, and beaded gowns will be of interest to vintage fashion buffs.

Jack London at the ruins of Wolf House. Courtesy of California State Parks.

Would-be writers can read London's first rejection letter and take comfort in the knowledge that he received over 600 of them before success found him.

The museum is located in Jack London State Historic Park, which covers more than 800 acres of London's original 1,400-acre Beauty Ranch and contains the remains of Wolf House, London's grave, the cottage where London wrote many of his later works, and several ranch buildings.

Gift Shop: The gift shop carries books by and about Jack London, and t-shirts.

HEALDSBURG

THE HEALDSBURG MUSEUM
221 Matheson Street, Healdsburg
Phone: (707) 431-3325
Hours: Tues.-Sun. noon-5:00 p.m.

From a charming, homegrown institution, the Healdsburg Museum has developed over the past decade into one of the finest regional history museums in California. Its high level of professionalism is a real joy for those museum-goers who are sticklers for proper museum protocol.

Located in a beloved local landmark, the restored 1910 Healdsburg Carnegie Library building, the large exhibition room presents permanent exhibitions highlighting the historical development of northeastern Sonoma County on one side, and temporary exhibits on the other. Photographs and fine examples of Pomo basketry and other skills describe the culture of the first inhabitants. Other exhibits chronicle the Mexican rancho era, the infamous Squatters Wars between the Mexican grantees and the American settlers, the pioneer journey across the Plains, and the founding of Healdsburg.

The illegal, immoral, or just plain unpleasant parts of history, although well-known to the people who live through them, tend to be swept under the carpet in history museums and books. "Sonoma County: The Untold Stories," the temporary exhibit on view during our visit, examined some of the less savory activities of the past, like bootlegging during Prohibition, drug addiction in proper Victorian society, prostitution, gambling, and racial prejudice in early Sonoma County. The exhibit brought forward little-known facts about the sanctioned form of Indian slavery in the mid-1800s, the kidnapping and sale of Indian children to local farmers, and the shameful treatment of the Chinese. It also took a look at customs of death in the nineteenth century and anti-unionism in Sonoma County agriculture. Although this striking exhibit may not be on view for your visit, the museum has three special exhibits a year, and you can look forward to one that is equally thought-provoking.

As with many small-town museums, the annual antique toy exhibition is a Christmas tradition here, taking on a new face each year. In 1991, "Toys of Christmas Past" featured toys of transportation along with the usual collection of dolls. "Toys of the Fabulous Fifties" in 1992 had rockets, planes, and cars of the 1950s fin-to-fin with robots, chubby-cheeked dolls, and Zorro and Lone Ranger memorabilia surrounding a 1954 Philco television set.

Library: The excellent Historic Research Library collection, open by appointment, includes local newspapers from 1865 to 1982, census records, city archives, family genealogy files, and over 5,000 photographs.

Gift Shop: The corner gift shop offers a wide selection of historical books, reproductions of Victorian children's literature and toys, fine jewelry, and replicas of early American and Native American crafts and tools.

PETALUMA

PETALUMA ADOBE
3325 Adobe Road, Petaluma
Phone: (707) 762-4871
Hours: Daily 10:00 a.m.-5:00 p.m.
Admission: Adults $2.00, children $1.00, good for the day at any of the Sonoma County state parks.

Of the four hundred land grants made to individuals by the Mexican government, General Mariano Vallejo's hundred-square-mile Rancho Petaluma was the largest and richest, a self-sufficient community raising cattle and sheep and growing great crops of wheat, barley, corn, and vegetables.

One hundred and fifty years later, a pair of newly shorn sheep and a frisky goat greeted us in the parking lot of the Petaluma Adobe State Park; a family of quail crossed our path as we climbed the hill to the Petaluma Adobe, where chickens hunted and pecked in the dust of the courtyard. Had we timed our visit for a weekend or holiday, we might have seen costumed docents spinning or weaving the sheeps' wool, or baking bread in the outdoor clay ovens. Nonetheless, excellent interpretive panels made it possible to imagine life as it was when this grand, two-story adobe served as the headquarters for Rancho Petaluma.

The Vallejo family living quarters, furnished with authentic rancho period furniture, reflect Vallejo's earlier Mexican lifestyle in contrast to the later American style of his house in the town of Sonoma. The restored blacksmith shop, where tools and nails were forged, the spinning and weaving rooms where blankets, carpets, and clothing were made, the leather shop where hides were turned into saddles, bridles, and other leather goods, great vats for rendering tallow, and a huge contraption for making candles recall the many activities that took place in the adobe.

PETALUMA HISTORICAL MUSEUM/LIBRARY
20 Fourth Street at B Street, Petaluma
Phone: (707) 778-4398
Hours: Thurs., Fri., Sat., Mon. 10:00 a.m.-4:00 p.m.; Sun. 1:00-4:00 p.m.; closed Tues., Wed.
Admission: Free

Like many small-town museums in California, the Petaluma Historical Museum occupies a former Carnegie library building. Constructed of locally quarried Roblar sandstone and white Alameda brick, the exceptionally beautiful interior features a unique, free-standing, stained-glass

dome, large Corinthian columns supporting a brass-railed mezzanine, and fine wood finishing of ash, pine, oak, and Douglas fir.

Gallery space on the ground floor is devoted to special exhibits, which change three times a year, and the vintage 1850 Knickerbocker Pumper fire engine on permanent display. Permanent exhibits on the mezzanine floor document Petaluma's history from Coast Miwok times through the 1950s. The wheel from the steamer *Petaluma*, the last commercial paddle wheel vessel on the West Coast, commemorates Petaluma's history as a river town. Letters and artifacts celebrate Sonoma County's best-known historical figure, General Vallejo. The recreated Victorian kitchen and 1870s schoolroom are popular with kids.

The exceptionally beautiful interior of the Petaluma Historical Museum features Corinthian columns and fine woodwork, not to mention artifacts from Petaluma's history of as the Egg Basket of the World. Courtesy of Petaluma Historical Museum.

Particularly interesting are the artifacts peculiar to Petaluma's heyday as the "Egg Basket of the World." Beginning with the invention of the first successful incubator, the local poultry industry spawned a dazzling array of gadgets and machinery to leave you amazed, amused, and awed by the richness of human ingenuity. Don't miss the 1950s egg-cleaning machine or the chicken beak trimmer.

Library: The research library boasts a complete collection of Petaluma's newspapers dating from 1851, as well as many other historical documents of local interest.

Gift Shop: Books and reproductions of paper toys are sold, along with an eclectic assortment of antiques and collectibles.

ROHNERT PARK

SONOMA COUNTY WINE & VISITOR CENTER
5000 Roberts Lake Road, Rohnert Park
Phone: (707) 586-3795
Hours: Daily 10:00 a.m.-5:00 p.m.

Grapes and wine have been a part of California history since Russian colonists planted grapes at Fort Ross in 1812. Oenophiles and visitors who want to learn about the wine industry can stop by the newly-opened Sonoma County Wine & Visitor Center, where a large electronic relief map gives an overview of the area, and a participatory computer system with touch-screen monitor provides information on wineries, hotels, restaurants, and recreational activities. Examples of trellising and other viticultural techniques are on view in the demonstration vineyards, and the demonstration winery traces wine production from the grape to the final bottled product.

Gift Shop: The Retail Shop carries over two hundred Sonoma County wines, t-shirts, posters, cookbooks, original artwork, and other wine country gifts.

Rental: The seminar, tasting, and exhibit rooms and the outside deck overlooking Roberts Lake, or the entire center, may be rented for meetings or food and wine events.

SANTA ROSA

LUTHER BURBANK HOME & GARDENS
Santa Rosa Avenue at Sonoma Avenue, Santa Rosa
Phone: (707) 524-5445
Hours: Gardens are open daily, dawn to dusk; house tours April-
**   October, Wed.-Sun. 10:00 a.m.-3:30 p.m.**
Admission: Gardens free, house $2.00

A framed photograph of Luther Burbank with Thomas Edison and Henry Ford places this American horticulturist among the giants of his time— men who changed the economic conditions of the United States. Born in Massachusetts on March 7, 1849 (in California we celebrate his birthday as Arbor Day), for fifty years Burbank made his home in Santa Rosa, which he considered "the chosen spot of all this Earth as far as nature is concerned." In his Santa Rosa garden and at his Sebastopol farm, the self-trained Burbank conducted plant breeding experiments that led to the introduction of more than 800 new varieties of plants, many improving the world's food supply.

Today, a stroll through Burbank's garden is an enjoyable way to discover the genius of this gardener to the world. Large interpretive panels depict Burbank's life and his most important plant introductions. The rose garden fills the air with the wonderful perfume of the Burbank rose, the successful outcome of Burbank's efforts to add more fragrance to flowers. The orchard area boasts a plumcot tree, created by crossing an apricot and a plum, and a multiple-grafted cherry tree which produces four different kinds of cherries. Under the straw on the potato bed you can see the famous Burbank potato that revolutionized the potato industry and gave us the Idaho potato we eat today. The cactus garden contains one of Burbank's less-appreciated endeavors, the spineless cactus. The lovely Victorian garden features flowers commonly found in home gardens in the late 19th century.

From April through October, visitors may tour the charming white house where Burbank lived with his wife, mother, and sister. The fragile glass greenhouse he built in 1889 survived the 1906 earthquake that leveled downtown

Hoping to create a new crop that would solve food shortages around the world, Luther Burbank created a cactus without spines. He told Paramahansa Yogsananda he had used mental persuasion on the plants, telling them, "You don't need your protective thorns, I will protect you..." Of Burbank's many contributions to humankind, the spineless cactus is perhaps the least appreciated. Photo by Lenny Siegel, courtesy of Luther Burbank Home & Gardens.

Santa Rosa, thereby enhancing Burbank's reputation as a man possessed of special, God-given powers.

Gift Shop: Located in the former carriage house, the gift shop sells items related to Burbank and to gardening, including seeds, books, and lovely, flowered t-shirts.

CALIFORNIA MUSEUM OF ART
Luther Burbank Center for the Arts
50 Mark West Springs Road, Santa Rosa
Phone: (707) 527-0297
Hours: Wed.-Sun. 11:00 a.m.-4:00 p.m.
Admission: Free

A small (2,000 square feet), friendly museum, the California Museum of Art has a loyal following who regularly attend its seven exhibitions a year—solo, group, and theme shows. By far the most popular show is the annual California Small Works exhibition, a juried show featuring pieces no larger than 12 inches. The show offers a comprehensive sampling of the contemporary California art scene, and a great opportunity to purchase art on a scale suitable for the home at reasonable prices. The museum also has a small but tasteful permanent collection of contemporary California art, and a slide registry is available for public viewing.

JESSE PETER NATIVE AMERICAN ART MUSEUM
Santa Rosa Junior College
1501 Mendocino Avenue, Santa Rosa
Phone: (707) 527-4479
Hours: Mon.-Fri. noon-4:00 p.m., mid-August through mid-June.
Admission: Free. Self-guided tour packages (elementary–college
    level) are available. Call for reservations.

Son of a pioneer Santa Rosa family, Jesse Peter began collecting geological specimens and Native American relics as a boy in the hills of Sonoma County, and as an adult continued assembling collections for the University of California and other institutions. In the early 1930s, at the request of the president of Santa Rosa Junior College, he installed a modest collection of rocks in display cases in the new science building. As the displays filled the cases and began to overflow into storerooms, the college applied to the WPA for assistance in building a museum. Opened in 1940, the museum operated as a natural history museum until 1979, when the focus was changed to Native American art.

The museum's collection encompasses fine examples of Native American art from California, the Southwest, the Great Plains, the Great Lakes, the Arctic, and the Northwest Coast. A life-size model of a Pomo roundhouse displays an extensive collection of Pomo baskets, including intricately woven miniature baskets. The Living Wall features contemporary photographs of Native American people, and the works of local Native American artists are featured in an artist-of-the-month case. The museum's center-piece, a large replicated pueblo, offers a view of Pueblo cultures through kachinas, Anasazi pottery, jewelry, and Pueblo polychrome and blackware.

A special annual event is "Day Under the Oaks," a Native American gathering held outside the museum the first Sunday in May.

Native American artifacts from California, the Southwest, the Plains, and the rest of North America are displayed at Santa Rosa Junior College's Jesse Peter Native American Art Museum. Courtesy of Jesse Peter Native American Art Museum.

RIPLEY'S MEMORIAL MUSEUM
492 Sonoma Avenue, Santa Rosa
Phone: (707) 524-5233
Hours: Wed.-Sun. 10:00 a.m.-4:00 p.m., March 1-October 23.
Admission: Adults $1.50, youth 7-17 & seniors 75¢

Across the street from the Luther Burbank home and gardens, in the lovely Julliard Park, is a memorial to another famous Santa Rosan, Robert L. Ripley, the "Believe It or Not" cartoonist. Housed in the Church Built from One Tree—a single California redwood yielded the 78,000 board feet of lumber used in the construction of this Gothic-style building—the museum contains an array of Ripley memorabilia: homey photos of young Bob receiving a haircut from his dad; a high school drawing; the slippers and yellow Chinese robe he wore at home while he worked, and a battered, old suitcase plastered with travel stickers that accompanied Ripley on his many journeys. A few items that didn't make it to one of the fifteen sensational Ripley's Believe It or Not museums located around the world are on view. A startlingly lifelike wax figure of Ripley looks out over the room where Ripley's family and the rest of the congregation worshiped when he was as a boy.

SONOMA COUNTY MUSEUM
425 - 7th Street, Santa Rosa
Phone: (707) 579-1500
Hours: Wed.-Sun. 11:00 a.m.-4:00 p.m.
Admission: Adults $2.00, seniors & students $1.00

Fortunately, some historic-minded individuals raised the funds to move this 1,800-ton building, a former post office and one of the few remaining examples of classic federal architecture in the area, to 7th Street, where it provides a splendid setting for the excellent Sonoma County Museum.

The main gallery features "The Dream Continues," a permanent display of Sonoma County history which begins with the native Pomo people and includes a tribute to the county's resort areas, among them the infamous Bohemian Club. The Russian presence in Sonoma County is represented by a model of Fort Ross and artifacts from the Russian-American fur trade. The "Dreamers" exhibit celebrates local heroes Jack London, Luther Burbank, Robert Ripley, and Fred Wiseman. The last and least-known of the four flew a homemade airplane but later gave up flying because he "didn't see any future in it."

An important collection of California landscapes is permanently displayed in the small Hart Gallery behind the gift shop. On the second floor, a handsome balcony gallery overlooking the main exhibition hall presents changing exhibitions. "Mount Tamalpais: An Artistic Interpretation" featured fifty paintings inspired by Mt. Tamalpais, created from 1850 to 1930. "The Hermitage Group of St. Petersburg: Paintings from the Russian Soul" was arranged as a cultural exchange between St. Petersburg and Sonoma County, and "Humor in a Jugular Vein: The Art, Artists and Artifacts of Mad Magazine" was originated here and toured the U.S., putting the Sonoma County Museum on the map.

Gift Shop: The Wild Oat keeps a full line of Sonoma County history books on its shelves, as well as one-of-a-kind jewelry, baskets made by local Pomo weavers, and unique craft items like elkhorn brushes.

SEBASTOPOL

Luther Burbank.
Courtesy of
Luther Burbank
Home & Gardens.

GOLD RIDGE EXPERIMENT FARM★
7781 Bodega Avenue, Sebastopol
Phone: (707) 829-6711
Hours: By appointment April 15-October 15.
Admission: Donation requested

America's great plant wizard, Luther Burbank, conducted most of his plant breeding experiments on an eighteen-acre farm outside Sebastopol. Three acres of the Gold Ridge farm and the small cottage where Burbank often stayed the night have been renovated and opened to the public. Many of the original plants remain and visitors can still see vestiges of the long rows Burbank used to walk. The cottage exterior has been restored and the interior furnished with items pertaining to Burbank's work.

WEST COUNTY MUSEUM
261 South Main Street, Sebastopol
Phone: (707) 829-6711
Hours: Fri., Sat., Sun. 1:00-4:00 p.m., and by appointment.
Admission: Free

Chartered in 1903 by the Spreckels sugar interests and the McNear family of Petaluma, the Santa Rosa and Petaluma Railroad provided rapid transportation for the west county communities in the days before the automobile dominated transportation. Known as the "Juice Line," the electric interurban rail system handled 2,000 passengers a day in its peak, and its depot was the hub of community life. The beautifully restored Mission-style Sebastopol Railroad Depot, built in 1917, now houses the West County Museum, which presents changing exhibits chronicling the history of western Sonoma County.

Library: The Triggs Reference Room contains research materials about western Sonoma County history.

SONOMA

DEPOT PARK MUSEUM
270 First Street West, Sonoma
Phone: (707) 938-1762
Hours: Wed.-Sun. 1:00-4:30 p.m.
Admission: Adults 50¢, children 25¢

Don't be misled by the name of this museum. Although it is located in a replica of the 1880 train depot, Depot Park Museum is not just about trains. While three restored railroad cars permanently stationed on the tracks outside and the reconstructed station agent's room at the east end of the building tell the story of the railroads in Sonoma Valley, displays in the rest of the building document the history of the valley, beginning with the Coast Miwok. A Victorian parlor, kitchen, and bedroom are replicated down to the last detail of a bride's trousseau handmade by French nuns. The main exhibit, "Manifest Destiny 1846," dramatizes the Bear Flag Rebellion, a quixotic moment in California history when a handful of American frontiersmen determined to take President Polk's policy of manifest destiny into their own hands rode into Sonoma and

The Depot Park Museum features restored railroad cars, but exhibits document local history as well, from the Coast Miwok to the Victorian era and beyond. Courtesy of Depot Park Museum.

declared California an independent republic. Authentically dressed mannequins are frozen in the act of raising the homemade Bear Flag, which flew over Sonoma for nearly a month, until it was replaced on July 9, 1846 by the Stars & Stripes.

Library: The reference library has over 10,000 photographs and works relating to Sonoma Valley and the railroads.

Gift Shop: The gift shop carries the best selection in town of local history books.

SONOMA STATE HISTORIC PARK
Sonoma Plaza, Sonoma
Phone: (707) 938-9560
Hours: Daily 10:00 a.m.–5:00 p.m.
Admission: Adults $2.00, children $1.00 (good on that day at any of the Sonoma County state parks).

During the 1830s and 1840s, three international interests concentrated on California: after 300 years of continental expansion, the Spanish were trying to push the northern frontier of "New Spain" to a new headquarters; the Russians, lured by the sea otter trade, established outposts on the California coast; and the United States, motivated by the vision of a nation that would span the continent from the Atlantic to the Pacific, moved ever westward. Today Sonoma State Historic Park marks the spot where these international interests came together.

General Mariano Guadalupe Vallejo with daughters Maria and Luisa and three granddaughters. Courtesy of Depot Park Museum.

LACHRYMA MONTIS
off Third Street West

Wherever you go in Sonoma County, you will come upon the name of Mariano Guadalupe Vallejo, a pivotal figure in California history. Statesman, soldier, scholar, and businessman, Vallejo was hailed as a military hero at 22 when he commanded an expedition that defeated Native Americans opposed to Mexican rule. Before he was 30, his position as Commander General of the Northern Frontier had earned him far-reaching military and civil powers and an enormous land grant which made him one of the wealthiest and most influential men in California. The Petaluma Adobe, headquarters of his agricultural empire, and La Casa Grande, his house in town, document this Mexican period of his life.

Captured and imprisoned by American frontiersmen during the Bear Flag rebellion, Vallejo was freed by U.S. officials and allowed to return home. He adapted to the new era, serving as delegate to the California constitutional convention and in the California Senate. In 1850, he purchased land half a mile west of Sonoma's central plaza, where he lived until his death in 1890.

The estate, named Lachryma Montis (mountain tear) for the artesian spring on the property, documents Vallejo's American period. His charming Victorian Gothic home, built of prefabricated materials brought

from Boston on a sailing ship and insulated with adobe bricks, reflects
Vallejo's transition from Mexican to American culture. Furnished with
many personal effects, the house looks much as it did when the Vallejo
family was in residence. Other attractions on the estate include the
cookhouse, where the Chinese cook lived and prepared meals; El Delirio,
a tiny retreat for family and guests; the Hermitage, a miniature house
built for Vallejo's artist son, Napoleon; the reservoir from which Vallejo
sold water to the city of Sonoma; and lovely gardens. The Swiss Chalet,
a special warehouse built to store wine, fruit, and other produce, now
serves as a museum and interpretive center.

LA CASA GRANDE
Only the low, two-story adobe servants' quarters remain of La Casa
Grande, Vallejo's first home here.

MISSION SAN FRANCISCO DE SOLANO
You can begin your visit on Spain Street at Mission San Francisco Solano,
the twenty-first and last mission built in California. Established in 1823
with the hopes of preventing further encroachment by the Russian
colony at Fort Ross, it became one of the most prosperous California
missions, consisting at one point of a 27-room building with over ten
thousand acres of land. Today only five of the original rooms remain:
the bell room, the dining room which now houses the Virgil Jorgensen
Memorial Collection of mission paintings, the priest's quarters, the
courtyard, and the 1834 chapel.

SONOMA BARRACKS
On the corner of East First and Spain Streets, facing Sonoma's large
central plaza, sits the two-story adobe barracks built to house Mexican
army troops under the command of General Vallejo. From the barracks
Vallejo and his men set out to subdue Native Americans opposed to
Mexican rule. Educational panels on the first floor recount the history
of the area. To get an idea of what a soldier's life was like, climb to the
second floor where uniforms hang from pegs in the walls, a loaf of bread
waits to be sliced, and the beds are outfitted with straw mattresses.

TOSCANO HOTEL
Hours: Sat. & Sun. 1:00–4:00 p.m.; Mon. 11:00 a.m.–4:00 p.m.

The wood-frame building next to the barracks at one time housed
a retail store and rental library. Today it is furnished as it might have
been at the turn of the century, when it functioned as an inexpensive
hotel. A separate building in the back served as the hotel kitchen and
dining room.

VASQUEZ HOUSE (JOSEPH HOOKER HOUSE)*
El Paseo Patio behind La Casa Restaurant, Sonoma
Phone: (707) 938-0510
Hours: Open Wed.-Sun. Call for hours.

Once the headquarters of Captain Hooker—later General Hooker of Civil War fame—this 1858 Victorian now houses a tiny museum dedicated to the history of Sonoma after California became a state.

Library: The small library features books on history and preservation.

Restaurant: The Sonoma League for Historic Preservation serves tea and cookies in this charming tea room.

Sacramento Valley

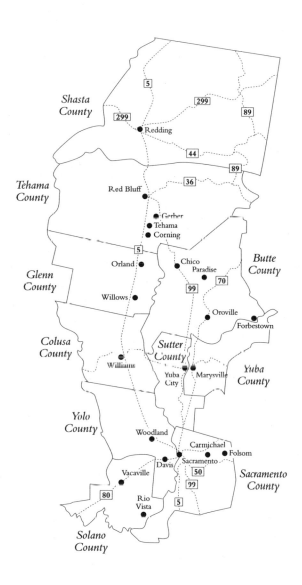

Shasta County

Tehama County

Glenn County

Colusa County

Yolo County

Solano County

Sutter County

Butte County

Yuba County

Sacramento County

Redding

Red Bluff

Gerber
Tehama
Corning

Orland

Chico
Paradise

Willows

Oroville
Forbestown

Williams

Yuba City
Marysville

Woodland

Carmichael
Folsom

Davis
Sacramento

Vacaville

Rio Vista

Sacramento Valley

SHASTA COUNTY

REDDING

CARTER HOUSE NATURAL SCIENCE MUSEUM
48 Quartz Hill Road (Caldwell Park), Redding
Phone: (916) 225-4125
Hours: Tues.-Sun. 10:00 a.m.-5:00 p.m.
Admission: $1.00

It may be small (1,500 square feet of exhibition space) but Carter House Natural Science Museum has a friendly, wholesome atmosphere and lots of hands-on exhibits the whole family can enjoy. The main gallery showcases two exhibits a year, either developed by the staff or borrowed from other institutions. Look for "Garbage... and all that trash" in 1994-95. Permanent exhibits include the Living Lab, with guinea pigs, a beehive, a pond, and "stuff for little kids"; the pitch-dark Nocturnal Room, inhabited by live night creatures; and Animal Discovery Time, when, every hour on the hour, wildlife from the museum's collection of non-releasable animals—snakes, turtles, rats, rabbits, guinea pigs, red-tailed hawk, great horned owl—are brought out for visitors to meet face to face. Pick up a map and brochure for a quarter-mile, self-guided nature walk through the Redding Arboretum after your visit.

Rental: Children can celebrate their birthdays at the museum—$25 for up to ten guests.

REDDING MUSEUM OF ART AND HISTORY
56 Quartz Hill Road (Caldwell Park), Redding
Phone: (916) 225-4155
Hours: Tues.-Sun. 10:00 a.m.-5:00 p.m., June 1-Aug. 31; Tues.-Fri.,
**   Sun. noon-5:00 p.m.; Sat. 10:00 a.m.-5:00 p.m., Sept. 1-May 31.**

In 1976, the Redding Art Federation and the Shasta Historical Society joined forces to create the Redding Museum of Art and History, designed

"End Times" by Michael Beck (watercolor). Photo by Richard Ray, courtesy of Redding Museum of Art.

by local architect Alan Martin in a style fondly dubbed "Redding Moderne" or "really adequate."

Major renovation five years ago brought the contemporary look of state-of-the-art exhibits to the history gallery. Native American baskets from the museum's extensive collection as well as gold-mining, logging, and railroad artifacts chronicle the area's history, from the first Wintu inhabitants to the present. A beautifully designed 1920s gas station featuring the front half of a Model T Ford pays homage to the economic force that saved the town—tourism.

The museum mounts nine art exhibits a year, showcasing mostly contemporary works of local, regional, national and international reputation, with occasional shows of 19th century art. In 1994 look for "Instant Memories," Polaroid images by Joyce Tennyson, John Reuter, Sandi Fellman and others, and "Paintings from Paradise," early 20th century California Impressionist painters including Granville Redmond, Guy Rose and William Wendt.

Library: Staffed by the Shasta Historical Society, the library has art and history texts, maps, papers, photographs (17,000), and microfilm relating to Shasta County.

Gift Shop: The four-star museum shop serves both Carter House and the Art and History Museum. Stock ranges from inexpensive children's science toys to one-of-a-kind, museum-quality pieces by local artists priced from $5 to $150.

TEHAMA COUNTY

CORNING

CORNING MUSEUM★
794 - 3rd Street, Corning
Phone: (916) 824-7033
Hours: Tues. 1:00-4:00 p.m., special tours by appointment.
Admission: Free

The one-room Corning Museum occupies the former council chambers in the city hall, once the Old Maywood Hotel. The museum displays "a little bit of everything about Corning" including the olive industry, Corning schools through the years, town churches, servicemen of various wars, businesses, and farming, and is working on histories of Corning area families.

Library: City records and information on the olive industry and farming are available for research.

GERBER

**SOUTH SHASTA
MODEL RAILROAD★**
The Humann Ranch
8620 Holmes Road, Gerber
Phone: (916) 385-1389
**Hours: Sunday noon–4:00 p.m.,
    April–May.**
**Admission: Adults $4.00,
    children $3.00**

Godfrey Humann began building a
quarter-scale model of the Southern
Pacific Gerber to Dunsmuir railroad in
1950. Forty-two years and 290,000 work hours later, he completed one
of the largest model train set-ups in the world, including 900 feet of
track, 16 steam locomotives, 100 railroad cars, and a miniature reproduction of the buildings, bridges and terrain from Gerber to Dunsmuir.
Visitors are treated to an hour-long miniature railroad show, a ride on a
2-foot gauge steam train, and a look at antique gas and steam-powered
farming equipment in the Antique Farm Machinery Museum.

*Godfrey Humann,
builder of the South
Shasta Model
Railroad, checks the
operation of a big
4-8-4, #4459,
with a northbound
freight crossing the
Sacramento River
north of Redding.
The bridge is built
on a curve and is
complete even to the
rivets. It took 300
hours of labor to
build. Courtesy of
South Shasta
Model Railroad.*

RED BLUFF

WILLIAM B. IDE ADOBE STATE HISTORIC PARK
21659 Adobe Road, Red Bluff
Phone: (916) 527-5927
Hours: Daily 8:00 a.m.-5:00 p.m.
Admission: $3.00 per car

William Brown Ide, an Illinois farmer, became the first and only president of the Bear Flag Republic on June 14, 1846; just 22 days after a
group of thirty American settlers captured Sonoma and declared themselves independent of Mexican rule, Commodore Sloat raised the
American flag at Monterey, and the California Republic became a
protectorate of the United States. After his brief term as president, Ide
joined the Gold Rush and managed to bring back $25,000, which he
used to purchase part of a Mexican land grant called Rancho de la
Barranca Colorada (Red Bluff Ranch).

While Ide's story is a fascinating one, it has nothing to do with the Ide
Adobe. Unfortunately for fans of accurate historical interpretation and its
first owner, Abraham Dibble, the building has been misidentified.
Nevertheless, the park, with its historic buildings set amidst a grove of
massive oaks overlooking the Sacramento River, is a charming place to
visit. The restored and furnished 1852 adobe home, hand-dug well,

adobe smokehouse, carriage shed, and small corral give a good idea of frontier life during early California's American period. Children are particularly fond of Lucy, the park's 27-year-old resident donkey, and the rare, white-tailed black Spanish hens.

KELLY–GRIGGS HOUSE MUSEUM★
311 Washington Street, Red Bluff
Phone: (916) 527-1129
Hours: Thurs.-Sun. 1:00-4:00 p.m.
Admission: Free

This classic, ten-room Victorian combines furnished period rooms and costumed mannequins with Tehama County history exhibits. The Pioneer Room displays early Chinese and pioneer artifacts. Yahi and Maidu artwork, baskets, and tools are on view in the Ishi Room; artwork dating back to the 1800s hangs in the Emmet Pendleton Stairway Gallery.

TEHAMA

TEHAMA COUNTY MUSEUM
C & 3rd Streets, Tehama
Phone: (916) 384-2420
Hours: Sat. & Sun. 1:00-4:00 p.m.
Admission: Free

From grinding rocks to pictures made with feathers to this 1870 wedding dress, the Tehama County Museum is packed with local historic artifacts. Courtesy of Tehama County Museum.

"You can't miss the Tehama County Museum," we were assured when we telephoned for directions. "It's the only two-story skyscraper in town." The museum's venerable 1859 building housed the Masonic Lodge for 117 years and one of the county's earliest schools. It now displays a fine collection of historic artifacts, including Nomlaki grinding rocks, the chopping knife given to William Ide as a wedding present by his mother, Dr. Fred Godbolt's famous pink dental chair, and the county's first post office—all of it—from Moon's Ranch. The natural history exhibits include mastodon bones, the Gem and Mineral Society exhibit, and a collection of Mrs. Nelda Dale Babb's pictures of birds made from feathers. This charming museum with a small budget and a big sense of humor manages just the right blend of homegrown folksiness and scholarly interpretation.

Gift Shop: Books, jams, sunbonnets and other home-made goodies are available at the gift shop at very reasonable prices.

GLENN COUNTY

ORLAND

HERITAGE TRAIL*
Glenn County Fairgrounds
Yolo Street, Orland
Phone: (916) 865-3902
Hours: call (916) 865-1168 for Fair and train schedules.

Visitors to the Glenn County Fair can recapture a bit of the past as they
walk along the Heritage Trail, established by the Orland Historical
Society. The first building to be restored and moved to the site was the
1891 Chrome Schoolhouse, with its original bell and pull-rope still intact.
The schoolhouse was soon joined by the Village Blacksmith Shop,
operated from 1913 to 1958 by village smithy Harry Strawn. The
Templeton Service Station, a mom-and-pop operation complete with
original pumps installed in 1927, displays memorabilia from several of
Orland's long-gone gas stations. The cluster of historic buildings also
includes the old Southern Pacific Depot, a 1917 tankhouse, a print shop,
and a windmill. The most recent addition is the Orland Newville &
Pacific Railroad, a miniature replica of an 1876 Baldwin three-foot
narrow gauge locomotive.

ALTA SCHMIDT HOUSE MUSEUM*
936 Fourth Street, Orland
Phone: (916) 865 5111
Hours: Sun. 2:00-5:00 p.m., April-October.
Admission: Free

Built in 1901 by C.F. and Katie Schmidt, the Alta Schmidt House
Museum is a small, gingerbread-trimmed Victorian cottage filled with
memorabilia of the Schmidt family and the town of Orland. Each of the
five rooms commemorates a part of Orland's past, from early businesses
to World War I veterans, to the town's famed Silver Coronet Marching
Band. From high-ceilinged Victorian bedrooms to the 1950s kitchen,
the rooms reflect changes in style as the house was remodeled over the
course of time.

WILLOWS

THE MUSEUM*
336 West Walnut, Willows
Phone: (916) 934-5644
Hours: Thurs. 1:00-4:00 p.m., October–May; Thurs. 9:00 a.m.-
   noon, June–September.
Admission: Free

A stately, neoclassic building on a shady corner in downtown Willows,

this former Carnegie Library now houses the museum of Glenn County.
Commonly known as the Willows Museum, its official name is simply
The Museum, to emphasize the fact that it does not belong to any one
town, but the entire county. Among the thousands of artifacts and
photographs on display are a grindstone made by Peter Lassen—the first
item to be donated—and a complete wedding ensemble worn by
Annabelle Compton Sexton.

SACRAMENTO NATIONAL WILDLIFE REFUGE
County Road 99-W, Willows
Phone: (916) 934-2801
**Hours: Daily 7:30 a.m.–4:00 p.m., October–February; open Mon.–
    Fri. 7:30 a.m.–4:00 p.m., March–September.**
Admission: Free

The Sacramento National Wildlife Refuge is the headquarters for four
separate refuges (Sacramento, Colusa, Delevan, and Sutter) that encompass 24,000 acres of wetlands, representing just a small portion of the vast
grasslands, seasonal marshes, and permanent ponds that once existed in
the Sacramento Valley. Today, most of the wetlands are gone, having
been drained and reclaimed for agriculture. Ironically, the refuges
established in the thirties to prevent waterfowl from raiding crops now
provide a winter home for migratory waterfowl and a year-round
residence for other birds and mammals (over 300 species). Visitors can
observe the wildlife from walking trails and auto tour routes. Stop at the
visitor center first for a look at posters and mounted specimens and to
pick up maps and guides, including a checklist of the 269 species of birds
recorded on the refuge since 1937.

BUTTE COUNTY

CHICO

BIDWELL MANSION STATE HISTORIC PARK
525 The Esplanade, Chico
Phone: (916) 895-6144
Hours: Daily 10:00 a.m.–5:00 p.m.
Admission: $2.00

Wherever you go in Chico, you will encounter the names of John and
Annie Bidwell. Arriving in California in 1841, John Bidwell found
employment as John Sutter's clerk. A master of being in the right place at
the right time, after he and Sutter confirmed that John Marshall had
indeed discovered gold, Bidwell himself found gold at Bidwell Bar. This
enabled him to purchase the 26,000-acre Rancho del Arroyo Chico, in
its day the most famous and diverse agricultural enterprise in California.

Active in politics, Bidwell was a member of California's first Senate, a member of Congress, twice a candidate for governor, and candidate for president on the Prohibition ticket. The Bidwells' prominence rested not just on wealth and politics, but on their commitment to righteous causes, and their generous hospitality. Prohibition, women's rights, education, and Christianity

Wherever you go in Chico, you'll run across references to the Bidwells, here seated on the south porch of their home, ca. 1893. Photo by Henry W. Henshaw, courtesy of Bidwell Mansion State Park and Special Collections Meriam Library, CSU Chico.

were among their causes. Susan B. Anthony, Rutherford B. Hayes, and General Sherman were among the notable guests at the Bidwell Mansion.

Begun in 1865, the 26-room, three-story brick building was designed in the romantic Italianate style by Henry Cleaveland, architect of the original Palace Hotel in San Francisco. Dark, polished furniture inhabits the cavernous rooms and the downstairs parlor door is draped with American flags. Guided tours are available on the hour, and you can learn all about the Bidwells in the recently opened visitor center.

CALIFORNIA STATE UNIVERSITY, CHICO
The second-oldest institution in the state system, CSU Chico was established in 1887 on an 8-acre cherry orchard donated by John Bidwell. Originally a teachers' college, Chico has become one of the state's largest universities, with a 15-acre campus and a student body of over 15,000. Historic buildings, museums, and galleries on campus are listed below.

MUSEUM OF ANTHROPOLOGY
Langdon Hall, CSU Chico
Phone: (916) 898-5397
Hours: Mon.-Fri. 8:00 a.m.-5:00 p.m., September–May.

Chico's Museum of Anthropology was set up as a teaching museum to showcase student-curated shows and provide practical experience in museum operation. A national, juried, thematic photo exhibit begins each academic year, followed by a show on an ethnographic, historic, or contemporary theme. Past exhibits have focused on Ancient Egypt, Polynesia, historic Chico, and women's roles.

UNIVERSITY ART GALLERY
Taylor Hall, CSU Chico
Phone: (916) 898-5861
Hours: Mon.-Fri. 10:00 a.m.-4:00 p.m.; Sun. 1:00-5:00 p.m.

The 2,000-square-foot University Art Gallery mounts eight shows a year, exhibiting the work of students, faculty, and nationally-known contemporary artists.

LIFE SCIENCES
Holt Hall, CSU Chico
Phone: (916) 898-5356

Holt Hall, designed by John Carl Warnecke, contains the University Herbarium, an instructional/research collection of over 26,000 plant specimens available only by guided tour; the Vertebrate Museum, a collection of birds, mammals, and reptiles available only by guided tour; the Marine Aquaria, changing displays of organisms collected from the northern California coast; the Edith V. Pennington Hooper Shell Collection; and the Hazel Schmidt Butterfly and Moth Collection.

JANET TURNER PRINT GALLERY
Mezzanine, Laxon Auditorium, CSU Chico
Phone: (916) 898-4476
Hours: Mon.-Fri. 10:00 a.m.-4:00 p.m.

Works from the Janet Turner collection of 3,000 prints are displayed on a rotating basis. Turner collected prints by outstanding artists from many regions and nationalities to illustrate print-making techniques.

CHICO CREEK NATURE CENTER
1968 East Eighth, Chico
Phone: (916) 891-4671
Hours: Tues.-Fri. 10:00 a.m.-5:00 p.m., Sat. & Sun. 11:00 a.m.-
   4:00 p.m., summer; Tues.-Sun. 11:00 a.m.-4:00 p.m., fall.
Admission: Free

Located in the heart of Bidwell Park, the third largest municipal park in the United States, Chico Creek Nature Center provides quality environmental education for children and adults via a nature museum, native plant gardens, nature walks, classes, and seminars.

The center and museum are located on the site of the second forestry station in California, established in 1888 on 37 acres of land donated by John Bidwell. The purpose of the forestry stations was to see which of many different types of trees from around the world would be suitable for commercial and ornamental use in California. Many of the original trees can be seen today on the "World of Trees" nature trail. Pick up a brochure and map to guide you along this half-mile loop.

Inside the Nature Museum you will see interpretive displays about the natural history of Bidwell Park, and the Living Museum, home to a lively group of non-releasable wild animals.

Library: Domestic animals—rabbits, guinea pigs, mice—can be checked out from the Animal Lending Library for one week. The center provides cages, bedding, food, and care instructions for $3.00.

Gift Shop: The museum store features the best selection of birdhouses and feeders in town, plus field guides and nature books.

CHICO MUSEUM
141 Salem Street, Chico
Phone: (916) 891-4336
Hours: Wed.-Sun. noon-4:00 p.m.
Admission: Free

From the Maidu exhibit to the ubiquitous blacksmith shop to an imaginative series of temporary exhibits, the Chico Museum creates sophisticated, high-quality shows of historical interest. Look for "Flight Through Time: Chico's Aviation History" in 1994.

The lovely, 1904 Spanish Colonial-style, Carnegie library building started out Romanesque, but according to one cynical museum member, they "taco-belled" it in 1939. The museum offers 6,000 square feet of exhibit space in two major galleries, a small video theater, and the beautiful Chinese Gallery, which features the main altar from the Chinese temple on Cherry Street.

Gift Shop: Local history books, games, gifts, and posters from museum shows are available in the gift shop.

COLEMAN MEMORIAL COMMUNITY MUSEUM*
13518 Centerville Road
**   (Butte Creek Canyon), Chico**
Phone: (916) 342-9124
Hours: Sat. & Sun. 1:00-4:00 p.m.
Admission: Free

Also known as the Centerville Museum, the Coleman Memorial Community Museum tells the story of Butte Creek Canyon—a tale "at once eloquent, brutal and prophetic, recalling a history of fire and flood, of savagery and exploitation, of brave dreams and wasted lives." The cement-block structure, built in 1976, displays a large collection of stone implements used by the Maidu people who lived in the canyon for centuries before the first white settlers arrived. An impressive basket display and an exhibit about Ishi, the last Yahi,

Ishi, the last member of California's Yahi tribe, spent his last years living at the University of California's anthropology museum, where he shared his knowledge of traditional skills with scholars and tourists. Courtesy of Phoebe Apperson Hearst Museum of Anthropology.

celebrate other Native American groups. Chinese artifacts commemorate the Chinese laborers who suffered at the hands of bigots a hundred years ago. Pioneer artifacts include furniture, farm equipment and the replicated interior of the one-room Centerville School. (The actual 1894 school building is now used as a community center.) Gold-mining equipment and a 5-1/2 ounce gold nugget chronicle the area's Gold Rush history.

THE STANSBURY HOUSE
307 West Fifth Street, Chico
Phone: (916) 895-3848
Hours: Sat. & Sun. 1:00–4:00 p.m.
Admission: $1.00, students 50¢

A visit to the Stansbury House today is like stepping back to 1883; almost nothing has been changed since the year it was built by Dr. Oscar Stansbury, one of Chico's first doctors. Set on one quarter of a city block that was purchased for $1,000, the Italianate Victorian home designed by Sacramento architect A.A. Cook featured wall-to-wall carpeting, indoor plumbing, and other modern conveniences, all at a cost of $7,200. This was a princely sum for an upper middle-class family home in those days. Daughter Angeline, a beloved art teacher at Chico High School, was born in the house and lived her entire 91 years there, maintaining things exactly as her parents had left them, right down to the original wallpaper.

Above all else, Angeline feared that her family home would become a fraternity house when she died. Fortunately, the city of Chico and the Stansbury Home Preservation Association have saved it from that fate.

Rental: Call for information.

FORBESTOWN

YUBA FEATHER HISTORICAL MUSEUM★
19096 New York House Road, Forbestown
Phone: (916) 675-1025 (summer); 675-2800 or 589-0218 (off-season)
Hours: Sat., Sun., holidays noon–4:00 p.m., Memorial Day–
**   Labor Day.**
Admission: Free

Housed in a replica of Forbestown's old schoolhouse, the Yuba Feather Historical Museum highlights the area's mining, ranching, and logging history with permanent and changing exhibits. The new Junior Museum features dioramas and family genealogies created by local schoolchildren. Outside are a country store, blacksmith shop, and exhibits of mining and logging equipment.

OROVILLE

BUTTE COUNTY HISTORICAL SOCIETY (THE EHMANN HOME)
1480 Lincoln Street, Oroville
Phone: (916) 533-5316
Hours: Sat. & Sun. 1:00-4:00 p.m.
Admission: $1.00 donation requested

The Ehmann Home serves as the headquarters and museum of the Butte County Historical Society. Historical exhibits feature Ishi, Robin Hood, Erle Stanley Gardner, and the Ehmann Olive Company.

Gift Shop: Ehmann olives and historical publications are the specialties of this shop.

BUTTE COUNTY PIONEER MEMORIAL MUSEUM
2332 Montgomery Street, Oroville
Phone: (916) 534-0198
Hours: Sunday 1:00-4:00 p.m., and by appointment.
Admission: Free

Florence Danforth Boyle, a mover and shaker in Oroville, started the Butte County Pioneer Memorial Museum in 1932. It is now lovingly maintained by her daughter, Betty Davis, practically single-handedly. Built on the site of Oroville's first sawmill with rocks from a nearby Native American village and metal doors from the Masonic temple, the 6,000-square-foot museum was designed to represent a miner's cabin. The eclectic range of collections includes dolls, guns, musical instruments, clocks, mining artifacts, Native American baskets, bootjacks, cameras, leather postcards, and clothing. Some of the most notable items are a handmade gold needle, an invitation to a hanging, an authenticated box stolen by Black Bart, and a tear jar from Oroville's Chinatown. Long on treasures but short on interpretation, the museum could use some help and sprucing up.

CHEROKEE MUSEUM*
4226 Cherokee Road, Oroville
Phone: (916) 533-1849
Hours: Weekends and by appointment
Admission: 50¢

Cherokee, founded in 1849 by Cherokee Indians, was once the site of the world's largest hydraulic gold-mining operation. Today it is a ghost town whose museum occupies a former miners' boardinghouse, displaying gold-mining artifacts, bottles, photos, fossils, minerals, and memorabilia relating to the town's founders. Outdoor attractions include grinding rocks, a caboose, a pioneer herbal garden, a cemetery, a school, and remarkable scenery.

LAKE OROVILLE VISITOR CENTER
917 Kelly Ridge Road, Oroville
Phone: (916) 538-2219
Hours: Daily 9:00 a.m.–5:00 p.m.
Admission: Free

The State Water Project supplies more than two-thirds of the people in California with their water, and irrigates hundreds of thousands of acres of farmland. With state-of-the-art graphic displays, videos, and push-button exhibits, this award-winning visitor center, jointly operated by the California Department of Water Resources and California State Parks, tells the story of the construction of the Oroville Dam and the State Water Project. The museum also features a replica miner's cabin and a diorama of a Maidu village.

The center's 47-foot viewing tower, the highest point in the area, gives visitors a sweeping view of the Oroville Dam, which is the tallest earthen dam in the United States; the Sutter Buttes, the smallest complete mountain range in the world; and the new Bidwell Bar Bridge. A self-guided nature walk begins at the center.

Gift Shop: Interpretive, educational books and souvenir items are available in the lobby.

C.F. LOTT HISTORIC HOME IN SANK PARK
1067 Montgomery Street, Oroville
Phone: (916) 538-2497
Hours: Sun., Mon., Tues., Fri. 1:00–4:00 p.m.
Admission: $2.00, groups of 15 or more $1.50, children
under 12 free

Forty-niner Charles Fayette Lott, a judge and state senator, built this Victorian Gothic revival cottage for his bride Susan in 1856. Many years later, in her fifties and after having reconciled herself to the idea of being a spinster, their daughter Cornelia married Jess Sank, who built many of the interesting features of the old-fashioned Victorian gardens that now comprise Sank Park. As an historic house museum, the Lott Home serves as a cultural repository for furniture, paintings, rugs, textiles, clothes, silver, and glassware from 1849 to 1910. Many of the Lotts' personal possessions are displayed in the Pioneer Museum.

Rental: Portions of Sank Park, the gazebo, and patio with kitchen may be rented for private parties, meetings, weddings, and receptions. Call the Department of Parks and Trees at (916) 538-2415.

OREGON CITY MUSEUM*
5 Oregon City Trail, Oroville
Phone: (916) 534-8237
Hours: Weekends and by appointment
Admission: Free

Emmett Galbraith started out collecting old things, like woodburning cookstoves, washing machines, old tools and such. Then he needed a place to keep his collection so he built a room lined with old lumber and collected some more old things—an 1870 piano, an old printing press, 58 monkey wrenches. Before you knew it word got out that it was a museum. Whenever the Galbraiths are home their museum is open and you are invited to stop by—it's next to the old school on the other side of the covered bridge on Tabletop Mountain.

OROVILLE CHINESE TEMPLE
1500 Broderick Street, Oroville
Phone: (916) 538-2415
Hours: Thurs.-Mon. 11:00 a.m.-4:30 p.m.;
  Tues. & Wed. 1:00-4:00 p.m.
Admission: $2.00, children under 12 free

Sent by their villages in China, a dozen men arrived in San Francisco in 1840, prepared to buy land and establish businesses. A slick salesman sold them riverfront property to the north, neglecting to tell them that the river flooded every year. Despite the floods the men prospered, sending over $5 million in gold back to China. In 1863, the Emperor Tung Chi sent gifts and money to build a temple for the Chinese community, which had grown to 10,000 members. In 1907, a major flood decimated the Oroville Chinese community, which today numbers less than 100. The temple complex was deeded to the city in 1937 and opened to visitors in 1949.

The restored temples represent the three major religious philosophies of China; the main temple of Liet Sheng Kong—Temple of Assorted Deities—served Taoists, Confucianists, and Buddhists. Its hand-carved teak panels, covered with gold leaf, were among the emperor's gifts. Upstairs behind the main temple, the Moon Temple is dedicated to Buddha, its round door representing the eternal circle of life. A council room used for conducting business affairs and a replica of a Chinese miner's shack illustrate the social and economic life of the once-thriving Chinese community.

The modern museum sits beyond the beautiful garden courtyard, one of the few authentic Chinese gardens open to the public in the United States. On exhibit is an extensive collection of embroidered tapestries, porcelains, bronzes, and folk art, and a rare collection of shadow puppets.

A handsome display of Chinese and American garments from 1850 to 1930 is arranged to show the contrast between the two cultures.

Gift Shop: The gift shop carries a fine selection of Chinese artifacts.

PARADISE

GOLD NUGGET MUSEUM*
502 Pearson Road, Paradise
Phone: (916) 872-8722
Hours: Wed.-Sun. noon-4:00 p.m.
Admission: Free

Named in honor of the Willard Nugget, a 54-pound gold nugget discovered in 1859, the Gold Nugget Museum collection of 19th century artifacts includes mining equipment, gun and doll collections, furniture, and an exhibit featuring the famous Indian guide Yellowstone Kelley. Reconstruction of the old mining town of Paradise and the surrounding area as it must have looked in the 1850s is in progress.

Rental: The reconstructed town is available for weddings and private parties.

YUBA COUNTY

MARYSVILLE

MARY AARON MUSEUM
704 D Street, Marysville
Phone: (916) 743-1004
Hours: Thurs.-Sat. 1:00-4:00 p.m.
Admission: Free

As the last stop on the way to the gold mines and the first stop on the way out, Marysville enjoyed a colorful past. A careless approach to historic preservation permitted the destruction of many of the town's old structures, leaving the Aaron house to be especially treasured.

The handsome, 1855 Gothic revival home of the Aaron family is the only example left in the West of the work of the prominent East Coast architect Warren Miller. It has been a Victorian house museum featuring local history exhibits for the past thirty years. Much-needed repairs shut the museum down for a while, but it reopened in 1992 for three days a week. It now features a carefully furnished parlor restored to its appearance in 1875 when the Aaron family moved in, and a bright and airy gallery space that showcases changing exhibits on local history. Restoration work continues on the days when the museum is closed. Long-time fans are especially looking forward to the wedding exhibit in 1994, which will celebrate the 119th birthday of an old favorite, a petrified wedding cake that was discovered, perfectly preserved, in a wooden Wells Fargo storage box.

Gift Shop: The small gift shop stocks local history books and Victorian items. Smart shoppers never miss the annual antique show and sale held the last weekend in February for the past 33 years.

EDWARD F. BEALE MUSEUM*
Beale Air Force Base, Marysville
Phone: (916) 634-2034
Hours: Mon.-Fri. 9:00 a.m.-5:00 p.m.; Sat. 10:00 a.m.-4:00 p.m.
Admission: Free

Established in 1942, Camp Beale housed German prisoners of war during World War II. The museum displays objects from the 13th Armored Division and the 9th and 100th Bomb Groups.

MUSEUM OF THE FORGOTTEN WARRIORS*
5865 A Road, Marysville
Phone: (916) 742-3090
Hours: Thurs. 7:00-10:00 p.m.; first Sat. 10:00 a.m.-4:00 p.m.
**   Veterans Day 10:00 a.m.-4:00 p.m., Memorial Day 10:00 a.m.-**
**   4:00 p.m., or phone for special group showings.**
Admission: Free

Established in 1985, the privately-owned Museum of the Forgotten Warriors is dedicated to all who served in the Vietnam War. On display are artifacts, photographs, and personal histories relating to Americans, South Vietnamese, and the Viet Cong. Exhibits in the three galleries tell the story of the war from a soldier's perspective. An OH-23 light observation helicopter, a UH1 "Charley" Huey helicopter, and a USMC "Ontos" tank stand outside the museum.

SUTTER COUNTY

YUBA CITY

COMMUNITY MEMORIAL MUSEUM OF SUTTER COUNTY
1333 Butte House Road, Yuba City
Phone: (916) 741-7141
Hours: Tues.-Fri. 9:00 a.m.-5:00 p.m.; Sat. & Sun. noon-4:00 p.m.

In 1841, just south of what is now Yuba City, John Sutter established Hock Farm, the first major agriculture project in northern California. To this day, Sutter County retains a rural, family-oriented character which is reflected in the Community Memorial Museum. Built in 1975, the spacious, modern structure showcases Sutter County treasures and memories in permanent exhibits, beginning with the Maidu and continuing into the mid-1900s, and emphasizing domestic and agricultural history. State-of-the-art exhibits combine a variety of ordinary and extraordinary artifacts with stories and quotations. Kids especially love the bearskin rug, vintage player piano, and toy collection. Study papers are provided to help you learn more. The museum mounts three to four changing exhibits a year. "Call for the Doctor," an exhibit about early medicine and health care in Sutter County which was up during our visit, showed admirable thoroughness and professionalism. From the graceful outdoor fountain to the gigantic guest register to the first-class exhibits and programs, the Community Memorial Museum is exactly what a small county museum should be.

COLUSA COUNTY

WILLIAMS

SACRAMENTO VALLEY MUSEUM★
1491 E Street, Williams
Phone: (916) 473-2978
Hours: Mon.-Sat. 10:00 a.m.-4:00 p.m., Sun. 1:00-4:00 p.m.,
April 1-October 31; Fri. & Sat. 10:00 a.m-4:00 p.m.,
November 1-March 31.
Admission: $1.00

The thirty-year-old Sacramento Valley Museum is housed in the former Williams High School, built in 1911. With 22 rooms on two floors, the museum has ample space to exhibit its many artifacts, dating from the 1800s through the 1920s. The women's room displays women's clothes from 1800 to 1920, the children's room has kids' clothing and toys, and a living room, parlor, kitchen, bedroom, and attic are furnished with period antiques. The quilt room displays the museum's quilt collection. There are also a document room, apothecary shop, barber shop, black-smith and saddlery shop, and a general store filled with merchandise from the 1800s.

SOLANO COUNTY

RIO VISTA

DUTRA MUSEUM OF DREDGING★
345 St. Gertrude Avenue, Rio Vista
Phone: (707) 374-6339
Hours: By appointment
Admission: Free

Housed in the Dutra family home, the Dutra Museum of Dredging tells the personal history of several generations of the Dutra family and their involvement with creating the canals that weave through today's San Joaquin Delta.

RIO VISTA MUSEUM
16 North Front Street, Rio Vista
Phone: (707) 374-5169
Hours: Sat. & Sun. 1:30–4:30 p.m.,
and by appointment.
Admission: Free

Created in response to the nation's Bicentennial, the Rio Vista Museum features a staggering assortment of artifacts donated by local residents. One wall displays a complete collection of California license plates from 1914 to 1990, along with front page headline stories of historical significance. Another wall, covered with photographs of Rio Vista farms, recalls the town's heyday as the asparagus capitol of the world.

Another example of the Sacramento Valley's homegrown culture, the Rio Vista Museum features a staggering assortment of artifacts donated by local residents. Photo courtesy of Rio Vista Museum Association.

WESTERN RAILWAY MUSEUM
5848 State Highway 12, Rio Vista Junction
Phone: (707) 374-2978
Hours: Wed.–Sun. 11:00 a.m.–5:00 p.m.
Admission: Adults $5.00, children 4–12 $2.00,
children under 4 $1.00.

Anyone who lived in the Bay Area between 1903 and 1958 will remember the sleek Key System trains that traveled from Richmond to Hayward via Berkeley, Oakland, and San Leandro, and from the East Bay to San Francisco on the lower deck of the Bay Bridge. BART, traveling much the same route as the former Key System, has replaced this bit of history, but train lovers and nostalgia buffs can still see and even ride the Key Route trains at the 25-acre Western Railway Museum. The museum has 110 pieces of historic rolling stock in addition to streetcars and trains from the Key Route collection, including a 1904 wooden interurban train that operated between Petaluma, Santa Rosa, and Sebastopol, and California's last nickel streetcar, from Chico. Admission includes unlimited rides on the vintage trains.

Gift Shop: Railroad books and memorabilia are available in the gift shop.

VACAVILLE

PEÑA ADOBE AND MOWERS–GOHEEN MUSEUM
Peña Adobe Park
Hwy 80, Vacaville
Phone: (707) 449-5198
Hours: Wed.-Sun. 9:00 a.m.-5:00 p.m. March-September.

In 1841, having crossed the Southwest on the Santa Fe Trail, Juan Manuel Vaca and Juan Peña arrived in what is today Vacaville. They built adobe houses on land grants received from General Vallejo and established successful ranchos. The Vaca adobe has long since disappeared (but by Vaca's express proviso, the town of Vacaville serves as his memorial) and today, only the Peña adobe remains. Restored to its original state, the three-room house, with two-foot thick adobe walls and hand-hewn redwood joists, doors, and lintels, exhibits ranching artifacts. One bedroom appears much as it might have over a century ago.

Near the adobe, the small, one-room Mowers–Goheen Museum exhibits Native American artifacts found near the adobe, maps, and photographs. A handful of 2,000-year-old beans found in a pot in Iowa are an intriguing, if incongruous, element of the display.

VACAVILLE MUSEUM
213 Buck Avenue, Vacaville
Phone: (707) 447-4513
Hours: Wed.-Sun. 1:00-4:30 p.m.
Admission: Adults $1.00, children 50¢; free on Wednesdays

An elegant table setting graces an exhibit at Vacaville's thoroughly up-to-date local history museum. Photo by Dar Spain, courtesy of Vacaville Museum.

Located in Vacaville's nicest residential neighborhood, the elegant, white-pillared, red brick Vacaville Museum was built in 1983 in a style fondly referred to as faux funeral home. The up-to-date facility houses the museum's collection of local artifacts, some of which are on permanent exhibit in the upstairs meeting room/gallery. The downstairs galleries offer visitors two new exhibits a year, focusing on aspects of Solano County history. The museum's exhibits consistently earn the highest marks possible for scholarship, interpretation, and exhibit design. Water will be the theme for 1994-95—Solano County is surrounded by water.

Historic exhibits on droughts, floods, and transportation will be enlivened by local artists' concepts of water.

The Vacaville Museum Native Plant Interpretive Garden includes plants and bedrock mortars used by Patwin people, who inhabited the area long before the arrival of European explorers, and rocks relocated from a stream bed in English Hills.

Library: Open by appointment for research.

YOLO COUNTY

DAVIS

UNIVERSITY OF CALIFORNIA AT DAVIS

Established in 1906 as the University State Farm for the University of California at Berkeley, UC Davis now ranks among the top twenty research universities in the country. A heritage of Davis' history of biological and agricultural research is the substantial number of world-class collections housed on the campus. Some welcome visitors; others are primarily available to researchers. We were graciously received by the staff in the museums reviewed below.

ARBORETUM

Arboretum Headquarters, LaRue Road, UC Davis
Phone: (916) 752–4880
Hours: Office, Mon.–Fri. 8:00 a.m.–4:30 p.m.; gardens are open
    24 hours a day, every day of the year.
Admission: Free

A campus landmark, considered by some to be the most beautiful place in Davis, the Davis Arboretum covers approximately 125 acres on the banks of Putah Creek, near the center of the Great Central Valley of California. More than just a pretty garden, this living museum contains 30,000 living specimens of trees and woody plants, and an important collection of California native plants. Gardeners can visit demonstration gardens and learn how to create a colorful, water-conserving garden using drought-tolerant native and Mediterranean plants. Visitors can wander through the gardens on their own, or stop by the arboretum headquarters for maps and self-guided tour brochures, or, on weekends during the academic year, take a free, guided tour. Among the seventeen different sections, including one for eucalyptus, one for redwoods, and one for drought-tolerant perennials, our very favorite is the Carolee Shields White Flower Garden. Modeled on a medieval Japanese garden, the garden is intended to be viewed at night, when the especially fragrant white flowers and leaves reflect the light of the moon.

The Annual Plant Faire, held the first Saturday of October, offers 1,000 varieties of uncommon garden plants for sale.

Library: A library of horticultural, botanical, and ecological reference works is open by appointment.

Rental: The hilltop gazebo in the Carolee Shields White Flower Garden is available for weddings. Call the Campus Events Office, (916) 752–2813, for rental information.

BOHART MUSEUM OF ENTOMOLOGY
1120 Academic Surge Building, UC Davis
Phone: (916) 752-0493
Hours: 8:30 a.m.-5:00 p.m., and by appointment.
Admission: Free

The Bohart Museum of Entomology collection has grown since 1947
from two wooden boxes to 3,500 feet of cabinet storage space containing
six million specimens—one of the major insect collections in the United
States. The rows upon rows of storage cabinets do not seem so very
impressive until the cabinet doors are opened, revealing glass-covered
wooden boxes containing beautifully mounted and labeled insects from
around the world. Although the majority of the specimens are from
California and the western United States, there are a number of exotic
creatures from Australia, Africa, and South and Central America.

Insects are the dominant form of life on earth, so you might want to
focus your visit on one aspect of entomology. You could, for example,
ask to see the camouflage displays illustrating the ways in which insects
keep from being eaten by their predators—some by resembling leaves,
twigs, thorns, and partially-eaten bark, others by mimicking toxic insects.

The museum even has a small petting zoo populated by spiders, hissing
cockroaches, and other creatures of the insect world. The busy museum
staff also performs a valuable public service by identifying household pests
and appropriate control methods.

CRAFT CENTER GALLERY*
South Silo, UC Davis
Phone: (916) 752-1475
Hours: Mon.-Thurs. noon-10:00 p.m., Fri. noon-7:00 p.m.,
     Sat. & Sun. 10:00 a.m.-6:00 p.m.
Admission: Free

Shows often represent the first public exposure for the work of artists
affiliated with the Craft Center. The center offers classes and studio
facilities for fine art, clay, photography, metal, textiles, and woodworking.

DESIGN GALLERY*
145 Walker Hall, UC Davis
Phone: (916) 752-6223
Hours: Mon.-Fri. noon-5:00 p.m., Sun. 2:00-5:00 p.m. Open only
     during exhibitions.
Admission: Free

Historical and contemporary design exhibits feature nationally and
internationally known designers, students, and faculty. Emphasis is on all
areas of environmental design: architecture, interiors, graphics, landscape,
costume, textiles, and folk art.

GEOLOGY MUSEUM
Department of Geology, UC Davis
PHone: (916) 752-0350
Hours: Mon.-Fri. 9:00 a.m.-5:00 p.m.
Admission: Free

A small sampling of the department's collection of 10,500 specimens, including fossils, rocks and minerals, is on display. Some 2,000 topographic and geologic maps are accessible to researchers by appointment.

C.N. GORMAN MUSEUM★
2401 Hart Hall, UC Davis
Phone: (916) 752-6567
Hours: Tues.-Fri. noon-5:00 p.m. and by appointment. Open only during exhibitions.
Admission: Free

The C.N. Gorman Museum features four changing art exhibitions by Native American and diverse artists each year. Featured artists have included Jean LaMarr, Frank LaPena, Frank Tuttle, Brian Tripp, Jimmie Durham, Malaquias Montoya, Edgar Heap of Birds, Enrique Chagoya, Diane Tani, Romare Bearden, and Masami Teroaka. The museum hosts opening receptions, artist lectures, and on-site t-shirt printing during public events.

MEMORIAL UNION ART GALLERY
2nd Floor, Memorial Union Building, UC Davis
Phone: (916) 752-2885
Hours: Mon.-Fri. 9:00 a.m.-5:00 p.m. Open only during exhibitions.

The gallery features a changing series of monthly exhibitions including work by UC Davis students, emerging and established California artists, and historical surveys.

RICHARD L. NELSON GALLERY
& THE FINE ARTS COLLECTION★
124-125 Art Building, UC Davis
Phone: (916) 752-8500
Hours: Mon.-Fri. noon-5:00 p.m.; Sun. 2:00-5:00 p.m. Open only during exhibitions.
Admission: Free

Distinguished for its program of changing exhibitions, the gallery features works of regional, national, and international artsists. Selections from The Fine Arts Collection, the campus' major collection of art, are frequently exhibited in the Entry Gallery and various campus locations.

HATTIE WEBER MUSEUM OF DAVIS
445 C Street, Davis
Phone: (916) 758-5637
Hours: Wed. & Sat. 10:00 a.m.-4:00 p.m.
Admission: Free

This small city museum opened in 1992 in the former Davis Free Library building. Named for Hattie Weber, the first paid librarian in Davisville (now Davis), the museum chronicles the history of the Davis Library System and the city of Davis. Miss Hattie, as she was known, is credited with teaching every kid in town how to read during her long career as the town librarian, from 1906 until 1953. The permanent exhibit, "The Role of the Library," follows the institution from its beginnings in 1870 in the upstairs hall of a private home, through the construction of the current building in 1911 under the charge of the Davis Bachelor Girls, to the present. Changing exhibits focus on the cultural life of the town.

Library: A small collection of oral histories, photographs, and memorabilia is available for research by appointment.

WOODLAND

A.W. HAYS ANTIQUE TRUCK MUSEUM
2000 East Main Street, Woodland
Phone: (916) 666-1044
Hours: Daily 9:00 a.m.-4:00 p.m.
Admission: Adults $5.00, children 14 & under $2.00

Starting with a battered 1929 Chevrolet truck, A.W. "Pop" Hays assembled the nation's largest collection of vintage trucks. Courtesy of A.W. Hays Antique Truck Museum.

A.W. Hays ("Pop") started his trucking business with a new, 1929 one-and-a-half ton Chevrolet truck. By the time he retired in 1977, he owned the largest agricultural carrier business in California. Worried that retirement might leave him with nothing to do, a friend presented him with a 1929 Chevrolet truck badly in need of restoration. Twenty-five years later, the A.W. Hays Antique Truck Museum has the largest collection of vintage trucks in the United States. At last count, 190 trucks representing 120 different manufacturers were on display, from a one-cylinder 1902 Knox to a 1967 Kenworth. Some of the trucks have been restored to their original condition, and many are preserved in street condition, a testimony to their years of hard labor as tankers, farm trucks, delivery, and pick-up vehicles. The Truck of the Month is apt to be a rare specimen like the 1916 C.T. Electric, manufactured by Commercial Truck Company of Philadelphia. One of a fleet used by the Curtis Publishing Company, it silently plied the streets of Philadelphia in the early morning hours, producing nary a puff of exhaust, delivering *Ladies' Home Journal* and the *Saturday Evening Post* until as late as 1962.

A.W. Hays died at age 91 in 1993 and his family has agreed to donate the museum and its collection to the Old Truck Town to be established in Sacramento on the capital's museum row. The museum will include interactive displays portraying the life of a trucker on the road, simulators to let visitors experience what it feels like to drive a truck, hands-on exhibits on truck safety and technology, and a demonstration workshop for truck restoration.

WOODLAND OPERA HOUSE STATE HISTORICAL PARK
340 Second Street, Woodland
Phone: (916) 666-9617
**Hours: Tues.-Fri. 9:00 a.m.-5:00 p.m. Tours Tues. 10:00 a.m.-
3:30 p.m.**
Admission: Free

Notables like Frederick Ward, John Philip Sousa, Walter Huston, and Sidney Greenstreet once trod the boards of the Woodland Opera House. Restored to its former splendor, the stately Victorian—northern California's oldest single-purpose theater building outside of San Francisco—is now the home of the award-winning Resident Theatre Company, with a year-round performance schedule of comedies, dramas, musicals, Shakespeare, and old time melodrama done in 19th century style. The Opera House bills itself as a living theater museum in action, but you can come in and have a look at the 1896 building during office hours, or take a 45-minute guided tour on Tuesdays, when you will see the original gas lighting system, 19th century clothing and accessories, handbills, and even graffiti left by turn-of-the-century performers.

Rental: The building may be rented for productions, meetings, weddings, and other special events when space is available.

From the Resident Company's production of "The Merry Wives of Windsor"— popular turn-of-the-century fare at the Woodland Opera House. Courtesy of Woodland Opera House State Historical Park.

YOLO COUNTY HISTORICAL MUSEUM
512 Gibson Road, Woodland
Phone: (916) 666-1045
**Hours: Mon. & Tues. 10:00 a.m.-4:00 p.m.; Sat. & Sun. noon-
4:00 p.m.**
Admission: $2.00; museum members and children under 12 free.

In the 1850s, Woodland settler William Byas Gibson built a ten-room brick house modeled after the southern mansions of his native Virginia, complete with massive wooden columns, formal pediment, and his name spelled out in cut-work decorations. Occupied by the family until 1963, the Gibson Mansion now houses the Yolo County Historical Museum. Rooms are furnished in different styles to represent successive generations of Gibsons. The outbuildings—a root cellar, dairy, and wash house— feature hands-on displays of functioning antique equipment. A separate

The great horned owl (Bubo virginianus) can see well at night, but it can hunt in total darkness. The rings of feathers around each eye collect sound in the same way that human ears do. Courtesy of Effie Yeaw Nature Center.

building houses farm equipment. Towering trees, historical plantings, and a sweeping lawn and picnic area surround the house.

Rental: The two and a half acres of grounds are available for weddings, receptions, family reunions, and other group activities.

Gift Shop: Sells books about Yolo County, reproductions of Victorian paper dolls, coloring books, stationery, and Gibson House soup, caps, t-shirts, and mugs.

SACRAMENTO COUNTY

CARMICHAEL

EFFIE YEAW NATURE CENTER
6700 Tarshes Drive, Carmichael
Phone: (916) 489-4918
Hours: Daily 10:00 a.m.-5:00 p.m.
Admission: $4.00 parking fee

This 77-acre riparian woodland preserve, located in Ancil Hoffman Park, is named for a Carmichael school teacher who fought to preserve the area from developers. The brown-shingled Effie Yeaw Nature Center offers outstanding programs for the public and changing exhibits. The permanent collection includes a great horned owl named Virginia, assorted snakes and toads and other non-releasable critters, and Nisenan and Maidu artifacts. A replica Maidu summer village has been constructed along the walkway to the center.

FOLSOM

FOLSOM HISTORIC POWERHOUSE*
Scott & Leidesdorff Streets, Folsom
Phone: (916) 988-0205
Hours: Wed.-Sun. noon-4:00 p.m., guided tours. State park is open daily.
Admission: Powerhouse free; $2.00 parking fee at park entrance

This site witnessed the technological breakthrough that ushered in the age of electricity in 1895, when three-phase, 60-cycle, alternating current was sent 22 miles to the city of Sacramento, to power street cars and light up the metropolis. The plant operated continuously until 1952, when Folsom Dam was completed. Today, it is the only intact 19th century powerhouse open to the public.

FOLSOM HISTORY MUSEUM
823 Sutter Street, Folsom
Phone: (916) 985-2707
Hours: Wed.-Sun. 11:00 a.m.-4:00 p.m.
Admission: Free

In 1959, just one year short of its hundredth birthday, Folsom's Wells
Fargo Assay Office was torn down to make way for a service station.
Outraged citizens saved the bricks, doors, ceiling, and facade of the
historic building, and when the gas station went out of business in 1960,
the resourceful residents gathered up the materials, which had been
scattered in the city park, and used them to reconstruct the building, now
the Folsom History Museum, on its original site. The large, two-room
museum opened in 1976 to retell many chapters of the town's history,
beginning with the original Maidu inhabitants of the area. The working
model of the Natomas Company Dredger No. 10 shows how gold was
excavated from the Folsom fields. A new addition to the museum, built
on the site of the Pony Express stables, presents six exhibitions a year.

Gift Shop: The large gift shop is filled with books and art prints on gold
mining, railroads, and local history, as well as handcrafted items.

FOLSOM PRISON MUSEUM
Folsom
Phone: (916) 985-2561
Hours: Daily 10:00 a.m.-7:00 p.m.
Admission: $1.00 charitable donation

*Folsom State Prison
standard cell
ca. 1950.* Photo
hand-printed at
Folsom Prison
Museum.

Folsom's most familiar landmark, the crenelated tower of Folsom Prison,
was built in 1878. The new prison was to ease overcrowding at San
Quentin. You may have seen it in the films "American Me"
or "Frankie and Johnny," or you might know it from
Johnnie Cash's rendition of "Folsom Blues." One of the
first maximum security prisons in the country, the massive,
blue-gray granite facility was designed to be escape-proof,
and was dubbed "the end of the world" by inmates.
You can learn more about its history in the museum,
located just inside the visitors' walk-in gate, across the street
from the handicraft store. A ten-minute video that plays
like a chamber of commerce public relations piece provides
a tour of the old and new prison, and tells you all about
opportunities for inmates, who can attend school or work
in one of the prison industries—Folsom turns out 40,000
license plates a day! Exhibits include a talking mannequin
in a mock cell describing living conditions in the original
prison, and a display of weapons manufactured by inmates.

Gift Shop: Souvenir items, including Folsom Prison mugs, ball & chain keychains, t-shirts, sweatshirts, caps, pencils, postcards and historic photos are available for purchase.

OLD SACRAMENTO

The old commerical district on the banks of the Sacramento River has been redeveloped, with wooden sidewalks, cobblestone streets, and restored buildings recalling the area's past as the commercial hub of the Gold Rush era, and plenty of museums. Over 100 shops and restaurants catering to the tourist trade lend an unfortunate Disneyland air to this historic district, but the museums are first rate.

THE CALIFORNIA CITIZEN–SOLDIER MUSEUM
1119 Second Street, Old Sacramento
Phone: (916) 442-2883
Hours: Tues.-Sun. 10:00 a.m.-4:30 p.m.
Admission: Adults $2.25, seniors $1.50, children under 17 $1.00

Operated by the California National Guard, the four-story California Citizen–Soldier Museum is located fifty feet from the original California Militia Headquarters. The museum chronicles California's military history with over 30,000 artifacts dating from the Mexican expeditions in the 1770s to Operation Desert Storm. Uniforms, weapons, battle flags, unit records, 19th century medical instruments, photographs, medals, personal letters, newspaper articles, and other items in chronologically-arranged displays introduce you to some surprising bits of information. Did you know, for example, that California had the greatest per capita percentage of volunteers to the Union Army of any state, including the two famous Civil War generals William "Tecumseh" Sherman and John Fremont? The museum proudly displays the country's largest collection of long arms, rifles dating back as far as the Revolutionary War, as well as California native son General George Patton's uniform. Military history buffs will have a field day here.

Library: The Library and Resource Center provides books, photographs, official and personal correspondence, and historical files with unit lineage for on-site research.

CALIFORNIA STATE RAILROAD MUSEUM
111 I Street, Old Sacramento
Phone: (916) 552-5252, ext. 7245
Hours: Daily 10:00 a.m.-5:00 p.m. (last admission 4:30 p.m.)
Admission: Adults $5.00, children 6-12 $2.00 (also good at the
     Central Pacific Passenger Station)

Although the automobile may be the dominant mode of transportation today, no other form has had more impact on the history of this nation than the railroad. Sacramento, which was the site of California's first railroad and the original terminus for the transcontinental railroad, is now the home of the largest and finest interpretive railroad museum in the country. Inside the 100,000-square-foot museum, visitors can expect to find not only interpretive exhibits and lavishly-restored locomotives and cars, but also showmanship and drama in the finest Hollywood tradition.

Begin your visit with the excellent orientation film in the theater. At the conclusion of the film the screen rises and you find yourself before a snowshed in the high Sierra. This dramatic exhibit pays tribute to the ten thousand Chinese workers who helped build the railroad and the one thousand who died on the project.

A walk through the mountain tunnel brings you to the vast Great Hall, housing 20 restored locomotives and cars dating from the 1860s to the 1960s. Children are particularly fascinated with the restored 1929 sleeping car: the gentle rocking motion, lights flashing past the blackened windows, and the sounds of railroad crossings create the sensation of a real Pullman car speeding through the night. Kids also love to board the post office car and see how the mail was collected, sorted, and distributed as late as 1967. The Gold Coast, Lucius Beebe's luxuriously decorated private car, so impressed Ronald and Nancy Reagan when they dined aboard in 1970 that funding was secured for the museum. The second floor of the museum displays an enviable collection of toy trains and models.

A 114,000-square-foot Museum of Railroad Technology is under development. The new facility will delve into the "nuts and bolts" of the railroad industry and house the rest of the museum's collection, as well as a restoration and maintenance shop.

Part of the Railroad Museum, the **Central Pacific Railroad Passenger Station** at Front and J Streets, is a reconstruction of the passenger station that served Sacramento from 1867 to 1879. The **Central Pacific Railroad Freight Depot** at Front and K Streets, a reconstruction of the original freight terminal in Sacramento, is the home of the museum's summer excursion train.

Library: Open Tues.-Sat. 1:00-5:00 p.m., located on the second floor of the Big Four Building, the library's non-circulating collection contains over one million books, periodicals, government documents, corporate records, blueprints, drawings, timetables, tickets, maps, and photographs dealing with all aspects of railroading: political, social, business history, technology, restoration, collecting, and modeling.

Gift Shop: The museum store offers the country's largest selection of railroad books, memorabilia, and gifts with a railroad motif.

DISCOVERY MUSEUM
SACRAMENTO MUSEUM OF HISTORY, SCIENCE
   AND TECHNOLOGY
101 - I Street, Old Sacramento
Phone: (916) 264-7057
Hours: Tues.-Sun. 10:00 a.m.-5:00 p.m., Memorial Day–Labor Day;
   Wed.-Fri. noon-5:00 p.m., Sat. & Sun. 10:00 a.m.-5:00 p.m.,
   winter. Open most Monday holidays—call for details.
Admission: Adults $5.00, children 6-17 $2.00, children under 6 free

The Sacramento Museum of History, Science and Technology, better known as the Discovery Museum, is the result of a merger between the Sacramento History Museum and the Sacramento Science Center.

Exhibits at Sacramento's Discovery Museum are lively, well-designed, and packed with unexpected details. Photo by Nikki Pahl, courtesy of Sacramento Museum of History, Science and Technology.

The splendid Sacramento History Museum, now the Old Sacramento home of the Discovery Museum, opened its doors in 1985. The two-story, 20,000-square-foot building, a reconstruction of Sacramento's 1854 City Hall and Waterworks building, offers a contemporary, light-filled interior with gorgeous, state-of-the-art exhibits.

The historical component focuses on the histories and cultures of the Sacramento Valley, beginning with the Miwok and Nisenan people who lived there for at least 2,500 years before Europeans arrived. Moving through the 19th century, exhibits feature the largest specimen gold collection in private ownership, Governor Leland Stanford's carriage, and a fully operational 1890s print shop. Striking a poignant, personal note is the trunk filled with the belongings of a thirteen-year-old girl who died of encephalitis in 1879. Her grief-stricken mother packed away clothing, needlework, books, invitations, and many other treasures.

The trunk was found a hundred years later, just where it had been left.

For innovative exhibit design, you can't do bettter than the Agricultural Technology Gallery, which focuses on what the Sacramento Valley is best known for. Photo murals, early agricultural implements, a recreated 1928 suburban kitchen, and a wall of crate and canning labels illustrates the exhibit's agricultural themes of planting, harvesting, processing, and marketing. The pièce de résistance is the mesmerizing conveyor belt installed by the Sacramento Almond Growers that circles endlessly above your head.

Plans are underway to improve the museum's long-term exhibits, adding more science-related information, and increasing hands-on and "minds-on" interaction for visitors. Exhibitions scheduled for the future include "The Legacy of Gold Mountain," a history of the Chinese in Sacramento, and "Puzzles and Places," an interactive exhibition about geography. Also scheduled are the "Science Carnival," "Body Wonderful," and a continuation of the popular "Adventures of Abby Quest," an extraordinarily creative exhibit that makes math fun and comprehensible to even the most mathophobic.

The Sacramento Science Center at 3615 Auburn Boulevard has become the Discovery Museum's Learning Center, with educational programs for students and teachers, a quarter-mile Nature Discovery Trail, and the only public planetarium in the region.

Gift Shop: The museum gift shop offers a large selection of books for children and adults, souvenirs, and a great selection of science toys.

B.F. HASTINGS BUILDING
1006 Second Street, Old Sacramento
Phone: (916) 445-4209
Hours: Tues.-Sun. 10:00 a.m.-5:00 p.m.
Admission: Free

In 1852, Benjamin Hastings purchased a building that was to play an important role in California history, for the sum of $1500 in a foreclosure auction. Wells, Fargo & Company, the California Supreme Court, California's first two communication companies, and Theodore Judah were among the early tenants. Purchased by the State in 1967 to be a part of the Old Sacramento restoration project, today the B.F. Hastings Building houses several museums.

In 1855, the **California Supreme Court** set up headquarters in the Hastings Building. With a few interruptions, the Court heard orators and legal tacticians plead their cases in the second-story courtroom until 1869. Restored by the State, the courtroom recaptures the opulence of its former days, with some of the original furniture and exact replicas of other 19th century pieces.

The Hastings Building also housed California's first communications enterprises. The short-lived Alta Telegraph Company, founded in 1852, was soon put out of business by a patent infringement lawsuit filed by Samuel Morse. In 1860, California Telegraph Company took over, to be replaced in turn by Western Union. Visitors to the **Communications Museum** can tap out messages to each other from two telegraph booths, reminders of this early history. (415) 668-3330.

The building also served as the western terminus for the **Pony Express**. Beginning in 1860, eighty young men on horseback completed the 1,966-mile transcontinental run in less than 10 days. The charge for delivering the mail was a mere $5.00 per half-ounce. Western Union's transcontinental telegraph line soon put the Pony Express out of business.

A lovely, batik-dyed map depicts the Pony Express routes to California, and a restored Concord Coach recalls the days of transportation by stagecoach.

Theodore Judah, a brilliant young engineer from the East, was in charge of building California's first railroad. In 1856, the line linking Sacramento to Folsom was completed, but Judah had greater plans: he envisioned a great, transcontinental railroad that would bring the nation together. It was Judah's determination that convinced the Big Four investors that his plan was possible, and his innovative design and engineering that enabled the railroad builders to cross the rugged Sierra Nevada.

Henry Wells and William Fargo, whose portraits grace the walls of the tiny, one-room **Wells Fargo History Museum**, would probably be pleased to see an automatic teller machine side-by-side with historic artifacts, reminders of the early years of Wells, Fargo & Company's presence in the Sacramento community.

HUNTINGTON HOPKINS HARDWARE STORE
Big Four Building
111 I Street, Old Sacramento
Phone: (916) 445-4209
Hours: Tues.-Sun. 10:00 a.m.-5:00 p.m.
Admission: Free

Collis Huntington, Charles Crocker, Leland Stanford, and Mark Hopkins—the Big Four—met here in the Huntington Hopkins Hardware Store with Theodore Judah to plan the first transcontinental railroad. Today Huntington, the purchasing agent, and his partner Hopkins, the shopkeeper, would feel right at home in their old shop, which is outfitted like a typical hardware store of the 1880s. Friendly clerks demonstrate sale items ranging from spinning tops, jacks, and marbles to lanterns and enamel coffee pots, and write up your purchases in an old-fashioned receipt book. In the back room a Museum of

Collis Huntington and Mark Hopkins did well as merchants before joining Leland Stanford and Charles Crocker to found the Central Pacific Railroad.

Hardware displays old tools—planes, spokeshaves, scythes, and axe handles, and horse-shoeing, blacksmithing, and barrel-making tools.

OLD EAGLE THEATRE
925 Folsom Street, Old Sacramento
Phone: (916) 446-6761
Hours: Daily 10:00 a.m.–4:00 p.m.
Admission: Free

A wooden and canvas reconstruction of the first building constructed as a theater in California, the Eagle Theatre occupies the site where the original Eagle opened to a full house on October 18, 1849. The California State Parks department offers a free, 14-minute Old Sacramento slide show during the day; contemporary plays are performed on weekends.

OLD SACRAMENTO SCHOOLHOUSE MUSEUM
Front & L Streets, Old Sacramento
Phone: (916) 483-8818
Hours: Mon.-Sat. 10:00 a.m.–4:00 p.m., Sun. 1:00–4:00 p.m.,
   volunteer staff permitting.
Admission: Free, tours $5.00 donation

This little museum, built in the style of the 1880s one-room school-houses, recreates turn-of-the-century life for the younger set.

SACRAMENTO

CALIFORNIA STATE CAPITOL MUSEUM
State Capitol, 10th & L Streets, Room 124, Sacramento
Phone: (916) 324-0333
Hours: Daily 9:00 a.m.–5:00 p.m. Tours on the hour.
Admission: Free

I consider myself pretty sophisticated, but I must admit I got quite a thrill the first time I visited the State Capitol. History is being made here, now as it has been for 125 years. You can watch the Senate and Assembly in action (when they're in session) in the 19th century legislative chambers, and Californians can visit their own legislators' offices in the east annex.

Californians came very close to losing this beautiful building, modeled after the nation's capitol. After a seismic study of the much-remodeled, hundred-year-old structure concluded that it was unsafe, money was appropriated to raze it and build a larger, modern capitol. After a lengthy battle, the Legislature decided to strengthen the existing building and restore it to its original, turn-of-the-century appearance. The six-year, $68 million reconstruction was completed in 1982.

The best way to see it all is to take one of the free, guided tours offered by the State Capitol Museum. Tickets are available in the basement tour office near the Museum Exhibit Room, where you can learn the inside story of the restoration process. Included on the tour is a visit to the seven historic offices once occupied by the governor, attorney general, secretary of state, and state treasurer, which have been restored to their 1906 appearance and furnished with authentic artifacts and beautiful antiques. Don't forget to look up at the 120-foot-tall ceiling of the rotunda or check out the displays, representing each California county, that line the hallways.

If possible, time your visit to coincide with one of the special programs. For the annual Restoration Day in January, craftsmen who worked on the building offer hands-on demonstrations of how the work was done. On Living History Day, in April, costumed docents re-enact the day in the capitol following the 1906 earthquake. Actors dressed as the governor and other state officers act out a scene from history on Living Portraits Days in August (call for exact dates).

Gift Shop: Capitol Books and Gifts, in the capitol basement, offers an endless supply of capitol souvenir items. Among them are a marble clock with the State seal, capitol Christmas ornaments, capitol cocktail napkins, old maps, copies of the California Constitution, jams, popcorn, and a large selection of travel and history books.

CALIFORNIA STATE INDIAN MUSEUM
2618 K Street, Sacramento
Phone: (916) 324-0971
Hours: Daily 10:00 a.m.–5:00 p.m.
Admission: Adults $2.00, children 6-12 $1.00

When the thirty-year-old California State Indian Museum was remodeled in the 1980s, California Indian elders were asked to help select objects and photographs that reflected the living culture of the state's earliest inhabitants. Native people donated many of the extraordinary photographs that help make a visit to the museum such a rich experience. The museum's collections are displayed in thematic areas that reflect the past and the present—baskets and basketmaking, the family, hunting and gathering, singing. Obliging docents will open drawers filled with contemporary versions of the artifacts on display so you can get a closer look. We were allowed to shake a rattle made of the tiniest of deer hooves, examine a flute made of birds' bones, and see a woodpecker trap up close. A few hours spent among the beautiful items on display will provide an introduction to the dozens of tribes of California Indians, their ways of life, and artistic accomplishments. A new gallery showcasing the Indians of the Central Valley offers hands-on exhibits.

Library: A small reference library is available by appointment.

Gift Shop: Jewelry, arrowheads, and books are available at the front desk.

CROCKER ART MUSEUM
216 O Street, Sacramento
Phone: (916) 264-5423
Hours: Wed.-Sun. 10:00 a.m.-5:00 p.m., Thurs. 10:00 a.m.-9:00 p.m.
Admission: Adults $4.50, children 7-17 $2.00, children under 7 free.

The Crocker Art Museum, the oldest public art museum in the West, is inextricably linked, like so many California art museums, to the Central Pacific Railroad. Founder Edwin Crocker, counsel for the Central Pacific and a well-known abolitionist lawyer, owed his fame to his brilliant legal career and his fortune to his investments in the railroad. When Edwin's brother Charles and the other members of the "Big Four," Leland Stanford, Mark Hopkins, and Collis Huntington, took their millions to San Francisco, Edwin and Margaret Crocker remained in Sacramento. The Crocker Art Museum is their most treasured legacy.

Climbing the double stairway and opening the massive doors, visitors are apt to gasp at the splendor of the English tile floors, trompe l'œil wall frescos, and sensuously curving banisters. California is rich in magnificent Victorian mansions, but Seth Babson's architectural masterpiece surpasses them all. At one time, the mansion included a 60-foot ballroom, an elaborately carved library, a skating rink, and a bowling alley. The stately, Italianate-style gallery was built to house the artworks that Edwin and Margaret Crocker amassed in Europe while construction was underway— probably the largest private art collection in the country at the time.

Today, the ground level houses the Hansen Library, a photography gallery, and the Discovery Gallery, which features a continuing exhibit that traces the evolution of museums from cabinets of curiosities to the present. Works from the original Crocker collection of 700 European and American paintings and over 1,000 drawings—arguably the finest collection of old master drawings in the United States—are exhibited on the main level in the original gallery. The Crocker Family Gallery recreates the family parlor with outstanding examples of Victorian decorative arts. In 1969, the R.A. Herold wing was built in the Brutalist style, to provide space for six changing exhibitions each year.

The most recent addition to the museum is the Crocker Mansion Wing, whose exterior recreates the original Crocker home. The light-filled galleries display the museum's California collection. Judge Crocker's fine collection of paintings by California artists of his day includes works by Charles Christian Nahl that capture the excitement of the Gold Rush, and landscapes by Thomas Hill and Albert Bierstadt. In keeping with the Crocker legacy, the museum also collects and displays sculpture, paintings, drawings, and ceramics by northern California artists from 1960 to the present.

Library: The Gerald Hansen Library, open Wednesday and Thursday from 11:00 a.m. to 1:30 p.m. and Saturday from 1:30 to 4:00 p.m., is a pleasant reference library housing more than 3,000 (non-circulating) art books.

"The Lost Pleiad," by Randolph Rogers. According to Greek and Roman myth, the Pleiades were seven sisters. Since we can only see six stars in the group, the seventh sister is sometimes called the lost Pleiad. Actually, there are about 250 stars in the Pleiades cluster. Courtesy of Crocker Art Museum.

Gift Shop: The splendid, glass-walled gift shop offers an exciting selection of art books, handcrafted silver and ceramic pieces, antique jewelry, art glass, museum replicas, cards, and children's art projects.

GOVERNOR'S MANSION
1526 H Street, Sacramento
Phone: (916) 323-3047
Hours: Daily 10:00 a.m.–5:00 p.m. Tours on the hour.
Admission: Adults $2.00, children 6-12 $1.00, children under 6 free.

Ronald Reagan was the last California governor to occupy the old Governor's Mansion, but yes, Jerry Brown did sleep here—to answer one of the questions visitors often ask—though only on weekend visits from college and the seminary when his father, Governor Pat Brown, was in residence. Later, when he became governor, Jerry Brown preferred a two-bedroom apartment across the street from the capitol to both the old mansion and the more modern one that Ronald Reagan's supporters had just had built in the suburbs. These are only a few of the interesting tidbits you will pick up when you tour the Second Empire Italianate Victorian that was home to thirteen California governors and their families from 1903 until 1967.

Built in 1877 as a private home for Albert Gallatin, who made his fortune in the Huntington & Hopkins Hardware Company, the three-story mansion was purchased by the state of California to be the governor's mansion in 1903. The first governor in residence, George Pardee, cemented over the dirt floor of the basement where some of Gallatin's servants had lived, and his daughters later used it for roller skating. Since the furnishings are public property, purchased with funds allotted to each first lady for redecoration, they remain in the mansion. As a result, the house is eclectically furnished, to say the least. Several first ladies' ballgowns and an Adolpho suit of Nancy Reagan's are on display in the upstairs bedrooms, as well as Governor Earl Warren's desk, which was made by inmates at San Quentin Prison. When you purchase your tickets at the refurbished Carriage House you will see the kidney-shaped swimming pool that friends presented to Governor Pat Brown in 1959 after learning of his ungovernorlike habit of crossing the street with a towel slung over his shoulder, to swim in the neighboring hotel's pool.

STANFORD MANSION STATE HISTORIC PARK
802 N Street, Sacramento
Phone: (916) 324-0575
**Hours: Tours Tues. & Thurs. 12:15, Sat. 12:15 & 1:30. Groups
    by arrangement.**
Admission: Free

By the late 1990s, the 1856 home of former California governor, senator, railroad magnate, and founder of Stanford University Leland Stanford should be restored to its original magnificence and open to visitors daily. In the meantime, California State Parks offers unique pre-restoration tours. The tours focus on the archaeological detective work used to piece together the mansion's past. Architectural drawings and historical photos show how the rooms will look in the future. When possible, hard hat tours allow visitors to watch some of the work in progress.

SUTTER'S FORT STATE HISTORIC PARK
2701 L Street, Sacramento
Phone: (916) 445-4422
Hours: Daily 10:00 a.m.-5:00 p.m.
Admission: Adults $2.00, children $1.00

Fleeing bad debts in his native Switzerland, John Augustus Sutter set out for America to make his fortune. Calling upon his business experience, diplomatic skills, and ability to get to know all the right people, including Mariano Vallejo, Ignacio Martinez, and the Russian governor at Fort Ross, he managed to acquire 150,000 acres of land. Sutter dreamed of an independent financial empire founded on the natural wealth of California: rich soil and a gentle climate that would yield enormous crops of fruit and wheat, waterways with prolific salmon runs, abundant grazing for livestock, and thickly timbered forests for large lumber mills.

When one of his employees, James Marshall, found gold on land Sutter had leased to build a sawmill, Sutter knew immediately that the news could destroy his empire. He tried to keep the discovery a secret, but soon the news was out and the California Gold Rush was on. While fortunes were made and the city of Sacramento grew and prospered, Sutter's dreams unraveled. Squatters settled on his land, butchered his cattle, and sold his horses. He was swindled out of his land, and by 1849 he no longer owned Sutter's Fort.

As the city of Sacramento grew up around its adobe walls, Sutter's Fort was abandoned and fell into disrepair until 1891, when the Native Sons of the Golden West acquired the property and immediately began reconstruction, making it the oldest recreated historic fort in the United States. Now managed by California State Parks, Sutter's Fort State Historic Park is a fine example of the impeccable restoration, fanatical attention to historic detail, and scholarly interpretation that characterize all of the state historic parks. Pick up a "soundstick" (no charge) at the entry gate and listen to lively dialogues, diary readings, and fascinating information as you move from station to station. You will see meticulous recreations of Sutter's living quarters, the kitchens, and the early "factories" that made Sutter's Fort California's first shopping center. Any day is a good day to visit, but history really comes alive on Living History Days and Pioneer Demonstration Days, when docents in period costumes act the parts of Captain Sutter leading musket drills and of other pioneers baking bread, dipping candles, spinning wool, weaving, cooking, hunting, and trapping. Visitors can join in the fun.

Gift Shop: The Trade Store, staffed by costumed clerks, stocks books and reproductions of items that might have been available a century ago— dress patterns, buttons, sundials, toys, games, jewelry, hats, clothing, and blankets.

TOWE FORD MUSEUM
2200 Front Street, Sacramento
Phone: (916) 442-6802
Hours: Daily 10:00 a.m.–6:00 p.m.
Admission: Adults $5.00, seniors $4.50, high school students $2.50,
    elementary school students $1.00, children under 5 free

Boasting the world's largest collection of antique Fords, the Towe Ford Museum uses 180 cars and trucks to tell an automotive version of American history, including the social, financial, ethnic, and commercial changes triggered by Henry Ford's car for the common man—the Model T.

The core of the collection was assembled by Edward Towe, a Montana banker who began his collection in 1952, restoring a 1923 Model T Runabout as a family project. The collection now encompasses almost every year and model Ford made through 1953, starting with the 1903 Model A Runabout and including 28 Model T's. Other makes are also well-represented, including three California Governors' cars— Earl Warren's Cadillac limousine, Ronald Reagan's staff car, and Jerry Brown's infamous 1974 blue Plymouth. The vehicles, in good original condition or beautifully restored, are arranged by decade with "time posts" offering information about the days when the cars were new. Car hobbyists will be enthralled by this museum, and even non–enthusiasts will find it entertaining. I felt suitably nostalgic when we came across a sleek 1955 Thunderbird just like the one my brother used to own, and an Edsel like the one that was once our family car.

Elegant workmanship from a bygone era: a Model T Ford steering wheel. Courtesy of Towe Ford Museum.

Library: The Frank Clock Memorial Automotive Library's extensive holdings in automotive research include over 25,000 magazines, newsletters, shop manuals, parts manuals, sales brochures, and other references on hundreds of makes of automobiles

Gift Shop: The enormous gift shop stocks a large automotive-related inventory.

Rental: The Special Event Area, which features a 1920s Mighty Wurlitzer Theatre Pipe Organ, offers banquet/ auditorium seating for up to 300 people, a 70-foot stage, and a spacious dance floor. The 6,400-square-foot space is available for private or public events.

VISIONARIUM CHILDREN'S MUSEUM
Sutter Square Galleria
2901 K Street, Sacramento
Phone: (916) 443-7476
Hours: Tues.-Sat. 10:00 a.m.-5:00 p.m., Sun. noon-5:00 p.m.
Admission: Adults $2.50, children $4.00. Grandparents are admitted
 free the first Saturday of each month.

This up-tempo children's museum fits a lot of hands-on exhibits for youngsters ages two through twelve into a relatively small space in a shopping mall. On our visit, kids (mostly pre-schoolers) and parents were having a great time blowing bubbles in the bubble machine and racing golf balls on the raceway track while learning about geometry, structural form, momentum, friction, and gravity. The popular Me Too Supermarket exhibit, sponsored by Lucky's, was crowded with kids weighing plastic fruits and vegetables on real scales and filling their shopping carts with groceries, to be checked out at real cash registers by their pals, wearing real checkers' hats. The dress-up corner offers a selection of uniforms from local community agencies. With crutches, wheelchairs and a braille typewriter, the "What if I Couldn't" exhibit gives young visitors a chance to experience briefly the challenges faced by people with physical disabilities.

Gift Shop: Kreative Kids Shop stocks hundred of fun, educational items, many under $1.00.

Rental: For a trouble-free children's birthday party, the Visionarium offers two birthday packages—Basic and Ultimate—for 10 to 25 children, ranging from $3 ($4 on weekends) to $7 and $8 per child. You can also rent the Visionarium at night for grown-up parties.

WELLS FARGO HISTORY MUSEUM★
400 Capitol Mall, Sacramento
Phone: (916) 440-4161
Hours: Mon.-Fri. 9:00 a.m.-5:00 p.m.
Admission: Free

Prominently displayed in the lobby of the Wells Fargo Building is a gleaming, fully restored Concord stagecoach surrounded by exhibits, including gold, a functioning telegraph, Sacramento postal history, and others that document Wells Fargo's role in the commercial history of Sacramento since 1852.

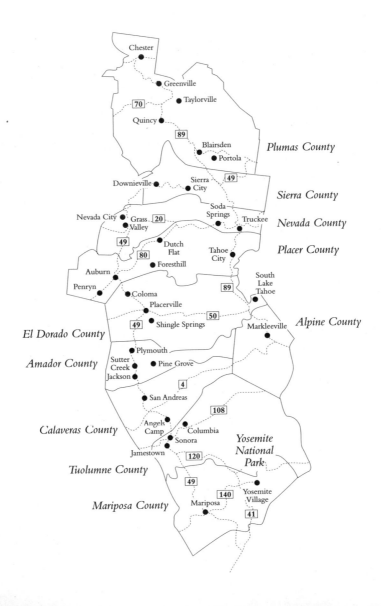

Chester

Greenville

Taylorville

70

Quincy

89

Blairsden

Portola

Plumas County

49

Downieville

Sierra City

Sierra County

Soda Springs

Nevada City Grass Valley 20 Truckee *Nevada County*

49

Dutch Flat

Tahoe City

Placer County

80

Auburn

Foresthill

South Lake Tahoe

Penryn

Coloma

Placerville

50

89

Alpine County

49 Shingle Springs

Markleeville

El Dorado County

Plymouth

Amador County

Sutter Creek Pine Grove

Jackson

4

San Andreas

108

Calaveras County

Angels Camp Columbia

Sonora

Yosemite National Park

Jamestown

120

Tuolumne County

49

Mariposa County 140 Yosemite Village

Mariposa 41

Sierra Nevada

PLUMAS COUNTY

BLAIRSDEN

PLUMAS–EUREKA STATE PARK AND MUSEUM
310 Johnsville Road, Blairsden
Phone: (916) 836-2380
Hours: Daily 8:00 a.m.–4:30 p.m., summer; as staff is available
during the rest of the year.

Rich in natural beauty and gold-mining history, Plumas–Eureka State Park is not one of those places you can breeze in and out of in fifteen minutes. A visit to this indoor/outdoor museum might begin with the museum proper, a red structure with white trim built in 1873 as a boarding house for miners, laborers, and mechanics who worked the nearby Mohawk Stamp Mill and Plumas–Eureka Mine operations. Here, mining exhibits display models of a stamp mill and arrastra. The natural history section contains the Science Discovery Center, a hands-on, child-friendly exhibit featuring discovery boxes, animal skins, skulls, and a microscope.

A modern-day paradise for skiers when winter snows blanket the area, the park enjoys a rich ski history. The first organized ski races in the western hemisphere were held on the slopes of Pilot Peak in 1856. When winter snows slowed down the mining operations, the miners amused themselves with early versions of today's skis. Racing on "long boards" or "snow shoes" twelve feet long and weighing up to 20 pounds, the miners traveled the 1,700 to 2,500 foot runs at speeds up to 80 miles per hour, carrying one long, large ski pole between their legs to serve as a brake. The museum's skiing exhibit displays skis used by Snowshoe Thompson, one of the most colorful figures of the Sierra Nevada.

A tour of the mill and other historic outbuildings helps you understand the mining process and what life was like when the mines flourished.

The serenity of the outdoors today gives a false idea of the atmosphere a hundred years ago, but you can try to imagine how earthshakingly noisy the Mohawk Stamp Mill was.

The park's interpreters like to focus on the human side of Gold Rush history: we found two docents forging dinner gongs and candleholders in the blacksmith shop, much as they might have been made a century ago. A tour of the Moriarty home emphasizes what life was like for renters in the tiny company houses almost a century ago. Imagine mother, father, grandmother, and eight children living together in the 220-square-foot, single-story house, and reserving the best room for company!

Gift Shop: T-shirts, sweatshirts, maps, books, gold, hand-forged candlesticks, and gongs are available.

CHESTER

CHESTER/LAKE ALMANOR MUSEUM
First & Willow Way, Chester
Phone: (916) 258-2426
Hours: Thurs.-Sat. 11:00 a.m.-2:00 p.m., June through Labor Day,
**   or by appointment.**
Admission: Free

The founders of the Chester Museum started out to write a book telling the history of Chester and Lake Almanor through photographs. Before they knew it, the book had become a museum. Primarily a photo museum, with information and artifacts from the Maidu culture through

The Chester post office at the Olsen Ranch, ca. 1908. The founders of the Chester/Lake Almanor Museum set out to publish a history book and ended up with enough historic photographs to start a museum. Courtesy of Chester/ Lake Almanor Museum.

the early dairy and cattlemen to the development of present-day timber and tourism industries, the museum is housed in a contemporary log structure designed to resemble the 1929 log cabin library building to which it is attached.

Gift Shop: Books about the Plumas County area and t-shirts are for sale in the gift shop.

GREENVILLE

GREENVILLE MUSEUM★
208 Main Street, Greenville
Phone: (916) 284-6633
Hours: Mon.-Fri. 8:30 a.m.-2:30 p.m.
Admission: Free

After many years in storage, the artifacts of the Greenville Museum can be seen in the museum's temporary home in the Chamber of Commerce building. Plans are to establish a permanent home in one of the town's historic buildings.

PORTOLA

PORTOLA RAILROAD MUSEUM
700 West Pacific Way, Portola
Phone: (916) 832-4131
Hours: Daily 10:00 a.m.-5:00 p.m., Memorial Day-Labor Day;
**   weekends during winter months.**
Admission: Free

Visitors come from around the world—as far away as Tasmania and Egypt—to the Portola Railroad Museum. The lure is a once-in-a-lifetime opportunity to operate a diesel locomotive—a dream come true for railroad buffs. One 87-year-old man stopped the engine and broke down in tears, saying, "I never thought I'd live long enough to do this. It's been my dream ever since I was a little boy to run an engine."

Visitors who don't want to pay $75 for an hour's train ride can still enjoy the museum,which covers 37 acres of an old railroad maintenance yard. A 16,000-square-foot shop building and two and a half miles of trackage display the country's largest collection of diesel locomotives—33, and an assortment of rolling stock that includes boxcars, freight cars, passenger cars, maintenance equipment, and cabooses. The museum's hands-on policy encourages visitors to climb up into the cabs of locomotives, sit in the engineers' seats, and browse through the Pullman cars to see the luxury of railroad travel in days gone by. In contrast to Sacramento's pristine Railroad Museum, the Portola museum has a faintly rusty junkyard look and a pronounced diesel smell, but it's full of railroad treasures—the Union Pacific's 6,600-horsepower Centennial (the largest diesel locomotive ever built), the only remaining California Zephyr, which was the premier passenger locomotive of its day, and a business car built for the president of Union Pacific Railroad in 1917.

Gift Shop: Books, videos, mugs, stamps, hats, t-shirts, and anything else you can think of connected to the railroad.

Restaurant: The Beanery features a model train exhibit and a display of Ken Roller's paintings depicting the locomotives of the Western Pacific Railroad. Since you will probably spend the better part of the day at this huge museum, plan to eat here. The profits from the cafe feed the volunteers who come for the weekend to help restore the engines and keep them running. It is operated by the wife of Bruce Cooper, our instructor for running the diesel engines, and she does *not* stint on quantity or quality. The hamburger is a full one-third pound of extra-lean ground beef, grilled to your order. The homemade chili is a don't-miss and there is usually a homemade soup. Unhappily, the food service is only on weekends from May through September.

*"Young Anglers":
a Western Pacific
Railroad photogra-
pher named Lawton
took this picture at
Mohawk in 1920.
It is part of the
Plumas County
Museum's extensive
archival collection.
Courtesy of
Plumas County
Museum.*

QUINCY

PLUMAS COUNTY MUSEUM
500 Jackson Street, Quincy
Phone: (916) 283-6320
Hours: Mon.-Fri. 8:00 a.m.-5:00 p.m.; Sat. & Sun. 10:00 a.m.-
**   4:00 p.m., June-September.**
Admission: Free

Stella Fay Miller, a former Quincy piano teacher, bequeathed the funds to establish the Plumas County Museum. The San Francisco architectural firm Osborne & Stewart designed the white clapboard structure in 1969 to fit in with the county's historic architecture and function as a "living museum." A large, open, first-floor gallery, whose only permanent exhibit is an outstanding collection of Maidu baskets, rotates period rooms, a country store, and mining and logging displays. In keeping with the living museum theme, concerts and recitals are a feature of the Victorian Music Room housing Miss Miller's piano. The mezzanine gallery presents changing exhibits by local artists and exhibits from the museum's collection of artifacts, textiles, costumes, etc.

Dolls and teddy bears, railroad memorabilia, and a button collection were on view during our visit.

Library: The museum is known for its state-of-the-art archives, which contain county records and documents, photographs, biographical studies, oral histories, rare books, sheet music, news clippings, ephemera, and a cartography room. Open for research by appointment.

Gift Shop: Historical publications, postcards, gold specimens, and jewelry.

TAYLORSVILLE

INDIAN VALLEY MUSEUM*
Cemetery Street, Taylorsville
Phone: (916) 284-6511
Hours: Sat. & Sun. 1:00-3:00 p.m., April-October;
or by appointment
Admission: Donation

The Indian Valley Museum, which shares a building with the Mt. Jura Gem and Mineral Club, shows a little bit of everything relating to the Indian Valley area. This includes Maidu baskets, and artifacts and historic photos of the now-closed Walker and Engle Mines—two of the richest copper mines in California. Taylorsville can be quite lively when the tourists arrive for the Mt. Jura Gem and Mineral Club show on July 4th and the Silver Buckle Rodeo, one of the largest in the West. The quilt show and hobby show in May draw large crowds from near and far.

SIERRA COUNTY

DOWNIEVILLE

DOWNIEVILLE MUSEUM
330 Main Street, Downieville
Phone: (916) 289-3261
Hours: Daily 10:00 a.m.-5:00 p.m.
Admission: Donation

Sleepy Downieville, population 400, the smallest county seat in America, was once a great gold-producing town that just missed being named the capital of California by a few votes. Today, it is famous as the first and only place where a woman was hanged in California. As the town founder, Major William Downie, put it, "Juanita, a dance-hall girl, was to bring more infamy upon Downieville than all the years and all the gold could remove." You can purchase a copy of the complete story of Juanita for $1.00 in the Downieville Museum.

Back in 1932, the Meroux family donated the historic, 1852 brick-front, mortarless schist structure to the people of Downieville for a museum to perpetuate the memory of Sierra County pioneers. The former Chinese store and gambling den is now filled to overflowing with a collection of the usual early Victorian odds and ends—sewing machines, wedding dresses, irons, tools, mining artifacts, and mourning jewelry—many displayed in delicate, curved glass cases that are historic artifacts themselves. Although the museum may suffer from a lack of up-to-date conservation techniques and state-of-the-art exhibition design, our knowledgeable guide, Margaret Gregory, demonstrated a genuine affection and great familiarity with the history behind every artifact. She proudly demonstrated a working stamp mill model constructed in the fifties by Downieville High School students, and regretted she couldn't show us the model of the town that occupies the entire basement of the building. This H-O scale model of the town as it was in 1900 was faithfully reproduced in detail from photographs, and can be seen by appointment or as part of a tour.

SIERRA CITY

KENTUCKY MINE MUSEUM
SIERRA COUNTY HISTORICAL PARK
Highway 49, one mile north of Sierra City
Phone: (916) 862-1310
Hours: Wed.-Sun. 10:00 a.m.-5:00 p.m., summer;
    weekends only in October; closed November-Memorial Day.
Admission: Museum $1.00, tour $3.00

Indoor exhibits at the folksy Sierra County Historical Society Museum focus on Native Americans, early-day mining (including a pair of 1908 levis), the Chinese community, logging, and pioneer recreation. A lovely array of Sierra County wildflowers was on display during our visit. However, the most compelling reason to visit is the outdoor museum, which encompasses the meticulously restored Kentucky Mine stamp mill.

Built at the base of the Sierra Buttes in 1853, the Kentucky Mine was one of the first hard rock gold mines in the area. Like many small mines, the Kentucky folded when government subsidy of gold mining stopped around the turn of the century. After lying idle and abandoned for twenty years, the claim was purchased by Emil Loeffler. In 1928 Loeffler and his son Dutch built a new mine and stamp mill using mostly salvaged materials and equipment, and ran the mine and mill as a hobby until Dutch was killed in an accident in the mine in 1944. In 1974 Sierra County purchased the mine and began restoration of the mill and development of the park and museum, operated since 1977 by the Sierra County Historical Society.

The hour-long tour led by curator Karen Donaldson may be one of the most thrilling experiences to be had in the gold country. Donaldson has the knack for making history come alive and explaining technical operations so that anyone can understand. The mill, of course, offers its own thrills, beginning as you cross the high trestle where ore cars once carried their loads, and continuing as you go down the six levels of processing and gold extraction and take your final look back at the spectacular peaks of the Sierra Buttes. If you time your visit right, you'll be treated to the sight of the Thompson big-eared bats that return every year for the mosquito hatch.

An amphitheater above the mine hosts the Kentucky Mine Summer Concert Series, ten evenings of music under the stars, each Friday from July 4th to Labor Day weekend.

The Kentucky Mine Museum, site of intense mining activity during the Gold Rush and a summer concert series today. Photo by Angel Hendrickson, courtesy of Sierra County Historical Society.

NEVADA COUNTY

GRASS VALLEY

EMPIRE MINE STATE HISTORIC PARK
East Empire Street, Grass Valley
Phone: (916) 273-8522
Hours: Daily 9:00 a.m.–5:00 p.m., May 1–June 6;
    9:00 a.m.–6:00 p.m., June 7–September 6;
    10:00 a.m.–5:00 p.m. September 7–April 30.
Admission: Adults $2.00, children 6-12 $1.00

Within two years of the discovery of gold, the great hordes of forty-niners who rushed to California had exhausted the easily-mined placer gold. When a rich vein of gold was discovered near what is now the Empire Mine State Historic Park, miners rushed to the area to stake out claims. Lacking the skills and equipment needed to reach the gold that lay hidden deep within the earth, the discouraged miners sold their claims to a group that was consolidating hundreds of small claims into a single operation. The Ohpir Hill Mine operated with varying degrees of success under a series of owners, until William Bourn, Jr. took over operations in 1869. With the help of his cousin, George Starr, who managed the mine until 1929, Bourne turned the Empire Mine into one of the largest, most progressive, best-managed gold mines in the country. The mine owed its great success to the skilled Cornish miners who dug 367 miles of tunnels—some angling downward almost a full vertical mile into the earth—and brought with them the latest technological advances in mining equipment. The Empire remained a prosperous operation until World War II, when it was shut down by the War Production Board as a non-essential industry. The mine reopened in 1945, but the fixed price of gold (at the 1934 level of $34 an ounce), inflation, and the 1956 miners' strike put it out of business.

The gold is still in the ground waiting for the day when deep, hard rock gold mining will again be profitable. But in the meantime, the greatest treasures are above ground in the 784-acre Empire Mine State Historic Park. Although only the foundations of many of the original buildings are left, the remaining industrial structures—a refinery, a rescue station, and welding, machine, and blacksmith shops—are fascinating. A good place to begin your tour is in the former carriage house, now the visitor center, where displays give you an overview of the mining industry. An intricate model of the underground workings of the mine, constructed in secret in 1938, is on view in the model room. The current price of gold—$407 per ounce on the day of our visit—is posted on a chalkboard outside the 1898 mine office, which is now a walk-through museum.

Set amidst acres of beautifully landscaped formal gardens, the Empire Cottage, designed by San Francisco architect Willis Polk, offers a striking contrast to the huge industrial sheds. The lovely, stone English manor house (called a cottage to distinguish it from Filoli, Bourn's lavish Woodside mansion) is furnished and open for guided tours.

Gift Shop: This is the place to pick up gold-mining souvenirs, including replicas of miners' candlesticks and lunch pails, gold-plated jewelry, little gold nuggets, and fool's gold.

GRASS VALLEY MUSEUM
Old Mt. St. Mary's Academy
Corner of Church & Chapel Streets, Grass Valley
Phone: (916) 272-4725
Hours: Tues.-Sun. 10:00 a.m.-3:00 p.m.
Admission: Free

Built by the townspeople of Grass Valley at the request of Father Dalton, the fine old building that now houses the Grass Valley Museum was first occupied by five Sisters of Mercy who had come from Ireland to start an orphanage. The boarding school for "select young ladies" that was opened to support the orphanage closed in 1965, but the parochial elementary school carries on as the oldest continuously operating Catholic school in California. In the second-floor museum, the music room, parlor, and school rooms are furnished much as they might have been during convent days. Oil paintings by Samuel Marsden Brookes, Julian Walbridge Rix, and Gustav Frederick Brock, as well as the nuns' art and needlework, line the walls. (The sisters were especially fond of painting on mirrors to avoid the temptations of vanity.) A lace-making exhibit, miniature room reproductions by Julia Thorne, and a charming collection of glass slippers add to the museum's appeal. Be sure to tour the pleasant formal gardens, which were originally laid out in the shape of a Celtic harp to make the Irish sisters feel at home. Many of the rosebushes are over one hundred years old.

Rental: St. Joseph Hall may be rented for concerts, weddings, classes, workshops, and special events.

NORTH STAR MINE POWERHOUSE MUSEUM
Corner of Mill Street & McCourtney Road,
Grass Valley
Phone: (916) 273-4255
Hours: Daily 10:00 a.m.-5:00 p.m., closed November
through April.
Admission: Free

The world's largest Pelton wheel, the invention that powered California's mining industry. Photo by John R. Harris, courtesy of North Star Mine Powerhouse Museum.

Camptonville resident Lester Pelton couldn't refuse when his landlady asked him to supply the foot power to run her treadle sewing machine. Looking out the window as he peddled away, Pelton was inspired to rig up a home-made waterwheel to run the machine. A little fiddling led to the discovery that dividing the cups into two parts made for greater efficiency. Thus was born the Pelton Wheel, the invention that provided the primary source of power for California's mining industry and the inspiration for today's electricity-generating water turbine.

Among the many examples of early mining equipment in the North Star Mining Museum you will find Pelton's first little iron demonstration wheel. The museum's star attraction is the world's largest Pelton wheel, a monster 30 feet in diameter that generated the power to run the now defunct North Star Mine. Housed in the mine's powerhouse, the city and county historical museum is packed full of old mining equipment and artifacts. Our exceedingly knowledgeable guide, Bob Gardiner, was able to help even the least mechanically minded among us understand and be interested in how everything works. Also on display is the country's largest working Cornish Pump (you'll need to supply four quarters to see it in action).

NEVADA CITY

FIREHOUSE MUSEUM
214 Main Street, Nevada City
Phone: (916) 265-5468
Hours: Daily 11:00 a.m.-4:00 p.m., April-October;
closed Wednesdays, November-March.
Admission: Free

One of the prettiest Victorians around, the little white jewel box orna-mented with a peaked belfry, slender columns, and balconies of carpenter's lace served as the Nevada City Firehouse from 1861 to 1938, and has been the historical museum since 1947. "We try to do a little bit of all the history," we were told by the curator. This includes the usual vintage clothes, toys, household items, and Gold Rush artifacts, plus a nice bottle collection and Donner Party relics. The pride of the museum is the altar from the Hou Wong Joss House in Grass Valley. Of the estimated fifty thousand Chinese in California in 1894, five thousand lived in Grass Valley. The Tinloys, one of only four Chinese families remaining in Grass Valley by the time the Firehouse Museum opened, dismantled the joss house altar and gave it to the museum. A curator from a big city museum identified the scroll that hangs beside the elaborately carved altar as a valuable 16th century piece. "He said that this is so important we shouldn't have it," said our guide.

MALAKOFF DIGGINS STATE HISTORIC PARK*
23579 North Bloomfield Road, Nevada City
Phone: (916) 265-2740
Hours: Daily 10:00 a.m.-5:00 p.m.
Admission: $5.00 per vehicle

More Pelton wheels: Miners' Foundry, a California historic landmark, is known as the first site where they were manufactured. Courtesy of Heritage Graphics and Miners Foundry.

Environmental controversies and protective legislation are not just a 20th century phenomenon. In 1884, after years of court battles, federal legislation outlawed hydraulic mining. The first major legal victory for the environment, the Sawyer Decision, closed Malakoff Diggins, the largest hydraulic gold mine in the world. Today you can still see the ravaging effects of the giant monitor nozzles that washed away the hillsides and filled the rivers with silt. The 3,000-acre park also includes the remnants of the mining town of North Bloomfield, and a small mining museum.

MINERS FOUNDRY CULTURAL CENTER
325 Spring Street, Nevada City
Phone: (916) 265-5040
Hours: Mon.-Fri. 10:00 a.m.-5:00 p.m. or
by appointment. Call for tour schedules.
Admission: Free

Built in 1856, birthplace of the famous Pelton wheel, the stone-walled Miners' Foundry housed the American Victorian Museum until recently. Although its primary function now is to provide a home for county arts organizations, it also provides tours for groups and individuals and has a permanent exhibit about the history of the foundry.

SODA SPRINGS

WESTERN SKISPORT MUSEUM
Boreal Ski Area, Soda Springs
Phone: (916) 426-3313
Hours: Weekends 11:00 a.m.-
    5:00 p.m.
Admission: Free

The Western SkiSport Museum's monument to Snowshoe Thompson, who carried mail across the perilous Sierra Nevada on his back for forty years. Courtesy of Western SkiSport Museum.

The fascinating Western SkiSport Museum traces the history of today's multi-million-dollar ski industry in the Sierra Nevada back to the Gold Rush. The winter of 1852—the worst in history—marked the start of Western skiing, as gold miners began to use snowshoes (forerunners of today's skis) to survive in the snow-bound mountains. Shortly afterward, miners pioneered sport skiing with the first organized ski competition in the western hemisphere. Skis from the 1860s to the present are on display, including the 8-foot-long cross-country skis belonging to the legendary Snowshoe Thompson, who for twenty winters made the perilous journey across the Sierra Nevada with a 40-pound mail sack on his back. Other exhibits include the Western Ski Hall of Fame, California's first chair lift, and artifacts from the Army's 10th Mountain Division. A large selection of ski films, some dating back to 1918, are shown on request at a moment's notice.

Library: Ski archives containing scrapbooks, annuals, and magazines are open for research by appointment.

TRUCKEE

EMIGRANT TRAIL MUSEUM
Donner Memorial State Park
12593 Donner Pass Road, Truckee
Phone: (916) 582-7892
Hours: Daily 10:00 a.m.-4:00 p.m.
Admission: Adults $2.00, children 6-12 $1.00

Built in 1962, the Emigrant Trail Museum includes exhibits about local Native Americans, the construction of the transcontinental railroad, lumbering, and ice harvesting, but all of this is overshadowed by the sensational story of the Donner Party. In 1846 this group of pioneers attempting to cross the treacherous mountain pass were trapped in the blizzards of what may have been the most severe winter ever to hit the Sierra. Many members of the group died of starvation or froze to death; the survivors were forced to resort to cannibalism to survive. Relics of the party, including a replica of Patty Reed's doll and a slide presentation, recount this tragic history.

SIERRA NEVADA CHILDREN'S MUSEUM
11400 Donner Pass Road, Truckee
Phone: (916) 587-KIDS
Hours: Wed.-Sun. 10:00 a.m.-4:00 p.m.; Mon. & Tues. group
   tours only.
Admission: $2.00 (under 2 free)

The Sierra Nevada Children's Museum offers hands-on learning exhibits. In the summer of 1994, the main exhibit invited children to experience the sights and sounds of a forest at night, listening for owls, sharing stories around a campfire, and learning how to make an emergency shelter. Children can don an engineer's cap and guide the G gauge Truckee Model Railroad over trestle bridges, through mountain tunnels, and into snowsheds, warning mountain animals with a whistle. Rotating projects in the Art Center, along with math, reading, and drawing software at the Computer Corner, can help round out the day's experiences.

PLACER COUNTY

AUBURN

The doll room
at Auburn's
Bernhard Museum
Complex.
Photo by
Nate Levine.

BERNHARD MUSEUM COMPLEX
291 Auburn-Folsom Road, Auburn
Phone: (916) 889-4156
Hours: Tues.-Sun. 11:00 a.m.-3:00 p.m.
Admission: Adults $1.00, seniors & children 6-16 50¢ (also good for
   Gold Country Museum)

Located on the main path to the gold country, Auburn was a popular stopover and the logical site for the Bishops Travelers' Rest Hotel built in 1851. In 1868 teamster Bernhardus Bernhard purchased the hotel and thirty surrounding acres. The land was planted with grapes and the hotel was converted into a family home occupied by Bernhard descendants until 1957. Now restored, the house, which is one of the oldest wooden structures in Placer County, depicts family life of the late Victorian era. Our delightful father-and-daughter docent team had us guessing the purpose of obscure kitchen gadgets, and oohing and ahhing over the doll room. Restored outbuildings feature exhibits on 19th century winemaking, blacksmithing, and coopering.

GOLD COUNTRY MUSEUM
1273 High Street (in the Gold Country Fairgrounds), Auburn
Phone: (916) 889-4134
Hours: Tues.-Sun. 10:00 a.m.-4:00 p.m.
Admission: Adults $1.00, seniors & children 6-16 50¢ (also good for
Bernhard Museum)

Three white plaster, larger-than-life figures symbolizing the spirit of the mines (one is an actual portrait of the museum's director, Dave Tucker) greet visitors at the entrance to the Gold Country Museum's 48-foot, walk-through hard rock mine shaft. Housed in a 1940s Works Progress Administration building, the museum provides a comprehensive and enlightening overview of the different mining techniques you will run across in other gold country museums.

Three figures symbolizing the spirit of the California gold mines greet visitors to the Gold Country Museum. Photo by Nate Levine.

Our docent turned on the working miniature stamp mill model and had us pick up a lead ingot (almost as heavy as gold) in the model assay office to give us an idea of the heft of it. A replica miner's cabin is complete with pine needle mattress and a table set with the miner's meager diet (onions cost $1.00 each, eggs $2.00 apiece). This and the recreated Union Saloon depict the spare lifestyle of those adventurous men who came to seek their fortunes. Mini exhibits: *"Gold,"* featuring coins, ingots, watches, and other items made of this most precious metal, "Men's Justice," and "The Spiritual Properties of Minerals" complement the larger exhibits in this beautifully designed museum.

The placer mining exhibit, complete with a forty-niner panning for gold, draws the greatest crowds. Many visitors come to the museum for the specific purpose of learning to pan. Almost everyone who sticks with it finds a speck or two of gold in the black sand bottom of the stream that flows in front of the diorama—pretty exciting stuff for kids and adults. You can also watch the video "How to Pan Gold" for more information.

DUTCH FLAT

GOLDEN DRIFT MUSEUM
32820 Main Street, Dutch Flat
Phone: (916) 389-2126
Hours: Wed., Sat., Sun. noon-4:00 p.m., Memorial Day-Labor Day
Admission: Free

You won't find a prettier town in the gold country than Dutch Flat. The tourist trade and all the commercialism it brings seem to have overlooked this perfectly preserved Victorian jewel, which has also had the rare good

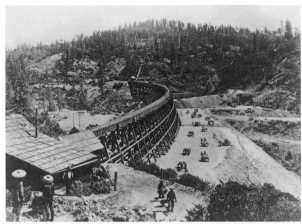

Chinese workers using hand tools and carts to fill in the Secret Town trestle west of Dutch Flat, 1877. Courtesy of Golden Drift Historical Society.

fortune of escaping destruction by fire. Many original 19th century buildings are still standing, among them the 1880s structure that houses the Golden Drift Museum. The museum chronicles the history of Dutch Flat, focusing on the native Maidu people, lumbering, gold mining, and the railroad. Theodore Judah, with local pharmacist D.W. Strong, worked out of Dutch Flat while mapping the trans-Sierra route for the Central Pacific transcontinental railroad, and the first subscription money for building it was raised here.

Gift Shop: You can purchase Golden Drift Museum photos, mugs, books, glasses, t-shirts, and homemade postcards.

FORESTHILL

FOREST HILL DIVIDE MUSEUM★
Harrison Street, Foresthill
Phone: (916) 367-3988
Hours: Sat. & Sun. noon-4:00 p.m., mid-May through October
Admission: Free

The history and geology of the Forest Hill and Iowa Hill Divides are showcased in exhibit modules featuring the Gold Rush, transportation, early business, recreation, and early firefighting. The logging exhibit includes a model of the Foresthill Logging Company.

PENRYN

GRIFFITH QUARRY MUSEUM★
Corner of Taylor & Rock Springs Road, Penryn
Phone: (916) 663-1837
Hours: Sat. & Sun. noon-4:00 p.m.
Admission: Free

The Welshman Griffith, realizing that the Gold Rush was destined to end, founded a granite mine here in 1864 on the site that would later furnish stones for the State Capitol, the San Francisco Mint, and Fort Point. The Griffith Quarry Museum, housed in the original offices of the Penryn Granite Works, chronicles the history of the Penryn-Loomis Basin. Exhibits focus on the granite industry and the Griffith family. Tours of the old quarry are available.

TAHOE CITY

GATEKEEPER'S MUSEUM
130 West Lake Boulevard, Tahoe City
Phone: (916) 583-1762
Hours: Daily 11:00 a.m.–5:00 p.m., summer; Wed.–Sun. 11:00 a.m.–
    5:00 p.m. May–June 15 & Labor Day–October 1.
Admission: Free

The Gatekeeper's Museum, a hand-carved log cabin built in 1981, stands
on the foundation of the original 1910 gatekeeper's cabin destroyed by
fire in 1978. Although the Federal Watermaster's Office is now in charge
of raising or lowering Lake Tahoe's water level, the hand-turned winch
system employed by the original gatekeeper is still used. The museum,
situated on the shores of Lake Tahoe in William B. Layton Park, is
dedicated to the social and natural history of the lake. A 170-year-old
rocking chair resting in front of the large stone fireplace lends a cozy
atmosphere. A premier Native American basket collection is exhibited
beside arrowheads found and labeled by second and third graders. A large
photo display and a child's toy train from the Ehrman Mansion are also
among the exhibits.

Library: The beautiful research library contains local history books,
photographs, and vintage newspapers.

WATSON CABIN MUSEUM
560 North Lake Boulevard, Tahoe City
Phone: (916) 583-8717
Hours: Daily noon–4:00 p.m., June 15–Labor Day.
Admission: Free

Built as a wedding present in 1909 for Robert and Stella Watson, the
unimposing Watson cabin is an excellent example of turn-of-the-century
log cabin construction in the Lake Tahoe region. Furnished with Watson
memorabilia, the tiny cabin depicts the life of one of the first families to
live at Lake Tahoe year-round.

EL DORADO COUNTY

COLOMA

MARSHALL GOLD DISCOVERY STATE HISTORIC PARK
Highway 49, Coloma
Phone: (916) 622-3470
Hours: Museum, daily 10:00 a.m.–5:00 p.m. Park, 8:00 a.m.–sunset.
Admission: $5.00/vehicle park use fee

This is where it all began: the California Gold Rush, an event that not

Like other 19th century spiritualists, James Wilson Marshall believed gold produced special emanations. John Sutter believed Marshall to be "notionall," but nonetheless capable of supervising construction of a sawmill on the American River, which is where Marshall found gold. Marshall did not profit from his discovery, and in fact spent the rest of his life in a series of marginal endeavors trying to strike it rich. Courtesy of Marshall Gold Discovery State Historic Park.

only altered the fate of California, but affected the entire nation. James Wilson Marshall and John Sutter were building a sawmill on the south fork of the American River to supply lumber for Sutter's agricultural empire in the Sacramento Valley. On January 24, 1848 Marshall was inspecting the tailrace when he found some shining yellow flecks in the water. Tests confirmed his suspicion that the metal was gold. Although Sutter and Marshall tried to keep the discovery a secret, the news leaked out. Sam Brannan, owner of a store in Sutter's Fort, ran through the streets of San Francisco waving a quinine bottle full of gold and shouting, "Gold, gold, gold, from the American River!" Men from San Francisco, and soon from all over the world, flocked to the sawmill at Coloma, and the Gold Rush was on. Coloma boomed to a population of five thousand, but soon the easy placer gold gave out and it became a sleepy agricultural village.

Today, fewer than two hundred people live in Coloma, most within the boundaries of the 275-acre Marshall Gold Discovery State Park, established in 1890. Up to the usual high standards of the California State Parks system, this indoor/outdoor facility offers sixteen historic buildings open to the public, and the Gold Discovery Museum with its excellent reference library. Outdoors, fifty small interpretive signs placed throughout the town describe its historic past.

To get oriented, we suggest you begin your visit at the museum, which tells the story of the discovery in a series of easy-to-read panels augmented with mining artifacts. You can begin your outdoor exploration with the stone Chinese stores next to the museum. The Man Lee store now houses a mining exhibit, and Wah Hop's store and bank building has been set up as a typical Chinese general store. The original sawmill was abandoned soon after the discovery of gold and ultimately disappeared, but an electrically-powered replica completed in 1968 is operated for visitors. Opposite the mill, the Mormon Cabin is a replica of the cabin built to house Marshall's Mormon workers. Work is underway to repair the 1890 Coloma Schoolhouse, which was destroyed by a logging truck after years of meticulous restoration work. When it is completed, the "living museum" will be staffed by a credentialed teacher who will teach the lessons a child would have studied in 1925.

Hikers will want to follow the 2.3-mile Monroe Ridge Trail, named in memory of Coloma's pioneer Monroe family who trace their origins to Nancy Gooch, brought to California as a slave in 1849. Pick up a brochure at the museum or the trailhead.

Library: Open for research by appointment, the library contains one of the best collections of scholarly Gold Rush literature in California.

Rental: Arrangements can be made to reserve either of the park's historic churches. Two group picnic sites are also available.

PLACERVILLE

EL DORADO COUNTY HISTORICAL MUSEUM
100 Placerville Drive, Placerville
Phone: (916) 621-5865
Hours: Wed.-Sat. 10:00 a.m.-4:00 p.m., Sun. noon-4:00 p.m.
Admission: Free

This sprawling museum, built in 1973 on the El Dorado County fairgrounds, is chockablock with authentic artifacts used to illustrate the
history of the county's mining and lumbering industries, its early inhabitants, and life in the 19th century. A mural by a local artist complements
the fine collection of Maidu and Washo baskets. The ubiquitous country
store exhibit, complete with cracker barrels and an authentic turn-of-
the-century kitchen, is filled to overflowing with period artifacts.
The museum's assorted collections include cameras, carnival glass, dolls,
tools, mustard jars, and miniature rooms. Outside you can roam through
the museum yard and view a wheelbarrow made by John Studebaker
(later of automobile fame), Pelton waterwheels that powered mines and
mills, a horse-drawn buggy, buckboard and express wagons, and a 1930s
gas pump, and watch the restoration in progress on a Diamond & Caldor
Shay #4 steam engine.

FOUNTAIN & TALLMAN SODA FACTORY MUSEUM
524 Main Street, Placerville
Phone: (916) 626-0773
**Hours: Fri.-Sun. noon-4:00 p.m., summer; Sat. & Sun. noon-
    4:00 p.m., winter.**
Admission: Free

Miners had pretty dull diets, which they sparkled up with carbonated
water. Built in 1852, the soda works was the only structure to survive the
fire that destroyed the rest of downtown Placerville in the early 1880s.
After chemical carbonation was replaced with mechanical means, the soda
factory closed and the building served a stint as a bookstore and antique
shop. Today, restored to its 1852 condition, the Fountain & Tallman
Soda Factory Museum houses within its thick, brick walls artifacts from
Placerville's Chinese community, baseball memorabilia from the town's
baseball mania of the twenties and thirties, and upstairs some fine china
and silver bequeathed to the county museum by Stella Ralston Tracy,
niece of San Francisco millionaire William Ralston.

HANGTOWN'S GOLD BUG PARK
One mile north of downtown Placerville
Phone: (916) 642-5232
Hours: Daily 10:00 a.m.–4:00 p.m., summer; closed in winter.
Admission: Adults $1.00, children 50¢

HANGTOWN'S GOLD BUG MINE
Resting on the eastern edge of the famous Mother Lode vein, the Gold
Bug Park area has yielded thousands of dollars in gold, and, so they say,
sixty to ninety percent of the Mother Lode is still in the ground today. A
visit to the Hangtown's Gold Bug Mine should help you decide if mining
is in your future: the country's only city-owned gold mine gives you a
feel for the rigors of the profession. Before you enter the 360-foot-long
illuminated shaft, pick up a hand-held cassette ($1) for a tour narrated by
the ghost of an old miner, who will tell you all you ever wanted to know
about geology and hard rock mining, and a few tall tales besides. The
mine is a cool 56 degrees year round and a bit damp from the constantly
dripping water.

JOSHUA HENDY STAMP MILL
One hundred years ago the gold country was dotted with stamp mills,
which crushed ores into a powder that was then washed and combined
with mercury to extract the gold. Local residents remember the thunder-
ous, crashing staccato of the Joshua Hendy Stamp Mill that could be
heard for miles in the narrow canyon. The "neighborhood mill" served
two hundred small mining operations once located on the 63 acres that
are now park land. A museum built around the reconstructed stamp mill
building houses the original mill. Tours are $25.00 for up to 15 people.

SHINGLE SPRINGS

SAM'S TOWN AMERICANA MUSEUM
Highway 50, Cameron Park exit, Shingle Springs
Phone: (916) 933-1671
Hours: Sun.–Thurs. 8:00 a.m.–8:30 p.m., summer; 8:00 a.m.–
     7:30 p.m., winter.
Admission: $1.00

Sacramento restaurateur and antique buff Sam Gordon built an annex
to his large Sam's Town Restaurant to house the Americana Museum,
a showcase for his vast collection of antiques. A purchase of wax museum
figures inspired the vignette format. Twenty-nine scenes recreate a
hodgepodge of memories of earlier days, ranging from Lillian Russell to
an old-time barber shop to Dwight David Eisenhower modeling a 1917
World War I uniform. Putting aside the overt commercialism and
carnival atmosphere generated by this restaurant cum video arcade cum

general store, you'll find the museum informative (the 25¢ guidebook helps) and well designed. A collection of horse-drawn vehicles purchased from 20th Century Fox is on display outside. A guaranteed kid pleaser.

Gift Shop: You can buy candy, dolls, toys, coffee, and more in the 19th century General Store.

Restaurant: Sam's Town Restaurant is probably the reason you stopped here. It is a full-service eatery with a museum on the side for your added enjoyment.

SOUTH LAKE TAHOE

BALDWIN MUSEUM
Tallac Historic Site
870 Emerald Bay Road, South Lake Tahoe
Phone: (916) 541-5227
Hours: Tues.-Sun. 11:00 a.m.-3:00 p.m., summer
   (10:00 a.m.-4:00 p.m., July–August); closed in winter.
Admission: Free

The first vacationers to enjoy beautiful Lake Tahoe were the Washo, who travelled there each summer from the Carson Valley. John Fremont is reported to have sighted the lake in 1844, but it wasn't until the transcontinental railroad arrived in the 1850s that Lake Tahoe became a popular retreat for the wealthy from San Francisco and Sacramento.

In 1880, Elias "Lucky" Baldwin, a California entrepreneur, established the lavish Tallac Resort and Casino, considered by some to have been the best mountain hotel in the world. By 1916 the era of opulence was drawing to an end; the resort was razed by Baldwin's heir as hundreds of elaborate private estates sprung up around the lake. Today, examples of these luxurious estates can be seen in the 150-acre Tallac Historic Site.

Built in 1921 by Dextra Baldwin, Lucky's granddaughter, the Baldwin Estate now houses the Baldwin Museum, with exhibits about the Baldwin family and the Washo people. Outside in the Washo Garden are three structures: a dome-shaped summer house constructed of tule woven together with willow branches, a winter house made of long poles set in the ground and interlocked at the top, and a simple sunscreen.

The Pope Estate, one of the largest and most luxurious in the area, offers historic tours, art exhibits, and a living history program in the summer. The Valhalla Estate is used for community events.

Library: Available for research, the archives contain photos and oral history tapes.

LAKE TAHOE MUSEUM
3058 Lake Tahoe Boulevard, South Lake Tahoe
Phone: (916) 541-5458
Hours: Daily 11:00 a.m.–4:00 p.m., summer; Sat. & Sun. noon–
   4:00 p.m., winter.
Admission: Adults $1, seniors 75¢, children 50¢

Exhibits chronicle the history of the Lake Tahoe Basin from the earliest
Washo inhabitants to the present in the old county library building,
which now houses the Lake Tahoe Historical Society Museum. Farming, logging, ice cutting, and the railroad all feature in the exhibits, as
well as artifacts from rustic resorts and fancy hotels which represent the
tourist industry in America's year-round playground. Be sure to ask to see
the film made in 1915 for the San Francisco Exposition depicting a
40-day trip to Tahoe. This and other films from the 1930s and 1940s
which have been transferred to video are enormously entertaining. Old-
time footage depicts the SS *Tahoe*, pride and joy of the lake, which sank
to the bottom in 1940.

   Just behind the museum is the oldest building still standing in the
Lake Tahoe Basin, the 1859 Osgood's Toll House, and a 1930s vacation
cabin, one of the last unchanged log cabins in the basin. This will be
open for viewing in 1994. A few blocks away in Bijou Park, there is a
railroad exhibit.

Library: A large photographic and archival collection, oral histories, and a
small library are available for research.

VIKINGSHOLM
Emerald Bay State Park
Highway 89, approximately 11 miles west of South Lake Tahoe
Phone: (916) 525-7277
Hours: Daily 10:00 a.m.–4:00 p.m., summer
Admission: Adults $2.00, children 6-17 $1.00

Lora Josephine Knight, who held large amounts of stock in the National
Biscuit, Continental Can, Diamond Match, Union Pacific, and Rock
Island Railroad companies, built a medieval Scandinavian castle on the
shores of Lake Tahoe's Emerald Bay in 1929. Designed by Swedish
architect Lennart Palme and constructed of materials native to the Tahoe
area, the 38-room mansion is said to be the finest example of Scandinavian architecture in the country. Palme paid scrupulous attention to
authenticity of the medieval details (with the addition of conveniences of
the early 1930s) and Mrs. Knight selected antique furnishings in
Scandinavia, hiring craftsmen to reproduce the historic pieces she could
not take home from Norway and Sweden. Weather permitting, the
grounds and magnificent scenery can be enjoyed year-round, and the

California State Parks department provides tours of the house in the summer. Unfortunately, it's a steep, one-mile hike to get there—and uphill on the way back.

AMADOR COUNTY

JACKSON

AMADOR COUNTY MUSEUM★
225 Church Street, Jackson
Phone: (209) 223-6386
Hours: Wed.-Sun. 10:00 a.m.-4:00 p.m.
Admission: Free.
  Kennedy Mine Model tour: adults $1.00, children 50¢

The historic Brown House, a two-story brick building constructed in 1859, exhibits the Amador County Museum's collection of mining memorabilia. Costumes and 19th century household goods are displayed in period rooms. A separate structure houses the museum's star attraction, a working model of the Kennedy Mine complete with ten-stamp mill, tailing wheel, and the wooden head frame from the Kennedy mine.

PINE GROVE

CHAW'SE REGIONAL INDIAN MUSEUM★
Indian Grinding Rock State Historic Park
Pine Grove-Volcano Road, Pine Grove
Phone: (209) 296-7488
Hours: Mon.-Fri. 11:00 a.m.-4:00 p.m.; Sat. & Sun. 10:00 a.m.-
  4:00 p.m.
Admission: $5.00 per vehicle

The Chaw'se Regional Indian Museum, located in the 135-acre Indian Grinding Rock State Park, offers visitors an introduction to the Miwok way of life, with artifacts representing the Miwoks and neighboring tribes. Films enhance the interpretive materials. The reconstructed Miwok village outside, with its large roundhouse, is used by many California Native American communities for celebrations and ceremonies. The park's star attraction is the enormous 7,700-square-foot grinding rock (chaw'se), used by the Miwoks for pounding acorns into meal. More than 300 petroglyphs and 1,158 mortar holes dot the rock.

PLYMOUTH

SHENANDOAH VALLEY MUSEUM
Sobon Estate
Shenandoah Road, Plymouth
Phone: (209) 245-6554
Hours: Daily 10:00 a.m.-5:00 p.m.

Workers pose with a giant drive wheel made at the historic Knight Foundry, where you can still watch foundrymen pour molten iron at the last water-powered foundry and machine shop in the U.S. Courtesy of Historic Knight & Co.

Using timber and rock cut and quarried on his property, Swiss emigrant Adam Uhlinger established one of California's oldest wineries in 1856. Almost 150 years later, new owners transformed the winery into a museum dedicated to the thriving wine industry of the lush Shenandoah Valley. The sprawling building, which incorporates the original stone cellars that Uhlinger dug into the hill, provides an ideal setting for displays of agricultural and winemaking artifacts. Enormous redwood fermenting tanks, a small, hand-cranked grape crusher, an old, motorized crusher-stemmer, wine casks coopered from native oaks, and an extensive display of coopering tools chronicle the history of winemaking.

In continuous operation since before the Civil War (they made sacramental wine during Prohibition) the winery, previously known as D'Agostini Winery, now operates under the Sobon Estate name. While adult visitors sample current production in the tasting room, children can check out the exhibit on spinning.

Gift Shop: Wine, prints, and gifts are for sale in the handsome gift shop.

SUTTER CREEK

HISTORIC KNIGHT FOUNDRY & MUSEUM★
81 Eureka Street, Sutter Creek
Phone: (209) 267-5543
Hours: Daily 9:00 a.m.-4:00 p.m.
Admission: Adults $2.50, children $1.50

The last water-powered foundry and machine shop in the country, Knight Foundry has been pouring molten iron since 1873. Visitors can stop at twenty display areas along the self-guided tour, and watch the foundrymen at work using traditional methods. Guided tours, hands-on workshops, and other special programs are available. Call ahead for the pouring schedule.

Gift Shop: Metal products produced on-site, as well as reprints of historical books related to foundry work, blacksmithing, steam engines, etc. are available in the gift shop.

J. MONTEVERDE GENERAL STORE MUSEUM
11 Randolph Street, Sutter Creek
Phone: (209) 267-1431
Hours: Thurs.-Fri. 11:00 a.m.-4:00 p.m., Sat. & Sun.
noon-5:00 p.m., if docents are available.
Admission: Donation

Rose Monteverde willed her family's general store to
Sutter Creek to be used as a museum in the 1970s. Almost
twenty years later, the 1,200-square-foot, single-story
Italianate frame building opened as the J. Monteverde
General Store Museum. It provides a nostalgic journey
back to the time when cheese came in wheels, crackers
were displayed in bins, shoppers scooped pickled pigs feet
and sauerkraut out of barrels, and Melody Mender tape for
repairing player piano music sold for 35¢ a roll.

Nostalgic packaging from a simpler time greets visitors to Sutter Creek's general store museum. Courtesy of J. Monteverde General Store Museum.

CALAVERAS COUNTY

ANGELS CAMP

ANGELS CAMP MUSEUM
753 South Main Street (Highway 49), Angels Camp
Phone: (209) 736-2963
Hours: Daily 10:00 a.m.-3:00 p.m.
Admission: Adults $1.00

Angels Camp, made famous by Mark Twain in "The Celebrated Jumping
Frog of Calaveras County," has another claim to fame—the Angels Camp
Museum. This sprawling affair, covering three acres of grounds, boasts an
assortment of indoor and outdoor exhibits chronicling the days of the
Gold Rush. My advice is to begin at the bottom of the property with the
carriage house and work your way up to the Upper Museum building.

With 9,184 square feet of exhibition space, the carriage house has
ample room to exhibit twenty five or so beautifully restored horse-drawn
carriages, wagons, and carts. A colorful popcorn wagon, a dairy wagon,
an undertaking wagon, Widow Marie Porter's coupe and others stand at
attention in the center of the dirt and gravel floor, while exhibits of
brands and branding irons, barber shop artifacts, household antiques, and
the like line the periphery.

Steam traction engines, 20-mule-team logging wagons, and horse-
drawn farm equipment are part of a collection of rolling stock housed in
corrugated metal sheds. Blacksmith and foundry exhibits demonstrate
craftsmanship of an earlier time. Mining equipment, including a huge
overshot waterwheel on its original site and a working stamping mill, and
a rock and mineral "garden" are part of the outdoor display.

A sign outside the Upper Museum advises visitors that the museum was started with a gift from Dan Daniels, who collected anything that wasn't nailed down. When his collections outgrew his home, he asked the city to help build a place to display them. The museum continues Daniels' passion for collecting and displaying artifacts—it's hard to believe that so many could be squeezed into one medium-sized museum. "If someone donated it, I want people to see it," explained the charming woman at the desk. You'll see shoes, Native American baskets, clocks, tools, a switchboard, a frog cage, bottles, guns, cameras, early patent medicines, celluloid vanity items, an early engraving machine, and an 1880s hearse complete with coffin, just to mention a few.

Library: Calaveras Genealogical Society Library.

Gift Shop: Rocks, books, and Mark Twain memorabilia.

SAN ANDREAS

CALAVERAS COUNTY HISTORICAL MUSEUM
30 North Main Street, San Andreas
Phone: (209) 754-6579
Hours: Daily 10:00 a.m.–4:00 p.m.
Admission: Adults 50¢, children 25¢

The handsome Calaveras County Museum occupies three restored historic buildings: the original county courthouse and jail; the hall of records, built in 1893; and the former IOOF and Masonic lodges, built in 1856. The restored courtroom and judge's chambers, witness to so much Gold Rush history, are best remembered for the trial of the notorious highwayman Black Bart. This wry stage robber, who ranged throughout the Gold Country writing poems to his victims, led a double life as Charles Bolton, a mining engineer and minor philanthropist. Captured in San Francisco, he was returned to the jail in San Andreas to await trial, tried in the courtroom of Judge C.V. Gottschalk, convicted, and sentenced to six years in San Quentin.

The jail features a Black Bart exhibit, and the jail yard, once the site of executions, is now a pleasant garden of native plants and early mining artifacts. Two second-floor museum galleries display geologic history of the gold country, a full-size bark house and artifacts of the Miwok Indians, the interior of a Mother Lode Catholic church, early mining artifacts, a replica of Camp Seco's general store, hand tools, a gamblers' corner, children's toys, and costumes. Photo murals and poetic signage enhance the excellent exhibits.

Library: The County Archives, open Thursday and Friday, 9:00 a.m. to 5:00 p.m., contain one of the most complete collections in the gold country. An archivist works with researchers interested in genealogy, mining claims, property records, and histories of early-day towns and events for a nominal fee.

Gift Shop: An excellent book selection and photographs are available.

ALPINE COUNTY

MARKLEEVILLE

ALPINE COUNTY MUSEUM AND HISTORICAL COMPLEX★
1 School Street, Markleeville
Phone: (916) 694-2317
Hours: Wed.-Mon. noon-5:00 p.m., Memorial Day through
October.
Admission: Free

Built in 1971, the Alpine County Museum and Historical Complex focuses on Alpine County history. In addition to an old country store and blacksmith shop, exhibits feature lumber and carpentry tools, toys and dolls, clothing, photographs, rocks and gems, old bottles, handmade skis, and a collection of scenic paintings by local artist Walt Monroe. The museum's highlight is the Spicer collection of artifacts and tools from one of the oldest known structures on the North American continent. Uncovered in an archaeological dig in 1988, this collection confirms the presence of Native Americans in the high Sierra over 10,000 years ago.

The one-room Old Webster School, built in 1882 and abandoned in 1929, has been restored to its original appearance. Original artwork by former students still adorns the walls. The Old Log Jail, with its hand-riveted iron cells, heavy iron bar doors, and iron slot windows, now houses an assortment of farming, lumber, and mining tools and artifacts.

Library: The Alpine County Library and Archives are housed in the new Webster School building at the western edge of Markleeville. The archival collection includes county records dating from 1864.

TUOLUMNE COUNTY

COLUMBIA

COLUMBIA STATE HISTORIC PARK
Main Street, Columbia
Phone: (209) 532-4301
Hours: Daily 10:00 a.m.-5:00 p.m.
Admission: Free

Americans aren't the only people who are fascinated with the Old West. Of the half a million people who visit Columbia State Historic Park every year, fifty thousand are from out of the country. Preserved by the State as a typical Gold Rush town, Columbia is the perfect place to relive the colorful past. Incidentally, the feeling of déjà vu that so often strikes visitors comes from having seen the town countless times in the movies ("High Noon") and on television ("Little House on the Prairie," Wells Fargo commercials).

Gold was discovered in Columbia in March 1850. One month later Columbia's population was over 5,000, and by the end of 1852 the town boasted more than 150 stores, shops, and saloons, as well as a church, Masonic lodge, and Sunday school. When the easily-mined placer gold was gone, the town declined and the population dropped to about 500. After two devastating fires, unlike many gold settlements that succumbed to fire and disappeared, Columbia was rebuilt with fireproof bricks and iron fire doors. As a result, it now looks much as it did during its Gold Rush heyday.

The historic core of the town—twelve square blocks of forty original buildings and historically accurate reconstructions—is a nice blend of living museum/tourist attraction. Under the strict guidelines of the park system, the enterprises aimed at the tourist's dollar reflect the types of businesses that existed in the 1800s: some have actually been in business since the town was established, some are new but historically accurate venues, and others are modern ventures with an old-time flavor. You can buy a ticket for a stagecoach ride at the old stage depot; purchase gifts at New York Dry Goods, where dry goods have been sold since 1855; have a drink at one of the two 1850s-era saloons; sample horehound drops and licorice sticks made from Gold-Rush-era recipes at the Nelson Candy Kitchen; watch the blacksmith turn out souvenirs, restorations, and

Photo of the town of Columbia courtesy of Columbia State Historic Park.

replicas; and even find lodgings for the night at the two-story City Hotel or the elegant Victorian Fallon Hotel, operated by students of resort management at Columbia Junior College.

You could pass an entire, activity-filled day in Columbia and not cover it all. Some visitors have been known to spend the entire day panning for gold. Others begin their visit at the William Cavalier Museum, which displays mining supplies and other relics of Gold Rush life. A replica of the 1855 *Columbia Gazette* office houses an operating newspaper and a basement museum with exhibits on early California printing and newspaper publishing.

Two firehouses, one containing the park's modern firefighting equipment, exhibit historic firefighting equipment including the hand-pumper Papeete manufactured in Boston in 1852. This fancifully decorated, two-cylinder fire engine with leather hoses and buckets was named for the capital of Tahiti, to which it was supposed to be shipped. Somehow it ended up in Columbia instead.

The Gold Rush brought about one of the biggest human migrations of all time. A quarter of the people who flocked to the California gold fields from all over the world came from China. A former bakery exhibits a Chinese herb shop and a small temple in memory of the Chinese who were brought to this country to work under contract and stayed on to mine their own diggings or open businesses.

Gift Shop: Several business sell gifts, souvenir items, and gold-panning equipment.

Restaurants: The full-service Columbia City Hotel restaurant features fresh California cuisine of high quality and an excellent wine list. Columbia House offers breakfasts and lunches daily, American dinners Thursday through Sunday. Fallon Ice Cream Parlor provides fresh-baked waffle cones for your favorite flavor of ice cream. Csarda's Deli-Bakery has sandwiches and desserts.

JAMESTOWN

RAILTOWN 1897 STATE HISTORIC PARK
End of 5th Avenue, Jamestown
Phone: (209) 984-3953
Hours: Weekdays 9:30 a.m.-4:30 p.m., weekends 9:30 a.m.-5:00 p.m.
Admission: Adults $9.00, children 3-12 $4.50

Not too many people nowadays remember when short line steam facilities like the Sierra Railway could be found in small towns all over the country. But many recall seeing these very trains in Hollywood's version of those bygone days, in films like "Unforgiven," "Back to the Future (Part III)," "Pale Rider," "High Noon," and the television series "Petticoat Junction."

The Sierra Railway, founded in 1897, connected the gold mines and lumber mills of Tuolumne County with the rest of the country until passenger service ended in 1930 and diesel engines replaced the steam locomotives for hauling freight in 1955.

In 1982, the State purchased the 27-acre Railtown complex and turned it into a living museum where visitors can ride the short line railroad (one of only two left in the country) and tour the historic roundhouse. Still in use today, the six-track roundhouse contains a variety of steam locomotives and antique passenger cars, and the tools and equipment used to maintain them. Other outbuildings include the blacksmith, machine, and carpenter's shops, and the motion picture prop storage area. Visitors can choose from a menu of steam train excursions, including the Mother Lode Cannonball, the Twilight Limited Bar-B-Que Train, and the Wine and Cheese Zephyr.

Gift Shop: You will find an excellent selection of train books, memorabilia, and gifts, and a bathtub full of iced sodas, in the large Freight House Gift Shop.

SONORA

SONORA FIRE DEPARTMENT MUSEUM
91 Washington, Sonora
Phone: (209) 532-7432
Hours: Daily 10:00 a.m.–4:00 p.m.
Admission: Free

The Sonora Fire Department Club Room does double duty as the Sonora Fire Department Museum. Cases lining the clubhouse perimeter display uniforms and trophies. Old lithographs, photos, and a poster collection cover the walls.

TUOLUMNE COUNTY MUSEUM AND HISTORY CENTER
158 West Bradford Avenue, Sonora
Phone: (209) 532-1317
Hours: Tues.–Sun. 10:00 a.m.–3:30 p.m., Memorial Day–Labor Day;
**   Tues.–Sat. 10:00 a.m.–3:30 p.m., winter.**
Admission: Free

Sonora was once known as "the wickedest camp in the mines," where drunkenness, gambling, stealing, violence, and general lawlessness prevailed. So the Tuolumne County Jail, which housed outlaws and desperados from 1857 until 1960, is a fitting site for the Tuolumne County Museum. Two jail cells now house an extensive collection of vintage firearms, and the east cellblock area houses an exhibit of "Overland Trails to California." The front gallery exhibits tell the history of Tuolumne County with artifacts and photographs, and spotlight the importance of gold in the area's history—in addition to the usual Gold Rush artifacts, the museum features the Tuolumne County Gold Country Collection of nuggets and quartz. You can also learn about modern-day gold mining from the museum's exhibits.

Library: The Tuolumne County Genealogical Society and Tuolumne County Historical Society maintain libraries at the museum. Genealogical Society members are available to help researchers Tuesday, Thursday, and Saturday during museum hours. On other days, use of their materials is by appointment. The Historical Society Library is open by appointment.

Gift Shop: There is no shop, but books on local history, a 25¢ local guidebook, and limited edition reprints of old lithographs are available for purchase.

MARIPOSA COUNTY

MARIPOSA

CALIFORNIA STATE MINING AND MINERAL MUSEUM*
Mariposa County Fairgrounds, Mariposa
Phone: (209) 742-7625
Hours: Wed.-Mon. 10:00 a.m.-6:00 p.m., May 1–September 30;
   Wed.-Sun. 10:00 a.m.-4:00 p.m., October 1–April 30.
Admission: Adults $3.50, seniors & students $2.50, children 13 and
   under free.

California, famous for her gold, is also one of the richest states in the nation for the value and diversity of other minerals and gems. The official State Gem and Mineral Collection, created by an act of the Legislature in 1880, was housed in San Francisco's Ferry Building from 1889 to 1983. In 1989 the State built a picturesque new home for the collection in the historic gold-mining town of Mariposa, in the Sierra foothills. An accurate replica of a turn-of-the-century ore-processing mill, the building is divided into three galleries connected by a 200-foot mine tunnel depicting underground mining techniques. The smell and dampness of the earth, the scent of burned blasting fuses, and the display of mannequins demonstrating the difficult work create an authentic feel for the rugged conditions in underground mines in the early 1900s.

A gallery devoted to mining and mineral development features a working model of a five-stamp gold processing mill and a replica of a 19th century assay office. Another gallery dedicated to minerals and their uses stages special traveling exhibits. Some of the oldest and most colorful specimens from the State's historic gem and mineral collection—one of the largest in the world—are displayed in the central gallery as you enter. Many of the specimens in this unique collection were discovered in the last century and are no longer available to collectors. An impressive display of gold in many of its varied forms—leaf gold, wire gold, gold nuggets, and crystalline gold—is accompanied by specimens of benitoite, the official state gem, and serpentine, the state rock, as well as Butte County diamonds, Monterey County jade, copper, lead, silver, and a host of semi-precious stones. The fabulous, 13-pound "Fricot Nugget," one of the largest and most beautiful ever found in California, is also on display.

This state-of-the-art museum is filled with hands-on activities, including a favorite exhibit where visitors learn how to pan for gold and take their discoveries home with them (summers only).

Gift Shop: You can buy gems, minerals, and jewelry in the stunning museum shop, as well as books on gems, minerals, mining, and Gold Rush history.

MARIPOSA COUNTY COURTHOUSE
5088 Bullion Street, Mariposa
Phone: (209) 966-2456
Hours: Mon.-Fri. 9:00 a.m.-5:00 p.m.; Sat. & Sun. tours
**   10:00 a.m.-5:00 p.m. (April-October)**
Admission: Free

Built in 1854 at a cost of $9,000, the Mariposa County Courthouse is the oldest county courthouse in continuous use west of the Mississippi. The two-story white structure was constructed of native white pine in a classic Grecian style. A cupola was added in 1861 to house a clock shipped around Cape Horn from the East Coast. The clock is still hand-wound today by cranking two weighted cables onto separate drums. During the week, visitors can walk the hallways and peek into the courtroom where some of the most celebrated civil, mining, and water cases were tried, including the Fremont land grant title case, and *Biddle Boggs* v. *Merced Mining Company.* The Mariposa Chamber of Commerce sponsors guided tours on weekends during the summer where you can get a closer look at the original furniture, and the original hand-planed boards on the walls.

MARIPOSA MUSEUM AND HISTORY CENTER
5119 Jessie Street, Mariposa
Phone: (209) 966-2924
Hours: Weekends 10:00 a.m.-4:00 p.m., February; daily 10:00 a.m.-
**   4:00 p.m., March; daily 10:00 a.m.-4:30 p.m., April-October;**
**   weekends 10:00 a.m.-4:00 p.m., Nov.-Dec.; closed January.**
Admission: Free

The Mariposa Museum and History Center, which bills itself as "the finest small museum to be seen anywhere," presents an authentic picture of the people and life of Mariposa County from its first inhabitants to the recent past. In the ranch-style building the museum shares with the Mariposa Library, you will see a typical one-room miner's cabin containing all his worldly possessions. Excerpts from the 1852-54 "Dear Charlie" letters, written by Horace Snow from Agua Fria to his boyhood friend Charlie in Cambridge, Massachusetts, offer a rare glimpse into the life of a miner over one hundred years ago. Original counters and shelves stocked with merchandise dating back more than one hundred years recreate the Gagliardo Store, operated by members of the Gagliardo family from 1854 until the death of the beloved "Miss Jennie" in 1960 at the age of 90.

Among the many buildings on the museum grounds are a pre-Civil War Temperance Hall that housed the *Mariposa Gazette* for over seventy years, a five-stamp mill used at the Golden Key Mine until 1953, a typical one-room schoolhouse, and the recently restored Counts House built in 1863. The Indian Village features bark houses and sweat houses recently constructed by Native Americans whose ancestors made their homes nearby. The Native Plant Garden is surrounded by a rock wall originally built in Cathey's Valley by Chinese laborers as they cleared the fields of rocks. Historic vehicles displayed in the Carriage House include a sparkling, black-lacquered doctor's buggy purchased in 1907 for $21.50, and the Cannon Ball carriage that transported passengers to Yosemite National Park from 1901 to 1915.

Gift Shop: You can pick up books, postcards, and maps of the area, as well as souvenir gift items.

YOSEMITE NATIONAL PARK

A place of unparalleled beauty, Yosemite National Park welcomes almost four million visitors a year, so expect a crowd. No museum on earth could compete with its magnificent valley, great domes and peaks, waterfalls, giant sequoias and flowering meadows. However, for an overview and orientation you may want to begin your visit to Yosemite with a stop at one of the visitor centers.

Of the four visitor centers in the park, the Valley Visitor Center (209/372-0299, open daily from 9:00 a.m. to 5:00 p.m. in winter, extended hours in summer) is the largest and most comprehensive, offering natural history displays and an orientation slide show. A multimedia program about the park is presented throughout the day. The other visitor centers are the Big Oak Flat Information Center, Tuolumne Meadows Visitor Center, and the Wawona Information Center. The Happy Isles Nature Center (open daily from 9:00 a.m. to 5:00 p.m., late spring through October) includes wildlife exhibits, a children's corner, a display of Yosemite at night, and books specially designed for youngsters.

YOSEMITE CLIMBING ARCHIVES★
Ahwahnee Hotel & Curry Village, Yosemite
    National Park
Phone: (209) 379-2810
Hours: Daily, 24 hours a day
Admission: Free

A private collection commemorating sixty years of
mountain climbing in Yosemite is on view in the
Winter Club Room and the Indian Room at the
Ahwahnee Hotel and in the Mountain Shop at Curry
Village. Artifacts donated by early Yosemite climbers
include the hammer of John Salathe, the father of big
wall climbing, a handmade leather vest worn by
Warren "Batso" Harding on the first ascent of El
Capitan in 1958, and homemade pitons. The large
collection of photographs and books on the sport are
available for research.

Cathedral Spire,
Yosemite Valley.
Photo by
Richard M.
Leonard,
courtesy of
Yosemite
Climbing
Archives.

YOSEMITE MUSEUM★
Yosemite National Park
Phone: (209) 372-0281
Hours: Indian Cultural Exhibit, daily 9:00 a.m.-4:30 p.m.,
    summer; daily 9:30 a.m.-noon, 1:00-4:00 p.m., winter.
    Museum Gallery, hours vary.
Admission: Free

The Yosemite Museum, located next to the Yosemite Valley Visitor
Center, has two exhibit galleries. The Indian Cultural Exhibit is devoted
to the culture of the Miwok and Paiute people of Yosemite, and includes
exhibits of basketry, ceremonial regalia, and other artifacts from the
region. Demonstrations of basketry, beadwork, and traditional Miwok
and Paiute games take place there daily. The Museum Gallery exhibits
changing shows of contemporary art and historic materials from the
museum's extensive collection. The Indian village of Ahwahnee, a
reconstructed Miwok–Paiute village of the 1880s, is located behind the
museum. This outdoor exhibit is open all year, from dawn to dusk.
Cultural demonstrations take place there daily during the summer, from
9:00 a.m. to 4:30 p.m.

Library: The Yosemite Research Library, focusing on the human and
natural history of Yosemite, has circulating materials as well as rare books
and pamphlets, maps, unpublished manuscripts, oral history tapes and
transcripts, news clippings, and more, as well as a large photo collection.
The library is open to the public Tuesday through Friday, 8:00 a.m. to
noon, and 1:00 to 5:00 p.m. Researchers wishing to make extensive use
of the library should contact the librarian in advance: (209) 372-0280.

Gift Shop: The museum shop, offering books about the Yosemite region and a selection of local Native American baskets, musical instruments, beadwork, and other objects, is open April through January.

YOSEMITE PIONEER HISTORY CENTER*
Wawona Ranger Station, Yosemite National Park
Phone: (209) 372-0563
Hours: Daily, all year, for self-guided tours; interpreters and stage rides, Wed.-Sun. 9:00 a.m.-4:30 p.m., late June-Labor Day.
Admission: Free

The Yosemite Pioneer History Center, a cluster of buildings representing different chapters in the Yosemite story, commemorates the people involved in establishing the park. The buildings, which were moved to Wawona in the 1950s, include the studio of painter Christian Jorgensen, a homestead cabin built by ranchers who grazed cattle in the valley, and the miner's cabin of George Anderson, an early Yosemite guide and the first man to climb Half Dome. Other buildings recount the development of tourism and travel in Yosemite: a blacksmith shop that served travelers who arrived on horseback or by horse-drawn stage; a ranger patrol building used as a check station as cars replaced horses (drivers paid $5.00 to enter the park in 1915!); and the powderhouse where blasting powder for road improvement projects was stored in the 1930s. During the summer, costumed interpreters portray the people and events that shaped Yosemite's history, and stage rides are available from the transportation building, which contains an old Wells Fargo Bank office. Call to verify hours, especially for stage rides. The buildings can be visited all year, however, with plaques at each site providing a self-guided tour.

Lucy Telles, (Yosemite Miwok and Paiute), with one of the many magnificent baskets she wove, 1933. Photo by Ralph Anderson, courtesy of Yosemite National Park Research Library

San Joaquin Valley

SAN JOAQUIN COUNTY

ESCALON

THE HORSELESS CARRIAGE GARAGE
1601 B Street, Escalon
Phone: (209) 838-3206 or (209) 529-3851
Hours: Call for hours or appointment.
Admission: Free

The sandwich board in front of the privately owned Horseless Carriage Garage proclaimed it to be an Antique Car Museum, so we checked it out. On display were a dozen or more beautifully-restored vintage automobiles dating from 1900 to 1930.

Gift Shop: Many of the artifacts on display (e.g., a 1908 Reo) are for sale.

LODI

SAN JOAQUIN COUNTY HISTORICAL SOCIETY AND MUSEUM
11793 North Micke Grove Road, Lodi
Phone: (209) 368-9154
Hours: Fri.-Sun. 1:00-4:45 p.m.
Admission: Adults $1.00, seniors & children 50¢

Thousands of artifacts at the San Joaquin Historical Museum, from Mason jars to gigantic farm equipment, illustrate the area's agricultural history. Courtesy of San Joaquin County Historical Society.

You might want to set aside a whole day for your visit to the San Joaquin County Historical Society and Museum, to take advantage of the swimming pool, zoo, Japanese garden, and picnic facilities at Micke Grove Regional Park. Allow at least a couple of hours to explore the museum's many buildings and the gardens covering fifteen acres of parkland.

The large, modern Erickson Exhibition Hall presents rotating exhibits—"Needle, Shuttle & Awl," an exploration

of technology employed by women to create utilitarian and ceremonial items from baskets to quilts, was on view at the time of our visit. Permanent exhibits chronicle the life of Charles Weber, founder of Stockton, presenting furnishings from the Weber and William Micke houses in a series of rooms depicting a typical middle-class Victorian home.

The remaining seven buildings are filled with thousands of artifacts, from mundane household utensils to gigantic farm machinery, arranged in accessible exhibits devoted to the agricultural history of the San Joaquin Valley. A wheelwright exhibit, a cooper shop, the saddler's and harness maker's shop, the rancher's blacksmithy, and the tractor corral develop the museum's "Man and the Soil" theme. In the Tree & Vine Building, a life-like mannequin is busy canning pears in the 1920s kitchen, where you learn that home canning did not become widespread until John Mason patented the zinc screw cap and rubber ring for sealing jars. Metal-roofed halls large enough to house, among other things, a gigantic Holt combine harvester also offer the extraordinary Floyd Locher Tool Collection, an assembly of nearly 4,000 different hand and foot-powered tools dating from the 16th century through the 1950s.

"Keep your face to the sunshine and you cannot see the shadow." This quotation from Helen Keller inspired the Sunshine Trail, a garden designed for the visually impaired. The songs of the birds, the splash of the waterfall, the fragrance of the plants and the texture of their leaves allow visitors to use their senses of hearing, smell, and touch to enjoy nature.

For kids: Local third to fifth graders love Valley Days at the Museum, where they live a day in the life of a child in an agricultural community of the 1880s, donning period costumes and attending class in the restored, one-room Calaveras schoolhouse. Also, for a nominal fee, museum docents will bring a Grandmother's Trunk and Suitcase exhibit to your site.

Library: The Gerald D. Kennedy Reference Library provides access to county records and local history by appointment for a small fee.

Gift Shop: The museum's book and gift shop operates in the carriage house at the entrance to the museum complex.

Rental: Several indoor and outdoor museum sites are available for classes, meetings, and special events.

STOCKTON

CHILDREN'S MUSEUM OF STOCKTON
402 West Weber Avenue, Stockton
Phone: (209) 465-4386
Hours: Tues.-Sat. 9:30 a.m.-5:00 p.m.; Sun. noon-5:00 p.m.
Admission: $4.00, $2.00 in groups of 10 or more

The Children's Museum of Stockton, "where every touch is a know-know," offers playful interactive exhibits in the arts, sciences, humanities, and technology. Toddlers can play in the Toddletown Park, an area set aside just for them, while older children explore real, grown-up equipment in themed exhibits featuring emergency room medical equipment, a real fire truck, television cameras, and the front end of a city bus. A dentist's office, barber shop, builder's office, restaurant, bank, post office, and stage dressing room complete with costumes, jewelry, and face-painting offer opportunities galore for role-playing. The pet store stocked with rabbits, rats, turtles, and birds, as well as a model hydroelectric plant, a spectacular cave, and the Water Company, an area devoted to bubble-making, introduce them to junior level geology, geography, physics, biology, and other sciences. Art-loving children will have the opportunity to create to their hearts' content in the recycling art center.

Library: A room filled with overstuffed chairs and lots of books provides a quiet getaway.

Gift Shop: The shop sells kids' items priced from 5¢ to $30.

THE HAGGIN MUSEUM
Victory Park
1201 North Pershing Avenue, Stockton
Phone: (209) 462-4116
Hours: Tues.-Sun. 1:30-5:00 p.m.
Admission: Free—donations appreciated

Set amidst the green lawns, shade trees, and serene ponds of Victory Park is an unknown jewel, Stockton's Haggin Museum—the least celebrated of California's major museums. Built in 1931, the gracious, three-story, neoclassic brick structure has 31,000 square feet of exhibition space and something to keep everybody happy.

For art lovers, an important collection assembled at the turn of the century by Louis Haggin focuses on late 19th and early 20th century American and European paintings. In the rotunda, you can enjoy the largest collection of Albert Bierstadt paintings in the United States, including the well-known and much-reproduced "Looking up at Yosemite Valley" and "Sunset in Yosemite Valley." Two first-floor galleries showcase works from the French Academic School, among them the striking "Unfolding the Holy Flag," a masterpiece of realism by Jean Leon Gerome, and "Gathering for the Hunt" by Rosa Bonheur, the most

"Looking Up the Yosemite Valley" Albert Bierstadt, (1863, oil on canvas, 35-7/8' x 58'). The Haggin Museum, the least celebrated of California's major museums, has the largest collection of Bierstadt paintings in the U.S. Courtesy of the Haggin Museum.

famous woman painter of her day. The second-floor arcade gallery displays landscapes from the Hudson River schools.

The history collection traces its roots to the San Joaquin Society of California Pioneers, a group founded in 1868 by residents dedicated to preserving the history they themselves were making; many of the objects they gathered are on display in the museum today. Recent renovations take advantage of state-of-the-art technology to appeal to museum-goers of all stripes—sprinters, strollers, and studiers.

Sprinters can race through the galleries, reading the large signs to get the gist of Stockton history from prehistoric times through the mid 1940s. First, an overview in the Pioneer Room, then a quick vision of Native American life, a swift journey back to a turn-of-the century California town and a Victorian farmhouse, a brief lesson in the history of farm equipment at the Holt Gallery, a glance at early fire engines, a horse-drawn carriage, and a high-wheeler bicycle in the Vehicle Gallery, and finally a hasty hello to the popular mummy from ancient Egypt (on loan from the de Young Museum since 1945) in the Ancient Arts Gallery on the way out.

Strollers can stop to examine exhibits that particularly interest them—the bark slab house in the full-scale Miwok environment perhaps, or the furniture in Jennie Hunter's 1860 parlor; antique dolls in the toy shop storefront; Old Betsy, the second-oldest steam-powered fire engine in the country; or the twelve-and-a-half ton, Stockton-built Holt "Caterpillar" track-type tractor, the largest item ever displayed by the museum.

Studiers who read every word and examine each item will enjoy the extensive collection of California Indian baskets. They can check out the fine stitching on crazy quilts laid out on the Victorian bed, wonder at the herbs and medicines displayed in the Chinese Herb Store—an exhibit the Smithsonian was dying to get its hands on—and learn all about the role of Stockton industry in the mechanization of American agriculture. As a reward for their efforts, only the studiers will know the details, such as the purpose of the gigantic brass contraption that resembles something from *Twenty Thousand Leagues Under the Sea*: it's actually an enormous pressure cooker used by Tillie Lewis to make tomato paste.

This 12-1/2-ton Caterpillar built in Stockton is displayed in the agricultural section of Stockton's Haggin Museum. Courtesy of Haggin Museum.

For kids: popular drop-in family programs on Saturdays feature hands-on activities throughout the galleries. The bi-monthly programs highlight aspects of the museum's permanent collections or special exhibitions.

Library: Three research libraries, including the Earl Rowland Art Library, the Holt Industrial Archives, and the Almeda May Petzinger Library of 7,000 volumes devoted to California history and an extensive

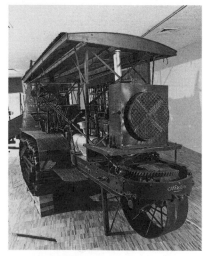

archival collection of maps, diaries, documents, and photographs, are open by appointment only.

Gift Shop: The cheerful basement gift shop carries books, Victorian reproductions, folk art, Bierstadt reproductions, and one-of-a-kind pieces by local artists.

STANISLAUS COUNTY

MODESTO

McHENRY MANSION
15th and I Streets, Modesto
Phone: (209) 577-5344
Hours: Tues., Wed., Thurs., Sun. 1:00–4:00 p.m.; Fri. 1:00–3:00 p.m.
Admission: Free

Built in 1883 by Robert McHenry, a rancher/banker and leading citizen, the ornate Italianate Victorian is one of the few 19th century buildings to survive in Modesto. After doing service as a sanitarium and apartment house, the mansion has been carefully restored to its former elegance and decorated to the period (1883–1896), right down to an entire stuffed peacock. An upstairs bedroom and sitting room reflect the period from 1896 to 1906, when the house was occupied by the McHenrys' son.

Gift Shop: The gift shop sells items reflecting the Victorian era.

Rental: The mansion may be rented for weddings, receptions, and special events.

McHENRY MUSEUM
1402 I Street, Modesto
Phone: (209) 577-5366
Hours: Tues.-Sun. noon–4:00 p.m.
Admission: Free

The McHenry Museum's 1912 Greek Revival building, designed by William Weeks, formerly housed the city library, a gift of the McHenry family. Now the 8,000 square feet of exhibit space chronicle the history of Stanislaus County, the home of the first municipal airport in the United States and the birthplace of crop dusting.

A pleasant gallery presents six changing exhibits a year that focus on local activities, special collections, and ethnic groups in the area. On exhibit during our visit, "Back to School" displayed a collection of 250 school lunch boxes together with drawings by schoolchildren in Modesto's sister city in Japan. Most popular with local residents is the Gallery of Pioneer Families, featuring panels and a carousel of old photos and documents. Two large back rooms celebrate life at the turn of the century (1880–1910) through a series of recreated rooms, including the barber shop from a local hotel, a 1906 dentist's office, a doctor's office equipped with a rare, early x-ray machine, a blacksmith shop, and a gold-mining exhibit. The museum's newest exhibit, a charming country store, boasts a post office and switchboard along with a host of old-fashioned items. A country store exhibit is a wonderful thing for a small museum, according to curator Heide Warner. "They sold everything," she explains, "So if you can't find a place for an artifact, you put it in the country store." Glass cases filled with personal collections display walking sticks, fans, pipes, and Weller pottery. The museum rotates its first-rate collection of clothing according to season.

The Central California Art League occupies the downstairs space, exhibiting the work of local artists and maintaining the largest sales and rental gallery in northern California outside of San Francisco.

Library: Open by appointment, the Museum Archives offer researchers an outstanding collection of photos, documents, and county records from 1854 to the 1920s.

Gift Shop: The gift shop features an extensive selection of local history books, including reprints of out-of-print volumes and charming Victorian reproductions.

OAKDALE

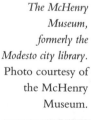

The McHenry Museum, formerly the Modesto city library. Photo courtesy of the McHenry Museum.

OAKDALE MUSEUM
212 West F Street, Oakdale
Phone: (209) 847-9229 or 847-5822
Hours: Tues. & Thurs. noon–4:00 p.m.; second Sat. 10:00 a.m.–
**   4:00 p.m.**
Admission: Free

Hershey Chocolate USA, the only Hershey Chocolate plant in the country offering tours to the public, is considered Oakdale's major tourist

draw. A lesser-known but still worthwhile attraction is the Oakdale Museum, housed in the oldest building in town. Built in 1869 for the town's first postmaster, the small Italianate farmhouse displays historic items, such as a bedroom furnished in the style of the late 1800s, featuring a rope bed and chamber pot, and a rare, letter-combination safe from the Stockton & Copperopolis Railroad, along with other items from the old train depot.

The Sandl Art Gallery, located in what was once the living room, showcases the work of local artists on a three-month rotating schedule.

Library: The museum has an outstanding collection of reference material on local history, including the Tim Haidlen collection of over 3,000 photographs and hundreds of oral histories, and a complete collection of Oakdale newspapers on microfilm.

MERCED COUNTY

ATWATER

CASTLE AIR MUSEUM
Castle Air Force Base, Atwater
Phone: (209) 723-2178
Hours: Daily 10:00 a.m.-4:00 p.m.
Admission: Free

Extending over 18 acres, Castle Air Museum is the largest Air Force museum in the western United States. Visitors can stroll outdoors through the varied collection of 42 faithfully restored planes from World War II and the Korean and Vietnam wars. These include the "Flying Fortress," the first four-engine bomber to perform successfully in daylight raids; and the biggest, fastest, and most technically-advanced bomber of World War II, the B-29. On the other end of the spectrum is the sleek, black SR-71 strategic reconnaissance aircraft, one of the highest flying planes in the world, which can fly more than three times the speed of sound—literally faster than a speeding bullet.

The indoor museum, housed in a vintage World War II wood structure, contains a large collection of uniforms, personal equipment, paintings, and photographs. Computer technology has replaced the Link Trainer and the once top-secret Norton Bomb Sight, but you can get a close look at these and other military relics.

Neighboring Castle Air Force Base is scheduled to close in 1995, but the museum will remain open. An admission charge may be instituted.

Library: Archives Research Center.

Gift Shop: Flight of Fancy, the large restaurant and gift shop, sells all things aeronautical including models, artwork, books, and aircraft memorabilia.

Restaurant: If you work up an appetite walking over the 18 acres of airplanes, go to the Flight of Fancy for a hearty lunch or snack. Located between the museum building and the planes, with both indoor and outdoor seating, this no-frills cafeteria offers simple, inexpensive food— hamburgers garnished with fresh lettuce and tomatoes, large-cut fries, meat sandwiches, chili, and clam chowder are all on the menu. You'll be eating with service people from the base as well as other museum visitors.

GUSTINE

GUSTINE MUSEUM★
397 Fourth Street, Gustine
Phone: (209) 854-2344
Hours: Thurs. & Sun. noon–4:00 p.m.
Admission: Free

In 1911, the first prisoner in the newly-built Merced County Jail was leaning against his cell door when it suddenly came open and he fell out. The model prisoner reported the incident to the constable, who notified the builder, who replaced the faulty lock, and there was never another jailbreak in Gustine. You can examine this very same iron door when you visit the Gustine Museum, housed in the former Merced County Justice Court/Jail Building. Other items of interest include displays of the Bald Eagle Mine, located in the hills west of Gustine, which contained the purest magnesite in the state. Cowboy tack and horseshoeing tools used by local cowboy Loren Tate recall the cattle industry in the area. Artifacts of the dairy industry commemorate Gustine's position as the dairy center of the San Joaquin Valley.

Library: The archival library features original documents relating to early Gustine and to western history.

MERCED

AGRICULTURAL MUSEUM OF MERCED COUNTY
4498 East Hwy. 140, Merced
Phone: (209) 383-1912
Hours: Tues.-Sun. 10:00 a.m.–4:00 p.m.
Admission: Adults $2.50, seniors $2.00, children 6-12 $1.50

Don't be misled by the name. The only way Charles Parish could get a permit to build a museum was to call it an Agriculture Museum. It really is a museum devoted to the gas engine, with a few miscellaneous collections (beauty salon equipment from the 1920s, dental equipment, tin toys, eye cups, stove-top washers, old radios, bicycles, horse-drawn buggies) thrown in for good measure. "My great-grandfather had a museum in

Randolph, Vermont," said Parish, "So I just had it in the back of my mind I'd build me one."

Opened in 1992, the museum's 6,000-square-foot building and three acres of land provide exhibit space for Parish's growing collection of antique gas engines, one of the best collections from Oregon to San Diego. "These engines are built to run for two or three centuries, not two or three years; they're made to last forever," says Parish. For the 20,000 engine collectors in the country, these machines are pure poetry, and this museum is their shrine. Parish is in the process of constructing an authentic blacksmith shop and restoring a 1915 gas station, which will broaden the appeal of this idiosyncratic museum.

MERCED COUNTY COURTHOUSE MUSEUM
21st and N Streets, Merced
Phone: (209) 723-2401
Hours: Wed.-Sun. 1:00-4:00 p.m.
Admission: $1.00 over age 12, children free when with adult, maximum family charge $3.00

The old Merced County Courthouse, an imposing, three-story Italianate structure, now houses the Merced County Museum. Designed by Albert A. Bennett, one of the architects of the State Capitol in Sacramento, the dome-topped, faux marble building is encrusted with symbolic trappings: the hand-carved wooden statue of Minerva, the Roman goddess of wisdom, is placed atop the cupola overlooking the goddess of justice, to symbolize the desire for wisdom to prevail over justice in the courthouse. The second-floor courtroom, a Superior Court venue until 1951, boasts the original furniture, including rocking chairs for the jury and a marble basin, which harks back to the ancient Roman ritual requiring a judge to wash his hands after sentencing.

The museum's 8,500 square feet of exhibition space are devoted to the history of Merced County and early settlers in the Central Valley. First-floor exhibits include a blacksmith shop, gambling artifacts, and a temple altar, a relic of Merced's Chinatown. A grist mill, a cowboy's fireless cooker, and other implements recall the days when the Del Monte cannery and the largest peach orchard in the world were located in Merced. On the second floor, a collection of Victorian furnishings and household appliances demonstrates life before electricity—kids are encouraged to try the hand-operated, wooden washing machine. The turn-of-the-century schoolroom displays a 1902 attendance record listing "measles and small pox—cause of quarantine," and a carousel of old school photographs.

Library: County archives are available for research by appointment.

Gift Shop: The first-floor gift shop sells books and gift items relating to the Central Valley and California.

YOSEMITE WILDLIFE MUSEUM
2020 Yosemite Parkway (Highway 140), Merced
Phone: (209) 383-1052
Hours: Mon.-Sat. 10:00 a.m.-5:00 p.m.
Admission: Adults $2.50, seniors & students $1.75,
**   children 5-12 $1.00**

The privately-owned Yosemite Wildlife Museum, also known as the
Hunters Hall of Fame, features two hundred taxidermied specimens of
North American wildlife set in 26 dioramas representing their natural
habitats. Hand-painted backgrounds, landscaped foregrounds, and a sound
track attempt to recreate the feeling of being in the great outdoors.
The creatures, some of which were donated by San Francisco's Academy
of Sciences, range in size from giant polar bears to tiny birds.
Gift Shop: The large gift shop specializes in country-style gifts.

MADERA COUNTY

NORTH FORK

SIERRA MONO MUSEUM
Intersection of Road 225 and Road 228, North Fork
Phone: (209) 877-2115
Hours: Mon.-Fri. 9:00 a.m.-4:00 p.m.
Admission: $1.50

Owned and operated by Mono Indians, the Sierra Mono Museum
focuses on the natural history of the area and the culture of the Mono
tribe, who were among the original inhabitants of the Sierra Nevada.
The Monos, who bought the land and built the museum with all-
volunteer labor, are justifiably proud of their fine museum.

A wall-to-ceiling case is filled with hundreds of Native American
baskets, many passed down through generations and on loan from Mono
families. Basketry is taught at the museum when materials are available.
The museum posts maps of areas that have been sprayed with pesticides
for the benefit of weavers who gather the native plants.

The large Tettleton Wildlife collection, featuring grizzly bears, mountain
lions, elk, moose, antelope, wolves, and many birds, fish, and reptiles
displayed in dramatic dioramas, is considered the finest in the state.

Two large dioramas chronicle traditional Mono hunting, fishing,
cooking, acorn gathering, basketmaking, healing, games, and ceremonies.
One features a small cedar-bark house, toy bows strung with milkweed
string and willow arrows, an acorn-filled basket granary, and a ramada
thatched with bay leaves, sheltering cooking utensils. A bachelor-size
cedar-bark house sits just outside the front entrance to the museum.

The Annual Indian Fair Days celebration, held the first week in August,
provides an opportunity to see and hear traditional Native American

songs and dances from all over the West, watch demonstrations of acorn gathering, basketmaking and other arts, and purchase handcrafted items.

Library: The Archives house artifacts from archaeological digs for scholarly research.

Gift Shop: You can purchase jewelry and cards from the small shop.

OAKHURST

FRESNO FLATS HISTORICAL PARK
School Road (Road 427), Oakhurst
Phone: (209) 683-6570
Hours: Wed.-Sat. 1:00–3:00 p.m., Sun. 1:00–4:00 p.m.
Admission: Adults $2.00, children 5-12 75¢

Charlie Meyers, the first mechanic in Fresno Flats (he switched from blacksmithing) was accused of robbing the stage. Although his guilt was never proven—he was acquitted after a year in jail—he and his alleged crime were thenceforth inextricably linked with the name of Fresno Flats. His wife, Kitty, got so tired of hearing people ask, "Fresno Flats—isn't that where Charlie Meyers robbed the stage?" that she got up a petition to have the name changed to Oakhurst in 1913.

The Sierra Historic Sites Association decided to preserve the old name when they created Fresno Flats Historical Park. Members of the all-volunteer association moved eight historic buildings to the site, restoring and furnishing them to capture the flavor of family life in central California's foothills and mountains a century ago. A family could easily spend the better part of a day here touring the buildings and enjoying a picnic on the banks of the nearby the Fresno River.

Our tour, led by the gracious and well-informed caretaker, Coletta Staigg, began in the Nathan Sweet Memorial Museum, which is housed in the 1874 Fresno Flats schoolhouse. Cases contain items from ranches, gold mines, logging camps, the Chinese settlement, the old Wawona Hotel, pioneer family memorabilia, and a model of Fresno Flats made out of popsicle sticks by third-graders.

The 1869 Taylor Log House, all handmade in a typical Ozarks design, was the home of Boot Taylor, the area's earliest forest ranger. Boot's diary gives visitors insight into the daily life of a forest ranger (he was paid $68 a month and a mule). Modern-day Taylor descendants often stop by to pencil in additions to the family tree on the wall.

The Old Barn houses an agricultural exhibit and a typical blacksmith shop from the late 19th century. The Raymond Jail, dating to the 1880s, still bears the original

"Fresno Flats—isn't that where Charlie Meyers robbed the stage?" Mrs. Meyers got so tired of hearing this that she got the town's name changed to Oakhurst. Wedding portrait of Charlie Meyers in San Francisco courtesy of Fresno Flats Historical Park.

leg irons fastened to the floor. The Dupzyk Barn, a typical stock barn of the early 1900s, now houses the museum's logging exhibit. Outside is a section of the flume which once extended some 50 miles from Sugar Pine to Madera. Filled with water, this amazing structure, tended by flume herders, was used to carry rough-cut lumber from the mountains to the sawmill. It also served as an early and dangerous version of the modern water slide. The Fresno Flats wagon–stage collection claims to contain the touring stage that carried Teddy Roosevelt on his visit to Yosemite.

The final building on the tour, the three-story, yellow Laramore-Lyman Home, is a typical "box house," built without studs or corner posts (the outside boards are simply nailed to the inside boards.) Occupied until 1973, the house boasts its original wallpaper, and an unusual assortment of furnishings from the 1870s to the 1920s, including a self-heating iron powered with white gas, a pump organ, and chairs made to fit individual bottoms by a traveling craftsman named Mr. Buckingham. Roses from antique stock dating from 1890 to 1950 grow outside in the well-tended garden.

Library: Open Thursday mornings and by appointment, the Uarda Hocker Memorial Library and Research Center, housed in an historic log cabin from an early resort, offers valuable reference material including many volumes dealing with the history of the area, and county records.

Gift Shop: The gift shop, located in the Nathan Sweet Memorial Museum, sells toys, inexpensive gift items for kids, and Victoriana, including paper doll reproductions and feather fans.

FRESNO COUNTY

COALINGA

R.C. BAKER MEMORIAL MUSEUM★
297 West Elm, Coalinga
Phone: (209) 935-1914
Hours: Mon.-Fri. 10:00 a.m.-noon, 1:00-5:00 p.m.; Sat. 11:00 a.m.-
    5:00 p.m.; Sun. 1:00-5:00 p.m.

Coalinga—originally known as Coaling Station A, for loading coal onto trains—eventually evolved into an oil town whose claim to fame is the cluster of fancifully-decorated oil rigs nine miles north of town. The Annual Horned Toad Derby and the R.C. Baker Memorial Museum share billing as the second most popular attractions. The museum is housed in the former machine shop of R.C. Baker, an oilman and inventor. Baker's personal memorabilia and a large collection of oil field equipment are featured, along with displays of fossils, a mastodon jaw and tusk, World War I artifacts, and western ranch hand equipment.

Baker's former welding shop now showcases a 1924 American La France fire engine, a 1929 Model A Ford, and an old grocery truck that used to supply the oil camps.

FRESNO

AFRICAN AMERICAN HISTORICAL AND CULTURAL MUSEUM OF THE SAN JOAQUIN VALLEY
1857 Fulton Street, Fresno
Phone: (209) 268-7102
Hours: Wed.,Thurs., Fri. 1:00-5:00 p.m.; Sat. & Sun. 11:00 a.m.-5:00 p.m.
Admission: Adults $4.00

Founder and president Jack A. Kelley long dreamed of establishing a museum to promote understanding, appreciation, and awareness of African-Americans in the San Joaquin Valley. In June 1993 his dreams became a reality when the African-American Historical and Cultural Museum opened with "Songs of My People," a landmark photography project documenting the experience of African-Americans. Future plans call for traveling exhibitions of the work of local artists, and an exhibit featuring success stories of local African-Americans and the legacies they have left throughout the San Joaquin Valley.

The second floor of the former bank is devoted to classrooms, meeting rooms, and a children's room featuring an African-American history mural.

DISCOVERY CENTER
1944 North Winery Avenue, Fresno
Phone: (209) 251-5533
Hours: Mon.-Sat. 11:00 a.m.-4:00 p.m.
Admission: Adults $3.00, children $2.00

An old winery barn, the oldest standing structure in Fresno, shares the 6-1/2 acres of former vineyard with a coyote, a pond, tortoises, and the 1954 building that houses the Discovery Center. This natural science museum offers hands-on science exhibits, dioramas of local habitats and wildlife, an indoor zoo, and a Native American room featuring an outstanding display of Yokuts baskets and artifacts.

Gift Shop: Offers a wonderful selection of science-related toys and gifts.

FORT MILLER BLOCKHOUSE MUSEUM*
Roeding Park
US 99, Fresno
Phone: (209) 498-1551
Hours: Fri.-Sun. 1:00-4:00 p.m.
Admission: Free

The Fort Miller Blockhouse Museum exhibits artifacts of pioneer life.

FRESNO ART MUSEUM
2233 North 1st Street, Fresno
Phone: (209) 441-4220
Hours: Tues.-Fri. 10:00 a.m.-5:00 p.m., Sat. & Sun. noon-5:00 p.m.
Admission: Adults $2.00, students and seniors $1.00, children under 16 free. Free on Tuesdays.

A recent remodel has given the Fresno Art Museum, founded in 1948, a stunning showplace building worthy of its reputation as a vanguard in the visual arts. The museum presents thirty temporary exhibitions a year, which complement and enhance permanent installations of pre-Colombian Mexican ceramic sculpture, French post-impressionist graphics, Ansel Adams photographs, and American sculpture.

Temporary exhibitions in 1994 and 1995 will include the new work of Sam Hernandez, Robert Cremean, John Battenberg, Kim Aboles, and Joy Johnson. Surveys of the work of George Hurrell and Jeannette Maxfield Lewis will also be presented. From May 1994 through summer, the world's most extensive collection of indigenous Amazon art will be featured. An exhibition of works by northern California women artists, "New World (dis)Order," will open in September 1994.

Gift Shop: The large, lovely gift shop features one-of-a-kind jewelry and pieces by local artists, toys, games, a large selection of art books, and a rental gallery.

An electrifying "trans-active" exhibit in the science gallery. Courtesy of Fresno Metropolitan Museum.

Restaurant: Cafe Thursday, open Thursdays from 11:30 a.m. to 2:00 p.m., serves salads, soup, entrees, and desserts.

FRESNO METROPOLITAN MUSEUM
1515 Van Ness Avenue, Fresno
Phone: (209) 441-1444

Hours: Tues.-Sun. 11:00 a.m.-5:00 p.m., summer (call for winter hours).
Admission: Adults $4.00; students, seniors, children 4-12 $3.00. Free first Wednesday of the month.

In 1979 the historic, 85,000-square-foot *Fresno Bee* newspaper building was saved from the wrecking ball and converted into the Fresno Metropolitan Museum. To date, approximately half of the total space has been developed into a first-class institution with so much to offer in science, art, and history, for both children and adults, that it's impossible to see it all in one visit.

As a new museum, able from the beginning to take advantage of state-of-the-art exhibit design techniques, the Fresno Metropolitan Museum has pioneered the "trans-active" exhibit, the latest word in hands-on learning. Exhibits are designed to engage visitors in the process of discovery, not to yield predictable results or simply present the discoveries of others. An excellent example is "Zap it. Move it. Make it!" A temporary exhibit that will probably return, it featured a physics lab designed to look like an amusement park, in which kids (and grown-ups) could take apart ordinary household appliances to see what makes them work (engineers call this reverse engineering). In another area, visitors were asked to re-design the human body, or make a model rocket that can touch the roof, or build their own alien from space. The permanent science gallery features forty hands-on activities, including an earthquake table, magnetic colors, and holograms.

The Met has not had the opportunity to establish much in the way of an art collection. Works from their collection of sixty European and American still life paintings dating from the 17th through early 20th centuries are on permanent display, as well as a delightful collection of snuff bottles. World-class traveling art exhibitions frequently make their way to Fresno.

Regional history is featured in richly detailed changing displays. One permanent exhibit devoted to Fresno's most famous son, William Saroyan, combines personal artifacts and photographs with wall panels that will have you reading every word.

KEARNEY MANSION
7160 West Kearney Boulevard, Fresno
Phone: (209) 441-0862
Hours: Fri.-Sun. 1:00-4:00 p.m. Tours at 1:00, 2:00 & 3:00 p.m.
Admission: Adults $3.00, students 13-17 $2.00, children 3-12 $1.00
(adult admission may vary during Christmas).

Built at the turn of the century, this French Renaissance-style house was the headquarters of raisin baron M. Theo Kearney. Featuring many of the original furnishings and French Art Nouveau wallpapers, the house is decorated to the nines for a Victorian exhibit at Christmas.

LEGION OF VALOR MUSEUM
1235 O Street, Fresno
Phone: (209) 498-0510
Hours: Mon., Wed., Thurs., Fri. 10:00 a.m.-3:00 p.m., or by appt.
Admission: Free

The Legion of Valor, formed in 1890 by veterans of the Civil War and Indian Wars, recognizes recipients of the Medal of Honor, Navy Cross, Distinguished Service Cross, and Air Force Cross, the nation's highest military honors. Opened November 11, 1992 (Veterans' Day) in the lobby of the Veterans Memorial Auditorium, the Legion of Valor Museum honors all veterans of all wars, as well as members of the Legion of Valor. Hung with stars and stripes and red, white, and blue bunting, the 10,000-square-foot museum features military uniforms, photographs, guns, ships' models, and a host of military memorabilia.

MEUX HOME
1007 R Street, Fresno
Phone: (209) 233-8007
Hours: Fri.-Sun. noon-3:30 p.m. Closed January.
Admission: Adults $3.00, students 13-17 $2.00, children 3-12 $1.00

The 103-year-old Meux Home, described in its day as "probably the most elaborate residence in Fresno," is the last of the prominent Victorian houses from Fresno's early years. Built by Thomas Meux of Tennessee, a Confederate surgeon and pioneer Fresno physician, the house was continuously occupied by the Meux family until 1970. To the Victorians, charm had to hold an element of surprise, and this solid, two-story edifice has many architectural surprises. The interior is also typically Victorian— no part of a wall or ceiling is left undecorated. The house, including Dr. Meux's office, is richly furnished to the period with many original family pieces.

Gift Shop: The Carriage House Gift Shop, in the original carriage house of Dr. Meux, offers Victorian memorabilia and remembrances of the Meux Home Museum for sale.

KINGS COUNTY

HANFORD

HANFORD CARNEGIE MUSEUM
109 East 8th Street, Hanford
Phone: (209) 584-1367
Hours: Tues.-Sat. noon-4:00 p.m.
Admission: Donation

Originally a Carnegie Library, the Hanford Museum building is considered the best example of Romanesque architecture in California outside of Stanford University. Exhibits and photographs highlight the region's history from the early Yokuts inhabitants to the present. Furnishings from two pioneer families are featured in a period parlor and kitchen. Apparel from the museum's large collection of vintage clothing is showcased in well-designed changing exhibits. A fine display of antique dolls, toys, and children's garments will interest young visitors. The Carnegie Courtyard so delighted Charles Garrigus, California's poet laureate, that he wrote a poem dedicated to the museum. You can read his "Interlude for Comfort" in the courtyard garden, engraved upon a stone monument that at first glimpse appears to be a tombstone.

Library: Kings County records afford an excellent opportunity for family research.

Gift Shop: The small museum store features local history publications, t-shirts, children's items, and children's books.

TAOIST TEMPLE AND MUSEUM
#12 China Alley, Hanford
Phone: (209) 584-3236
Hours: By appointment
Admission: Free

Upon completion of the transcontinental railroad in 1869, many Chinese workers came to settle in Hanford, a town created by the Southern Pacific Railway Company. These early Chinese pioneers formed the Sam Yup Association and bought large tracts of land, which have been handed down over the generations. Because the Chinese weren't allowed to own businesses downtown, they created their own city-within-a-city, complete with herb stores, restaurants, laundries, boarding houses, and gambling establishments.

The L.T. Sue Herb Store, recreated at Hanford's Taoist Temple and Museum. Courtesy of Taoist Temple and Museum.

Constructed in 1893, the building that houses the Taoist Temple originally functioned as a community center, providing housing for single men on the first floor and a place for worship and education on the second. The first floor now houses a recreation of the L.T. Sue Herb Store, a gaming room displaying mah-jong, dominoes, lottery tickets, and other forms of gambling, and a wall of family photos. Upstairs, the original temple furnishings include an altar dedicated to Kuan Kung, the God of Courage, hand-carved cherrywood staves representing the eight immortals of the Taoist religion, teak and marble chairs, embroideries, and the Tung Sing, an almanac with advice on business, health, and personal affairs. Volunteer members of the Taoist Preservation Society lead tours of the temple, recounting anecdotes and memories of the lively past.

Gift Shop: The gift shop has a unique assortment of Chinese art goods, tea cups, rice bowls, and teapots, all extremely reasonably priced.

Restaurant: The Imperial Dynasty building, adjacent to the Taoist Temple, has been in the Wing family since Gong Shu Wing opened the restaurant in 1883. The multi-room building is filled with museum-quality Chinese artifacts and art, including the chef/owner's collection of metal and ceramic sculpture. Not to be missed is the second-floor ladies' room decorated with a carved rosewood screen and brightly colored walls and furniture. Open for dinner Tuesday through Sunday, Imperial Dynasty features an extensive menu of continental cuisine, with items like Escargots à la Bourguignonne, Dace Chinoise, Roast Prime Ribs of Beef, and Pasta Lo Mein. The address and phone number are 406 China Alley #2, (209) 582-0087.

KINGSBURG

KINGS COUNTY MUSEUM
Burris Park
6500 Clinton Avenue, Kingsburg
Phone: (209) 582-3211, ext. 2690
Hours: Sat. & Sun. 10:00 a.m.–4:30 p.m. Easter to November 1,
** or by appointment.**
Admission: Adults $1.00, children under 12 free

The Kings County Museum is housed in two buildings in rural Burris
Park, on land that once held a Native American village, and was later part
of the Burris Ranch. The museum's collections of artifacts and memorabilia chronicle the area's natural history and the cultural history of the
local Tachi Yokuts people and the early settlers. Items of special interest
include portraits of two men, James Harris and Daniel Rhodes. Rhodes
was one of the Donner Party rescuers, and Harris was killed in the
Tragedy of Mussel Slough, a gunfight between settlers and the sheriff,
who was trying to evict them on behalf of the railroad. The natural
history displays include birds' eggs, minerals, and mastodon fossils, and the
spectacular Dying Eagles: these two magnificent birds became entangled
in flight while fighting each other, fell to earth and perished, locked
together in final combat.

A second building contains blacksmith and wheelwright shops and the
wagon collection. The museum's founders began collecting anything and
everything in the twenties, with the result that the museum is now
"an amazing place—kind of like a swap meet of artifacts," to quote one
visitor. Although this little bit of the past is a charming representation
of a state-of-the-art museum circa 1929, it is currently being reorganized
and upgraded to contemporary museum standards.

LEMOORE

SARAH A. MOONEY MEMORIAL MUSEUM★
542 West D Street, Lemoore
Phone: (209) 924-6401
Hours: By appointment
Admission: Free

The only Victorian left in Lemoore, home of the largest navy jet base in
the state, is a charming, one-story brick building with white gingerbread
trim. Built by the Mooney family in 1893, the house is furnished to the
period with artifacts and vintage fashions, including Mrs. Sarah Mooney's
dresses. The original brick outhouse has been plumbed and now serves as
the museum's public restroom. Museum docents have many tales to tell
of the early days of Lemoore to make a visit worth your while.

TULARE COUNTY

PORTERVILLE

PORTERVILLE HISTORICAL MUSEUM
257 North D Street, Porterville
Phone: (209) 784-2053
Hours: Thurs.-Sat. 10:00 a.m.-4:00 p.m.
Admission: Free

This 1913 Southern Pacific passenger depot, now the Porterville Historical Museum, still has its original lights and beams, and two signs reading "Women exclusively" and "Men," a reminder of the time when the waiting room was strictly segregated by gender. The former waiting room also features the museum's excellent collection of Yokuts baskets, cradleboards, mortars and pestles, and other Native American artifacts. A large painting by Porterville native son Louis Velasquez, done at the age of 16, hangs over the entrance to the Wilcox Room, a repository of Western memorabilia such as cattle brands of local ranchers, a 1785 flintlock rifle, saddles, barbed wire, and Wild Bill Hickock's gloves.

A kitchen exhibit at the Porterville Historical Museum recaptures life a hundred years ago. Courtesy of Porterville Historical Museum.

Period rooms recapture life a hundred years ago: a large Victorian bedroom, a kitchen, a drugstore, and lawyer's, doctor's, and dentist's offices exhibit memorabilia from the town's early settlers, including the dental tools of Porterville's founder, Royal Porter Putnam. Generous townspeople have donated collections of silver, crystal, porcelain, and the best collection of moustache cups in the area to the museum. One room is dedicated to changing exhibitions. On view during our visit was a popular movie exhibit hung with colorful movie posters, photographic histories of past and present local theaters, and memorabilia from the 1947 film "So Dear to my Heart," which was filmed in Porterville.

ZALUD HOUSE MUSEUM
393 North Hockett, Porterville
Phone: (209) 782-7548
Hours: Wed.-Sat. 10:00 a.m.-4:00 p.m., Sun. 2:00-4:00 p.m.
Admission: Adults $1.00, children 50¢

From the time is was built in 1891 by John and Mary Zalud, this Victorian house was occupied only by members of the Zalud family. It is one of the few historic house museums in the country furnished entirely with the original owners' possessions. The eccentric Pearle, the last of the

Zaluds to inhabit the house, traveled the world accumulating souvenirs when she wasn't teaching piano and holding a salon in town. According to the curator, she never threw anything away. A collector's paradise, the museum's rooms, cupboards, closets, and pantries are bursting with treasures—furniture, original art, linens and laces, Bohemian glass, china, dolls, postcards, clothing—you name it. The decor of the house is changed seasonally (the Valentine's Day display is a special favorite) and the famed Zalud flower garden retains its original design from the 1930s.

Rental: The Zalud garden and kitchenette may be reserved for weddings by calling the Porterville Parks & Leisure Service Department at (209) 782-7461.

TULARE

TULARE COUNTY MUSEUM
2700 South Mooney Boulevard (Mooney Grove Park), Visalia
Phone: (209) 733-6616
Hours: Mon., Wed., Thurs., Fri. 10:00 a.m.-4:00 p.m.; Sat. & Sun.
**   noon-6:00 p.m. Call for information about seasonal changes.**
Admission: $2.00 adult, $1.00 children

A larger-than-life version of James Earl Fraser's "End of the Trail" statue (he also designed the buffalo head nickel) is one of the many treasures of the Tulare County Museum. The complex of historic buildings, located on two enclosed acres of Mooney Grove Park, offers two turn-of-the-century schools, two farmhouses, a blacksmith shop, a building housing restored wagons, a large display of farm equipment, and a wooden caboose used by the Visalia Electric Railroad. The museum proper boasts a fine collection of Yokuts baskets and artifacts, toys, eyeglasses, guns, and replicas of a general store, barber shop, and doctor's and dentist's offices.

TULARE HISTORICAL MUSEUM
444 West Tulare Avenue, Tulare
Phone: (209) 686-2074
Hours: Thurs.-Sat. 10:00 a.m.-4:00 p.m., Sun. 12:30-4:00 p.m.
Admission: Adults $1.50, students $1.00

The Tulare Historical Museum, touted as "the most modern small historical museum in the state," tells the history of Tulare through carefully-researched and meticulously-prepared exhibits.

A diorama of a Yokuts village, with baskets and cradleboards (the first child safety seats) represents the area's earliest inhabitants. The first Euro-American settlers came in 1860, and the arrival of the Southern Pacific railroad in 1872 led to the establishment of Tulare, a rough-and-tumble town with more bars than churches. The subsequent departure of the railroad shops and roundhouse for Bakersfield turned Tulare into a very small town forced to change its focus from railroading to agriculture. Displays featuring photographs of Old Tulare and historically significant artifacts recount the town's colorful if somewhat traumatic history.

Miniature rooms replicate home life in early Tulare. Mrs. Lawler's millinery shop (complete with a hat worn by Lillian Russell), Dr. Lasch's pharmacy, Frank Willes' barber shop, and a blacksmith shop capture the flavor of period businesses. An extensive collection of American art glass is on display, and Tulare's heroes—Bob Mathias, Sam Iness, General Maurice Preston, Tex Rankin, Bryan Alan (he flew the English Channel in a man-powered plane), and Admiral Elmo Zumwaldt, U.S. Chief of Naval Operations under President Nixon—are celebrated in another exhibit.

Library: Open by appointment, the Audio-Visual Room/Library contains historical volumes, photographs, slides, newspapers, and memorabilia of Old Tulare.

VISALIA

THE CENTRAL CALIFORNIA CHINESE CULTURAL CENTER
500 South Akers Road, Visalia
Phone: (209) 625-4545
Hours: Wed.-Sun. 11:00 a.m.-6:00 p.m.

Lured by the promise of Gum Sahn, "Gold Mountain," the Chinese came to California in the mid-1800s like other forty-niners, to strike it rich. They worked in the mines, railroads, laundries, and later on the farms, always planning to make a stake and return to China. As Chinese laborers entered other job markets after the completion of the railroad, their reputation for working harder than others for less money engendered profound resentment. In reaction to the nationwide fear of the "yellow peril," Congress passed the Chinese Exclusion Act in 1881. In response, Chinese-American society became ever more insulated, taking little from the dominant culture and displaying a stoic willingness to persevere, enduring the indignities proffered by America. Within this society, bolstered by Confucian ideals, the Chinese worked to provide a good education and better life for each new generation.

The alliance of China with the United States in World War II bolstered the image of Chinese-Americans on a national level, and many Chinese-Americans today have succeeded in the dominant American culture as businesspeople and professionals. Confronted with a world in which the push for homogeneity makes it difficult for people to retain their heritage, a group of central California businessmen of Chinese descent got together to create a center to reeducate the younger generation of Chinese-Americans, who had been losing their culture and language, and to expose other Americans to Chinese traditions.

Opened in 1990, the Central California Chinese Cultural Center, a large modern structure, celebrates Chinese architecture. Symbols of Chinese deities, dragons, and warriors line the tiled roof, while gargoyles on the beams ward off evil spirits. Two six-foot, marble Tzu-Shih lions guard the main entrance, and an eight-foot bronze statue of Confucius oversees the back courtyard. Inside, cases lining the walls of the main exposition room hold changing exhibits of artifacts, paintings, and archaeological findings.

Rental: The center, with its up-to-date caterer's kitchen, is available for weddings, receptions, and other special events.

San Francisco Peninsula
and South Bay

Daly City

South San Francisco

280

101

Burlingame

San Mateo

1

92

Belmont

Redwood City

San Carlos

Menlo Park

Palo Alto

Woodside

Mountain View

Los Altos

Milpitas

84

Cupertino

101

880

680

Sunnyvale

*San Mateo
County*

280

Santa Clara

San Jose

Saratoga

Los Gatos

Campbell

*Santa Clara
County*

17

New Almaden

Morgan Hill

San Martin

101

Gilroy

San Francisco Peninsula and South Bay

SAN MATEO COUNTY

BELMONT

RALSTON HALL
College of Notre Dame
1500 Ralston Avenue, Belmont
Phone: (415) 508-3501
Hours: Tours Mon.-Fri. by appointment only.
Admission: Adults $5.00, seniors & students $3.00

Today a favorite spot for weddings, as well as the administrative offices of the College of Notre Dame, Ralston Hall looks back on a colorful past as a girls' finishing school, a sanitarium, and the country showplace of one of the most important and powerful men in the West, William Chapman Ralston, founder of the Bank of California. The lavish Italian villa, modified with touches of Steamboat Gothic and Victorian details, suggests the work of John Gaynor, architect of San Francisco's Palace Hotel, one of Ralston's many projects.

The four-story, 55,000-square-foot mansion boasts a dining room large enough to seat 75 guests, a mirrored ballroom, and a grand staircase overlooked by an opera box gallery from which, it is said, Ralston liked to observe his guests' reactions to his opulent country estate.

Rental: The ground floor, available for wedding receptions, parties, luncheons, and dinners, can accommodate up to 250 people.

BURLINGAME

KOHL MANSION*
2750 Adeline Drive, Burlingame
Phone: (415) 992-4668
Hours: By appointment

Fashioned after the great baronial estates of England and situated on the secluded, 40-acre site of the Mercy High School campus, this elegant,

When friends decided to name a town in the San Joaquin Valley after him, William Chapman Ralston declined the honor, so they named the town Modesto (Spanish for modest) instead. This megalethoscope, a 3-D viewer similar to a stereopticon, is among the items displayed at Ralston's immodestly opulent country estate. Courtesy of Ralston Hall.

authentic Tudor mansion was built in 1914 by Charles and Elizabeth Kohl. The stately, oak-filled grounds include a lovely rose garden and a swimming pool.

Rental: This estate can be rented for weddings, private parties, corporate events, photo sessions, press conferences, and picnics.

DALY CITY

DALY CITY/COLMA HISTORY MUSEUM*
Serramonte Library
40 Wembley Drive, Daly City
Phone: (415) 755-5123
Admission: Free

The Serramonte Library has allotted the Daly City/Colma History Museum space in its reference area to showcase memorabilia of Daly City and the historical cemetery town of Colma. This mini-museum occupies two walls and three display cases chockablock with memorabilia, documents, maps, vintage photographs, scrapbooks, photo albums, old campaign buttons, and other fun things to look at.

MENLO PARK

SUNSET PUBLISHING CORPORATION
80 Willow Road, Menlo Park

In California, the name Sunset has come to stand for, even define, the quintessential California style. *Sunset,* the magazine, enjoys a readership of five million Westerners, who look to it for guidance on gardening, building, foods, and travel.

Sunset Publishing Corporation, which produces *Sunset* and a host of other western living publications, gladly welcomes visitors to their Menlo Park headquarters, a sprawling complex designed in 1952 by architect Clifford May, known as the father of the ranch-style home. The guided tour begins with a seven-minute video outlining the history of *Sunset,* from its conception in 1898 as a Southern Pacific public relations piece to promote the West, to a brief stint as a literary magazine featuring such notables as Sinclair Lewis, Jack London, and Mark Twain, to its acquisition by the Lane family, under whose direction it became the magazine of Western living.

A view of the test kitchens shows cooks deftly preparing dishes from recipes under consideration for publication. Each recipe is prepared three times and sampled by a taste panel (a green flag indicates the staff can have a taste—but not the visitors). The tour concludes with a visit to the gardens designed by Thomas Church, a scaled-down horticultural journey from Baja California to Washington state. This tour may not be your average child's cup of tea, but it is a fascinating experience for anyone interested in the what goes on behind the scenes of publishing *Sunset* magazine.

REDWOOD CITY

AMPEX MUSEUM OF MAGNETIC RECORDING
411 Broadway, Redwood City
Phone: (415) 367-3127
Hours: Call for hours.
Admission: Free

The Ampex Museum of Magnetic Recording—closed, temporarily, we hope—occupies three small rooms in Ampex's main headquarters. Museum exhibits chronicle the history of magnetic recording from the first telephone answering machine, invented in 1911, to today's ultra-sophisticated equipment.

LATHROP HOUSE
627 Hamilton Street, Redwood City
Phone: (415) 365-5564
Hours: Tues.-Thurs. 11:00 a.m.-3:00 p.m.; closed in August.
Admission: Free

Lathrop House, a classic example of early Steamboat Gothic, was built in 1863 by Benjamin Lathrop, San Mateo County's first clerk-recorder-assessor, and later occupied by Civil War General Patrick Edward Connor. It is furnished to the period.

Gift Shop: Tarnished Doorknobs sells antiques and collectibles.

MARINE SCIENCE INSTITUTE
500 Discovery Parkway, Redwood City
Phone: (415) 364-2760; (800) 444-7275 for camping reservations
Hours: By reservation
Admission: Shoreside program $7.00.
  Discovery Voyage: adults $30.00, children $20.00.

Educators believe that if kids haven't become excited about science by the time they reach fifth grade, they probably never will be. The folks at Marine Science Institute are doing their best to develop a passion for science in students from kindergarten through college, and the adults accompanying them.

One of the world's great natural harbors, the San Francisco Bay is a rich habitat for marine life and many species of birds and other wildlife. Founded in 1970, the Marine Science Institute takes a hands-on approach to understanding the bay's ecosystem. When we visited in 1993 their headquarters were so unimpressive (the office is a trailer) that we almost missed them. This doesn't really matter, as an important part of their program takes place aboard the *Inland Seas*, a refurbished, fifty-year-old, 85-foot, wooden-hulled Navy rescue vessel. Students from fifth grade and up can sign up for a four-hour course on the bay. Time is divided among three stations: Benthic, where they scoop up samples of mud from the bottom of the bay to examine the marine life within; Ichthyology, where they net fish to study in an on-board aquarium; and Plankton/ Hydrology, where they study the microscopic creatures in bay water. Younger children can participate in the shoreside program, in which the same activities take place on the dock and beach. Although the program is designed for classes and groups, it can accommodate individuals.

The Marine Science Mobile takes interactive presentations to schools and community groups. A new, floating classroom and lab and an onshore Marine Science Center are in the planning stages.

SAN CARLOS

SAN CARLOS HISTORY MUSEUM
533 Laurel Street, San Carlos
Phone: None
Hours: 2nd & 4th Sat. 1:00-4:00 p.m., special tours available.
Admission: Free

A reconstruction of San Carlos' original firehouse now serves as the San Carlos History Museum. Among the artifacts and photographs on permanent display are memorabilia of the pre-Silicon Valley electronic industry, a video of the town's older homes, and a Seagraves fire engine. Changing exhibits have featured baseball cards, antique dolls, and mementos of early San Carlos history.

SAN MATEO

COYOTE POINT MUSEUM
1651 Coyote Point Drive, San Mateo
Phone: (415) 342-7755
Hours: Tues.-Sat. 10:00 a.m.-5:00 p.m.; Sun. noon-5:00 p.m.
Admission: Adults $3.00, seniors $2.00, children 6-17 $1.00.
Free first Wednesday of the month. Park entrance fee $4.00.

"Human beings must learn again how to adapt themselves to the natural order of the life sphere or their inventions may carry them and all other organisms to extinction" is written large at the entrance of the Environmental Hall in Coyote Point Museum. The country's first ecology museum makes use of each exciting exhibit to get the message across— we must think about the world we live in and act to preserve it before it's too late.

Located in the heart of 670-acre Coyote Point Park, the museum is housed in a modern structure featuring wood surfaces inside and out. The 8,000-square-foot Environmental Hall is a good place to begin your visit. A huge, 60-foot mural depicting the history of life on earth greets you at the top entry level. Three descending levels depict the ecological communities of the Bay Area, and paired representations of plant and animal communities illustrate ecological concepts in a simulated walk from the San Francisco Bay up over the Santa Cruz Mountains and down to the Pacific shore. Hands-on models, dioramas, sculptures, films, graphics, aquaria, live insect colonies, and computer games capture your attention at every turn.

You can listen in on a buzzing beehive, an example of living together in harmony, and learn that a tired bee buzzes the note "E" while an energetic bee hums "A." A twenty-foot tower of small animals representing the diet of one red-tailed hawk for a year illustrates the numbers game in the food chain. Pick the right answer on the computer games and you will earn enough trees to reforest an entire mountain. Non-electronic games let you load Noah's Ark or take a Big Mac apart. An electronic scoreboard keeps track of world population growth—5,497,064,447 as I stood there, and increasing at the rate of three per second. The Environmental Hall and changing exhibits in the North Gallery and the Concourse can keep children and adults enthralled for hours, but you will want to leave time to explore the outdoor exhibits.

The one-acre Wildlife Habitats exhibit houses birds in a walk-through aviary, and mammals, reptiles, and amphibians native to the area in realistic, rock-like settings. The river otters playing under their waterfall and swimming by in their glass-walled pond are especially captivating. The new hummingbird garden, ablaze with color, attracts the tiny birds with a year-round supply of flowers.

The scenic, bayside Coyote Point Park surrounding the museum provides a marina, yacht club, fishing pier, swimming beach, playing field, playground, picnic areas, wind-surfing area, and winding paths—in other words, you will find enough indoor and outdoor activities for at least a full day's visit.

For kids: Family Day on the second Saturday of every month offers crafts, games, and demonstrations on different themes from science wizardry to dinosaurs. Kids 7 to 10 can attend Summer Discovery Day camp.

For teachers: Teachers may visit the museum free at all times and reserve environmental education materials.

Library: Reference library available by reservation.

Gift Shop: All the merchandise in the large, well-stocked store relates to the museum's nature/ecology theme, from gem stones to games and stuffed animals.

The one-acre wildlife habitat exhibit at Coyote Point Museum houses birds, mammals, reptiles, and amphibians. This and other innovative ecology exhibits, as well as the marina, yacht club, fishing pier, swimming beach, playing field, wind-surfing area, and more at Coyote Point Park will bring you back for more than one visit. Courtesy of Coyote Point Museum.

SAN MATEO ARBORETUM
Central Park
El Camino & 5th Avenue, San Mateo
Phone: (415) 579-0536
Hours: Mon.-Fri. 10:00 a.m.-4:00 p.m.; Sat. & Sun. 11:00 a.m.-
    4:00 p.m.
Admission: Free

Old stands of pine, oak, cedar, and redwood planted over 100 years ago
as part of the William Kohl estate still flourish in San Mateo's Central
Park Arboretum. The turn-of-the-century Kohl pumphouse now serves
as the headquarters of the San Mateo Arboretum Society. A more recent
addition to the park, the lovely walled Japanese garden, is graced with
reflection pools, a waterfall, a shrine, and bridges from which you can
watch the koi swimming below. The sound of Japanese music floats from
the tea house.

SAN MATEO COUNTY HISTORICAL MUSEUM
College of San Mateo, Building 5
1700 West Hillsdale Boulevard, San Mateo
Phone: (415) 574-6441
Hours: Mon.-Thurs. 9:30 a.m.-4:30 p.m.; Sun. 12:30-4:30 p.m.
Admission: Free

The San Mateo County Historical Museum has a knack for making
history fun, with hands-on exhibits interspersed among the artifacts.
The 7,500 square feet of exhibition space are divided into seven areas—
Indian, Spanish, Mexican, American, Whaling, Logging, and Mansions.
Visitors can handle stone tools used by Ohlone Indians, and pick up
tiles and adobe used to build Spanish homes, and the hides and tallow
they traded. Kids get a kick out of setting the parts of the intricate
model of a sawmill in motion—lumbering was the area's first industry—
or Mr. Murry's dairy farm. Grown-ups will be amused by the list of
whippings in Belmont School, dated 1872, e.g., "Willie Reed for fighting
and stubbornness." The museum also has a fine collection of antique
vehicles, including bicycles, horse-drawn carriages, a governess cart,
a magnificent park drag carriage, and a fire engine.

The Keyston Gallery features changing exhibits. A relocation and
possible merger with the Hiller Northern California Aviation Museum
is under consideration.

Library: Research Library

SOUTH SAN FRANCISCO

SOUTH SAN FRANCISCO HISTORICAL SOCIETY MUSEUM*
Magnolia Center
601 Grand Avenue, South San Francisco
Phone: (415) 877-5344
Hours: Tues. & Thurs. 1:00–3:00 p.m.
Admission: Free

A former elementary school building renovated to serve as a senior center also houses the South San Francisco Historical Museum. The small (600 square feet) room on the main floor displays historic photographs and artifacts from the city's past. Cases in the lobby display 1920s wedding dresses and a cup and saucer collection. "South San Francisco Industries," "75 years of South San Francisco High School," "The 3 R's, Then and Now," "Military Memories," and "Treasures from the Attic" have been the subjects of changing exhibitions.

WOODSIDE

FILOLI
Cañada Road, Woodside
Phone: (415) 364-2880
Hours: February–November, Tues.–Sat. Guided tours by reservation only. No reservation required for self-guided tours each Friday, first Saturday, and second Sunday of the month.
Admission: Adults $8.00, children $4.00

Television viewers and movie buffs will recognize Filoli from the soap opera "Dynasty" and the film "Heaven Can Wait." Built in 1915, the 43-room Georgian mansion evinces a stately elegance that makes it a popular setting for movies and catalog shoots. San Francisco millionaire William Bourn II, who made his fortune in gold, wine, and water, selected the 654-acre site for his estate because of its proximity to the protected Crystal Springs watershed. He engaged noted California architect Willis Polk to design the mansion, which he named Filoli, an abbreviation of "FIght-LOve-LIve." In 1975 the property was given by Mrs. William Roth to the National Trust for Historic Preservation. The house is lavishly furnished with priceless antiques, oriental rugs, chandeliers, and works of art. Special volunteers keep the rooms filled with breathtaking bouquets from Filoli's own cutting garden.

As spectacular as the house is, to my mind the major attraction of Filoli is the magnificent, 16-acre formal garden. Designed by Bruce Porter and Isabella Worn and brought to full maturity by Mrs. Roth, the garden is actually a succession of separate areas or garden rooms, each with a distinct character. The walled garden, enclosed by a handsome brick wall, displays the elegance of formal garden design, highlighted by the Italian Renaissance-style tea house. The rose garden, in full bloom for our May visit, presents a symphony of color and fragrance. In contrast, the Sunken Garden relies on shades of green ranging from gray-green olives to yellow-green sunburst locust for classic effect. The stiff formality of the Chartres Garden offers a perfect foil for the natural ease of the Woodland Garden. From the first bold display of color as 360 camellias burst into bloom in early spring to the last of the fall chrysanthemums, plantings have been selected to present a splendid display throughout the year.

Nature hikes, open to all, take place on wide trails in the undeveloped portions of Filoli beyond the formal gardens. Points of interest include

Ohlone sites, the San Andreas Fault, and the Nature Center, with displays of Native American artifacts, birds, and wildlife indigenous to the area.

Gift Shop: The Garden Shop is filled with baskets, garden books, potted plants, cunning accessories for home and garden, and potpourri made from Filoli garden plants.

Restaurant: The Tea Shop offers light refreshment—tea, cookies, and muffins.

The dining room at Filoli, the Woodside estate of William Bourn II, may look familiar to viewers of "Dynasty." The house is spectacular, but the gardens are the main attraction. Courtesy of Filoli.

WOODSIDE STORE HISTORIC SITE
3300 Tripp Road, Woodside
Phone: (415) 851-7615
**Hours: Tues. & Thurs. 10:00 a.m.–4:00 p.m.; Sat. & Sun.
    noon–4:00 p.m.**
Admission: Free

Many small county museums feature a "General Store" as a catch-all exhibit for artifacts and old stuff that doesn't fit anywhere else. This is not the case, however, with the Woodside Store. The curators of this meticulous reconstruction operated by the San Mateo County Historical Association are fanatical about historical accuracy in recreating the store exactly as it was when Dr. Tripp established it in 1854. Store merchandise has been replicated precisely as it was described in an old ledger—accurate in sight, smell, and touch down to the labels on the cans, the apples in the barrels, and the potatoes in the bins. Kids especially enjoy the hands-on aspects of the Living History program available to school classes.

SANTA CLARA COUNTY

CAMPBELL

CAMPBELL HISTORICAL MUSEUM AND AINSLEY HOUSE
51 North Central Avenue, Campbell
Phone: (408) 866-2119
Hours: Call for hours.
Admission: Carriage House exhibits and gardens free, docent-led
tour of Ainsley House $4.00.

Campbell old-timers remember when orchards stretched as far as the eye
could see, and innumerable prunes lay on trays in the largest drying yard
in the country. Now a bedroom community to the high-tech Silicon
Valley, the city of Campbell is preserving the memories of its farming
and canning past. The Campbell Historical Museum will soon be housed
in the restored Ainsley House, a beautiful example of the 1920s English
Tudor revival style, to be furnished with artifacts from 1926 to 1937.
Exhibits in the Carriage House will interpret the history of the
Campbell area from the early days to today's 20th century setting.
The historic gardens surrounding the museum have been recreated in
keeping with the 1926 plans of renowned San Francisco landscape
architect Emerson Knight.

Library: Research archives for local and family history are open to the
public by appointment.

Gift Shop. Located in the Carriage House, the store features carefully
selected merchandise that reflects the themes of the changing exhibits and
the history of the area.

CUPERTINO

CALIFORNIA HISTORY CENTER
21250 Stevens Creek Boulevard, Cupertino
Phone: (408) 864-8712
Hours: Call for hours.
Admission: Free

Dedicated to preserving the history of California and the Santa Clara
Valley and bringing it to life, the California History Center offers a
variety of enriching opportunities. You can use the outstanding research
library, attend classes on subjects ranging from the wine industry to local
history, enjoy changing exhibits on themes from local agriculture to
children's art, or tour the unique building. The former party house and
country getaway of San Francisco millionaires Charles and Ella Hobart
Baldwin, later owned by Harriet Pullman Carolan, was designed by Willis

Polk in the 1890s. The pavilion, now known as "le Petit Trianon," consists of four rooms—a ballroom, (now an exhibition hall), dining room, library, and grand entrance hall, which also served as the Baldwins' bedroom.

Library: The Louis E. Stocklmeir Regional History Library/Archives is an excellent resource for California history, containing 10,000 photographs, 2,000 books, student research papers, oral histories, maps, prints, clippings, pamphlets, and manuscripts. The library is open to the public for a small daily fee.

Gift Shop: A good place to pick up the center's publications.

CUPERTINO HISTORICAL MUSEUM
10185 North Stelling Road, Cupertino
Phone: (408) 973-1495
Hours: Wed.-Sat. 10:00 a.m.-4:00 p.m.
Admission: Free

Housed in the Quinlan Community Center, the Cupertino Historical Museum presents a new exhibition every year that interprets the history of Cupertino and the surrounding Santa Clara Valley. The area has seen many historical transformations, from the native Ohlone people to the de Anza expedition, through the Californio era to the orchard and cannery culture of the late 1800s and early 1900s, to its present status as part of the Silicon Valley.

The Museum History Gallery, a satellite museum located in a small retail space on the lower level of the Vallco Shopping Center (Wolfe Road at Stephens Creek Blvd.) offers a permanent exhibit interpreting Cupertino's cultural past, circa 1890. Hours at the satellite museum are Tuesday and Saturday, noon to 3:00 p.m.

Gift Shop: Both facilities maintain museum stores with history-related items about the Cupertino area's past.

ENVIRONMENTAL STUDIES AREA
De Anza College
21250 Stevens Creek Boulevard, Cupertino
Phone: (408) 864-8346
**Hours: First Sunday of the month, 10:00 a.m.-2:00 p.m., and by
    appointment.**

Twenty-five years ago, when annoying mosquitoes were breeding in a pond at De Anza College, biology Professor Doug Cheeseman threw in some mosquito fish and got a great idea. With the help of volunteers, the California Native Plant Society, a $12,000 matching grant, and plants donated by Joshua Tree National Monument and many local nurseries, he created an Environmental Studies Area, where twelve different

California native plant communities thrive on one and a half acres. On our tour, in the space of an hour we passed from the sweltering desert to the shady woodlands, while our enthusiastic and knowledgeable student guide pointed out native plants and visiting birds, and filled us with information. Biology was never this fascinating when we were in school.

Docent-led natural history tours are available to school and community groups.

EUPHRAT MUSEUM OF ART
De Anza College, Cupertino
Phone: (408) 864-8836
Hours: Tues.-Thurs. 11:00 a.m.-4:00 p.m. & Wed. 6:00-8:00 p.m.;
   Sat. 11:00 a.m.-2:00 p.m. Open October–May.
Admission: Free

A desert willow graces one of twelve native plant communities at De Anza College's Environmental Studies Area. Courtesy of Doug Cheeseman, Environmental Studies Area.

In partnership with De Anza College, the Euphrat Museum presents three shows a year featuring works in many media by nationally and internationally known as well as emerging artists. Exhibition themes often reflect issues of contemporary society, such as "The Fourth R: Art." The 1994 schedule includes an exhibition on art and technology, work by elementary, high school, and De Anza College students, and an exhibition on art by recent immigrants to the United States, presented in collaboration with the Bronx Museum of the Arts.

MINOLTA PLANETARIUM
De Anza College, Cupertino
Phone: (408) 864-8814
Hours: Call for show times.
Admission: Laser shows: adults $6.00, children $5.00.
   Planetarium "Star" shows: adults $4.00, children $3.00.

"The mind finds no limits in an expanding universe," said the president of Minolta when he dedicated the second largest planetarium in northern California. State-of-the-art sound and star projection equipment let you travel to distant galaxies, into the future, or back in time to experience the birth of the cosmos, while sitting beneath the 50-foot dome. Friday and Saturday evening laser shows starting at 8:00 include rock and roll as well as family shows. Planetarium shows are at 6:30 on Saturday evenings, and an astronomy lecture series on Friday evenings is presented at least twice a year.

Gift Shop: Stellar shoppers can pick up books, space toys, posters, NASA patches, laser shades, and more in the planetarium gift shop.

Rental: The 170-seat planetarium is available for weddings, birthday parties, receptions, ceremonies, and other special events.

GILROY

GILROY HISTORICAL MUSEUM
195 Fifth Street, Gilroy
Phone: (408) 848-0470
Hours: Mon.-Fri. 9:00 a.m.-5:00 p.m., some Saturdays 11:00 a.m.-
**   3:00 p.m.**
Admission: Free

A computer printout of the family tree of California's first permanent English-speaking settler, John Gilroy, is posted just inside the door of the Gilroy Historical Museum. Gilroy's descendants occasionally come into the museum to pencil in births, marriages, and deaths—this is a "people museum," the director explained. Using pieces from the museum's collection of over 22,000 objects, exhibits trace the development of the Gilroy area from the Ohlone people of at least 7,000 years ago, to the era of Spanish and Mexican land grant families, to the town's success as an agricultural center, presently the garlic capital of the world. One exhibit features Gilroy resident Henry Miller, the father of California agri-business, who owned more land and cattle than any other man who ever lived in the United States. A cigar-store Indian and rare cigar molds point to the time when Gilroy boasted a thriving tobacco industry and the world's largest cigar factory. Kids will love the children's room, which is packed full of dolls, toys, clocks, and other curiosities from the past.

Library: The museum includes the South Santa Clara Valley Archives, including tax records, photos, and every edition of the Gilroy newspapers published since 1868.

Gift Shop: The small gift shop sells books, maps, postcards and drawings.

LOS ALTOS

LOS ALTOS HISTORY HOUSE MUSEUM★
51 South San Antonio Road, Los Altos
Phone: (415) 948-9427
Hours: Wed. 1:00-5:00 p.m.; Sat. noon-4:00 p.m.
Admission: Free

In the pre-Silicon Valley days, before subdivisions blanketed the area, the Santa Clara Valley bloomed with magnificent orchards. The Los Altos History House Museum, located in what was once a thriving apricot orchard, is a remnant of the old way of life. The brown-shingled, Craftsman-style farmhouse was built in 1905 and is furnished in the style of the 1930s—before television and computers took hold. An outdoor agricultural exhibit depicts the processes of cutting and drying apricots.

Library: Archival materials documenting early 20th century life are available for research.

LOS GATOS

FORBES MILL MUSEUM
75 Church Street, Los Gatos
Phone: (408) 395-7375
Hours: Wed.-Sun. noon-4:00 p.m.
Admission: Free

The tide of history that swept over so much of northern California changed Los Gatos from the homeland of a group of Costanoan Indians to a sleepy provincial town founded on part of a Mexican land grant. With statehood, the little town evolved into a thriving agricultural and railroad community, then a residential suburb dependent on the high-tech electronics and aerospace industries of the Santa Clara Valley.

Forbes Mill, the first business in Los Gatos, is now the Regional History Department of the Los Gatos Museum. Dedicated to preserving the history of Los Gatos, the Museum displays artifacts and memorabilia: both the common objects you'll find in other historical museums of the area—splendid Victorian costumes, household goods, a fine doll collection, old agricultural implements, a foot-operated printing press, lots of old photos—and those unique to Los Gatos. Inside the door hangs a larger than life portrait of beloved local legend Charles Henry McKiernan, a mountain man turned entrepreneur. Dressed like the successful businessman he became, "Mountain Charley" wears his flat-brimmed black hat pulled low on his forehead to cover the scars where a grizzly bear took a chunk out of his skull.

THE LOS GATOS MUSEUM
4 Tait Avenue, Los Gatos
Phone: (408) 356-2646
Hours: Wed.-Sun. noon-4:00 p.m.
Admission: Free—donations accepted

Things I never knew until I visited the Los Gatos Museum: State gem, benitoite; State mineral, gold; State fossil, saber-toothed cat; State rock, serpentine. I also learned from an ingenious exhibition on organic dyes that you can get purple from the rare murex shell. Folksy but fascinating (the birds are stored in the bathroom closet), the Los Gatos Museum is a treasure trove of collections—rocks, shells, insects, fossils, wildflowers, gems, minerals—displayed in a way to make learning about the natural history of the area fun.

Upstairs in this former firehouse, built in 1927, the art department mounts six or more changing exhibitions a year, by artists from Los Gatos, the region, or occasionally the nation.

YOUTH SCIENCE INSTITUTE—VASONA DISCOVERY CENTER
296 Garden Hill Drive, Los Gatos
Phone: (408) 356-4945
Hours: Mon.-Fri. 9:00 a.m.-4:30 p.m.; Sat. & Sun. (March-Oct.)
**   noon-4:30 p.m.**
Admission: Parking fee $3.00

The Youth Science Institute opened this, their second Discovery Center, in 1980 in a modern octagonal wooden structure. The emphasis is on water ecology, aquatic life, animal adaptation, and conservation. A habitat cube features local aquatic critters—fish, reptiles, and amphibians—and a corner devoted to dinosaurs has fossils and fossil replications. The Viola Anderson Native Plant Trail winds past the center and overlooks Vasona Lake. Free nature walks are held on alternate Saturdays, March through October, starting at 9:30 a.m.

MILPITAS

THE RECYCLERY
1601 Dixon Landing Road, Milpitas
Phone: (408) 432-1234
Hours: Mon.-Fri. 7:30 a.m.-5:00 p.m.; Sat. 7:30 a.m.-4:00 p.m. by
**   appointment—please call.**
Admission: Free

The 100-foot-long Wall of Garbage at the Recyclery— Santa Clara County residents generate this much trash every three minutes. Courtesy of The Recyclery.

At The Recyclery, a state-of-the-art center for commercial recycling, you can find out what happens to your garbage after it leaves your home. The Recyclery's centerpiece, the $1 million Education Center, is a veritable museum of garbage featuring hands-on exhibits and interactive electronic displays. The most striking exhibit, a 100-foot-long Wall of Garbage, offers a panorama of what gets tossed by the average family of four in a year, or three minutes' worth of trash generated by Santa Clara County.

Other exhibits include the History of Garbage from 500 B.C. to the early 1900s; "Buried Treasure," a look at what's in landfills today and how much could be recovered for other uses; and "Magnet Fishing," a demonstration of how the magnetic properties of different metals are used in commercial recycling to separate aluminum and other metals from tin cans. "Shoot the Loot" lets kids zap recyclable materials with a laser gun.

You can stay in the Education Center and see the rest of The Recyclery—the landfill, the compost site, methane recovery system, and commercial operations—on video, or you can sign up for a tour of the plant, which includes a stop at the Materials Recovery Facility Observation Room, where you can watch this $10 million, 80,000-square-foot facility process up to 1,600 tons of recyclables per day!

MORGAN HILL

PINE RIDGE MUSEUM
Henry W. Coe State Park, Morgan Hill
Phone: (408) 779-2728
Hours: Fri.-Mon. 8:00 a.m.-4:30 p.m.
Admission: Free

With 68,000 acres, this is the largest state park in northern California, yet hardly anyone knows about it. Well, 30,000 visitors a year isn't exactly "nobody," but it's a drop in the bucket compared to other state parks. Although the rugged and varied terrain, abundant wildlife, and numerous fishing spots are the park's greatest attraction for most visitors, the Pine Ridge Museum, named for Henry W. Coe's 12,000-acre ranch, should appeal to history buffs.

Designed to blend in with the historic structures, the visitor center houses the museum, which features ranching history and artifacts. A replica of the house's original living room displays the elegant furniture, rugs, and fine china that helped Coe's bride maintain her household in the wilderness in the style she was accustomed to. The park ranger now inhabits the 1905 ranch house, and the long metal barn is used as a display and storage site for pioneer farm equipment and vehicles awaiting restoration. The blacksmith shop, the hay barn, the stone cooler where perishable food was kept in the days before refrigerators, and the bunkhouse, furnished simply with a bunk, a nail in the wall for a closet, and a lantern, document early ranch life.

Gift Shop: T-shirts, books, nature guides.

MOUNTAIN VIEW

THE LACE MUSEUM
552 South Murphy, Mountain View
Phone: (408) 730-4695
Hours: Tues.-Sun. 10:00 a.m.-4:00 p.m.; Mon. by appointment.
Admission: Free—donations accepted

Recently moved to a new home, the Lace Museum is now able to display their extensive collection, which includes examples of every technique of lace making. Among the many lace gowns and accessories are pieces dating back to the 18th century. Classes on several techniques of lace making are also available, as well as private tours.

Gift Shop: A small museum gift shop carries lace-related merchandise.

RENGSTORFF HOUSE
Shoreline at Mountain View
3070 North Shoreline Boulevard, Mountain View
Phone: (415) 903-6392
Hours: Tues., Wed., Sun. 11:00 a.m.-5:00 p.m.
Admission: Free

Two years after the Civil War ended, successful German immigrant Henry Rengstorff built this elegant, twelve-room farmhouse. Restored and relocated to its current site near Rengstorff Landing, Mountain View's oldest house is one of the finest examples of Victorian Italianate architecture around. Ornate marble fireplaces, period reproduction wallpapers, brass chandeliers, and authentic Victorian furniture recall its former grandeur. Visitors can tour the lovely gardens and the downstairs rooms. The upstairs serves as Shoreline staff offices.

Rental: The first floor, which has a modern catering kitchen, and the beautifully landscaped gardens can be rented for weddings, meetings, and special events.

NEW ALMADEN

NEW ALMADEN QUICKSILVER MINING MUSEUM
21570 Almaden Road, New Almaden
Phone: (408) 268-1729
Hours: Saturdays noon-4:00 p.m.
Admission: $1.00 donation

Long before the Spanish came to California, native Ohlone people used the red mineral cinnabar to paint their bodies. In 1845, a Mexican cavalry officer recognized cinnabar, the principal ore of mercury, and staked the first mining claim in California. The mine, named the Nueva Almaden after the centuries-old Almaden mine in Spain, produced $70 million dollars worth of quicksilver (equal to the richest 19th century gold mine) before mining ceased in 1976.

In 1949 Constance Perham, who grew up in New Almaden, established the museum to display her collection of mercury mining artifacts, memorabilia, and photographs. Located in the New Almaden National Historic District, the museum gives visitors a complete picture of the technology used to extract mercury from cinnabar, and the uses of the metal (it's not just for thermometers). Beginning with the blacksmith shop where mine tools were forged, the history of the mine is portrayed with tools of yesteryear, photographs, and documents like the large specimen map showing hundreds of miles of mine tunnels. Everyday artifacts from home, school, and church portray the lives of the people who worked the mines—the Mexicans who knew where to find the ore, and the Cornish who knew how to get it out.

After a tour of the museum, visitors can sit at a table in the folksy community room and peruse scrapbooks filled with newspaper articles dating from 1910. Youngsters are welcome to climb on the outdoor display of larger 20th century mining equipment.

The museum plans to relocate to a reconstruction of the old mining office on the site of the Hacienda furnace yard in 1995.

Library: The New Almaden is the most documented mine in California. Some materials are available at the museum, many more (15 boxes) can be examined at the Green Library on the Stanford University campus.

Gift Shop: Besides t-shirts, mine publications, and postcards, the gift shop sells handsome copies of Freidolin Kessler's linoleum prints made to document the mine for the Civilian Conservation Corps ($3.00).

PALO ALTO

BARBIE DOLL HALL OF FAME
433 Waverley Street, Palo Alto
Phone: (415) 326-5841
Hours: Tues.-Fri. 1:30-4:30 p.m.; Sat. 10:00 a.m.-noon, 1:30-4:30 p.m.
Admission: $4.00

Enter the hearing center, buy your ticket from the audiologist, and ascend a narrow flight of stairs to Barbie heaven, otherwise known as the Barbie Hall of Fame, the first and only museum dedicated to one of the most popular dolls of all time. Although small in square footage—after all, it's for small people—the privately-owned museum showcases the world's largest public collection of Barbiana, over 16,000 items. Floor-to-ceiling glass cases packed with dolls and accessories recreate Barbie history from the original 1959 model through four major face lifts (how else could she manage to look 17 at age 34) to the 1993 Totally Hair Barbie, complete with ankle-length tresses and a tube of styling gel.

Be sure to strike up a conversation with owner Evelyn Burkhalter, who not only can recite chapter and verse on Barbie history, but also provides philosophical, psychological, and sociological

The more than 16,000 Barbie dolls and accessories at the Barbie Doll Hall of Fame have more to say than you might expect about U.S. history and culture since 1959, when Barbie first appeared. Courtesy of Barbie Doll Hall of Fame.

Their opposition to elitist fraternities led Herbert Hoover and friends in the Stanford class of 1895 to be referred as to Barbs—short for barbarians. While at Stanford, the enterprising Hoover started a laundry and newspaper delivery service, subcontracting the work out. Stanford now houses the massive Hoover library and archives. Photo of Hoover Tower courtesy of Hoover Institution Archives.

commentary on the Barbie phenomenon. Barbie has received her share of criticism over the years, but, as Burkhalter points out, Barbie only follows fads, she doesn't start them.

Girls two to twelve, the major Barbie consumers, are delighted to spend the entire afternoon in this tiny museum. Mothers and grandmothers also seem happy to keep them company. Strange as it may seem, young boys who zero in on Tarzan Barbie or Soccer Barbie can be kept busy for a good half hour. Burkhalter hopes to move to larger quarters before long, so call before you go.

BAYLANDS NATURE INTERPRETIVE CENTER
East Embarcadero Road, Palo Alto
Phone: (415) 329-2506
Hours: Tues. & Wed. 9:00 a.m.-1:00 p.m., 2:00-5:00 p.m.;
**   Thurs. & Fri. 2:00-5:00 p.m.; Sat. & Sun. 1:00-5:00 p.m.**
Admission: Free

The simple wooden structure sitting on stilts in the salt marsh is a good place to begin your exploration of the 120-acre Palo Alto Baylands Nature Preserve. Videos, slide shows, wildlife charts, and a few cases of stuffed birds, mammals, and baylands insects prepare you for the major attraction, the wildlife outside. Join park rangers and staff naturalists on guided walks to find out more about marshland plant and animal life.

HOOVER TOWER
Stanford University, Palo Alto
Phone: (415) 723-2053
Hours: Daily 10:00 a.m.-4:30 p.m. during
**   the academic year. Call ahead to confirm.**
Admission: Free; fee to ride the elevator
**   to the observation deck $1.00 adults,**
**   50¢ seniors & children.**

A tour of the Stanford University campus should include a visit to the Hoover Tower, which houses the Herbert Hoover and Lou Henry Hoover exhibit rooms and the renowned Hoover Library and Archives. The exhibits include a video interview with Herbert Hoover, photographs, documents, and an assortment of artifacts assembled by the Hoovers, including a Russian drinking vessel that once belonged to Alexander I, Hoover's medicine ball, Belgian lace tablecloths, and a model of Hoover Dam.

Be sure to ask about the current exhibition in the adjacent Exhibit Pavilion, which features treasures from the Hoover Institution Archives, a vast source of historical materials such as posters, photographs, films, and original documents.

Children will enjoy the elevator to the 250-foot-high observation deck and the model of Hoover Dam, but will find the rest of little interest.

Library: The Hoover Library and Archives, open to the public Monday through Friday from 8:00 a.m. to 5:00 p.m., comprise one of the largest and most complete private collections in the world on economic, political, and social change in the twentieth century— 1.6 million volumes and 40 million documents.

MUSEUM OF AMERICAN HERITAGE
275 Alma Street, Palo Alto
Phone: (415) 321-1004
Hours: Fri.-Sun. 11:00 a.m.-4:00 p.m.
Admission: Free

One day in the early sixties, Frank Livermore picked up an old Standard Vacuum Sweeper in a junk shop and became a collector of all things mechanical and electrical. Thirty years and 75 typewriters, 40 cameras, 30 radios, dozens of adding machines, calculators, vacuum cleaners, phonographs, hair dryers, toasters, kitchen tools, and cash registers later, he founded the Museum of American Heritage in a former BMW agency. The 7,000 square feet of exhibit and warehouse space allowed Livermore to clear out his house and display his hundreds of artifacts.

The Museum of American Heritage celebrates human technical ingenuity in the past with four permanent exhibits and quarterly changing exhibitions. Three period rooms and hundreds of historic artifacts inspire nostalgic sighs from adults and laughter of disbelief from electronic-age kids. The Kitchen of the 1930s is up-to-date with the latest appliances—a Wedgewood gas/wood stove, GE Monitor top refrigerator, and a washing machine with a copper tub and the latest labor-saving gadgets. The 1920s law office displays state-of-the-art technology—a candlestick telephone with the first rotary dial, a wax-cylinder Dictaphone, and a Royal typewriter. The equipment in the grocery store exhibit came from a 1920s neighborhood business in southside Chicago.

The museum sponsors crystal radio and other science education workshops for kids 10-14.

Gift Shop: A tiny store sells mechanical things, car models, a special edition Hot Wheels ($15), and "Make Your Own Time Capsule."

Rental: Call for information.

The 1903 Edison Standard Cylinder Phonograph played recordings made on wax cylinders. The Museum of American Heritage celebrates human technical ingenuity with a vast array of historic phono-graphs, vacuum cleaners, office equipment, kitchen tools, and much, much more. Courtesy of Museum of American Heritage.

PALO ALTO CULTURAL CENTER
1313 Newell Road, Palo Alto
Phone: (415) 329-2366
Hours: Tues.-Thurs. 10:00 a.m.-5:00 p.m. & 7:00-10:00 p.m.;
    Fri. & Sat. 10:00 a.m.-5:00 p.m.; Sun. 1:00-5:00 p.m.
Admission: Free

Serving the Bay Area for twenty-two years, the sprawling, airy Palo Alto Cultural Center offers outstanding exhibitions and educational programs featuring contemporary art. Imaginative, theme-based exhibitions display works in a surprising range of media by some of California's most talented artists. The Cultural Center also offers an extensive studio art program of classes and workshops for adults and children, and a children's art education program of docent-led tours and hands-on activities.

Rental: The Auditorium, Greenroom, Patio, Sculpture Garden, and meeting rooms are available to residents and non-residents for $30 to $100.

Restaurant: The Cultured Cappuccino, in the patio, sells pastries, soup, salad, and sandwiches to go, not to mention foam-topped lattes and cappuccinos.

"Walking Woman with Staff" (detail, color monotype with watercolor, 26-1/2" x 22", collection of Harry W. & Mary Margaret Anderson), from a printmaking exhibit at the Palo Alto Cultural Center. The center features imaginative exhibits of contemporary art and an extensive studio arts program. Courtesy of Palo Alto Cultural Center.

PALO ALTO JUNIOR MUSEUM
1451 Middlefield Road, Palo Alto
Phone: (415) 329-2111
Hours: Tues.-Sat. 10:00 a.m.-5:00 p.m.; Sun. 1:00-4:00 p.m.
Admission: Free

From the look and sound of it, the kids were having a great time exploring the electronic tree house, crossing the swinging bridge, and observing the caged boa constrictor in the forest exhibit created by volunteers in the city-run Palo Alto Junior Museum. Quarterly arts and science classes, star shows in the inflatable planetarium, and constantly changing exhibits, plus a pretty little zoo housing turtles, snakes, crows and ravens, waterfowl, a rabbit, and carnivorous plants make this a popular outing for younger children.

STANFORD MUSEUM OF ART
Museum Way, Palo Alto
Phone: (415) 723-4177
Hours: Closed until 1997

Dedicated in 1891, the Stanford Museum was, in its day, the largest private museum in the world. Virtually destroyed in the 1906 earthquake, it lay fallow until the 1960s. Struck again by earthquake in 1989, the museum will be closed until 1997. You can still enjoy the Rodin sculpture garden and changing exhibitions in the small Stanford Art Gallery, which features works from the museum's collection and the Masters of Fine Arts show.

SAN JOSE

ALUM ROCK PARK VISITOR CENTER
16240 Alum Rock Avenue, San Jose
Phone: (408) 259-5477
Hours: Call for hours.
Admission: Free

The oldest municipal park in California, Alum Rock was founded in 1872 and became a nationally-known health spa, with 27 mineral springs, mineral baths, an indoor swimming pool, a tea garden, a restaurant, and a dance pavilion. The stone baths and a gazebo sheltering a fountain are all that remain of its former splendor, but it still offers 700 acres of natural, rugged beauty and a visitor center that provides educational displays. "We try to do a little bit of everything here," explained the ranger who was kind enough to open the large hall for us (funding cuts have led to fewer hours). "Everything" includes live residents Owliver the owl, Penny the Opossum, and king snakes Boris and Natasha; a model of the park; stuffed birds and animals; a history corner featuring an Ohlone hopper and a large rock; and the remains of a 2,000-ton "meteorite" found in 1800. The meteorite turned out to be a hunk of manganese that provided 39 tons of high-grade ore for the war effort of 1918.

AMERICAN MUSEUM OF QUILTS AND TEXTILES
766 South 2nd Street, San Jose
Phone: (408) 971-0323
Hours: Wed.-Sat. 10:00 a.m.-4:00 p.m.; Sun. 1:00-4:00 p.m.
Admission: Adults $2.00, seniors & students $1.50, free to children
under 13 and museum members.

"Gather Ye Rosebuds" (1988, 83" x 98", muslin, pattern by Jean Johnson, quilt by Claire Moses). There are 1566 diamonds and hexagons in this handpieced quilt—over 200 hours went into the quilting alone. Courtesy of American Museum of Quilts and Textiles.

Along with wedding gowns, christening dresses, and family Bibles, quilts are said to be the most common objects donated to museums. But it wasn't until the landmark exhibition of American quilts at the Whitney Museum of American Art in 1971 that quilting burst upon the art scene as an aesthetic expression valued beyond its historical and cultural context. The Santa Clara County Quilters' Guild followed hard upon this explosion with the founding, in 1977, of the American Museum of Quilts and Textiles.

Quilting has so long been considered a women's pastime, and is such an important part of the study of women's history, that

you might think of this as a women's museum. Not so. The exhibitions encourage visitors to view the works on several levels—as art forms, as historic documentation, and as social commentary.

Currently located in a 1925 Spanish-revival house in a residential neighborhood, the museum makes good use of its 2,400 square feet of space to showcase quilts from around the world as well as from their own collection. Regularly changing exhibits range in scope from the historic to the contemporary.

As this book goes to press, the museum is planning to relocate but does not yet have a new address—call for information.

Gift Shop: In addition to the extensive selection of quilt books and publications, the museum shop sells their own quilting kits ($5-$15), and a delightful assortment of quilt-related gift items.

CHILDREN'S DISCOVERY MUSEUM OF SAN JOSE
180 Woz Way, San Jose
Phone: (408) 298-5437
Hours: Tues.-Sat. 10:00 a.m.-5:00 p.m.; Sun. noon-5:00 p.m.
Admission: Adults $6.00, seniors $5.00, children 2-18 $4.00, members and children under 2 free.

The provocatively purple Children's Discovery Museum of San Jose features exhibits designed to keep kids entertained and engaged as they discover how things work. Photo by Nate Levine.

"Nothing is fun for the whole family unless the parents are under ten." The Children's Discovery Museum of San Jose may just be the exception that proves this cynical rule. Although I did, at one point, express the wish that they would send the children home so I could enjoy the museum in peace and quiet, this rare place operates successfully on both an adult's and child's level.

Set on two acres of parkland, the museum's provocatively purple building of playful shapes, amazing angles, and striking profiles was designed by Ricardo Legorreta, a pre-eminent Mexican architect.

Its 42,000 square feet are packed with kid-pleasing exhibits designed to encourage children to discover for themselves how and why things work.

"The Streets" exhibit on the first floor, a 5/8-scale replica of an actual city street complete with traffic lights, parking meters, fire hydrants, a fire truck, ambulance, and sewer structure, lets visitors try out the systems that keep the city humming. Kids can climb on the fire truck, sound the siren, wire up their own networks on the microcomputer that controls the museum's traffic lights, or slide down a culvert and explore life under the city streets. In the Kids' Bank they can try to crack the combination to the vault, or examine the contents of safe deposit boxes. The Kids' Care Clinic lets them compare the bones of the resident skeleton to images on actual x-ray films.

Active youngsters can experiment with water and sand by operating a variety of pumps in the Waterworks exhibit—this can get wet! Or children may prefer to "Step into the Past," where they can watch a bee colony, sit on a porch swing, try on costumes from the dress-up trunk, crank up a phonograph, or do laundry the old-fashioned way, in a washtub with a hand-operated wringer. This can get slightly wet, too.

The pace is a little slower on the second floor, where the glass-enclosed Early Childhood Resource Center offers age-appropriate play for children from one to four, and an oasis of quiet and networking opportunities for parents.

A satisfied fourth grader wrote, "I have visited your museum three times and it was better and better each time." For the young at heart, the Children's Discovery Museum is well worth a trip to San Jose.

Gift Shop: A large, well-stocked store sells creative books, toys, and games. A separate entrance allows you to shop without paying admission fees.

Rental: The Kids' Cafe offers three party packages ($5 to $9 per child, museum admission additional) which include lunch, birthday cake, party hats and favors, and reserved tables in the cafe. Exclusive use of the museum for evening events may be arranged.

Restaurant: The small Kids Cafe, operated by Hope Rehabilitation Services, offers family cuisine—nachos, PB & J, pizza, hot dogs, and hamburgers. Located right in the heart of the downstairs exhibition space, seating is limited and the noise level high, but the menu is a winner and the price is right.

EGYPTIAN MUSEUM & PLANETARIUM
Rosicrucian Park
1342 Nagle Avenue, San Jose
Phone: (408) 947-3636
Hours: Daily 9:00 a.m.-5:00 p.m.
Admission: Adults $6.00, seniors & students $4.00,
**   children 7-15 $3.50**

EGYPTIAN MUSEUM

A major San Jose tourist attraction, the Egyptian Museum and Planetarium are located in Rosicrucian Park, an exotic setting of Egyptian-style buildings, rose gardens, papyrus-lined paths, and colossal statues of Egyptian gods.

Sphinxes line the approach to the museum, which was inspired by ancient Egyptian temple architecture. Beyond the polished bronze doors guarded by the hippopotamus deity Taurt, the largest collection of Egyptian, Babylonian, and Assyrian artifacts on exhibit in the West awaits you. (The UC Berkeley Hearst Museum collection is seldom on display.)

The Egyptian Museum houses the largest collection of Egyptian materials on exhibit on the West Coast, in addition to Assyrian, Sumerian, Babylonian, and Persian collections, and a contemporary art gallery. Courtesy of Egyptian Museum.

Four large galleries on three levels feature objects dating from pre-dynastic times through Egypt's early Christian era. The most popular galleries explore the ancient Egyptians' view of the afterlife through canopic jars, ushabtis, funerary boats and models, and an exceptional collection of mummified cats, birds, crocodiles, fish, a baboon, and the head of a sacred bull, as well as humans. Ancient Egyptian life is portrayed through jewelry, scarabs, pottery, glass and alabaster vessels, bronze tools, and sculpture, including an excellent reproduction of the famous Nefertiti bust. The highlight of our visit, an experience designed to thrill the timid, was a tour of a rock-cut tomb, a replica based on fifteen tombs dating from 2000 B.C. Illuminated only by the guide's flashlight, we passed from the upper offertory chamber deeper into the burial chamber, its walls adorned with colorful hieroglyphics, its sarcophagus desecrated by thieves.

Gift Shop: The small museum store carries a wonderful assortment of jewelry, reproductions, books, and gift items with an Egyptian theme. The Alexandria Bookstore offers a large selection of metaphysical books and gifts reflecting the spiritual values of many world cultures.

PLANETARIUM
Hours: Open intermittently—call for schedule.
Admission: Adults $4.00, children 7-15 $3.00, children 5 & 6 free.
    Children under 5 not admitted.

One of the first planetariums in the United States, since 1936 the Rosicrucian Star Theater has offered programs exploring the mysteries of the cosmos, from the mythologies of ancient peoples to the latest findings of astronomy.

For more information on the Rosicrucian philosophy, ask for a free copy of their booklet, "An Introduction to AMORC, The Ancient Mystic Order Rosae Crucis."

MILITARY MEDAL MUSEUM AND RESEARCH CENTER
448 North San Pedro Street, San Jose
Phone: (408) 298-1100
Hours: By appointment
Admission: Free

Established in 1979 to showcase the private collection of owner John Langton, San Jose's Military Medal Museum is a tiny, one-room affair located in a vintage (1878) building that used to be a railroad saloon. Floor-to-ceiling glass-framed boxes display medals and related documents

from 57 countries. On display is an 1820 Boston Fusiliers medal,
the oldest American decoration in existence. Only a small portion of
Langton's collection—40 years' worth—can be displayed at one time.
His 5,000-volume library is no longer open to the public (books kept
disappearing), but Langton will be happy to research any question that
sounds interesting to him.

OVERFELT BOTANICAL GARDENS
McKee & Educational Park Drive, San Jose
Phone: (408) 251-3323
Hours: Daily 10:00 a.m.-sunset.
Admission: Free

In 1959, 33 acres of land were donated to the city of San Jose to establish
"a place of solitude, beauty and education." The park contains three small
lakes, a palm grove, a camellia garden, a wildflower path, and, most
notably, the five-acre Chinese Cultural Garden. A statue of Confucius
overlooks a large pond. Two small marble pavilions flank the imposing
Dr. Sun Yat Sen Memorial Hall. Marble lions guard the entrance to the
tile-roofed, pagoda-like structure. Given the painful history of San Jose's
Chinese community—Chinatown was deliberately destroyed by fire in
1887 and their beautiful Taoist temple razed by the city—the creation
of the Chinese Garden is a welcome effort.

SAN JOSE HISTORICAL MUSEUM
1600 Senter Road
Kelley Park, San Jose
Phone: (408) 287-2290
Hours: Mon.-Fri. 10:00 a.m.-4:30 p.m.; Sat. & Sun. noon-4:30 p.m.
Admission: Adults $4.00, seniors $3.00, youth 4-17 $2.00

Five minutes from the capital of Silicon Valley—renovated, up-to-the-
minute downtown San Jose—is a turn-of-the-century recreation of the
same city. The remarkable San Jose Historical Museum, located on 25
acres in Kelley Park, has restored or faithfully reproduced twenty houses,
businesses, and historical landmarks from the city's past. The master plan
calls for the restoration of 75 buildings.
     A 115-foot, half-scale replica of San Jose's famous Electric Light
Tower dominates Market Street, along with Banca D'Italia, forerunner
of Bank of America, and the elegant Pacific Hotel, which presents a
comprehensive exhibit tracing the history of the area from the Ohlone
through the 1920s.
     Around the corner on San Fernando Street, a 1927 gas station; a stable
complete with blacksmith shop, carriages, and buggies; and the trolley
barn give an idea of turn-of-the-century transportation. Several Victorian
homes have been moved to the site, including the Umbarger House,

which remains exactly as it was in the early 1870s, without indoor plumbing or running water. Kids can pump water at the well by the kitchen garden where sits the outhouse. In contrast, the Chiechi House, built in 1876, is faithfully furnished as it was in 1924, down to the original living room suite from Sears. The neoclassic 1905 Nelson-DeLuz House displays "Vintage Reflections" from the museum's textile collection, which contains many fine examples of period costumes and household textiles. The Stevens Ranch Fruit Barn, a relic from the bygone agricultural glory of the area, has been relocated to the museum.

Our guide concluded our tour with his and our favorite building, the replica of the 1888 Chinese temple located in Heinlenville, San Jose's last Chinatown. The first-floor exhibit traces the history of the Chinese community in San Jose, covering the injustices of the immigration system, the untimely demise of the first Chinatown by arson, and life in the Heinlenville Chinatown, a tiny, fenced community in the middle of one of the richest agricultural regions in California. The second story houses the pièce de résistance, the Ng Shing Gung altar in all its restored splendor. The altar was made in Canton in 1889.

This delightful and informative museum offers more than enough to interest adults and entertain children for at least half a day. After your visit you can go on to the Happy Hollow Park and Zoo, also located within Kelley Park.

Library: A research library containing archival and photographic collections relating to Santa Clara County is open by appointment.

Gift Shop: The large, attractive City Store, located in the Pacific Hotel, sells Victorian souvenirs and an excellent selection of local history books. Vintage Reflections, the museum's costuming program, rents Victorian-era reproduction costumes for men, women, and children.

Rental: The grounds and meeting rooms can accommodate picnics, weddings, cultural events, and receptions for a nominal fee.

Restaurant: Old-fashioned O'Brien's Ice Cream and Candy Store, the first establishment to serve ice cream sodas west of Detroit, offers old-time candies and a menu of sandwiches, soup, salads, nachos, chili, and chili dogs for under $4.00.

SAN JOSE MUSEUM OF ART
110 South Market, San Jose
Phone: (408) 294-2787
Hours: Tues.-Sun. 10:00 a.m.-5:00 p.m., Thurs. 10:00 a.m.-8:00 p.m.
Admission: Adult $5.00, seniors & students $3.00, children under 5
free. Free first Thursday of the month.

The San Jose Museum of Art opened in 1969, in a historic building (formerly the city's post office and then the public library) that boasts solid oak doors with bronze hinges, marble floors, and a heavy facade of local sandstone carved by Italian artisans. In 1991 the museum added a modern, 45,000-square-foot wing which tripled the exhibition space and provides an elegant complement to the historic structure.

The museum's collection is modest, and a limited number of works are on permanent display, but beginning in 1994 the best of American art will be right here in San Jose. In collaboration with New York's Whitney Museum of American Art, the museum will draw from the largest collection of 20th century American art in the world for four 18-month exhibitions, beginning with a survey of American art from 1900 to 1940. California art lovers will no longer have to travel to New York to see works by seminal figures.

For kids: Family Sundays, the first Sunday of every month, feature activities designed to introduce kids (and adults) to the world of contemporary art. Free for children and those accompanying them.

Library: 4,125 volumes.

Gift Shop: The large gift shop sells art books, toys, cards, gifts, jewelry, and accessories, many of them one-of-a-kind pieces designed by artists.

Rental: The museum is available for rental for private receptions, corporate events, and meetings for groups of 10 to 1,000.

Restaurant: You can relax with a cup of coffee and biscotti or a muffin at the The Artfull Cup, the small coffee bar which seats about ten patrons.

Beginning in 1994, the San Jose Museum of Art will host four major, 18-month exhibitions of 20th century art from New York's Whitney Museum. The San Jose Museum also features activites designed to turn children (and their parents) on to contemporary art. Photo by Diane Levinson, courtesy of San Jose Museum of Art.

THE TECH MUSEUM OF INNOVATION
145 West San Carlos Street, San Jose
Phone: (408) 279-7150
Hours: Tues.-Sun. 10:00 a.m.-5:00 p.m. Open Mondays on school holidays.
Admission: Adults $6.00, seniors, youth 6-18, & college students with ID $4.00, groups of 12 or more $1.00 off.

The Tech Museum's large exhibit hall, divided into six sections highlighting space, microelectronics, materials, robotics, bicycles, and biotechnology, features spell-binding exhibits guaranteed to fascinate science junkies and computer illiterates alike. A 23-foot double helix made from 500 telephone books replicates a giant strand of DNA; a nine-foot square "microchip" can tell you what day your birthday will fall on in the year 2000; a computer helps you create a better bicycle and print out your design. In the Info Lounge, visitors can use laser-video disc players and computers, and access the electronic highway.

Unlike traditional science museums, which concentrate on basic scientific principles, The Tech focuses on real-life uses of advanced technologies: how gene-splicing helped a young boy grow, how robots can be commanded to cook for a paraplegic, how space research results in a lighter, more aerodynamically effective bike.

For the technologically impaired, a host of patient volunteers, many of them Silicon Valley engineers, are on hand to guide you through exhibits and answer your questions.

Patient volunteers are on hand to guide the technologically impaired through exhibits at San Jose's Tech Museum of Innovation. Photo by Nate Levine.

Formerly known as the Technology Center of Silicon Valley and The Garage, the present museum is a prototype for a 120,000–square–foot facility scheduled to open in San Jose's Guadalupe River Park in 1998.

Gift Shop: The Tech Museum Store offers unusual and educational gifts, gadgets, and clever devices, as well as books, software, special publications, and Silicon Valley souvenirs.

Rental: The Tech is available for exclusive rental Monday through Sunday from 6:00 p.m. to midnight. Call (408) 279-7156. For birthday party information and other group reservations, call (408) 279-7176.

Restaurant: We traveled with our photographer to The Tech Museum and stopped in the Cafe Tech for a quick meal. The sandwiches were made to order with fresh lettuce and tomato. The soup was canned, but hot. The total check for all three of us came to under $15. Not gourmet dining, but a wholesome, inexpensive lunch.

WINCHESTER MYSTERY HOUSE
525 South Winchester Boulevard, San Jose
Phone: (408) 247-2101
**Hours: Daily 9:00 a.m.–8:00 p.m., summer; 9:00 a.m.–4:30 p.m.,
  spring/fall; 9:30 a.m.–4:00 p.m., winter.**
Admission: Adults $12.50, seniors $9.50, children 6-12 $6.50.

Sarah Pardee Winchester, widow of the heir to the Winchester rifle fortune, was obsessed with the untimely deaths of her husband and infant daughter. A Boston medium convinced her that the ghosts of the victims of the Winchester rifle, the "gun that won the West," would haunt her unless she built a large house and fixed it up according to the wishes of the spirits. If work went on continuously, the good spirits would keep the bad spirits at bay; as long as the hammers rang out night and day, every day of the year, Sarah would never die. She purchased an eight-room farmhouse in the Santa Clara Valley and for the next forty years spent her $20 million inheritance and $1,000-a-day income on construction as dictated by the spirits in her nightly seance.

Acting as her own architect and contractor, Sarah kept carpenters busy building 40 bedrooms, 13 bathrooms, 47 fireplaces, blind closets, secret passageways, staircases leading nowhere, 2,000 doors, and 10,000 windows. These days, the rambling, 160-room structure on six acres at the outskirts of San Jose has been turned into such a tourist attraction that serious-minded museum lovers seldom visit. This is unfortunate: kids expecting a Disneyland-like haunted house may be disappointed, but architecture enthusiasts will be pleasantly surprised. Despite a promotional campaign that focuses on the mysterious and bizarre aspects of the labyrinthine palace, the Winchester mansion is a unique jewel of Victorian architecture, created by a remarkable artist with no architectural training.

A house so complex that even the owner needed maps to find her way around requires a guided tour. Visitors can also take a self-guided tour of the restored gardens and back buildings, the Winchester Historic Firearms Museum, which contains the largest collection of Winchester rifles on the West Coast, and the Antique Products Museum, which offers a sampling of antique Winchester products.

Gift Shop: The Winchester Gift Shop features books about the mansion and Winchester souvenirs.

Rental: To make your birthday party a real scream, the mansion offers a birthday package for $10.95 per child, including cake, beverage, and reserved picnic area. A private group tour is included.

Restaurant: We visited the Winchester House in the morning, so all we needed was a little breakfast snack. Our bagel was a bit stale. You will probably do much better with the Winchester Cafe's prepared snacks: nachos or a chili, cheese, or corn dog, available for under $3. For a group, you can get pizza and a pitcher of soft drink for about $13. Hot sandwiches—fried chicken, polish sausage, ham & cheese, or breast of turkey—are under $5, and the dessert menu offers lots of choices under $2.50. You can eat at the cafe without paying the entrance fee to see the mystery house.

An aerial view of the Winchester Mystery House, built for $5.5 million by Sarah L. Winchester, heiress to the Winchester rifle fortune. Courtesy of Winchester Mystery House.

YOUTH SCIENCE INSTITUTE
ALUM ROCK NATURE CENTER
16260 Alum Rock Avenue, San Jose
Phone: (408) 258-4322
Hours: Tues.-Sat. noon–4:00 p.m.; Sun. (summer) noon–5:00 p.m.
Admission: Adults 50¢, children 25¢, parking $3.00

Founded in 1953 by the Junior League of San Jose to augment science
education in the schools, Youth Science Institute now has three discovery
centers offering hands-on programs that give children a chance to
discover why science is a part of their everyday lives. Located within
Alum Rock Park in a 1920s stone building that once served as a bathhouse for the Alum Rock mineral springs, the original Discovery Center
specializes in local natural history. One room is devoted to hands-on
exhibits and the recently acquired Homes Bird Collection, an astonishing
assembly of taxidermied avians collected at the turn of the century. A live
animal room features native birds of prey (red-tailed hawk and great
horned owl), chipmunks, a hedgehog, a ferret, common house mice,
and other assorted mammals, birds, and reptiles including, on our visit,
two-week-old baby rats.

While Youth Science Institute focuses on school programs, they do
offer Summer Science Day Camps for children (pre-kindergarten through
7th grade) and Science Safaris for families.

Gift Shop: A lot of goodies are crowded into the tiny counter that serves
as a gift shop. In addition to nicely done t-shirts, you will find arrowheads
(Mexican-made), gemstone collectors' cards, optic wonders, and hand-
carved wooden king snakes.

SAN MARTIN

CALIFORNIA ANTIQUE AIRCRAFT MUSEUM
12777 Murphy, San Martin
Phone: (408) 683-2290
Hours: Sat. 10:00 a.m.–2:00 p.m., or by appointment.
Admission: Free—donation suggested

Northern California is rich in aviation history. Santa Clara College
professor John Montgomery was building and flying gliders long before
the Wright brothers took off; Californian Harriet Quimby, the first
licensed woman pilot, was also the first woman to fly across the English
Channel; and of course the aviation pioneers Allan, Victor, and Malcolm
Loughead (now spelled Lockheed), who grew up in the area, are still well
known in the field.

Although the California Antique Aircraft Association has sponsored
the West Coast Antique Fly-in at Watsonville on Memorial Day weekend for the past 30 years, the museum was just getting off the ground at

the time of our visit. Plans for a major museum of antique aircraft by the end of the decade are underway and meanwhile, the museum staff and volunteers do an excellent job at the present, two-acre site near the South County Airport, collecting old planes and artifacts before they disappear forever. Classes are offered in restoration techniques, and restoration work is proceeding on several old flying machines. Twenty aircraft from World War I through the 1950s are on display, as well as instruments, replicas, and models. Visitors can try out the Link Trainer flight simulator. For anyone interested in airplanes, this museum is a must.

Library: The reference library's collection includes books, magazines, photographs, personal log books, newspaper clippings, and other aircraft memorabilia.

Gift Shop: T-shirts, hats, posters, cups, water bottles, and old airplane magazines (50¢ each) are available.

SANTA CLARA

DE SAISSET MUSEUM
Santa Clara University
500 El Camino Real, Santa Clara
Phone: (408) 554-4528
Hours: Tues.-Sun. 11:00 a.m.-4:00 p.m.
Admission: Free

A recent bequest of photographs by such outstanding artists as Ansel Adams, Imogen Cunningham, Annie Leibovitz, and Edward Weston enhances the de Saisset Museum's permanent collection of works in a wide range of media and periods. The 14,400-square-foot museum, adjacent to Mission Santa Clara de Asis on the Santa Clara University campus, was built in 1955 thanks to Isabel de Saisset, whose bequest underwrote the construction with the stipulation that the museum permanently house 95 oil paintings by her brother, Ernest de Saisset. The museum also boasts the largest public collection of works by Henrietta Shore, an early 20th century painter hailed as one of the great women artists of her time. Works from Stanford University ranging from classical Greece to the early 20th century will be on view at the de Saisset through 1997.

Visually spare but dramatic exhibits in the California History Collection, on permanent display in three galleries on the museum's lower level, trace Costanoan (Ohlone) culture, the Spanish missionary era, and the early days of Santa Clara College. The displays feature Native American artifacts ranging from simple

"Fortune Teller" by Arnold G. Mountfort (oil on canvas, 36" x 28-1/4", 1930, bequest of Patricia O'Neill Mountfort). The de Saisset Museum features a lively range of paintings, photographs, and a sculpture, as well as local history exhibits. Photo by Charles Barry, courtesy of de Saisset Museum.

domestic utensils to beautifully handcrafted baskets, the recreation of
a Mission altar, vaquero gloves and spurs, and photos and memorabilia
documenting the transformation of the Mission into Santa Clara College.
Younger visitors will be intrigued by the full-sized replica of a tule house
created with the same native plants, wild grasses, and willow poles used
by the Ohlone. An exhibit of scientific instruments used at the college
between 1845 and 1875 includes an early seismograph and the Jesuit
Seismological Record for 1914–1915.

HARRIS-LASS HISTORIC MUSEUM*
1889 Market Street, Santa Clara
Phone: (408) 249-7905
Hours: Sat. & Sun. noon-4:00 p.m.
Admission: Adults $3.00, seniors $2.00, children 6-12 $1.00

Located on the last farm site in the city of Santa Clara, the two-story,
Italianate Harris-Lass house with barn, tank house, summer kitchen, and
chicken coop is a reminder of the days when the Santa Clara Valley was
known not for computer chips but for orchards.

MISSION SANTA CLARA*
Santa Clara University
500 El Camino Real, Santa Clara
Phone: (408) 554-4023
Hours: Church (for self-guided visits): Mon.-Fri. 8:00 a.m.-6:00 p.m.
Office: Mon.-Fri. 1:00-5:00 p.m.
Admission: Free

Founded in 1777, Mission Santa Clara de Asis was destroyed successively
by flood, earthquake, and fire. The present building, constructed in 1926
and now a part of Santa Clara University, is a replica of the third mission,
which was built in 1825. The bell tower contains the original three bells
sent by the king of Spain.

TRITON MUSEUM OF ART
1505 Warburton Avenue, Santa Clara
Phone: (408) 247-3754
Hours: Tues. 10:00 a.m.-9:00 p.m.; Wed.-Fri. 10:00 a.m.-5:00 p.m.;
Sat. & Sun. noon-5:00 p.m.
Admission: Free

Set on a seven-acre park with rolling green lawns and stately palm trees,
the elegant Triton Museum building is perhaps the most prized jewel of
its own collection. Designed by San Francisco architects Barcelon and
Jang, the sand-colored stucco exterior, banded with sky blue and capped
by pyramidal skylights, has been called a post-modernist reference to early

California missions. The felicitous blend of architectural styles culminates in the gorgeous, light-filled rotunda, whose curved wall of windows looks out on a sculpture garden. The flood of natural light pouring down from the skylights and in through the windows, unexpected in an art museum, can be controlled by a high tech baffling system, which provides flexible exhibition options.

The Triton's permanent collection emphasizes historic California painting, contemporary works on paper, and the Austen Warburton Native American Collection. Two galleries present rotating exhibitions, either of works from the permanent collection or traveling exhibitions selected to complement it. On view during our last visit were works from a drawing and printmaking competition, and a powerful exhibition of large installation pieces made specifically for the Triton by master Japanese printmaker Arinori Ichihara.

The Triton's continued commitment to regional artists is reflected in upcoming exhibitions of new works by California artists and the Bay Area Masters Series. Other exhibits will feature Diego Rivera, David Alfaro Siqueiros, Jose Clemente Orozco, Georgia O'Keeffe, and Toulouse-Lautrec and his contemporaries.

For kids: The education wing exhibits children's art, and the museum's Artreach program provides hands-on experiences for children, docent tours, and in-service training for teachers.

Library: The research library, open by appointment, includes materials on American and California artists, art history, Native American art and history, and Triton-related history.

Gift Shop: The Collectors' Gallery is a lovely place to find one-of-a-kind pieces by California artists, hand-crafted jewelry, whimsical Mexican folk art, beautiful African masks, Native American baskets, quilts, and more.

Rental: The facilities are available to individuals and groups and can accommodate up to 400 for a reception.

The Triton Museum of Art may be the best piece in its own collection, which also features California painting, contemporary works on paper, and Native American art. Rotating exhibitions feature local and internationally known artists. Courtesy of Triton Museum of Art.

SARATOGA

HAKONE GARDENS
21000 Big Basin Way, Saratoga
Phone: (408) 741-4994
**Hours: Mon.-Fri. 10:00 a.m.-5:00 p.m.; Sat. & Sun. 11:00 a.m.-
5:00 p.m.**
Admission: Free weekdays, $3.00 parking weekends

Northern California offers many lovely Japanese gardens, but for design, attention to detail, and authentic use of Japanese garden art, none can compare to Saratoga's Hakone Gardens, considered by many to be the finest in the United States.

Captivated by the beauty and simplicity of gardens she had seen in Japan, San Francisco art patron Isabel Stine brought an architect from Japan and an imperial gardener to create her summer retreat in the Saratoga foothills. Patterned after a 17th century Zen garden, it is arranged for contemplation and tranquillity.

The Upper, or Moon Viewing House, built in 1917 in the traditional samurai style without nails, overlooks a waterfall, reflecting ponds stocked with koi, an arched bridge, and a pavilion. The Lower House, built in 1922 as the family's summer residence, was remodeled in 1980 to include two tea ceremony rooms. The Zen or dry garden facing the Lower House consists of five large stones, a shrine lantern, black pine, azaleas, and gravel raked into waves. The main gate, Mon, was added in 1932 by Hakone's second owner, Charles Lee Tilden of Berkeley's Tilden Park fame. The newest garden, the Kizuna-En or Bamboo Garden, was created in partnership with Saratoga's Japanese sister city, Muko-shi.

It was pouring rain the day of our visit and the gardens, deserted except for a lone gardener, were unbearably beautiful. It's hard to imagine a more delightful place to spend an hour in any weather. Children will enjoy the tea and snacks served in the teahouse on weekends, April through September.

Gift Shop: Beautiful gift items from Japan, one-of-a-kind Japanese-inspired pieces by local artists, Hakone notecards, Happi coats, prints and postcards are available. The gift shop is open Tuesday through Thursday, 9:00 a.m. to 5:00 p.m.

Rental: The Lower House, multi-purpose room, and deck of the Cultural Exchange Center are available for weddings, receptions, luncheons, dinners, and business retreats.

SARATOGA HISTORICAL MUSEUM
20450 Saratoga–Los Gatos Road, Saratoga
Phone: (408) 867-4311
Hours: Wed.-Sun. 1:00-4:00 p.m.
Admission: Free

The oldest commercial building in town, with its painted white facade, has been at various times the Saratoga Drug Store, a restaurant, a creamery, a variety store, and a dress shop. The turn-of-the-century building is now home to the Saratoga Historical Museum, a repository of photographs, artifacts, and memorabilia relating to Saratoga's history. Sparse but nicely arranged displays chronicle Saratoga's agricultural past, early school days, local politics, and small-town life from the 1850s to 1900. When you've finished examining the old store cabinets filled with domestic ware from another time—cookbooks, apple peelers, waffle irons, darning eggs, glove stretchers—and the glass-topped counter displaying temperance literature and a Women's Christian Temperance Union pledge card, you can sit at a table and page through photo albums featuring early Saratogans. The museum has a friendly, folksy feel.

VILLA MONTALVO
15400 Montalvo Road, Saratoga
Phone: (408) 741-3421
Hours: Call for hours.
Admission: Adults $1.00, children under 18 free

James Phelan, a passionate Californian, three times mayor of San Francisco and the first popularly-elected U.S. senator from California, named his lush, 175-acre estate for the popular 16th century Spanish author Garcia Ordonez de Montalvo, whose tale of "California," a fabulous golden island ruled by Califia, queen of the Amazons, inspired Spanish explorers who named the state. A generous patron of the arts, Phelan surrounded himself with prominent figures of his day—Jack London, Douglas Fairbanks, and Joaquin Miller among others. When he died in 1930, he left his estate to be used as a public park and for the development of the arts.

Today, the main rooms of the Mediterranean-style villa house an art gallery showcasing the works of established and emerging Santa Clara Valley artists, and occasional touring exhibitions of major artists. The artist-in-residence program, established in 1942, provides six studio apartments for visual artists, musicians, and writers. The octagonal carriage house has been transformed into a theater presenting an impressive calendar of performing arts events.

Formal gardens populated by marble statues, fountains, tiled and paved verandas, wisteria-covered trellises, and sweeping lawns surround the villa. The remainder of the estate has been made into an arboretum and

Audubon Society bird sanctuary. A one-and-a-half-mile nature trail winds through three separate plant communities: chaparral, evergreen forest, and redwood forest. From the lookout point on a clear day you can see the Santa Clara Valley floor from the bay to the Almaden Valley.

Gift Shop: The Griffin Shop offers art, garden and children's books, hand-crafted gifts, cards, and jewelry.

Rental: The Oval Garden, with its Temple of Love Pavilion, may be rented for outdoor weddings. The villa interior is available to Montalvo Circle donors for weddings.

YOUTH SCIENCE INSTITUTE
SANBORN DISCOVERY CENTER
16055 Sanborn Road, Saratoga
Phone: (408) 867-6940
Hours: Wed.-Fri. 9:00 a.m.-4:30 p.m.; Sat. & Sun. noon-4:30 p.m.,
    and by appointment.
Admission: Parking $3.00

The newest of the three Youth Science Institute Centers in Santa Clara County, Sanborn Discovery Center specializes in invertebrates, botany, redwood ecology, and geology. Housed in Sanborn–Skyline County Park's former rangers' quarters, the Center's four rooms feature an insect zoo complete with hissing cockroaches and a tarantula; a live vertebrate room—snakes and other reptiles; the popular geology room, where kids can simulate an earthquake on the shaking table; and a one-third-acre organic demonstration garden. Budding entomologists won't want to miss the annual Insect Fair each May, during which the entire center is devoted to hundreds of different species of insects, with exhibits and demonstrations. During the last two weeks of October, thrill-seekers flock to the Haunted Woods, a quarter-mile trail set with theatrical scenes of zombies, Dr. Frankenstein's lab, "Terminal Jeopardy," and other frights with a scare quotient geared to eight years and older.

SUNNYVALE

SUNNYVALE HISTORICAL MUSEUM
260 North Sunnyvale Avenue, Sunnyvale
Phone: (408) 749-0220
Hours: Tues. & Thurs. noon-3:30 p.m.; Sun. 1:00-4:00 p.m.,
    and by appointment.

"In a rapidly changing community such as Sunnyvale, a museum is a constant. People in search of roots will find them here. A museum is a place where answers are found, where information is gathered, where knowledge is enhanced." So says Pat Plant, a member of the Sunnyvale Historical Society's board of directors.

Sunnyvale traces its origins to the first wagon train to successfully cross the Sierra Nevada, in 1844. Martin Murphy, Jr. and his wife Mary, members of that pioneer party, founded the city of Sunnyvale on their Bayview Ranch. The Sunnyvale Historical Museum occupies 700 square feet in the modern community center in Murphy Park, a few feet away from the site of the historic Murphy home. In 1961 a proposal to the city council to provide $30,000 needed to restore the house lost by one vote and the home was demolished. Historic consciousness has risen considerably since that unfortunate decision and members of Sunnyvale's Historical Society have put forth a lot of effort to preserve the city's past.

The museum displays many Murphy family heirlooms, as well as memorabilia, historic photographs, and artifacts documenting the area's transformation from the Valley of Heart's Delight to the Silicon Valley. The roles of the Libby and Del Monte canning companies, Hendy Iron Works, Ampex, Atari, and Moffett Field are all documented in the museum's exhibits on the history of canning, military establishments, and the aerospace, electronics, and computer industries.

Gift Shop: Reproductions of vintage aprons, bonnets, and other articles of clothing made by Sunnyvale Historical Society members are on sale here.

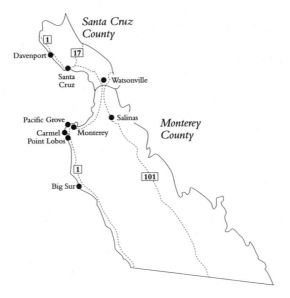

Monterey Bay Area

SANTA CRUZ COUNTY

DAVENPORT

DAVENPORT JAIL MUSEUM*
Highway 1, Davenport
Phone: (408) 429-3663
Hours: Sat. & Sun. 10:00 a.m.-2:00 p.m., and by appointment.
Admission: Free

Built in 1914, the tiny, two-cell Davenport Jail was rarely used before being abandoned in 1936. Since 1987 it has housed a small, local history museum with exhibits on native people, the natural environment, major industries, early settler families, and community life.

Gift Shop: A selection of books, cards, and gift items is available.

SANTA CRUZ

LIGHTHOUSE SURFING MUSEUM
West Cliff Drive, Santa Cruz
Phone: (408) 429-3760
Hours: Wed.-Mon. noon-4:00 p.m.
Admission: Free

The spectacular view of Monterey Bay from Lighthouse Point, the sight of surfers in their day-glo wetsuits catching waves, the sound of sea lions barking, and the salty smell of sea air should get you in the mood for a visit to this unique museum. Housed in the tiny, brick Mark Abbott Memorial Lighthouse, the Santa Cruz Surfing Museum traces over one hundred years of surfing history, with videos illustrating the sport's evolution and photographs of Santa Cruz surfers from the 1930s through today. Surfing memorabilia and a full range of boards from redwood planks to today's high-tech fiberglass designs document the development of the surfboard. If you visit on "Old-Timers' Day," Friday from noon to

DON PATERSON | HARRY MURRY | RICH THOMPSON | ALEX HOKAMP | BLAKE TURNER | BILL GRACE | BUSTER STEWARD | FRED HUNT | HARRY MAYO | PINKY PEDEMONTI | TOMMY ROUSSELL

Santa Cruz Surfing Club, 1941. The Lighthouse Surfing Museum traces more than a hundred years of surfing history. Photo courtesy of Harry Mayo and the Santa Cruz Museum Association.

four, you'll get a chance to talk to some living legends—museum volunteers who first rode the waves more than fifty years ago.

Gift Shop: Books, t-shirts, sweatshirts, posters, and other items, all having to do with surfing, are available.

JOSEPH M. LONG MARINE LABORATORY
100 Shaffer Road (at the end of Delaware Street), Santa Cruz
Phone: (408) 459-4308
Hours: Tues.-Sun. 1:00-4:00 p.m.
Admission: Free

At the Joseph M. Long Marine Laboratory, a research facility for UC Santa Cruz, faculty and students study esoteric topics like marine vertebrate physiology and energetics. Fortunately for the rest of us, the laboratory has expanded its mission to educating the public. Visitors of all ages are welcome to tour the facility with a docent and visit the small aquarium. An exciting array of Monterey Bay marine life and a popular touch tank, where the bold can examine the underside of a sea star or peek in at a hiding hermit crab. Exhibits inside the tiny museum include a model of the Monterey Bay submarine canyon and outside is the skeleton of a blue whale, the largest animal in today's world. This is an extraordinary opportunity to witness a working marine lab in action at no cost—you won't want to miss it.

Gift Shop: The large store has a wonderful selection of books for all ages, posters, cards, t-shirts, and delightful gift items with a marine theme. Teachers can find marine education curriculum development material.

McPHERSON CENTER FOR ART AND HISTORY

As a symbol of their emergence from the devastation of the 1989 Loma Prieta earthquake, Santa Cruz proudly opened the McPherson Center for Art and History in 1993. The elegant, postmodern structure, joining the old county jail and a new building with a dramatic, three-story, glass and steel atrium, houses the county's art museum and the history museum. The 1,000-square-foot gallery space in the Octagon Museum, built in 1882 as the County Hall of Records, is shared on a rotating basis by the art and history museums.

Rental: The auditorium, meeting rooms, courtyard, and ground floor are available for rent. Call (408) 454-0697.

THE ART MUSEUM OF SANTA CRUZ COUNTY
McPherson Center for Art and History
705 Front Street, Santa Cruz
Phone: (408) 429-1964
Hours: Tues.-Sun. 11:00 a.m.-4:00 p.m.; Thurs. 11:00 a.m.-8:00 p.m.
Admission: Adults $2.50, students & seniors $2.00, children free
   (good at both museums). Free first Thursday of the month.

The Art Museum's Solari Gallery presents a wide variety of art in its eight-week exhibits, including one-person shows of internationally recognized artists such as Judy Chicago, Christo, David Hockney, Manuel Neri, Wayne Thiebaud, and Jack Zajac, and group exhibitions representing the art of other countries or demonstrating various art techniques, media, crafts, and historic periods. Occasional exhibitions present works from the permanent collection, which emphasizes contemporary art since the 1940s, particularly works on paper and work by regional artists.

Gift Shop: The Museum Shop, a joint venture of the Historical Trust and the Art Museum, features the best of what's old and new in art and history, from postcards to jewelry, with prices to fit every budget. The Art Museum Rental Gallery offers a comprehensive selection of works by Santa Cruz County artists for sale or rent.

THE HISTORY MUSEUM OF SANTA CRUZ COUNTY
McPherson Center for Art and History
705 Front Street, Santa Cruz
Phone: (408) 425-7278
Hours: Tues.-Sun. 11:00 a.m.-4:00 p.m.; Thurs. 11:00 a.m.-8:00 p.m.
Admission: Adults $2.50, students & seniors $2.00, children free
   (good at both museums). Free first Thursday of the month.

Step across the 1873 map of the Monterey Bay region sandblasted onto the granite floor into one of the finest county museums in northern California. The History Museum brings to life the county's multi-cultured

Original ad from F.W. Swanton Pharmacy, Santa Cruz. Courtesy of The History Museum of Santa Cruz County.

past, beginning with the native Ohlone, whose history goes back at least 10,000 years, up to the devastating Loma Prieta earthquake of 1989. Historical artifacts, rare photographs and photo murals, meticulous recreations, and colorful anecdotes enliven exhibits on the Spanish explorers and missionaries who claimed California for "God, Glory and Gold," the Californios, forty-niners, early settlers, loggers, tourists, and recent local residents. Children can climb a short staircase to Grandmother's Attic, a hands-on exhibit with heaps of toys, clothes, a guitar, and other knickknacks for them to play with, while grown-ups watch the engrossing "Santa Cruz County—A Home Movie Scrapbook," a professionally produced video incorporating local home movies.

Library: Located in a bright, new room on the third floor, the local history research archives containing books, unpublished manuscripts, photographs and postcards, public records (including immigration, naturalization, voter registration, marriage, and incorporation records), newspapers, cemetery records, and much more are open to the public by appointment.

SANTA CRUZ ART LEAGUE GALLERY
526 Broadway, Santa Cruz
Phone: (408) 426-5787
Hours: Wed.-Sat. 11:00 a.m.-5:00 p.m.; Sun. noon-4:00 p.m.
Admission: Free

Founded in 1919, the Santa Cruz Art League is headquartered in a large facility built in 1951. The league mounts nine exhibitions a year featuring regional and local artists working in many media, an annual high school exhibition, and an annual statewide juried exhibition.

Gift Shop: The lobby gift shop sells fine prints and local crafts.

SANTA CRUZ CITY MUSEUM OF NATURAL HISTORY
1305 East Cliff Drive, Santa Cruz
Phone: (408) 429-3773
Hours: Tues.-Fri. 10:00 a.m.-5:00 p.m.; Sat. & Sun. 1:00-5:00 p.m.
Admission: Donations appreciated

Located in the old Seabright Library, the Santa Cruz City Museum is the oldest museum in the area, with a collection dating back to the turn of the century. The main focus is the natural history of the northern Monterey Bay area, with exhibits grouped by natural communities. Live snakes, a working beehive, and a touch pool of live tide pool creatures are on display, along with traditional dioramas. A recent addition to the geology collection is a mastodon skull discovered by an Aptos resident, who spotted the giant molars protruding from a creek bank.

The museum's history collection emphasizes Native Californians. One satisfied young visitor wrote, "We learned more than just about Indians. We learned about the way they lived and the things they ate. I learned more than I thought." A favorite play spot of many young visitors is the life-size model of a California gray whale on the lawn.

UNIVERSITY OF CALIFORNIA AT SANTA CRUZ ARBORETUM
High Street, Santa Cruz
Phone: (408) 427-2998
Hours: Daily 9:00 a.m.–5:00 p.m.
Admission: Free

The delicious scents and colors of lavender, thyme, sage, and other familiar plants greet you at the Arboretum's Mediterranean garden as you enter, but the pride of the place are the Australian and South African collections, considered the best in the world outside their native lands. Any flower lover who has ever purchased the exotic protea (they look vaguely like an artichoke and cost you an arm and a leg at the florist) will be amazed at their profusion and variety.

Started in 1964 with a gift of 90 species of eucalyptus, the 150-acre arboretum now boasts 50 acres planted with 6,000 species from all over the world, and thousands more in greenhouses waiting for planting areas to be prepared. With plant species as well as animals facing extinction around the world, arboreta are playing an increasingly important role in conservation. A visit to the UCSC Arboretum will give you an idea of the diversity of plant life on this planet.

Pick up a map at the docent hut near the entrance for a self-guided tour, or schedule your visit for a Wednesday, Saturday, or Sunday between 2:00 and 4:00 p.m., when docents are on duty.

WATSONVILLE

ELKHORN SLOUGH NATIONAL ESTUARINE RESEARCH RESERVE
1700 Elkhorn Road, Watsonville
Phone: (408) 728-2822
Hours: Wed.–Sun. 9:00 a.m.–5:00 p.m.
Admission: Adults (16 or older) $2.50. Free with current hunting or fishing license.

"For all at last returns to the sea," said Rachel Carson. During the last century, nearly ninety percent of California's estuaries, the places where rivers meet the sea, were destroyed by human activity. Fortunately, we have begun to learn the importance of preserving these resources. Elkhorn Slough, one of the few remaining coastal wetlands in California, is home to hundreds of species of birds, fish, and invertebrates, and at least six endangered species. A 1,400-acre portion of the slough has been

Henry Miller, 1969, Carmel. Miller moved from Europe to Big Sur in 1941 to overcome the writer's block that followed completion of Tropic of Cancer *and* Tropic of Capricorn *(both banned in the U.S. at the time).* Miller's *Big Sur and the Oranges of Hieronymus Bosch, published in 1957, describes the heightened reality and unique cultural milieu of Big Sur in the forties and fifties. Photo by William Webb, courtesy of the Henry Miller Library.*

designated as a National Estuarine Research Reserve, managed by the California Department of Fish and Game.

You can cover a good portion of the reserve on one of several hiking loops dotted with interpretive signs, boardwalks, and benches. Pick up a trail map at the handsome visitor center and check out binoculars and field guides. A relief model of the Monterey Canyon, an aquarium, taxidermied birds, and please-touch exhibits fill the visitor center. You can even try their recipe for estuary soup—take billions of plants, add millions of animals, stir with a tide spoon.

WILLIAM H. VOLCK MEMORIAL MUSEUM
261 East Beach Street, Watsonville
Phone: (408) 722-0305
Hours: Tues.-Thurs. 11:00 a.m.-3:00 p.m.
Admission: Free

The five-room Victorian, designed by noted California architect William Weeks in 1901, was given to the Pajaro Valley Historical Association by Helen Volck Tucker to house the association's collection of historical artifacts. The museum is dedicated to the donor's first husband, William Volck, who earned a place in Watsonville history by developing a spray to combat the codling moth, thus saving the local apple industry. A case of artifacts is dedicated to Mr. Volck. Other exhibits showcase the museum's historic costume and textile collection, spanning over a century of fashions from 1860 on. Displays of clothes, quilts, toys, and family memorabilia change quarterly. When we were there, the historical association was trying to sell their present museum building to move to 332 East Beach Street—call to verify their location before you visit.

Library: The museum archives, available by appointment only, contain historical photos, maps, and materials relating to Pajaro Valley. The fee for research from the archives is $10/hour, waived for students and Pajaro Valley Historical Association members.

MONTEREY COUNTY

BIG SUR

THE HENRY MILLER LIBRARY★
Highway 1, Big Sur
Phone: (408) 667-2574
Hours: Daily 11:00 a.m.-5:00 p.m., May-October; weekends, holidays, and by appointment, November-April.
Admission: Free

Big Sur artist Emil White founded the Henry Miller Library in 1981 as a memorial to his friend, the writer and artist Henry Miller, who lived in

Big Sur from 1944 to 1962. Housed in White's Japanese-style residence, set amidst towering redwoods and a beautiful garden, the library contains an extensive permanent collection of books, artwork, and memorabilia relating to Miller and the artistic and cultural heritage of Big Sur. Changing shows include art and historical exhibits.

CARMEL

MISSION SAN CARLOS BORROMEO DEL RIO CARMELO (CARMEL MISSION)*
3080 Rio Road, Carmel
Phone: (408) 624-3600
Hours: Mon.-Sat. 9:30 a.m.-7:30 p.m.; Sun. 10:30 a.m.-4:30 p.m., summer; Mon.-Sat. 9:30 a.m.-4:30 p.m.; Sun. 10:30 a.m.-4:30 p.m., winter.
Admission: Free

Established in 1771, the Carmel Mission was the favorite of Father Junipero Serra, and his home and headquarters until his death.

Robinson Jeffers stands in the doorway of his self-contructed Hawk Tower, the symbol of his life and work, 1925. Photo from the collection of Pat Hathaway, courtesy of Tor House Foundation.

TOR HOUSE
26304 Ocean View Avenue, Carmel
Phone: (408) 624-1813 (Mon.-Thurs.), 624-1840 (Fri.-Sat.)
Hours: Fri. & Sat. 10:00 a.m.-4:00 p.m., by reservation only
Admission: Adults $5.00, college students $3.50, high school students $1.50

"If anyone was ever bored, which is incredible, let him get five acres and grow a wood on them, and produce a stone house and twins and a book of verses," wrote the poet Robinson Jeffers. Jeffers built a home for himself, his wife, Una, and their twin sons on a craggy knoll on Carmel Point. Apprenticing himself to the building contractor, he learned the art of stonemasonry, and a year after Tor House was completed in 1919, he began construction on Hawk Tower. Working alone, adapting the block-and-tackle system used by the Egyptians to build the pyramids, Jeffers moved boulders from the beach to construct a towering granite retreat for his wife and a magic place for his sons.

Lee Jeffers, the wife of Jeffers' son Donnan, still lives on the property. Tor House is furnished just as it was when the poet and his family lived there. In the first level of Hawk Tower, you can sit in the sturdy chair at the desk where the poet created virtually all of his mature work. Energetic visitors who climb to the fourth level of the tower will be treated to a matchless view of all of Carmel Point.

MONTEREY

MARITIME MUSEUM OF MONTEREY
Stanton Center
5 Custom House Plaza, Monterey
Phone: (408) 373-2469
Hours: Daily 10:00 a.m.–5:00 p.m.
Admission: Adult $5.00, youth 13-18 $3.00, children 6-12 $2.00

Designed by Esherick, Homsey, Dodge & Davis of San Francisco, the architects of the Monterey Bay Aquarium, the two-story, adobe-inspired

Maritime Museum building is an elegant newcomer in historic Custom House Plaza on Monterey's waterfront. Seven thematic exhibits trace the region's maritime history, from the Ohlone people and Spanish conquistadores to Monterey's heyday as the sardine capital of the world.

A six-foot-long model of Commodore John Drake Sloat's ship, the *Savannah*, priceless navigational instruments, ships in bottles, photographs of shipwrecks, and treasures brought up from the ocean's depths are among the historic artifacts displayed. As you walk around the exhibits, make sure to look down at the intricate, colorful floor inserts

Volunteers Dick McFarland (front) and Ian Perry painstakingly sanded and polished the Maritime Museum's first order Fresnal Lens in preparation for the museum's 1992 opening. Now fully assembled, the 18-foot-tall lens rotates on its original turning mechanism from Point Sur in the 1890s. Courtesy of Maritime Museum of Monterey.

depicting maritime images. Impossible to overlook is the first order Fresnal lens from Point Sur Lighthouse, standing more than 18 feet tall and weighing nearly 10,000 pounds.

The second floor boasts a well-equipped workshop for model ship building and restoration. Free school tours for kids include an opportunity to learn to tie sailor knots and work in the model shop.

Library: The 4,000-volume maritime research library, open Tuesday through Friday, 10:00 a.m. to 5:00 p.m., contains beautiful and rare books, carvings, and scrimshaws. The extensive film and print collection is often used to trace genealogy or find information on relatives in World War II.

Gift Shop: A fine selection of nautical items includes model ships, scrimshaw replicas, and even cunning little ships in bottles for $5 and up.

Rental: The entire facility or just the library or theater are available.

MONTEREY BAY AQUARIUM
886 Cannery Row, Monterey
Phone: (408) 648-4888
Hours: Daily 10:00 a.m.–6:00 p.m.; summer, 9:30 a.m.–6:00 p.m.
Admission: General $11.25, students & seniors $8.25,
children 3-12 $5.00

When I hear rave reviews about a movie, book, or museum, my expectations are sometimes so high that I'm disappointed when I see it with my own eyes. Have no fears in this regard about the Monterey Bay Aquarium. It deserves every superlative ever applied, and more.

The museum building, noteworthy in itself, reflects the historic flavor of its famed Cannery Row location on the outside, while the interior is stunningly modern. Outdoor decks, an open-air aviary, and an enormous tide pool that opens on one side to the ocean create the feeling that the aquarium is very much an extension of Monterey Bay.

Life-size models of a 43-foot gray whale and her 22-foot calf, dolphins, and porpoises suspended from the soaring ceiling greet you as you enter. To your right, three orphaned sea otters turn somersaults and frolic in their two-story home. If you turn to your left, you will come upon the towering, three-story Kelp Forest exhibit, where leopard sharks and a host of other fishes weave among the kelp fronds. A school of sardines with anchovies tagging along for the ride were circling in perfect drill-team formation during my visit.

Behind the Kelp Forest, large sharks, bat rays, salmon, halibut, striped bass, and other fishes roam the 90-foot long, hourglass-shaped Monterey Bay Habitats exhibit. As you move along, you'll see kids and adults crowded around the Touch Tide Pool, where you can get a feel for starfish, chitons, and abalone—a sea cucumber feels just like Jello. Bat rays, kissing cousins to sharks, swim in their own pool. The greatest thrill of my visit was a particularly friendly fellow who followed me around the pool, came up to the edge, and stuck his head out of the water to be petted.

From the second floor you can get an overview of what you saw below. Watch the aquarists at work, or follow the antics of the sea otters above the water's surface. The Kelp Lab lets you get down to details with microscopes and magnifiers.

The three-story Kelp Forest at the Monterey Bay Aquarium. Photo by Nate Levine.

Step outside, where the aquarium's three levels of outdoor decks, including the "Watching the Bay" exhibit on the third floor, offer a crow's nest view of the bay—ideal for watching whales, sea otters, sea lions, harbor seals, and dolphins. Volunteer guides can help you spot passing whales and other wildlife.

A hundred other smaller exhibits and galleries, films, videos, discovery carts, and narrated feeding shows offer an almost inexhaustible source of entertainment. In 1996 the aquarium will open a new wing whose centerpiece will be a one-million-gallon exhibit devoted to the mysteries of the open waters of Monterey Bay.

Free, on-site school programs (K–12) include tours, classroom/laboratory programs, auditorium presentations, and classroom materials. The outreach program's Aquaravan carries educational materials to preschools, libraries, fairs, parks, and farm labor

The leopard shark makes its home along the California coast, finding food and shelter in muddy bays, kelp forests, and rocky reefs. Leopard sharks can be found in several exhibits at the Monterey Bay Aquarium, gliding gracefully through the water. In the wild, they are nomads, feeding on everything from schools of anchovies to buried prey found by detecting the animals' electrical fields. Photo courtesy of Monterey Bay Aquarium.

camps in the Monterey Bay region. Free teacher education programs include field, shipboard, laboratory, aquarium, classroom, and project experiences.

Library: The library collection focuses on high school and undergraduate level marine biology, oceanography, and environmental science resources, as well as teaching resources, juvenile literature, and research material.

Gift Shop: Several gift shops and bookstores stock every kind of marine-related object imaginable, from fish potholders and fish ties to art prints and stuffed toy sea otters. Field guides, binoculars, and other items for the amateur naturalist are available. The store is so successful (and deservedly so) that at one point it was in danger of losing its tax-exempt status.

Restaurant: Several dining options are available, from catching a quick bite at the express window to a leisurely, sit-down lunch in the elegant, ocean view restaurant, or a casual meal in the cafeteria. Portola Cafe Express features kid-pleasing items: pizza $3, clam chowder $1.50, shrimp salad $4.95, and brownies $1.50. The more elegant Portola Cafe's Italian-inspired menu, heavy on the ocean fare, offers seafood appetizers—crab cakes, prawn and shrimp cocktails, fried calamari, and clam chowder—in the $6 range, and seafood and other entrees from $8 to $12.

MONTEREY PENINSULA MUSEUM OF ART AT CIVIC CENTER
559 Pacific Street, Monterey
Phone: (408) 372-5477
Hours: Tues. 10:00 a.m.–8:00 p.m.; Wed.–Sat. 10:00 a.m.–4:00 p.m.;
**   Sun. 1:00–4:00 p.m. Gallery tours: Sun. 2:00 p.m.**
Admission: $5.00 (includes entry to La Mirada), $3.00 students &
**   active duty military, children under 12 accompanied by an adult**
**   and members free.**

Henry Hopkins called the Monterey Peninsula Museum of Art "the best small-town museum in the United States." It is, indeed, a charming place. Housed in a two-story, Spanish-style building, the museum concentrates on presenting American art with an emphasis on the Monterey region and California, as well as art from Asia and the Pacific Rim, photography, graphics, and international folk art. Exhibits are first-class.

Museum on Wheels, the mobile component of the museum's bilingual educational outreach program, brings selections from the folk art collection to elementary schools in Monterey and the surrounding counties.

Library: A small, non-circulating research library is open to the public.

Gift Shop: A cheerful shop stocks cards, posters, art books, folk art, and interesting gift items.

MONTEREY PENINSULA MUSEUM OF ART AT LA MIRADA
720 Via Mirada, Monterey
Phone: (408) 372-3689
Hours: Tues.-Sat. 10:00 a.m.-4:00 p.m.; Sun. 1:00-4:00 p.m.
   Gallery tours: Sat. & Sun. 1:00 p.m.
Admission: $5.00 (includes entry to Civic Center location), $3.00
   (La Mirada only), $1.50 students & active duty military, children
   under 12 accompanied by an adult and members free.

The historic Castro Adobe and Frank Work Estate, deeded to the
Monterey Peninsula Museum of Art Association in 1983 and now known
as La Mirada, offer fine antique furnishings, exquisite rose and rhododen-
dron gardens, and richly planted courtyards. Permanent and changing
exhibitions include California regional artists, Chinese ceramic tomb art,
and Japanese netsukes.

Gift Shop: The shop stocks art and garden-related gift items.

SPIRIT OF MONTEREY WAX MUSEUM
700 Cannery Row, Monterey
Phone: (408) 375-3770
Hours: Daily 9:00 a.m.-9:00 p.m.
Admission: Adults $5.00, seniors $3.95, children 6-12 $2.95

For the same reasons they prefer comics to classics, kids will probably
prefer the Spirit of Monterey Wax Museum to the Path of History. As
wax museums go, this is a small one, but unless you're willing to stumble
around in the dark, you have to follow the slow pace set for you. Allow
about 20 minutes for John Steinbeck to guide you through a sensational
version of Monterey history. By means of special animation technology,
the life-size figures move.

*"Surf and Rock,
Monterey County
Coast, California,"
Ansel Adams
(gelatin silver print,
c. 1951, gift of
James and Mary
Alinder). Courtesy
of Monterey
Peninsula
Museum of Art.*

OLD MONTEREY

MONTEREY STATE HISTORIC PARK
VISITOR CENTER
Stanton Center
Custom House Plaza, Old Monterey
Phone: (408) 649-7118
Hours: Daily 10:00 a.m.-5:00 p.m.
Admission: Free

In historic interest, Monterey claims to be to the Pacific
coast what Plymouth, Jamestown, and St. Augustine
together are to the Atlantic seaboard. A lot of history took
place in this lovely town and a good part of it is accessible
via an easy walking tour through the old town. The best
place to begin is at the Monterey State Historic Park

Visitor Center and History Theater, where a free, 14-minute film gives you an easy-to-digest history lesson. Although historic reenactments can fall on the hokey side, this film does introduce you to the key players whose names come up again and again.

As you follow the "Path of History" through Old Monterey, white plaques on poles and decorative paving tiles alert you to the historic sites. More than a dozen beautifully restored structures are open for your inspection as part of the Monterey State Historic Park. I highly recommend the half-hour guided tours offered at minimal cost by the Department of Parks and Recreation, Old Monterey Preservation Society, and Monterey History and Art Association. Every tour leader I encountered had the ability to make history come alive.

THE BOSTON STORE/CASA DEL ORO
Scott & Olivier Streets, Old Monterey
Phone: (408) 649-3364
Hours: Wed.-Sat. 10:00 a.m.-5:00 p.m.; Sun. noon-5:00 p.m.
  Garden open daily.
Admission: Free

Once a general store with the only iron safe in town, the Boston Store now sells ribbons, linens, crockery, soaps, antiques, and reproductions of merchandise that could have been purchased in 1849 when the store first opened for business. The adjoining herb garden supplies the herbs for fragrant potpourri, sachets, and teas.

CASA AMESTI
516 Polk Street, Old Monterey
Phone: (408) 372-2608
Hours: Guided tours Sat. & Sun. 2:00-4:00 p.m.
Admission: $2.00

One of the best examples of Monterey colonial architecture in California, Casa Amesti was built in the 1840s by José Amesti. The renowned interior decorator Frances Elkins bought the two-story adobe in 1928 and decorated it to the nines with French and English antiques. Her brother, famed architect David Adler, designed the formal walled gardens. Old Capital Club leases the building from the National Trust for use as a men's club. You can see the tables set for the gentlemen's lunch.

CASA GUTIERREZ
590 Calle Principal, Old Monterey
Phone: (408) 375-0095
Hours: Mon.-Thurs. 11:00 a.m.-9:00 p.m., Fri.-Sun. 11:00 a.m.-
  10:00 p.m.

Built in 1841, originally the home of Joaquin and Josefa Gutierrez, and now a Mexican restaurant, this is one of the few remaining adobes built in the simpler Mexican style.

CASA SERRANO
412 Pacific Street, Old Monterey
Phone: (408) 372-2608
Hours: Sat. & Sun. 2:00-4:00 p.m.
Admission: Free

An 1845 adobe filled with antiques and early California paintings, Casa Serrano is now the headquarters of the Monterey History and Art Association.

Rental: The house, lovely gardens, and two small patios are available for weddings and parties.

CASA SOBERANES
336 Pacific Street, Old Monterey
Phone: (408) 649-7118
Hours: Tours Fri.-Mon. & Wed. 10:00 & 11:00 a.m., winter;
10:00, 11:00, & noon, summer.
Admission: $2.00

Known as "The House of the Blue Gate," Casa Soberanes, with its lovely gardens, is a fine example of Mexican period adobe architecture

COLTON HALL MUSEUM & OLD MONTEREY JAIL MUSEUM
Civic Center
Pacific Street at Madison, Old Monterey
Phone: (408) 646-3851
Hours: Mon.-Fri. 10:00 a.m.-4:00 p.m.; Sat. 10:00 a.m.-noon; Sun.
10:00 a.m.-noon & 1:00-5:00 p.m. (Closes at 1:00 p.m. Nov.-Feb.)
Admission: Free

Colton Hall, considered the only building in California suitable to the purpose at the time, was the site of the convention called to draft California's constitution. Forty-eight men gathered in the white stone building in 1849 to debate the complex issues of statehood. Entering the second floor assembly hall, its tables strewn with historic documents (photo-copies), quill pens, red sealing wax, cigars, candles, and antique eyeglasses, you would swear you had journeyed back in time and that the delegates who had adjourned for recess would be returning momentarily.

Forced into extraordinary measures by internal conflicts, the Mexican government appointed a Yankee, Walter Colton, mayor of Monterey shortly after his arrival as Chaplain aboard the USS Congress in 1845. It was at Old Monterey's Colton Hall that California's constitution was drafted in 1849. Courtesy of Colton Hall Museum.

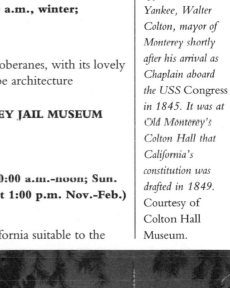

At the rear of Colton Hall, built of Monterey granite and the best ironwork that San Francisco could furnish, is the Old Jail, with each cell depicting an event from the jail's history.

COOPER-MOLERA ADOBE
525 Polk Street, Old Monterey
Phone: (408) 649-7118
Hours: Tours Tues.-Sun. 10:00 & 11:00 a.m.
Admission: $2.00

The three-acre complex enclosed by a fine adobe wall houses private dwellings, business establishments, a barn, farm animals, and historic vegetable and flower gardens. The house is luxuriously furnished with original pieces, including an 1865 custom-made king-size bed with the coverlet embroidered by the original owner.

Gift Shop: Charming antique reproductions, toys, tea sets, and white dresses are for sale in the gift shop.

CUSTOM HOUSE
Custom House Plaza, Old Monterey
Phone: (408) 649-7118
Hours: Daily 10:00 a.m.-4:00 p.m., winter; 10:00 a.m.-5:00 p.m.,
**   summer.**
Admission: Free

Monterey's Custom House—California Historical Landmark Number One—is the oldest government building on the West Coast. Built in 1827, the two-story adobe was in continuous use as a custom house under the Mexican and American governments until 1867. It was here, on July 7, 1846, that Commodore John Drake Sloat raised the American flag and declared "henceforth California will be a portion of the United States." The building is now maintained as a museum with displays of early trade goods—items manufactured in Europe that were exchanged for California hides and tallow.

FIRST BRICK HOUSE
Decatur Street, Old Monterey
Phone: (408) 649-7118
Hours: Daily 10:00 a.m.-4:00 p.m., winter; 10:00 a.m.-5:00 p.m.,
**   summer.**
Admission: Free

After building the first house of kiln-fired brick in Monterey, Gallant Dickenson left to find his fortune in the gold fields, and the two-story house was sold at auction for $1,091. Now operated by the Junior League of Monterey County, the house contains an historic display commemorating Mama Garcia's restaurant, famous for homemade tamales, enchiladas, and Spanish rice.

FIRST THEATRE
Pacific & Scott Streets, Old Monterey
Phone: (408) 375-4916
Hours: Wed.-Sat. 1:00-5:00 p.m.; summer, Fri. & Sat. 1:00-8:00 p.m.

This old adobe started life as a saloon and boardinghouse, then became the first building in California to hold commercial theatrical performances. Troupers of the Gold Coast have been performing old-time melodramas here since 1937. Performances are held Friday and Saturday evenings, and in July on Wednesday evenings also. Call for reservations and admission prices.

LARKIN HOUSE
510 Calle Principal, Old Monterey
Phone: (408) 649-7118
Hours: Guided tours Fri.-Mon. & Wed. 1:00, 2:00, & 3:00 p.m.,
  winter; 2:00, 3:00, & 4:00 p.m., summer.
Admission: $2.00

This two-story adobe was built by Thomas Larkin, the United States' first and last counsel to Mexican California, and one of the people who were instrumental in bringing California into the Union. An early example of Monterey adobe architecture, it is filled with an eclectic assortment of antiques from around the world acquired by Larkin's granddaughter, who lived here from 1922 to 1957.

Thomas Larkin, a Yankee trader, settled in Monterey in 1832, where he amassed a fortune throughout the years leading up to the Bear Flag Rebellion and the fall of the Mexican government in upper California. The Larkin House, California's first two-story home, is now a part of the "Christmas in the Adobes" celebration. Courtesy of California State Parks.

The small, one-room Sherman-Halleck adobe, which sits inside the walled area of the Larkin House property, served as an office for the U.S. military in the early months of American occupancy. Its most famous occupant was William Tecumseh Sherman, a lieutenant at the time.

MAYO HAYES O'DONNELL LIBRARY
155 Van Buren Street, Old Monterey
Phone: (408) 372-1838
Hours: Wed., Fri., Sat., Sun. 1:30-3:30 p.m.
Admission: Free

This tiny historic building, the first Protestant church in Monterey, now houses the Mayo Hayes O'Donnell Library of California history, a research library specializing in Californiana.

OLD WHALING STATION
Decatur Street (in Heritage Harbor), Old Monterey
Phone: (408) 649-7118
Hours: Tues.-Thurs. 8:30 a.m.-1:00 p.m.; Fri. 9:30 a.m.-2:00 p.m.
Admission: Free

Once a boardinghouse for Portuguese sailors, who would watch for whales from the second-story balcony, the charming, wisteria-covered adobe boasts the only remaining whalebone sidewalk in Monterey.

Rental: The Junior League, which has its office here, makes the site available for special events. The rose garden is a favorite site for weddings.

PACIFIC HOUSE
Calle Principal, Old Monterey
Phone: (408) 649-7109
Hours: Daily 10:00 a.m.-4:00 p.m., winter; 10:00 a.m.-5:00 p.m.,
**   summer.**
Admission: Free

After having served as a hotel, courtroom, newspaper office, ballroom, and church, the two-story Pacific House adobe is now a history museum. Historic artifacts from Monterey's Spanish, Mexican, and American periods are on display on the first floor, and the Holman Collection of Native American artifacts is housed on the second floor. Behind Pacific House, the tranquil, walled Memory Garden features a central fountain surrounded by four stately magnolia trees.

Rental: The garden can be rented for special events and will accommodate up to 250 guests. The fee is $2.50 per person or $100, whichever is greater, for four hours.

Stevenson House honors the author of A Child's Garden of Verses *and other favorite childhood books.* Courtesy of California State Parks.

STEVENSON HOUSE
530 Houston Street, Old Monterey
Phone: (408) 649-7118
Hours: Tours Tues.-Sun. 1:00, 2:00, & 3:00 p.m., winter;
**   2:00, 3:00, & 4:00 p.m., summer.**
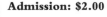
Admission: $2.00

Although he spent a scant four months here in 1879, the two-story adobe known then as the French Hotel houses the largest collection in the world of Robert Louis Stevenson's possessions. Your tour guide will tell you everything you ever wanted to know about the famous Scottish author of so many favorite childhood books, including *Treasure Island*, *A Child's Garden of Verses*, and *Dr. Jekyll and Mr. Hyde*.

The rooms—kitchen, bedrooms, family parlor—are fetchingly furnished with period antiques. The young visitors on my tour had a difficult time tearing themselves away from the enticing display of antique toys—dolls and teddy bears sitting down to tea, and games, a paint set, and Noah's ark spread out ready for play in the children's room.

At its peak in spring, the garden full of old-fashioned flowers—pansies, hollyhocks, cineraria, forget-me-nots, and deliciously fragrant roses—is a symphony of color.

PACIFIC GROVE

PACIFIC GROVE ART CENTER
568 Lighthouse Avenue, Pacific Grove
Phone: (408) 375-2208
Hours: Tues.-Sat. noon-5:00 p.m.; Sun. 1:00-4:00 p.m.
Admission: Free

Built in 1904 to house retail stores on the ground floor and assembly halls above, the historic Pacific Grove Art Center now contains four exhibit galleries and sixteen artists' studios. Hundreds of artists exhibit in the ten or more shows held each year.

PACIFIC GROVE MUSEUM OF NATURAL HISTORY*
165 Forest Avenue, Pacific Grove
Phone: (408) 648-3116
Hours: Tues.-Sun. 10:00 a.m.-5:00 p.m.
Admission: Free

Pacific Grove's claim to fame is the annual arrival of thousands of monarch butterflies. The colorful, orange and black Lepidoptera over-winter in the pine trees on Ridge Road from October through March. Housed in a beautiful, Spanish-style building from the thirties, the Pacific Grove Museum of Natural History details the phenomenon of the "butterfly trees" with a short film and diorama. The museum, recognized as one of the finest of its size in the country, also features permanent exhibits that deal with local birds, mammals, reptiles, amphibians, insects, and geology, and the Costanoan (Ohlone) Indians. Traveling exhibitions present data from farther afield. Kids enjoy climbing on the life-size sculpture of Sandy the Gray Whale in front of the museum and exploring the native plant garden, which contains a number of the Monterey Peninsula's rare and endangered species.

Gift Shop: The gift shop stocks merchandise pertaining to natural history—books, posters, minerals, and the like.

POINT LOBOS

POINT LOBOS WHALING STATION*
Point Lobos State Reserve
Highway 1, Point Lobos
Phone: (408) 624-4909
Hours: 10:00 a.m.-4:00 p.m. (hours may vary)
Admission: $6.00 auto fee, walk-in free

The 1,300 acres of rugged seacoast at Point Lobos include a 550-acre underwater reserve, home to sea lions, harbor seals, gray whales, sea otters, and thousands of sea birds. A turn-of-the-century whaler's cabin is the sole reminder that the area was the center of the whaling and abalone industry in California. Displays inside the cabin document Ohlone, Chinese, Portuguese, and Japanese settlements.

POINT PINOS LIGHTHOUSE*
Ocean View Boulevard, Pacific Grove
Phone: (408) 648-3116
Hours: Sat. & Sun. 1:00-4:00 p.m.
Admission: Free

The oldest continuously operating lighthouse on the West Coast, Point Pinos has been shining its beacon from the northernmost tip of the Monterey Peninsula since February 1, 1855. The present building, lenses, and prisms are all original.

SALINAS

JOSÉ EUSEBIO BORONDA ADOBE
333 Boronda Road, Salinas
Phone: (408) 757-8085
Hours: Mon.-Fri. 9:00 a.m.-3:00 p.m.
Admission: Free

After the 6,700-acre Rancho San José was granted to him in 1839, José Eusebio Boronda spent a great deal of his time defending his claim from the new American government and from his children, who fought against him for control of the property. (Boronda emerged victorious.) A typical example of Monterey colonial architecture, the one-room Boronda adobe, the oldest building in Salinas, features a four-sided shake roof and an open veranda surrounding the house. The adobe, now owned by the Monterey County Historical Society, has been restored to its original condition and furnished with many original artifacts.

Library: The Robert B. Johnston Archival Vault houses over 5,000 photographs (many dating back to the 1800s), the historic Mexican archives, county records, Monterey County family records, and newspaper files from 1900 to 1950. Researchers and genealogists are welcome to use the facility by appointment.

HARVEY-BAKER HOUSE*
238 East Romie Lane, Salinas
Phone: (408) 757-8085
Hours: First Sunday of the month, 1:00–4:00 p.m. or by appt.
Admission: Free

Missouri merchant Isaac Harvey moved to California in 1853 to capitalize on the prosperity engendered by the Gold Rush. He soon established a successful general store and became an influential citizen, the first mayor of Salinas. His house, built in 1868 with redwood lumber hauled from Moss Landing, has been restored and furnished by the Monterey County Historical Society.

LAGUNITAS SCHOOLHOUSE*
333 Boronda Road, Salinas
Phone: (408) 757-8085
Hours: Sundays 1:00–4:00 p.m.
Admission: Free

Children from grades one through eight were educated in the little red Lagunitas Schoolhouse from 1898 until 1967, when it was replaced by a look-alike modern structure. The original one-room building has been moved to the grounds of the Boronda Adobe and restored, and now serves as a museum depicting school days at the turn of the century.

STEINBECK CENTER FOUNDATION
371 Main Street, Salinas
Phone: (408) 753-6411
Hours: Mon.-Fri. 8:00 a.m.-5:00 p.m.
Admission: Free

Salinas pays homage to her most famous native son, John Steinbeck, by hosting the annual Steinbeck Festival and featuring his life and work in displays at the Steinbeck Public Library and the Steinbeck Foundation. (Although Steinbeck was the recipient of both the Pulitzer Prize for Fiction and the Nobel Prize for Literature, all this hometown adulation is posthumous—he was not so popular here during his lifetime.) Currently under development is the Steinbeck Center, a $7 million project to be located in the heart of Oldtown Salinas, which will house three museum-quality galleries with exhibits on the author's life and work, and the Salinas region.

Library: The Steinbeck Archives, housed in the basement of the Steinbeck Public Library, are available by appointment. The library is at 350 Lincoln Avenue in Salinas, phone (408) 424-2735.

Restaurant: Steinbeck's childhood home has been restored and opened as a restaurant: Steinbeck House, 132 Central Avenue, Salinas. It is open for lunch, served at 11:45 and 1:15 Monday through Friday. Reservations are necessary—phone (408) 424-2735.

Index

About the Authors

Charlene Akers has worked as a museum development director, corporation controller, and free-lance
writer. A person of eclectic tastes and interests, she has
also written *Never Buy Anything New*, a guide to 400
secondhand, thrift, and consignment stores in the San
Francisco Bay Area. She lives in Oakland with her
husband, son, and dog.

For over twenty years, food critic Jobyna Akers Dellar
travelled throughout Northern California for her own
sales agency, eating in fine restaurants and fast food
outlets for 23 years. She is a member of the Dellar
restaurant clan, and lives in San Francisco with her
husband.